Are pardons a thing of the past? Is mercy a prerogative of monarchs? This book answers these questions with a resounding 'no'. Edited by two leading legal scholars of clemency, this unmatched collection ranges across the world, demonstrating the breadth of discretionary practices that modify punishment. As it points the way toward the just use of executive power, this book is essential reading for scholars and activists.

Carolyn Strange, Professor of History, Australian National University.

This essential collection of writings on the use and power of clemency could not be more timely. *Executive Clemency* fills a long-standing gap in criminal justice research and provides us with the deepest and most extensive analysis of clemency procedures across global legal and political systems for more than 40 years. Not only does it fill a significant gap in our knowledge and understanding, it has the potential to inform and improve clemency laws and practices worldwide. It should be read and discussed by policymakers, practitioners, researchers and students concerned with the lives and deaths of prisoners.

Dr Catherine Appleton, Senior Research Fellow at the School of Law, University of Nottingham.

Executive Clemency

Nearly every country in the world has a mechanism for executive clemency, which, though residual in most legal systems, serves as a vital due process safeguard and as an outlet for leniency in punishment. While the origins of clemency lie in the historical prerogative powers of once-absolute rulers, modern clemency laws and practices have evolved to be enormously varied. This volume brings comparative and empirical analysis to bear on executive clemency, building a sociological and political context around systematically collected data on clemency laws, grants, and decision-making. Some jurisdictions have elaborate constitutional and legal structures for pardoning or commuting a sentence while virtually never doing so, while others have little formal process and yet grant clemency frequently. Using examples from Asia, Europe, Latin America, the Caribbean, and the USA, this comparative analysis of the law and the practice of clemency sheds light on a frequently misunderstood executive power.

Executive Clemency: Comparative and Empirical Perspectives builds on existing academic scholarship and expands the limited geographical scope of previous studies on clemency. It relays the latest state of knowledge on the topic and employs case studies, doctrinal legal analysis, historical research, and statements by clemency decision-making authorities, in explaining why clemency varies so considerably across global legal and political systems. In addition, it includes contributions encompassing international law, transitional justice, innocence and wrongful convictions, as well as on jurisdictions that are historically under-researched.

The book will be of value to practitioners, academics, and students interested in the fields of human rights, criminal law, comparative criminal justice, and international relations.

Daniel Pascoe is Associate Professor of Law at the School of Law, City University of Hong Kong. He is the author of *Last Chance for Life: Clemency in Southeast Asian Death Penalty Cases* (Oxford University Press 2019). He holds a DPhil in Law from the University of Oxford.

Andrew Novak is Term Assistant Professor of Criminology, Law, and Society at George Mason University, and is the author of six books, including *Comparative Executive Clemency* (Routledge 2015). He holds a PhD in Law from Middlesex University.

Routledge Research in Human Rights Law

Women and International Human Rights Law
Universal Periodic Review in Practice
Gayatri H Patel

International Law and Violence Against Women
Europe and the Istanbul Convention
Edited by Johanna Niemi, Lourdes Peroni, and Vladislava Stoyanova

The Human Rights Council
The Impact of the Universal Periodic Review in Africa
Damian Etone

Domestic Judicial Treatment of European Court of Human Rights Case Law
Beyond Compliance
Edited by David Kosař, Jan Petrov, Katarína Šipulová, Hubert Smekal, Ladislav Vyhnánek, and Jozef Janovský

Hate Speech and Human Rights in Eastern Europe
Legislating for Divergent Values
Viera Pejchal

Collective Punishment and Human Rights Law
Addressing Gaps in International Law
Cornelia Klocker

Executive Clemency
Comparative and Empirical Perspectives
Edited by Daniel Pascoe and Andrew Novak

For more information about this series, please visit: www.routledge.com/Routledge-Research-in-Human-Rights-Law/bookseries/HUMRIGHTSLAW

Executive Clemency

Comparative and Empirical Perspectives

Edited by
Daniel Pascoe and Andrew Novak

Routledge
Taylor & Francis Group
NEW YORK AND LONDON

First published 2021
by Routledge
52 Vanderbilt Avenue, New York, NY 10017

and by Routledge
2 Park Square, Milton Park, Abingdon, Oxon OX14 4RN

Routledge is an imprint of the Taylor & Francis Group, an informa business

Library of Congress Cataloging-in-Publication Data
Names: Pascoe, Daniel, 1983- editor. | Noval, Andrew, editor.
Title: Executive clemency : comparative and empirical perspectives / [edited by] Daniel Pascoe, Andrew Noval.
Description: New York : Routledge, 2020. |
Series: Routledge research in human rights law | Includes bibliographical references and index.
Identifiers: LCCN 2020007917 (print) | LCCN 2020007918 (ebook) | ISBN 9780367243579 (hardback) | ISBN 9780367243586 (ebook)
Subjects: LCSH: Clemency. | Executive power. | Pardon. | Comparative law.
Classification: LCC K5135 .E94 2020 (print) | LCC K5135 (ebook) | DDC 345/.077--dc23
LC record available at https://lccn.loc.gov/2020007917
LC ebook record available at https://lccn.loc.gov/2020007918

ISBN: 978-0-367-24357-9 (hbk)
ISBN: 978-0-367-24358-6 (ebk)

Typeset in Galliard
by Taylor & Francis Books

To Christopher Ruckman and John Ruckman, may you find forgiveness.

Contents

Acknowledgements

This book began as a conversation at George Mason University School of Law, Virginia, in the summer of 2016. After deciding to combine our (African and Southeast Asian) regional expertise on executive clemency, and to focus on clemency in comparative and empirical perspective, we were fortunate to find such a knowledgeable and far-flung cast of contributors to write about clemency's location at the intersection of law and politics. While this view is contested by scholars (including within this volume), we both believe that maintaining flexibility in the application of the criminal law through timely recourse to executive clemency can ultimately boost justice, rather than detract from it. Clemency still deserves a prominent place in the criminal justice systems of the twenty-first century.

Now that the manuscript has been completed, we have several people to thank for their help and advice. First are our contributors, and the editorial team at Routledge, whose patience with the volume we greatly appreciated. Several research assistants have helped us throughout the course of the project, particularly in compiling the appendix and revising the footnotes. On Andrew's side, Chelsea van Dijk, a PhD student in the Department of Criminology, Law and Society at George Mason University, helped with the appendix to the book and with a joint presentation at the Academy of Criminal Justice Sciences conference in Baltimore in March 2019. On Daniel's side, several research assistants have contributed to the project since its inception, including Carol Zhang Xiaofeng, Toni Tong Yihan, Ada Hung Ching, Sungbin Michelle Choi, Benjamin Chong Kin Chiu, Herbert Cheng Hoi Fai and Mark Law Hiu Fung. Much of the funding for the project was provided by an Early Career Scheme Grant from the Research Grants Council of the Hong Kong Special Administrative Region, China (Project Number CityU 9048110). With the continued support of the Research Grants Council, our clemency research will expand to novel and timely themes in the near future.

Institutionally, we would like to thank the Human Rights Law and Policy Forum at the School of Law, City University of Hong Kong, for providing the opportunity to present and receive feedback on our preliminary findings during a lunchtime seminar in March 2019. The authors also presented earlier versions of Chapters 1 and 9 at a seminar organised at Fordham University School of Law (New York City, June 2017), at the Annual Conference of the Australian and New Zealand Society of Criminology (Melbourne, December 2018), and most recently, at the Conference of the International Society of Public Law (Santiago de Chile, June 2019). To spread the word on this globally focused volume and to receive important feedback from other like-minded scholars, our conference attendance was almost as geographically eclectic as our chapters themselves!

Finally, several individuals provided advice on the direction of the project and on recommendations for contributors. To Professor Bin Liang (Oklahoma State University); Dr Jacqueline Wilson (United States Institute for Peace); Dr Josepha Close (Middlesex University); Dr Sung Yong Kang (Korea National Police University); and Professor Philippe Lagassé (Carleton University) – thank you for your help. We will pay it forward.

Daniel Pascoe and Andrew Novak
Hong Kong and Fairfax, Virginia

Editors and Contributors

Daniel Pascoe is Associate Professor of Law at the School of Law, City University of Hong Kong. He is the author of *Last Chance for Life: Clemency in Southeast Asian Death Penalty Cases* (Oxford University Press 2019). He holds a DPhil in Law from the University of Oxford.

Andrew Novak is Term Assistant Professor of Criminology, Law, and Society at George Mason University, and is the author of six books, including *Comparative Executive Clemency* (Routledge 2015). He holds a PhD in Law from Middlesex University.

Sonsoles Arias Guedón is Assistant Professor in Law at IE University in Madrid. She is also an Advocate with Elizalde & Barrie, specialising in litigation and arbitration practice.

Bikramjeet Batra is a lawyer and independent researcher, currently Research Associate at the SOAS School of Law, London. Previously, he worked with the United Nations Human Rights Office and with Amnesty International. He has published widely on the death penalty in India.

Arif Bulkan is Senior Lecturer at the Faculty of Law at the St Augustine campus of the University of the West Indies. He has published on democracy, the rule of law and constitutionalism in the Caribbean, the rights of indigenous persons, environmental law, and Caribbean human rights law.

Hannah Burrows is a dual US–UK qualified lawyer and holds degrees from the University of Oxford, University College London, and the University of Southern Denmark.

Sarah Lucy Cooper is a Reader in Interdisciplinary Legal Studies at Birmingham City University, the Director of Research in the School of Law, and a Senior Fellow of the UK Higher Education Authority. She is the editor of *Controversies in Innocence Cases in America* (Routledge 2014) and has published widely on the relationship between science and law.

Antonios Kouroutakis is Assistant Professor in Law at IE Law School in Madrid. He was most recently the author of *The Constitutional Value of*

Sunset Clauses (Routledge 2016). He was previously a postdoctoral fellow at Aristotle University of Thessaloniki and at the Free University of Berlin.

Nedžad Smailagić (LLB, LLM University of Sarajevo) is a doctoral candidate in criminal sciences at the Faculty of Law of the University of Zagreb. His previous affiliations include lectureships at the University of Sarajevo and Sarajevo School of Science and Technology, as well as research visits at the Institute of Criminal Sciences of the University of Poitiers and the Max Planck Institute for Foreign and International Criminal Law in Freiburg. He has published extensively on international and comparative criminal law.

Moulin Xiong is Chair of the Institute of Criminal Law and Associate Professor of Law at Southwestern University of Finance and Economics in Chengdu. He holds a PhD from the same institution. Xiong has published quantitative research on China's death penalty and sentencing practices and was previously a visiting scholar in sociology at the University of California, Irvine.

Foreword

Leslie Sebba

I was surprised and gratified to be informed that an article I published in the 1970s on pardoning power[1] was the departure point for this scholarly project by Daniel Pascoe and Andrew Novak on clemency (a sequel to the latter's earlier monograph *Comparative Executive Clemency*)[2] and that nothing comparable had been published in the intervening decades. On reflection, three factors contributed to my surprise: (1) considerations relating to the processes of knowledge production and prevailing academic practices; (2) the nature, circumstances, and parameters of the publication of my 1977 article; and, more particularly, (3) the expansive international and sociopolitical contexts of the development of criminal justice and human rights norms and practices over the past half-century, and their potential impact on the character and institutions of clemency powers.

With regard to the first point, the possibility that an individual publication from more than 40 years ago would be perceived as having a significant bearing on a contemporary research project must surely be remote given the exponential increase in academic publications during the intervening period,[3] a phenomenon related to the development of information technologies

1 Leslie Sebba, 'The Pardoning Power: A World Survey' (1977) 68(1) *The Journal of Criminal Law and Criminology* 83. See also Leslie Sebba, 'Clemency in Perspective' in Simha F Landau and Leslie Sebba (eds), *Criminology in Perspective: Essays in Honour of Israel Drapkin* (Lexington Books 1977).

2 Andrew Novak, *Comparative Executive Clemency: The Constitutional Pardon Power and the Prerogative of Mercy in Global Perspective* (Routledge 2015).

3 See, for example, Diana Crane, *Invisible Colleges; Diffusion of Knowledge in Scientific Communities* (University of Chicago Press 1972). Thus, a fairly recent search for publications in a related area (victimology) which I became involved in during the 1970s identified more than 10,000 academic articles relating to victims published between 1960 and 2012 (Leslie Sebba and Tamar Berenblum, 'Victimology and the sociology of new disciplines: A research agenda' (2014) 20(1) *International Review of Victimology* 7, 19). However, while the same growth phenomenon would surely apply to criminal justice in general, it may not be applicable to the specific topic of clemency as an object of academic research. Indeed, Crane (ibid., 1–3) noted variations in the patterns of growth among different scientific communities.

following World War Two. A related factor here is the expansion and transformation of academic structures,[4] particularly in newly recognised academic fields such as criminology and criminal justice.[5] Against this background, contemporary scholarship tends to lay emphasis on the *novelty* of its orientation and methodology rather than *continuity* or adherence to the models and methodologies of previous eras. Indeed, as an article tracing the historical development of victimology noted,[6] the 1970s—during which my work on the pardoning power was published—was a period in which two new criminal justice paradigms were emerging—an orientation to the victim and an emphasis on retribution and 'just deserts'. These developments are indicative of a dynamic of *transformation* rather than of *continuity* in criminal justice institutions during the decades in question, a topic on which I will expand further below.

As to the second factor, although exercise of the clemency powers was the field of my doctoral dissertation, I have devoted little attention to this topic since then. Indeed, even my 1977 article ('The Pardoning Power: A World Survey')[7] evolved somewhat by chance. My doctoral dissertation at the Hebrew University's Law Faculty, on pardons and amnesties,[8] was inspired by a general amnesty enacted in the wake of the Six Day War in Israel in 1967,[9] and focused on the structures of common law clemency powers as applied in Israel, which between 1917 and 1948 was a British Mandate. The dissertation included an account of the manner in which these powers were implemented and of the penological effects of the amnesty. However, the head of the Institute of Criminology to which I was affiliated, Professor Israel Drapkin, also offered to approach his numerous international contacts to provide me with materials relating to the norms and practices in this field in other parts of the world. Alas, these were insufficiently systematic to incorporate in the dissertation. Thereafter, during the initial stage of my postdoctoral fellowship at the University of Pennsylvania's Center of Criminology, I was able to enlarge my comparative sources on the basis of Peaslee's *Constitutions of Nations* and

4 See Andrew Abbott, *Chaos of Disciplines* (University of Chicago Press 2001).

5 A possible explanation for the paucity of academic publications on the topic of clemency as discerned by the editors of this volume may be that, while on the one hand this topic has never been focal to the relevant areas traditionally taught in law schools, such as constitutional law, criminal law and procedure, international law (given the dominantly domestic character of the exercise of the clemency powers), or legal theory, it also did not feature in these 'newly recognised academic fields'. The indisputable relevance of clemency to both the 'old' and the 'new' areas has, however, now been made evident in the authors' chapters and is the main focus of this Foreword.

6 Sebba and Berenblum (n 3) 12, 14.

7 Sebba, 'The Pardoning Power' (n 1).

8 Leslie Sebba, 'Pardon and Amnesty: Juridical and Penological Aspects' (Doctor of Law Thesis, Faculty of Law, Hebrew University of Jerusalem 1975).

9 See Leslie Sebba, 'Amnesty: A Quasi-Experiment' (1979) 19(1) *The British Journal of Criminology* 5, 5.

Blaustein and Flanz's *Constitutions of Countries of the World*, located in the University of Pennsylvania Law School Library.[10] These sources, however, were more concerned with formal structures than actual practice,[11] when compared with many of the analyses in the present volume.

Above all, however, I would have expected that radical transformations in the norms and practices of clemency would have taken place since the publication of an article of mine from the 1970s, not only by virtue of the passage of time, and the somewhat random changes which might therefore occur, but in particular because of the specific changes in the prevailing sociological, geopolitical, cultural, and constitutional norms and practices affecting the world's legal systems during the course of the intervening years. As a result of these changes, one might anticipate significant modifications in the patterns and practices of clemency—as well as new paradigms governing its institutions.

Two types of dynamic were envisaged here. In the first place, it should be recalled that the pardoning power has historically fulfilled a 'residuary' role in complementing the existing criminal justice systems and compensating for their deficiencies, such as the inability of the routine processes to correct miscarriages of justice or to take into account unusual personal circumstances, whether at the sentencing stage or during or after the implementation of sentence. In modern times, institutional reform has on occasion been specifically designed to correct these deficiencies, thereby ostensibly reducing the need for clemency powers. Thus, reforms have been adopted to deal with issues for which clemency had been the only available solution in the past, such as the adoption of provisions for appeals against conviction or retrials, the availability of new general defences, or the addition of discretionary powers to formerly mandatory sanctions (such as the revocation of driving or other licences).

However, in many other areas less ostensibly related to the pardoning power, new ideologies or specific reforms within the criminal justice system or its wider sociopolitical environment may also have possessed the potential to impact clemency powers or practices, though the extent and direction of this impact may be difficult to predict. Identification of the most relevant changes and reforms may be a problem, given the wide range of societal and legal contexts in which they take place. By way of illustration, consider my earlier reference to the two significant reorientations of the criminal justice system which took place in the 1970s, with the emergence of (a) victimology and (b) the 'just deserts' model of sentencing. The latter is analytically more closely linked to clemency and its impact on criminal punishment, since the policy being advocated was to move away from the penological model of individualised sentencing that had prevailed since the rise of the positivist school in the 1870s, in favour of a desert-based philosophy predicated on severity of

10 Amos Jenkins Peaslee, *Constitutions of Nations* (3rd edn, Martinus Nijhoff 1965); Albert P Blaustein and Gisbert H Flanz (eds), *Constitutions of Countries of the World* (Oceana Publications 1971). See Sebba, 'The Pardoning Power' (n 1) 84.

11 See Sebba, 'The Pardoning Power' (n 1) 121.

punishment proportional to the seriousness of the offence.[12] This was to be achieved by establishing sentencing commissions which would issue guidelines to courts. Whether explicitly or only implicitly, this policy proved antagonistic to the exercise of parole discretion.[13]

As we know, these proposals had a substantial impact on the US criminal justice system and further afield. Insofar as these policies were directed against the individualisation of the sentence, they could also be seen as hostile to the invocation of executive clemency powers (even though the grounds for individualisation in the two cases may be different). On the other hand, insofar as one of the objects of the reforms was to render judicial sentences less malleable, the need for clemency as a mechanism for evading an unjust or oppressive outcome may have, ironically, been enhanced.

The 1970s was also the decade in which the new (sub-) field of victimology began to emerge, one expression of which was the victims' rights movement, which generally contributed to the increasing harshness of sentences and to greater involvement on the part of the victims in the criminal justice system—sometimes extending to clemency procedures.[14] However, victimology has also given rise to a greater use of conciliation procedures such as restorative justice, sometimes advocating alternative processes outside the state-dominated criminal justice system.[15] This potential diversity of the impact of the victim's role is typical of the variety of directions in which clemency powers can develop in different locations from similar stimuli—given global variation in social, legal or political cultures.[16]

The text of the chapters comprising this publication—and the identification of the authors invited to contribute—indicate that the editors and authors were well aware of the transformations likely to have occurred in relation to the clemency powers since the 1970s. While I have here been emphasising the *a priori* uncertainty as to the specific impacts of the victimology and 'just deserts' trends in criminal justice, the authors—whose focus is *a posteriori*—have noted unexpected outcomes, and in particular the variations in patterns

12 Andrew von Hirsch, *Doing Justice: The Choice of Punishments* (Northeastern University Press 1976).

13 American Friends Service Committee, *Struggle for Justice: A Report on Crime and Punishment in America* (Hill and Wang 1971) 143–148; Alexander B Smith, Harriet Pollack and E Warren Benton, 'Sentencing Problems: A Pragmatic View' (1987) 51 *Federal Probation* 67, 67.

14 See Pascoe and Novak, this volume, and Novak and Pascoe, this volume, for legislative and constitutional examples from around the world.

15 See Nils Christie, 'Conflicts as Property' (1977) 17(1) *The British Journal of Criminology* 1. Restorative justice advocates also opposed the 'just deserts' movement, for example John Braithwaite and Philip Pettit, *Not Just Deserts: A Republican Theory of Criminal Justice* (Clarendon Press 1992).

16 Thus, several chapters make reference to the historically significant role of the victim in Muslim-majority states which incorporate Islamic Law into their criminal justice systems (see Sangiorgio, this volume; Novak and Pascoe, this volume; Appendix).

adopted by the states on which they have focused. For example, looking back on the last four decades, the authors have discerned the decline in the death penalty as a reliable source of clemency grants (contrary in some respects to the victim-centric and 'just deserts' trends evident in the 1970s), the rise of judicial review, and clemency's interaction with the 'innocence revolution' trend since the 1980s, among other developments.[17]

It would be of considerable intellectual interest to attempt to identify, by means of a detailed survey, the global changes and reforms which have taken place over the last four decades and which may have had a potential impact on clemency powers—i.e., an *a priori* list of significant developments since the 1970s. We could then compare these political, socio-legal and cultural changes with the actual (*a posteriori*) transformations of the clemency powers as identified by the authors of the chapters included in this volume. The results of such a comparison would tell us much about the timeless and, perhaps, anomalous place of clemency in global criminal justice systems. However, for brevity, below I restrict myself to a list of potentially relevant *a priori* developments[18]—some of which I have already alluded to above. Hopefully this list will serve to spur further academic debate, and will emphasise the significance of the authors' and editors' *a posteriori* analyses.

Constitutional, Criminological and Socio-Legal Contexts Affecting the Development of Clemency Powers and Practices

A. *Constitutional structures*—given clemency's historic identification with centralised monarchical regimes, what has been the impact of constitutionalism, democratisation, and professionalisation, and to what extent have clemency institutions become internationally standardised?

B. How far have contemporary *criminal justice processes* succeeded in replacing clemency procedures with, for example, appeals and rehearings to prevent miscarriages of justice?

C. What has been the role of reform of the *aims of punishment* and *sentencing structures* on the evolution of clemency?

D. How has *penal reform* affected clemency practice and structures, in particular through the restriction and abolition of capital and corporal punishment, limits placed on the duration of imprisonment (including life sentences), and the reform of prison conditions (such as concerning solitary confinement and overcrowding)?

E. How have changes in the scope and content of the *criminal law* and the allocation of penalties to various forms of deviance impacted clemency?

F. What has been the impact of *international human rights norms*, in particular since 1976, when the International Covenant on Civil and Political Rights entered into force? Moreover, has the expansion of the UN Human

17 See Novak and Pascoe, this volume, for a full summary.

18 Where appropriate I add a clarification as to the relevance of the topic.

Rights Committee's General Comments regulating the Covenant's implementation since the 1980s also affected clemency?

G.Has executive clemency changed since the emergence of *international criminal law*, and in particular *transitional justice,* including the controversial role of amnesties and 'positive obligations'?

Most of these issues have emerged or developed since the 1970s (items F and G and much of D even more recently), thus emphasising the importance of a contemporary academic focus on the institutions of clemency—and the timeliness of the present volume. This eclectic list of potential conceptual ties ensures that, in spite of a possible inclination to identify the clemency power with archaic and bygone regimes, the many academic questions associated with this topic seem unlikely to disappear any time soon.

Indeed, some of the more controversial issues within the list above appear to be at the peak of their academic interest, notably the topic of life imprisonment, which in some jurisdictions is already superseding capital punishment as the most problematic sanction.[19] Clemency is relevant both to the imposition and to the ultimate commutation of life imprisonment. Other topical issues pertain directly to the traditional image of the all-powerful sovereign controlling the penal system. This image is threatened (as noted by the authors) by the increasing expansion of international norms relating to penal sanctions, as also by the advent of international crimes. International jurisdiction has given rise to controversy in relation to the validity of domestic amnesty powers, thus possibly undermining the resolution of international disputes through truth-seeking processes or negotiation. A 'positive obligation' to prosecute and punish is sometimes seen as a boon to victim's rights. Thus, transitional justice situations raise questions as to which party has the authority to grant clemency, or to refuse to grant it. In an age of post-modernism and identity politics and the increasing fluidity of established legal institutions, such struggles may even play out within 'peaceful' constitutional regimes—relevant at the time of writing to US President Donald Trump's impeachment procedures and Israeli Prime Minister Benjamin Netanyahu's indictments—in both cases while seeking re-election.[20]

19 Dirk van Zyl Smit and Catherine Appleton, *Life Imprisonment: A Global Human Rights Analysis* (Harvard University Press 2019) 2, 87–88.

20 As Prime Minister of Israel, however, Netanyahu does not formally possess clemency powers, so (despite having wide powers to make and influence appointments) will not be in a position to 'pardon himself'—a threat often attributed to President Donald Trump. See further Jeffrey Crouch, 'President Donald J. Trump and the Clemency Power: Is Claiming "Unfair" Treatment for Pardon Recipients the New "Fake News"?' in Charles M Lamb and Jacob R Neiheisel, *Presidential Leadership and the Trump Presidency: Executive Power and Democratic Government* (Palgrave Macmillan 2020) 105–110; Brian C Kalt, 'Pardon Me: The Constitutional Case Against Presidential Self-Pardons' (1996–1997) 106 *Yale Law Journal* 779; Yonah Jeremy Bob, 'Rivlin will consider pardon if Netanyahu resigns, confesses' *The Jerusalem Post* (5 December 2019).

I was invited to contribute this Foreword by the editors of this volume on the basis of my survey of this topic in the 1970s, owing to the absence—despite the explosion in academic publishing at about that time—of additional publications since then analysing the global patterns and practices of clemency. While I have speculated as to how and why this should have come about,[21] this conundrum is surely intensified by the facility with which it has been possible to identify the many aspects of clemency that are highly relevant to contemporary aspects of 'punishment and society' and other important legal or sociopolitical topics. Hopefully my 1977 essay was nevertheless helpful in stimulating the questions which occupied the editors and authors in the planning of this volume. Its publication will surely be perceived by posterity as a turning point, providing a comprehensive basis for rethinking the changing historic role of clemency in the light of radical sociopolitical changes at both the national and international levels, thereby restoring the visibility of this topic in the international academic literature.

21 See note 5.

1 Executive Clemency

A Ubiquitous Part of the Constitutional Scheme

Daniel Pascoe and Andrew Novak

> [The] abolition of clemency may be a utopian aim—constantly to be pursued but never to be attained. [Cesare] Beccaria was undoubtedly correct in his view that a clemency power would be unnecessary when laws were perfected; but even the enlightened thinking of the eighteenth century philosophers could not produce perfect laws.
>
> Leslie Sebba, 1977[1]

Despite its anachronistic appearance, the power to grant clemency to persons convicted or accused of criminal offences 'remains an integral part of the constitutional scheme in almost every jurisdiction'.[2] This volume compares global executive clemency laws, and uncovers clemency practices in hitherto under-researched jurisdictions. Our aim is to demonstrate that executive clemency, despite its ancient origins, still plays an important and relatable role across the criminal justice systems of the world. So long as criminal laws remain imperfect, and are enforced and interpreted by human beings, clemency will persist as a necessary remedy to achieve more lenient punishments.

The starting point for comparative legal research on executive clemency is Leslie Sebba's 1977 journal article comparing clemency mechanisms globally.[3] More recently, publication of Andrew Novak's *Comparative Executive Clemency* in 2015 provided book-length treatment of the constitutional and legal

1 Leslie Sebba, 'Clemency in Perspective' in Simha F Landau and Leslie Sebba (eds), *Criminology in Perspective: Essays in Honour of Israel Drapkin* (Lexington Books 1977) 234.

2 Leslie Sebba, 'The Pardoning Power: A World Survey' (1977) 68(1) The Journal of Criminal Law and Criminology 83, 120; Carolyn Strange, 'Introduction' in Carolyn Strange (ed), *Qualities of Mercy: Justice, Punishment, and Discretion* (UBC Press 1996) 14–15; David Tait, 'Pardons in Perspective: The Role of Forgiveness in Criminal Justice' (2000) 13 Federal Sentencing Reporter 134, 135–136.

3 Sebba, 'The Pardoning Power' (n 2). See also Sebba, 'Clemency in Perspective' (n 1). For the reasons we describe below, within the collection our presumptive definition of clemency is as 'executive clemency', granted by a political actor from the executive branch of government.

mechanisms for executive clemency in the English-speaking world.[4] However, further empirical and comparative research on executive clemency is scarce, particularly given the secrecy of the decision-making process and the scarcity of data. The lack of academic scholarship on comparative clemency studies belies clemency's historical significance and its importance as a vital due process safeguard, particularly in death penalty cases. Though the clemency processes of US states and the US federal government are relatively well researched,[5] little scholarship exists on clemency practices in much of the rest of the world.

Good reasons exist for the scarcity of empirical literature on executive clemency. Deliberations are frequently performed in secret and clemency authorities rarely provide reasons for grants or denials. Even aggregate statistics on clemency outcomes may not be available. Traditionally, executive clemency was not subject to judicial review or to freedom of information laws, though this is changing.[6] Interviews providing personal perspectives from final

4 Andrew Novak, *Comparative Executive Clemency: The Constitutional Pardon Power and the Prerogative of Mercy in Global Perspective* (Routledge 2015).

5 A small selection includes the following works: Rachel E Barkow, 'The Ascent of the Administrative State and the Demise of Mercy' (2008) 121 Harv L Rev 1332; Rachel E Barkow, 'The Politics of Forgiveness: Reconceptualizing clemency' (2009) 21 Federal Sentencing Reporter 153; Margaret Colgate Love, 'Reinvigorating the Federal Pardon Process: What the President Can Learn from the State' (2013) 9 University of St Thomas Law Journal 730; Novak, *Comparative Executive Clemency* (n 4); Austin Sarat, *Mercy on Trial: What it Means to Stop an Execution* (Princeton University Press 2009); Austin Sarat and Nasser Hussain, 'Toward New Theoretical Perspectives on Forgiveness, Mercy, and Clemency: An Introduction' in Austin Sarat and Nasser Hussain (eds), *Forgiveness, Mercy, and Clemency* (Stanford University Press 2007); Jeffrey Crouch, *The Presidential Pardon Power* (University Press of Kansas 2009); Michael Radelet and Barbara Zsembik, 'Executive Clemency in Post-Furman Capital Cases Symposium: Clemency and Pardons' (1992) 27 University of Richmond Law Review 289; Hugo Adam Bedau, 'The Decline of Executive Clemency in Capital Cases' (1990) 18 New York University Review of Law & Social Change 255; Elizabeth Rapaport, 'Retribution and Redemption in the Operation of Executive Clemency' (1998) 74 Chicago-Kent Law Review 1501; Cathleen Burnett, 'The Failed Failsafe: The Politics of Executive Clemency' (2003) 8 Texas Journal of Civil Rights and Civil Liberties 192; Daniel T Kobil, 'Due Process in Death Penalty Commutations: Life, Liberty, and the Pursuit of Clemency' (1993) 27 U Richmond L Rev 201; Daniel T Kobil, 'Compelling Mercy: Judicial Review and the Clemency Power' (2011) 9 University of St Thomas Law Journal 698; Elkan Abramowitz and David Paget, 'Executive Clemency in Capital Cases' (1964) 39 New York University Law Review 136; Molly Clayton, 'Forgiving the Unforgivable: Reinvigorating the Use of Executive Clemency in Capital Cases' (2013) 54 Boston College Law Review 751; Jonathan Harris and Lothlórien Redmond, 'Executive Clemency: The Lethal Absence of Hope' (2007) 3 Criminal Law Brief 2; Michael Heise, 'Mercy by the Numbers: An Empirical Analysis of Clemency and its Structure' (2003) 89 Virginia Law Review 239; Michael Heise, 'The Geography of Mercy: An Empirical Analysis of Clemency for Death Row Inmates' (2013) 39 Thurgood Marshall Law Review 3; Michael Heise, 'The Death of Death Row Clemency and the Evolving Politics of Unequal Grace' (2015) 66 Alabama Law Review 949.

6 Andrew Novak, 'Transparency and Comparative Executive Clemency: Global Lessons for Pardon Reform in the United States' (2016) 49 U Mich JL Reform 817, 829–844. See also Cooper and Burrows, this volume; Bulkan, this volume.

decision-makers are also unusual given their high political status as heads of state or government, or as members of Cabinet. Clemency decisions are therefore 'shrouded in mystery and often fraught with arbitrariness' at a time when other aspects of criminal justice systems around the world have opened to academic scrutiny.[7] Yet, clemency decisions ultimately determine life or death for prisoners in death penalty retentionist jurisdictions and may be the last opportunity to prevent miscarriages of justice in all jurisdictions, whether retentionist or not.

This collection, with comparative and empirical contributions on executive clemency from around the world, will help to fill a longstanding gap in criminal justice research given clemency's relative opacity. The authors not only hope that academic scholarship will benefit from these findings, but also that the observations contained within this book's chapters will contribute to more transparent, enlightened and compassionate clemency laws and practices in the future.

Why Does Clemency Exist, and Why Is It Important?

Clemency is as old as centralised political authority itself: if crimes were committed against a sovereign, then the sovereign alone could forgive them. Ancient civilizations recorded acts of clemency as the prerogative of the rulers in ancient Rome, precolonial Africa, the pre-Columbian Americas, the early Islamic world, and elsewhere.[8] Clemency's durability across geographical space and time reflects its inherent political advantages. After the fall of the Roman Empire, when the Roman Catholic Church absorbed many functions of state through ecclesiastical law, popes, bishops, and other clergy could forgive transgressions on behalf of the divine.[9] Clemency is hardly unique to the Christian world, but it no doubt accorded well with the divine right of European royal dynasties. The political purposes for granting clemency went beyond solving crime or

7 Kobil, 'Due Process in Death Penalty Commutations' (n 5) 202.

8 Kathleen D Moore, *Pardons: Justice, Mercy and the Public Interest* (OUP 1989) 15–17; Daniel F Caner, 'Clemency, A Neglected Aspect of Early Christian Philanthropy' (2018) 9(8) Religions 2, 8; Carlo G Cereti, Mauro Maggi, and Elio Provasi, *Religious Themes and Texts of Pre-Islamic Iran and Central Asia: Studies in Honour of Professor Gherardo Gnoli on the Occasion of His 65th Birthday on 6th December 2002* (Reicher 2003) 208; Maria Vaiou, *Diplomacy in the Early Islamic World: A Tenth-century Treatise on Arab-Byzantine Relations* (IB Tauris 2015) 30; Zola Sonkosi, 'Amnesty from an African Point of View' in Erik Doxtader and Charles Villa-Vicencio (eds), *The Provocations of Amnesty: Memory, Justice, and Impunity* (New Africa Books 2003) 156; Pedro Sarmiento De Gamboa, *History of the Incas and the Execution of the Inca Tupac Amaru* (Cosimo Inc 2007) 148; James Robert Moriarty, *Ritual Combat: A Comparison of the Aztec "War of Flowers" and the Medieval "Mêlée": and The Origin and Development of Maya Militarism* (Colorado State College, Museum of Anthropology 1969); Novak, *Comparative Executive Clemency* (n 4) 14. See also Cooper and Burrows, this volume.

9 Adriano Prosperi, *Justice Blindfolded: The Historical Course of an Image* (Brill 2018) 98–99; Moore (n 8) 17.

exonerating the innocent; grants of pardon could end wars, co-opt political opponents, reward loyalists, or win favour from unruly subjects. In one grant of mercy, a ruler could forgive a supplicant on behalf of the divine and simultaneously bolster his or her legitimacy by appearing benevolent.[10]

Although clemency has been nearly universal among societies with centralised political authority, the modern institution of clemency has less varied origins. Because so much of the world was colonised by so little of it, modern clemency is, like the nation-state itself, almost entirely a product of European rule. This is not to say that modern clemency bears much resemblance to the medieval versions seen in England or France. The English monarch's ability to pardon goes back to the Anglo-Saxon period, as early as the seventh century, though the common use of compensation (the *wergild*) for homicide and other injurious offences ensured that clemency was infrequent.[11] It was only when punishments imposed by central authorities such as transportation or corporal and capital punishment became common that the importance of clemency increased, especially seeing as the payment of *wergild* declined after the Norman conquest.[12] However, in the medieval period, pardons had to be paid for. In England, a subject would purchase a copy of the pardon from the chancery and present the endorsed paper in court in the event of a subsequent prosecution.[13] Across the channel in France, the grovelling supplicant had to purchase from the chancellor a letter of remission, signed and sealed in green wax with silken threads, which he or she would present in court.[14] In all instances, the inability to pay for the pardon was a significant obstacle to redress, though pardons could be issued to the indigent or sold on credit. A lack of access to the ruling classes or to well-connected intermediaries like artisans or soldiers posed an even greater challenge to those who sought mercy.[15]

As their empires expanded across Africa, Asia, and the Americas, European rulers exercised the pardon power over their increasing numbers of colonial subjects. In practice, however, a trend toward depersonalising the power began. In France, this process was dramatic: the revolutionaries abolished the king's pardon power and transferred it to parliament in 1789. It was restored to Napoleon Bonaparte in 1802, but with intermittent parliamentary oversight

10 Daniel T Kobil, 'Quality of Mercy Strained: Wresting the Pardoning Power from the King' (1991) 69 Texas L Rev 569, 586; Novak, *Comparative Executive Clemency* (n 4) 20–21; Prosperi (n 9) 96–98.
11 Naomi D Hurnard, *The King's Pardon for Homicide before AD 1307* (OUP 1969) 1.
12 Ibid., 1–5.
13 Ibid., 55–62.
14 Natalie Zemon Davis, *Fiction in the Archives: Pardon Tales and Their Tellers in Sixteenth-Century France* (Stanford University Press 1987) 7–12.
15 Hurnard (n 11) 33, 41, 55; Helen Lacey, *The Royal Pardon: Access to Mercy in Fourteenth-Century England* (Boydell & Brewer 2009) 21, 27, 44–45; Novak, *Comparative Executive Clemency* (n 4) 18–20.

thereafter.[16] In Britain the adjustment of the clemency power to the modern administrative state was more gradual. With Queen Victoria's reign in 1837, Parliament delegated the royal prerogative of mercy to the Home Secretary, who was to exercise the power in the queen's name. From that point on, by convention, the clemency power has been exercised by a bureaucratic and politically accountable actor rather than the monarch personally.[17] In Spain, the clemency power dates to at least 1291.[18] The Spanish king frequently granted both general and individual pardons: the former were often tied to commemoration of religious holidays, while the latter were conditioned on one's noble service, good deeds, or payment of money.[19] Since 1870, the pardon power has been regulated by statute. Under a law promulgated during that year, the Ministry of Justice presents a pardon application to the Cabinet, which in turn makes a recommendation to the king.[20]

The bureaucratisation of the clemency power in Europe accompanied the expansion of clemency to the colonies. In British colonies, the pardon power was transmitted to colonial governors with only rare intervention from the London-based Colonial Office. Among the earliest colonies established by joint-stock corporations, such as the Massachusetts Bay or East India Companies, the pardon power was contained in the companies' royal charters.[21] In later colonies, the pardon power was written in the letters patent creating the colony. The governor-general, the monarch's colonial representative, would typically consult with a Cabinet or executive council in making a pardon decision on the monarch's behalf.[22] Only in situations of gross excess, such as after the Upper Canada rebellion in the 1830s, the Mau Mau war in Kenya in the 1950s, or the executions of African nationalists in Rhodesia in the 1960s, did the Colonial Office attempt to interfere.[23] All former British colonies inherited

16 René Lévy, 'Pardons and Amnesties as Policy Instruments in Contemporary France' (2007) 36 Crime and Justice 554 (noting that each of the five French constitutions created a different balance between the executive and legislature).

17 ATH Smith, 'The Prerogative of Mercy, The Power of Pardon and Criminal Justice' (1983) PL 398, 426.

18 Juan Luis Jiménez and José Abreu, 'Pardon Does Not Forgive Democracy: Econometrical Analysis of Pardons in Spain' (2016) 216 Review of Public Economics 81.

19 Ruth Pike, 'Capital Punishment in Eighteenth-Century Spain' (1985) 18 Histoire Sociale Social History 375, 379.

20 Law 1/1988, 14 January, updating Law 18 June 1870, establishing rules for the exercise of pardon.

21 Norman D Lattin, 'The Pardoning Power in Massachusetts' (1931) 11 Boston University Law Review 505, 507–508; Bikram Jeet Batra, '"Court" of Last Resort: A Study of Constitutional Clemency for Capital Crimes in India' (2009) Jawaharlal Nehru University Centre for the Study of Law and Governance Working Paper Series CSLG/WP/11, 6–8 <https://www.jnu.ac.in/sites/default/files/u63/11-Court%20%28Bikram%29.pdf> accessed 21 August 2019.

22 Novak, *Comparative Executive Clemency* (n 4) 25.

23 For the Upper Canada Rebellion, see Barry Wright, '"Harshness and Forbearance": The Politics of Pardons and the Upper Canada Rebellion' in Carolyn

some version of the colonial clemency practice in their independence constitutions. The Colonial Office assisted in drafting more than thirty 'Whitehall constitutions' for newly independent colonies that contained a clemency provision based on the British model, many of which still provide for Cabinet review or an advisory mercy committee to make clemency recommendations to the president.[24]

The other European colonial powers were similarly influential in transmitting their clemency structures to their former colonies. In an 1880 decree, persons condemned to death in French colonies could appeal their verdicts directly to the French president, which was a lengthy process albeit one that frequently led to commutation of the sentence. French colonial governors could no longer execute without approval from Paris.[25] At independence, this centralised model of clemency was replicated in the colonies. France's unitary state with a strong executive, a hallmark of the Constitution of the Fifth Republic (1958), was reflected in the template for colonies that had become autonomous members of the new French Community. In 1959, for instance, Côte d'Ivoire adopted a French-style constitution that preserved executive dominance over the legislature in a unitary state.[26] Although a second constitution was summarily adopted at full independence in 1960, the new version kept the strong executive structure. Article 20 of the 1960 Ivorian constitution was identical to Article 17 of the 1958 Constitution of the French Fifth Republic: 'The President of the Republic has the right to pardon' ('*Le président de la République a le droit de faire grâce*').[27]

Strange (ed), *Qualities of Mercy: Justice, Punishment, and Discretion* (UBC Press 1996) 81. The Canadian government granted a large number of conditional pardons to the rebels and then attempted to leave the expense of transporting the rebels to the Australian penal colonies to the Colonial Office. For the Mau Mau War, see David Anderson, *Histories of the Hanged: The Dirty War in Kenya and the End of Empire* (WW Norton & Co Inc 2005) 7, 111 (describing Governor Sir Evelyn Baring's refusal to spare Mau Mau rebels even when the trial judge recommended mercy). For Rhodesia, see Andrew Novak, 'Abuse of State Power: The Mandatory Death Penalty for Political Crimes in Southern Rhodesia, 1963–1970' (2013) 19 Fundamina: Journal of Legal History 28, 45. After their unilateral declaration of independence from Great Britain, Queen Elizabeth II attempted to pardon several African nationalists sentenced to death on the advice of the Commonwealth Secretary. However, Rhodesian courts found that only the Rhodesian government had the right to pardon after the unilateral declaration of independence and the nationalists were executed thereafter.

24 William Dale, 'The Making and Remaking of Commonwealth Constitutions' (1993) 42 ICLQ 67, 80–81.

25 Stephen A Toth, *Beyond Papillon: The French Overseas Penal Colonies, 1854–1952* (University of Nebraska Press 2006) 113.

26 AS Alexander 'The Ivory Coast Constitution: An Accelerator, not a Brake' (1963) 1 Journal of Modern African Studies 293, 296.

27 Constitution of Côte d'Ivoire 1960, art 20; Constitution of France 1958, art 17. Côte d'Ivoire enacted a new constitution in 2016. The pardoning power is identical to the 1960 constitution but is now located in art 66. By contrast, a constitutional amendment in France in 2008 limited the president's pardon power

In many jurisdictions around the world, the clemency power has gradually evolved from a personal prerogative of the ruler to a democratically accountable and constitutionally defined power. What is more striking is that the original array of justifications for granting executive clemency have changed little over the last millennium. Clemency still forms the final procedural avenue separating life and death in capital cases and a prisoner's final avenue of 'appeal' in all cases, capital and non-capital. This final safety valve is particularly important not just to redress violations of due process, but also in claims of actual innocence. Clemency may also be used to further individualise punishment on retributive grounds and to encourage and reward rehabilitation and demonstrated remorse in prison. Outside of ordinary judicial parameters, clemency can also be used as a utilitarian tool to benefit the broader populace, such as by reducing prison overcrowding, making peace between both sides of a civil conflict, or by rewarding police informants. Finally, as has been true over the centuries, clemency may be granted by political leaders to boost their own legitimacy in the eyes of domestic constituents and foreign governments.[28]

What Is Executive Clemency?

In the common law world, the term 'clemency' generally refers to the four traditional components of the royal prerogative of mercy, inherited from the United Kingdom, namely pardons, commutations of sentence, reprieves, and remissions of fines or forfeitures. The sovereign possessed the prerogative to replace one punishment with a lesser one, or with no punishment at all.[29] However, the conception of legal mercy is broader than this, and traditional forms of clemency overlap with conditional pardons and parole; exonerations or expungements; restoration of rights where criminal convictions result in continuing legal disabilities; and innocence pardons to correct wrongful convictions. Moreover, as described in further detail below, the civil law 'amnesty' in the continental European tradition shares many characteristics with a group or general pardon in English history.[30]

only to *individual* cases. The new art 17 states, *Le Président de la République a le droit de faire grâce à titre individuel* ('The President of the Republic has the right to pardon individually') (Loi constitutionnelle no 2008–724 de modernisation des institutions de la Ve République, JUSX0807076L (23 July 2008)).

28 Daniel Pascoe, *Last Chance for Life: Clemency in Southeast Asian Death Penalty Cases* (OUP 2019) 45–50; Novak, *Comparative Executive Clemency* (n 4) 20; Sebba, 'Clemency in Perspective' (n 1) 227–232.

29 Novak, 'Transparency and Comparative Executive Clemency' (n 6) 819.

30 Lacey (n 15) 85–89; Carolyn Strange, *Discretionary Justice: Pardon and Parole in New York from the Revolution to the Depression* (NYU Press 2016) 145; Andrew Novak, 'The Pardon Power' in *Max Planck Encyclopedia of Comparative Constitutional Law* (2016) para 4 <https://oxcon.ouplaw.com/view/10.1093/law:mpeccol/law-mpeccol-e405> accessed 15 June 2019.

Most of this book's contributions focus on pardons and commutations,[31] as these are the legal mechanisms effecting permanent changes to a sentence of death or imprisonment handed down by a court. Pardons generally connote freeing the prisoner altogether, sometimes accompanied by the restoration of civil rights or even a declaration of innocence, whereas commutation refers to one sentence being supplanted by another (such as a death sentence becoming a life sentence), or a sentence being reduced—often a prison sentence being reduced without entitling the prisoner to immediate release. In this sense, the book concerns the quasi-legal power of clemency afforded to executive decision-makers, be those presidents, monarchs, boards, ministers and so forth, rather than the lay definition of 'clemency', which refers to any leniency or mercy by someone in a position of power.[32] As traditionally understood by constitutional lawyers and political scientists, the power of clemency is a key component of the separation of powers, as an executive 'check' on the powers of the judiciary to punish.[33]

Other than the effect of the grant, the legal structures for executive clemency also vary widely. In some systems, an executive's decision is unfettered, while in others he or she must consult with an advisory board or with another political actor. In still others, the executive is bound by the recommendation of a pardons board or a justice ministry; in a handful of jurisdictions, the board itself makes the final decision.[34] Yet, the legal frameworks for clemency decision-making provide few clues as to the actual *practice* of clemency. In practice, elaborate clemency structures are moribund or dormant in some systems, while in others clemency is routine, expected, and frequent, despite few governing procedures. Absent comparison of empirical trends between jurisdictions, we have no way of knowing what is normal or exceptional within any criminal justice system.[35] In addition, comparative study can reveal systematic patterns, such as whether race, gender, nationality, or other characteristics are correlated to the exercise of the clemency power. Study of

31 Nonetheless, several of the contributions employ the term 'pardon' to refer to both releases from prison and commutations of sentence (Arias and Kouroutakis, this volume; Smailagić, this volume; Cooper and Burrows, this volume; Bulkan, this volume).

32 Austin Sarat and Nasser Hussain (eds), *Forgiveness, Mercy and Clemency* (Stanford University Press 2007) 3–5; Nicole F Dailo, '"Give Me Dignity by Giving Me Death": Using Balancing to Uphold Death Row Volunteers Dignity Interests Amidst Executive Clemency' (2014) 23 Southern California Review of Law and Social Justice 249, 260.

33 Peter M Shane, 'Presidents, Pardons, and Prosecutors: Legal Accountability and the Separation of Powers' (1993) 11(2) Yale L & Poly Rev 361, 363; Rachel E Barkow, 'Clemency and Presidential Administration of Criminal Law' (2015) 90 NYU L Rev 802, 831. Contrast Sebba, 'The Pardoning Power' (n 2) 83.

34 Novak, 'Transparency and Comparative Executive Clemency' (n 6) 823–829.

35 David Nelken 'Why Compare Criminal Justice?' in Mary Bosworth and Carolyn Hoyle (eds), *What Is Criminology?* (OUP 2011) 395–396; David T Johnson and Franklin E Zimring, *The Next Frontier: National Development, Political Change, and the Death Penalty in Asia* (OUP 2009) 38.

comparative clemency may even provide clues as to what works best, from a procedural point of view.[36]

Clemency has always been defined by the tension between the 'charismatic' and the 'legal-rational', to use Max Weber's terminology.[37] Is clemency like a lightning bolt, a benevolent and unexpected act of grace? Or is clemency rule-bound, subject to administrative and constitutional limitations, guided by narrow, impartial criteria?[38] The current answer, of course, is both. However, we propose that in world-historical terms, clemency has gradually become more legal-rational over time. As clemency has become more defined and rule-bound, it becomes increasingly indistinguishable from other forms of institutionalized legal mercy like parole, probation, remission of sentence, and expungement, all of which are subject to formal procedure, strict criteria, and public scrutiny.[39] This is not to necessarily predict clemency's terminal demise. Clemency has adjusted to the times, just as punishment has: conditional pardons were more common when transportation to a penal colony was used as punishment, and commutations of sentence were particularly useful in systems with the mandatory death penalty. But perhaps in the future, in a world of growing incarceration, closed borders, and budget austerity, clemency may be used more frequently to address prison overcrowding, save money within the criminal justice system, or prevent deportation of a convicted immigrant, for instance. We believe that clemency still has lives left to live.

What Is Clemency's Relationship with Amnesty?

Although its boundaries are hard to define, the classic conception of 'clemency' involves an individual supplicant seeking mercy from the monarch for forgiveness—it conjures an image both of individual applicant and benevolent, autocratic sovereign. The classic representation of 'amnesty' is quite different: in the popular imagination, an amnesty suggests a group of former rebels agreeing to lay down arms in exchange for peace.[40] A basic etymological distinction exists between clemency and amnesty: one comes from Latin and the other from Greek. The word 'pardon' comes from Vulgar Latin *perdonare*, 'to forgive'. The Latin word *clemens* means 'merciful, lenient, and gentle', while

36 Pascoe, *Last Chance for Life* (n 28) 22–23; David Hirschel, William Wakefield and Scott Sasse, *Criminal Justice in England and the United States* (2nd edn, Jones & Bartlett Learning 2008) 350; Novak, *Comparative Executive Clemency* (n 4) 198.

37 Max Weber, *On Charisma and Institution Building* (SN Eisenstadt ed, University of Chicago Press 1968) 46–47.

38 Novak, *Comparative Executive Clemency* (n 4) 148. For example, see Batra, this volume.

39 Novak, 'Transparency and Comparative Executive Clemency' (n 6) 818.

40 Louise Mallinder, *Amnesty, Human Rights and Political Transitions: Bridging the Peace and Justice Divide* (Bloomsbury Publishing 2008) 4, 29; Louise Mallinder, 'Amnesties and International Criminal Law' in William Schabas and Nadia Bérnaz (eds), *The Handbook of International Criminal Law* (Routledge 2010) 417, 419.

the ancient Greek word *amnestia* or ἀμνηστία means 'forgetfulness, failure to mention, or passing over', as with the derivative English word 'amnesia'.

That amnesties and pardons have evolved into comparable legal devices in modern constitutional systems is something of a historical accident. National constitutions and academic writings are inconsistent about the boundary between 'amnesty' and 'pardon'. Some commentators have viewed amnesty as a type of clemency, alongside commutations, pardons, and reprieves,[41] or vice versa.[42] Where constitutional systems do not create separate amnesty and clemency powers, executives sometimes claim the ability to grant both. This is particularly true in those nations like the United States where the executive can pardon before conviction. US Presidents, for instance, have used the constitutional pardon power to grant proclamations of mass amnesty at the end of the Civil War and the Vietnam War, though the US Congress may also exercise a legislative amnesty power.[43] The President of Zimbabwe has issued 'Clemency Orders' that pre-empted prosecutions for human rights abuses after election violence—something that looks suspiciously like an amnesty.[44] By contrast, in countries where an executive is not empowered to pardon before conviction, such as with the President of India, the distinction between clemency and amnesty more closely aligns with the original etymological distinction between forgiving and forgetting.

Generally speaking, clemency and amnesty may be distinguished on four separate grounds. First, the clemency authority is often (but not always) located within the executive branch in a system adopting a separation of powers. By contrast, amnesty is often (but not always) legislative in nature. Second, clemency is often (but not always) made after conviction, while amnesties are designed to pre-empt prosecution. Third, clemency is often (but not always) provided to individuals, while amnesty is for classes or groups of potential offenders. However, general and group pardons existed at common law and individual amnesties, those for a 'class of one', have also

41 Adam Sitze, 'Keeping the Peace' in Austin Sarat and Nasser Hussain (eds), *Forgiveness, Mercy and Clemency* (Stanford University Press 2007) 3–5; Louis Joinet, 'Study on Amnesty Laws and Their Role in the Safeguards and Protection of Human Rights' (ECOSOC 1985); Mary Bosworth (ed), *Encylcopedia of Prisons and Correctional Facilities* (SAGE Publications Inc 2005) 135.

42 Mallinder, *Amnesty, Human Rights and Political Transitions* (n 40) 6; Faustin Ntoubandi, *Amnesty for Crimes against Humanity under International Law* (Brill 2007) 11.

43 Novak, *Comparative Executive Clemency* (n 4) 192; Murray Illson, 'At Least 12 Presidents Involved in Pardon or Amnesty Moves' *New York Times* (22 January 1977) 10.

44 'Use of the Presidential Pardon in Zimbabwe' (2001) 45 Journal of African Law 231, citing Clemency Order No. 1 of 2000 (General Notice 457A) (Zimbabwe). The Clemency Order granted a 'free pardon' to 'every person liable to criminal prosecution for any politically motivated crime committed' after the 2000 elections, excluding murder, sexual offences, robbery, and a handful of other crimes.

been granted by legislatures in civil law countries.[45] Finally, amnesties and pardons may be distinguished by their purpose, though this is probably the weakest of the four distinguishing criteria. Often, pardons are issued for ordinary crimes while amnesties are used for political crimes or in a transitional justice context.

The position this book adopts is that the power's formal legal name is not as important as who exercises it. Where the power of leniency is exercised by the executive branch of government, we consider it as falling within a broad definition of 'clemency', whether the national constitution labels this 'commutation', 'pardon', 'amnesty', or indeed 'clemency' itself. Likewise, it is possible, depending on the accuracy of translation, that some national systems designate 'pardons' and 'commutations' as the province of the legislative branch, and therefore outside of our presumptive definition.[46] In the book, our chapter authors define clemency as executive clemency by default, unless they affirmatively depart from this presumption for reasons explained in their chapters.[47]

We limit this study of 'clemency' to the power of the executive rather than the legislature for several reasons. First, executive clemency is accorded greater recognition under international law, albeit only within death penalty cases. The International Covenant on Civil and Political Rights ('ICCPR') guarantees an individual condemned prisoner's 'right to seek' relief at the post-judicial stage in Article 6(4) via 'pardon' or 'commutation',[48] whereas the Inter-American Court of Human Rights considered the 'right to grace' as forming part of the international 'corpus juris'.[49] It is much more difficult for a single prisoner to request

45 Sebba, 'Clemency in Perspective' (n 1) 232; Novak, 'The Pardon Power' (n 30) para 4; Novak, *Comparative Executive Clemency* (n 4) 9–10.

46 To take one example, 40 US state constitutions exclude impeachment from the scope of the pardon power and 22 US state constitutions exclude treason. Many of these constitutions require a 'legislative pardon' for crimes of impeachment or treason, so as to prevent self-pardons. This was also the practice in England after Charles II attempted to pardon Thomas Osborne, the Earl of Danbury and Lord High Treasurer, in 1678 after Osborne faced impeachment for treason: see Novak, *Comparative Executive Clemency* (n 4) 102–104, 110–111.

47 See also note 31, on terminology.

48 See UN Human Rights Committee, 'General Comment No. 36 (2018) on art 6 of the International Covenant on Civil and Political Rights, on the Right to Life' (2018) CCPR/C/GC/36, para 47. ICCPR art 6(4) states in full: 'Anyone sentenced to death shall have the right to seek pardon or commutation of the sentence. Amnesty, pardon or commutation of the sentence of death may be granted in all cases.'

49 *Fermin Ramirez v Guatemala* (Inter-American Court of Human Rights, 20 June 2005), para 109: 'The Court considers that the right to grace forms part of the international corpus juris'. See also Anti-death Penalty Asia Network, 'When Justice Fails: Thousands executed in Asia after unfair trials' (*Anti-Death Penalty Asia Network*, AI Index ASA/01/023/2011, 2011) 31 <https://adpandotnet.files.wordpress.com/2011/11/adpan-unfair-trials-asa-010232100-final-pdf.pdf> accessed 17 November 2017 and William Schabas, *The Abolition of the Death Penalty in International Law* (3rd edn, CUP 2002), 168, on the right to apply for pardon or commutation and customary international law.

action from the legislature to relieve the death sentence (or a prison sentence), and this is presumably not what the ICCPR's drafters had contemplated in including the first sentence of Article 6(4).[50] The (legislative) 'amnesty' power is present with Article 6(4)'s second sentence, but the final draft of the ICCPR did not include a 'right' to seek amnesty, as with commutation or pardon—it is offered as a unilateral remedy only. While the 'positive' right to seek clemency in death penalty cases does not necessarily apply to amnesty, the negative prohibition in the ICCPR, however, applies to both.[51]

Second, while it risks overgeneralisation, we propose that executive clemency is unique precisely because it is such a personal power, resistant to institutional oversight, and revealing of the executive's policy preferences and motivations. Legislative amnesties primarily suit political or utilitarian aims rather than criminological ones. Legislation is by nature a compromise, revealing a collective viewpoint and one that is not specific to any individual case, no matter how gross the injustice.

Third and finally, we also observe that amnesty has been the subject of a growing global comparative literature, especially in transitional justice contexts.[52] The empirical and comparative study of clemency law and practice is,

50 Note 48. See further Sangiorgio, this volume.
51 Ibid.
52 See e.g. Roman Boed, 'The Effect of a Domestic Amnesty on the Ability of Foreign States to Prosecute Alleged Perpetrators of Serious Human Rights Violations' (2000) 33 Cornell International Law Journal 297; Jessica Gavron, 'Amnesties in the Light of Developments in International Law and the Establishment of the International Criminal Court' (2002) 51 ICLQ 91; Louise Mallinder, 'Can Amnesties and International Justice be Reconciled?' (2007) 1 International Journal of Transitional Justice 208; Mallinder, *Amnesty, Human Rights and Political Transitions* (n 40); Darryl Robinson, 'Serving the Interests of Justice: Amnesties, Truth Commissions and the International Criminal Court' (2003) 14 European Journal of International Law 481; Josepha Close, 'Amnesty Provisions in the Constitutions of the World: A Comparative Analysis' (*International Law Blog*, 5 January 2015) <https://aninternationallawblog.wordpress.com/2015/01/05/amnesty-provisions-in-the-constitutions-of-the-world-a-comparative-analysis/> accessed 21 September 2016; Josepha Close, *Amnesty, Serious Crimes and International Law: Global Perspectives in Theory and Practice* (Routledge 2019); William W Burke-White, 'Reframing Impunity: Applying Liberal International Law Theory to an Analysis of Amnesty Legislation' (2001) 42 Harv Intl LJ 467; Tricia D Olsen, Leigh A Payne and Andrew G Reiter, 'Transitional Justice in the World, 1970–2007: Insights from a New Dataset' (2010) 47(6) J Peace Research 803; Francesca Lessa and Leigh A Payne (eds), *Amnesty in the Age of Human Rights Accountability: Comparative and International Perspectives* (CUP 2012); Roldan Jimeno, *Amnesties, Pardons and Transitional Justice: Spain's Pact of Forgetting* (Routledge 2017); Renee Jeffrey, *Amnesties, Accountability, and Human Rights* (University of Pennsylvania 2014); Mark Freeman, *Necessary Evils: Amnesties and the Search for Justice* (CUP 2009); Ntoubandi (n 42); Kieran McEvoy and Louise Mallinder, 'Amnesties in Transition: Punishment, Restoration, and the Governance of Mercy' (2012) 39 Journal of Law and Society 410; Kieran McEvoy and Louise Mallinder, 'Rethinking Amnesties: Atrocity, Accountability and Impunity in Post-Conflict Societies, Contemporary Social Science' (2011) 6 Journal of the Academy of Social Sciences 107; Margaret Popkin and Nehal Bhuta, 'Latin American Amnesties in Comparative Perspective: Can the Past Be

we believe, less developed.[53] For these reasons, this book focuses on executive pardons and commutations, even though, in a given system, legislative amnesties may benefit more people given their collective application, and will therefore attract greater media attention and public scrutiny.

Sebba's Findings in 1977

Our historical frame of reference for this book is Leslie Sebba's journal article on comparative clemency across the world, authored in 1977, and based upon data from 1970–1976.[54] This collection forms the next attempt to compare clemency over such a global scale, albeit some 40 years after Sebba first did so. In the preceding 40 years, other scholars have compared executive clemency across national borders within regional or more limited international contexts,[55] including Novak's book-length treatment of comparative executive clemency in the common law world.[56] However, Sebba's work remains the

Buried?' (1999) 13 Ethics & International Affairs 99; Priscilla B Hayner, 'Fifteen Truth Commissions—1974 to 1994: A Comparative Study' (1994) 16 Human Rights Quarterly 597.

53 On the existing comparative and empirical literature, see e.g. Rob Turrell, 'It's a Mystery: The Royal Prerogative of Mercy in England, Canada, and South Africa' (2000) 4 Crime, History & Societies 83; Daniel Pascoe, *Last Chance for Life* (n 28); Daniel Pascoe, 'Towards a Global Theory of Capital Clemency Incidence' in Carol Steiker and Jordan Steiker (eds), *Comparative Capital Punishment Law* (Edward Elgar 2019); Daniel Pascoe and Marie Manikis, 'Making Sense of the Victim's Role in Clemency Decision Making' (*International Review of Victimology*, 9 November 2018) <https://doi.org/10.1177/0269758018805567> accessed 21 August 2019; Jody C Baumgartner and Mark H Morris, 'Presidential Power Unbound: A Comparative Look at Presidential Pardon Power' (2001) 29(2) Politics and Policy 209; The Parliamentary Monitoring Group, 'The Power to Pardon' (2004) <http://pmg-assets.s3-website-eu-west-1.amazonaws.com/docs/2004/appendices/040218pardon.htm> accessed 2 September 2017; Ariane M Schreiber, 'States That Kill: Discretion and the Death Penalty—A Worldwide Perspective' (1996) 29 Cornell International Law Journal 263; Claudia Ilona Dascalu, 'Elements of Comparative Law on the Individual Pardon, Between Constitutional Constraint and Discretionary Prerogative of the Head of State' (2012) 2(2) Union of Jurists of Romania Law Review 1; Strange 'Introduction' (n 2); Tait (n 2); Heise, 'Mercy by the Numbers' (n 5); Heise, 'The Geography of Mercy' (n 5); Heise, 'The Death of Death Row Clemency' (n 5); Novak, *Comparative Executive Clemency* (n 4); Novak, 'Transparency and Comparative Executive Clemency' (n 6); John Kraemer, 'An Empirical Examination of the Factors Associated with the Commutation of State Death Row Prisoners' Sentences between 1986 and 2005' (2008) 45 American Criminal Law Review 1389; William A Pridemore, 'An Empirical Examination of Commutations and Executions in Post-Furman Capital Cases' (2000) 17(1) Justice Quarterly 159.

54 Sebba, 'The Pardoning Power' (n 2) 83. See also Sebba, 'Clemency in Perspective' (n 1), which deals with similar themes.

55 See note 53.

56 Novak, *Comparative Executive Clemency* (n 4).

only truly global comparative study of executive clemency laws, whether applicable to capital or non-capital cases, during the twentieth and twenty-first centuries. The remainder of this chapter observes and explains changes in the constitutional provisions regulating executive clemency since Sebba's scholarship was first published, in order to set the stage for the comparative and empirical analyses presented within later chapters of the book.

In conducting his comparative study of national constitutions from the mid-1970s, Sebba surveyed the following components of national constitutions as they related to executive clemency:[57] the identity of the formal clemency decision-maker, recommending or countersigning bodies, other advisory bodies, allowances for special categories of offender and offence, and the categories of clemency mentioned in each constitution.[58] In brief, his findings published in 1977 were as follows.

1. Clemency Is Ubiquitous

Sebba observed that the power to grant post-judicial 'clemency' in some way, shape, or form existed in all of the 100 jurisdictions he studied,[59] with the possible exception of the People's Republic of China ('PRC'). In 1975, shortly before Sebba's article was published, the PRC had adopted a new stripped-down constitution, which made it unclear whether executive or legislative authorities would have any authority to pardon.[60] At the time of writing, Sebba was unsure whether the Chinese authorities would update the newly promulgated document with specific reference to a power to pardon or commute sentences.[61] Looking back at the PRC's first constitution from 1954 (Articles 27(12) and 40), this appeared likely at the time, given that 'special amnesties' or 'general amnesties' could be promulgated by the head of state, on the instruction of the legislature.[62] As it was, the PRC's third constitution rectified this omission in 1978, restoring the power to grant 'special amnesty' to the Standing Committee of the National People's

57 Sebba also analysed non-constitutional sources such as penal codes and codes of criminal procedure, albeit in selected cases (Sebba, 'The Pardoning Power' (n 2) 84). For several nations he provided statistics on clemency grants.

58 Ibid., 84–85.

59 Sebba included within his survey New South Wales and Queensland (Australia), Netherlands Antilles (Netherlands), Ukraine (USSR), and Rhodesia (UK), none of which were independent sovereign states at the time.

60 Sebba, 'Clemency in Perspective' (n 1) 222. The PRC's 1975 Constitution did allow for the Standing Committee of the National People's Congress to enact unspecified 'decrees' (art 18) and for the State Council to 'issue decisions and orders' in accordance with laws and decrees passed by the legislature. The PRC's fourth and most recent constitution, enacted in 1982, postdates Sebba's analysis.

61 Sebba, 'The Pardoning Power' (n 2) 84, 88.

62 Constitution of the PRC 1954, art 27(12), 27(15) and 40. The Chinese term 赦 (shè) may be translated as either 'amnesty' or 'commutation' or 'pardon' (Charles Sanft, 'Concepts of Law in the Shangshu' in Martin Kern and Dirk Meyer (eds), *Origins of Chinese Political Philosophy: Studies in the Composition and Thought of the Shangshu* (Brill 2017) 463–464).

Congress ('SCNPC'), a legislative body, with the special amnesty decision to be ratified by the Chairman of the SCNPC—at the time, the PRC's head of state.[63] Other than Sebba's doubts over the PRC, the royal prerogative of mercy existed as an 'unwritten' conventional power in two jurisdictions of the British Commonwealth, namely in Australia (and its constituent states) and New Zealand. Sebba included both of these nations in his analysis.[64]

Nevertheless, if Sebba's own definition of 'clemency' had excluded states where the sole power to intervene to reduce or abrogate punishment was allocated to the legislature, or even to the judiciary itself, the total number of states under analysis would have fallen to less than 100. Other than the PRC, at a minimum, Switzerland (legislature) and Uruguay (judiciary, for non-military offences)[65] would not have fallen within the definition of clemency that we adopt for the purposes of this book.[66]

2. Clemency Is Typically Exercised by the Head of State

Further to clemency being a ubiquitous constitutional power around the world, Sebba next observed that:

> In the overwhelming majority of countries, clemency powers are vested in the head of states, be it the president or the monarch ... Indeed, in this respect there appears to be a degree of historical continuity with the powers of the formerly autocratic monarch having been transferred to his constitutional successor.[67]

In other words, even if the clemency power was originally an autocratic, monarchical invention, it nonetheless survives in democratic or semi-democratic constitutional systems. Furthermore, the clemency power typically reflects the head of state's authority as *chief executive*, rather than as a figurehead. In rare systems where a ceremonial head of state had no formal executive power at all,[68] the clemency power was specifically allocated to the elected government, to be exercised by a Cabinet of ministers. In 14 other systems, extending primarily to socialist countries and those under military dictatorship, the formal clemency power was vested in a collective executive body rather

63 Constitution of the PRC 1978, art 25(11) and 26.
64 Sebba, 'The Pardoning Power' (n 2) 85, 86, 91, 98, 111.
65 Constitution of Switzerland 1874, art 85(7) and 92; Criminal Code 1934 (Uruguay), s 109.
66 Sebba, 'The Pardoning Power' (n 2) 106, 108, 119. Turkey allowed the President to pardon only on limited grounds. In circumstances other than 'chronic illness, infirmity or old age', the Turkish legislature alone possessed the power to pardon (ibid., 106–107). Nicaragua vested the pardon power primarily in the legislature, but allocated to the president and the judiciary supplementary powers (ibid., 112).
67 Ibid., 111.
68 Sweden was the only example fitting Sebba's description (ibid., 112).

than in an individual.[69] Nevertheless, the most common model was that, no matter who made the decision in practice, it was promulgated by the head of state him or herself.

Sebba also pointed to four cases where the *legislature* exercised the power to grant 'pardon' for most purposes (Switzerland, Uruguay, Turkey, Nicaragua).[70] In this sense, he employed a different definition to the one we adopt in this volume. While his definition was not demonstrably clear, Sebba seemed to define the power to 'pardon' by reference to its application to individuals, rather than to groups,[71] and the fact that it is exercised by a non-judicial body.[72] He made no differentiation between commutations and pardons, as we understand these terms, and brought together post-judicial lenient authority in individual cases under the broad banner of 'pardon'.[73]

By contrast, Sebba defined 'amnesties' in the following manner, although the inverse definition does not necessarily match his definition of 'pardon':

> The term 'amnesty' generally connotes an institution differentiated from pardon in the following respects: (a) it is general, in that it applies to categories of offenders and not to named individuals; (b) it removes the effects of the conviction and not merely of the sentence; and (c) it applies primarily to political offences.[74]

As most chapters do in this book, Sebba excluded amnesties from his comparative analysis,[75] albeit for different reasons, as he preferred a focus on individual acts of leniency. Nevertheless, he still appeared to countenance the possibility of clemency awarded by 'category'.[76] The gulf between his and our definitions is therefore not as wide as it first appears, especially seeing that Sebba further acknowledged that the characterisation as a legislative power 'has almost become an additional identifying characteristic of an amnesty'.[77]

69 Ibid., 112, 112 n 18: Bulgaria, Burma, East Germany, Poland, Romania, South Korea (State Council); Costa Rica (Council of Government); Ghana (National Redemption Council); Dahomey and Hungary (Presidential Council); Libya (Revolutionary Command Council); Albania, Mongolia and Ukraine (Praesidium of the Legislative Assembly).
70 Ibid., 112. As discussed above (note 66), the legislature and the executive shared the power to 'pardon' in Turkey and Nicaragua.
71 Ibid., 118.
72 Ibid., 112.
73 See the above section entitled 'What is Executive Clemency?'.
74 Ibid., 118.
75 Ibid. This may be the reason that Sebba excluded the Constitution of Syria 1973, art 71(6) and 105 ('amnesty' issued by the president, 'general amnesty' issued by the legislature) from his analysis.
76 Ibid., 118–119. See also Sebba, 'Clemency in Perspective' (n 1) 232.
77 Sebba, 'The Pardoning Power' (n 2) 118.

3. The Head of State (Sometimes) Receives Advice

Sebba noted that in exercising the power of clemency, the decision-maker (usually the formal head of state), sometimes receives either non-binding advice or mandatory instruction or recommendation from other governmental bodies, in line with the 'increasing professionalisation of the pardoning power'.[78] He labelled these the 'secondary' decision-making bodies as opposed to the 'primary' decision-maker.[79] Despite the power of clemency originating from absolute monarchs, it is now unusual for the decision in favour of leniency to be left to a single individual, at least on paper. Even at the time Sebba was writing, it was more likely that heads of state would legally 'share or transfer their effective authority to governmental figures who are more directly accountable to the legislature and/or to the electorate.'[80] Effectively, the *actual* decision-maker on clemency may be the 'secondary' body, rather than the head of state. A later re-count of Sebba's data reveals that 57 per cent (53 of 93) of national jurisdictions with a constitutional executive clemency power mentioned a secondary decision-maker in some capacity, whether the advice given was determinative or merely influential, or whether it was optional or compulsory.

According to the results of Sebba's research, this secondary decision-maker was typically an elected member of the executive branch, such as a minister or the collective Cabinet of ministers.[81] Sebba counted ten jurisdictions which possess this type of constitutional system, not including members of the Commonwealth relying upon constitutional convention.[82] Within the latter jurisdictions, a Cabinet minister typically provided advice to the colonial governor, the former being the effective decision-maker and the latter being the actual decision-maker. In other cases, where no executive recommending body was mentioned in the constitution, ministerial countersignature was sometimes required instead. Effectively, this results in two decision-makers: the head of state and the minister, who must reach agreement before granting clemency. Sebba counted at least eight systems that exhibited some variation of this practice.[83]

Nonetheless, sometimes the body dispensing advice or instruction will be a different branch of government altogether. In what Sebba labelled 'presidential-executive' systems,[84] the head of state will make the decision as chief executive, whereas in 'parliamentary-executive' systems, the head of

78 Ibid., 112, 114.
79 Ibid., 114.
80 Ibid., 120.
81 Ibid., 114.
82 Ibid.: Austria, Greece, Ireland, Japan, New Zealand, Niger, Rhodesia, Singapore, South Africa, Sri Lanka.
83 Ibid.: Belgium, Burundi, Italy, Lebanon, Luxembourg, Mauritania, Spain, and Turkey.
84 Sebba, 'The Pardoning Power' (n 2) 113 n 28. Now typically called 'presidential systems' (or else 'semi-presidential systems') in the political science and

state will act on the advice of the legislature, or a committee thereof.[85] The constitution may also list judicial or quasi-judicial bodies that must provide advice, or may provide for any 'ad-hoc' combination of the three branches of government.[86] Based on Sebba's survey, four jurisdictions (all African) possessed judicial or quasi-judicial advisory bodies,[87] whereas in seven other systems from eclectic parts of the world, a specially constituted committee or board provided advice.[88]

Sebba concluded this section by observing that an investigatory body, charged with gathering and sifting information relevant to the actual decision-maker, may or may not have been listed in the constitution itself. He labelled institutions such as these, which perform an important non-decision-making function, as 'tertiary' decision-makers.[89]

4. *Types of Clemency*

Sebba observed that a majority of 1970s constitutions did not elaborate on the *type* of clemency that might be granted, leaving this to primary or secondary legislation, or even to judicial interpretation. Exceptions were typically constitutions of Commonwealth countries, which described the effect of clemency in detail. For those jurisdictions that did elaborate on various types of clemency, Sebba identified four categories of constitutional power:[90]

(a) pardon, free or conditional;
(b) respite of execution for a specified or indeterminate period;
(c) substitution of a less severe form of punishment (commutation);
(d) remission of the whole or part of the punishment.[91]

Category (a) could be further broken into systems which allowed pardon grants which affect the existence of the conviction itself, and systems in which grants could only affect punishment.[92] There were even systems whose constitutions enunciated one type of pardon which would release a prisoner from incarceration, whereas another type operated to 'remove the stigma of past convictions'.[93]

constitutional law literature (Ilona Mária Szilágyi, 'Presidential versus parliamentary systems' (2009) 8 AARMS 307, 307–310).

85 Sebba, 'The Pardoning Power' (n 2) 113 n 28. Now typically called 'parliamentary systems' in the political science and constitutional law literature (Szilágyi (n 84) 311–313).
86 Sebba, 'The Pardoning Power' (n 2) 115.
87 Ibid.: Algeria, Upper Volta, Zaire, Chad.
88 Ibid.: Kenya, Nigeria, Uganda, Zambia, Malaysia, Ivory Coast, Greece.
89 Ibid.
90 Ibid., 116.
91 Ibid.
92 Ibid., 117, 119–120.
93 Ibid., 117.

5. Scope of the Power

Finally, Sebba discussed whether clemency was restricted in each jurisdiction for particular offenders or offences. Typically, the constitutional provisions that Sebba surveyed described the clemency power in broad terms. Aside from regulation of the decision-making process, described above, there were usually no limits placed on the power to grant or refuse clemency in individual cases.[94] As always, there were exceptions: there were partial or absolute restrictions on clemency for cases of impeachment (nine jurisdictions),[95] special provisions dealing with prisoners sentenced to death, such as mandatory clemency review (eight jurisdictions)[96] or restrictions on clemency (two jurisdictions),[97] a power to pardon *only* political crimes (two jurisdictions),[98] and provisions that enabled pardons for accomplices who provided information leading to the conviction of the primary offender (three jurisdictions).[99] Further provisions concerning scope provided that a clemency grant would not affect the rights of third parties, such as victims in obtaining compensation for their injuries.[100]

Constitutional Provisions for Clemency in 2018

We now turn to the constitutional situation in 2018, which is of greatest relevance for this book and its constituent chapters. Not only have the number of worldwide constitutions mushroomed since 1977 with the continued demise of colonialism and the breakup of the Soviet Union, but moreover there have been subtle changes in the worldwide picture for the kinds of clemency characteristics that Sebba originally identified through his survey. The present section explains these changes, as well as attendant similarities over time.

Approximately 150 new national constitutions went into force or were reinstated between 1970 and 2018.[101] Indeed, Sebba only considered the constitutional provisions of 100 different jurisdictions,[102] whereas in 2018 there were 193 UN member states, the Holy See and Palestine as UN observer states, plus other territories whose international status remains

94 Ibid., 115.
95 Ibid.: Belgium, Denmark, Greece, Iceland, Liechtenstein, Luxembourg, Finland, Chile, Norway.
96 Ibid., 116: Kenya, Malawi, Uganda, Zambia, Malta, Singapore, Sri Lanka, Jordan.
97 Ibid., 115–116, 120: New Zealand and Turkey.
98 Ibid.: Colombia, Panama.
99 Ibid., 117: New Zealand, Singapore, Sri Lanka.
100 Ibid., 120.
101 Appendix. We have relied primarily upon the text of national constitutions logged within the Constitute Project database: <https://www.constituteproject.org/search?lang=en>, except where the constitutions listed did not include the latest amendments to 31 December 2018.
102 Sebba, 'The Pardoning Power' (n 2) 84. However, see also note 59.

disputed (the most important being Taiwan and Kosovo). The vast majority of these territories have written constitutions, providing a 2018 pool of data almost twice the size. The tabulated constitutional data we have collected and coded to update Sebba's findings is found in the Appendix at the end of this book. As is initially obvious, while many provisions remain the same, much has also changed. Novak, in his 2015 monograph, documented some of the ways in which constitutional provisions on clemency have changed over the past 40 to 45 years.[103] We add to his findings with our observations in this section.

As with Sebba's own work, a couple of caveats must initially be borne in mind. First, we limit our 2018 analysis to national constitutions, thereby excluding provincial constitutions (e.g. those of US, Indian, Australian or Malaysian states), and largely ignore the more detailed regulation of clemency procedures which may occur at the legislative level or even within formalised administrative procedures. The main reason for both restrictions in scope is to achieve parity across jurisdictions in terms of source material, particularly for languages other than English. Furthermore, constitutional clemency regulation, as with other constitutional provisions, evinces a greater permanence and symbolic significance as part of each nation-state's fundamental law than do the easily amendable clemency laws passed by national legislatures.[104] Nevertheless, there are several exceptions where we do include observations from domestic legislation and convention. These are for cases where the national constitution provides no reference to executive leniency, or where there is no codified constitution at all, but yet executive clemency is still practised. This group presently consists of the following eight nations: Australia, Canada, Israel, Libya, New Zealand, Saudi Arabia, United Kingdom, and Yemen.[105]

Within the same five categories that Sebba originally examined in 1977, the following are the relevant constitutional trends in clemency to 2018, and our views on the reasons for such longitudinal variation or stasis.

103 Notably: constitutional codification of the prerogative power to grant clemency, an increased role for crime victims in the process, exceptions to the executive's general power to grant clemency in all cases, the growing influence of international law, bureaucratically guided rather than charismatic decision-making, an increasing trend towards judicial review, and the involvement of a specially appointed mercy committee (Novak, *Comparative Executive Clemency* (n 4) 5, 9–16, 197–198).

104 James Willard Hurst, *The Growth of American Law: The Law Makers* (The Lawbook Exchange Ltd 2007) 203; Tom Ginsburg, 'Written Constitutions and the Administrative State: On the Constitutional Character of Administrative Law' in Susan Rose-Ackerman and Peter L Lindseth (eds), *Comparative Administrative Law* (Edward Elgar Publishing 2010) 118; Erwin Chemerinsky, 'Amending the Constitution' (1998) 96 Michigan Law Review 1569.

105 See Appendix.

1. Clemency Is Still Ubiquitous

In 2018, nearly every national constitution still made provision for executive clemency. However, of the 197 jurisdictions that we coded for,[106] there do remain exceptions. The nations without any constitutional provision for clemency are Australia, Canada, El Salvador, Guatemala, Israel, Libya, New Zealand, Nicaragua, San Marino, Saudi Arabia, Switzerland, United Kingdom, Uruguay and Yemen. Six of the aforementioned 14 are countries that do not have a single codified constitution in any case.[107] Yet even those nations without a codified constitution or without an executive clemency provision within their constitution typically provide an executive clemency power via legislation, or via convention.[108]

As a result, at least on paper, clemency is still fairly ubiquitous in 2018, despite the many other changes and trends that have shaped worldwide constitutions over the past 40 to 45 years.[109] The only true exceptions as countries with no constitutional allowance at all for executive clemency in 2018 are: El Salvador, Nicaragua, Guatemala, Switzerland, San Marino, and Uruguay. Each of these six nations allocates through its legislation or constitutional provisions the power to grant individual or collective leniency to the legislature only, rather than to the executive,[110] following the continental European tradition.[111] The operative differences from Sebba's 1970s data come in the shape

106 The 193 UN member states, plus the Holy See (Vatican City State), Palestine, Taiwan (Republic of China), and Kosovo.

107 Canada, Israel, New Zealand, San Marino, Saudi Arabia and the United Kingdom.

108 Canada, New Zealand and the United Kingdom each rely upon the common law royal prerogative of mercy as states with no singular codified constitution. The Israeli President's power to pardon or lighten penalties is provided in the Basic Law: The President of the State 1964 (Israel), s 11(b), whereas Saudi Arabia relies upon the king's power to pardon certain offences provided for in Islamic Law (Richard N Merenbach, 'Religious Law and Religious Freedom in Saudi Arabia and Israel: A Comparative Study' (1988) 12 Hastings Intl & Comp L Rev 235, 242 n 75; Anthony H Cordesman, *Saudi Arabia Enters the 21st Century* (Greenwood Publishing Group 2003) 154; Law on Criminal Procedure 2001 (Saudi Arabia) art 1, 22–23). Australia, with a written constitution that does not make reference to clemency, also relies upon the royal prerogative of mercy. Libya's and Yemen's pardon provisions are found within legislation, rather than constitutional provisions (Libya Penal Code 1954 art 124–125; Republican Decree for Law No 12 for the Year 1994 Concerning Crimes and Penalties, art 48 (Yemen)).

109 See generally Jenny S Martinez, 'Inherent Executive Power: A Comparative Perspective' (2006) 115 Yale LJ 2480; Julian Go, 'A Globalizing Constitutionalism?: Views from the Postcolony, 1945–2000' (2003) 18 International Sociology 71, and David S Law, 'Globalization and the Future of Constitutional Rights' (2008) 102 NW UL Rev 1277.

110 Constitution of El Salvador 1983, art 131(26); Constitution of Nicaragua 1987, art 138(3) (legislative amnesty or pardon 'on the initiative of the President of the Republic' remains possible); Constitution of Guatemala 1985, art 171(g); Constitution of Switzerland 1999, art 157, 173; Criminal Code 1975, art 52, 112–113 (San Marino); Constitution of Uruguay 1967, art 85(14).

111 Novak, *Comparative Executive Clemency* (n 4) 7.

of the PRC (with 'special amnesty' reinstated within its 1978 and 1982 Constitutions),[112] San Marino, and the Central American jurisdictions El Salvador, Nicaragua, and Guatemala. None of the latter four nations appeared in Sebba's original survey. The striking conclusion is that approximately 97 per cent of sovereign nations make legal provision for executive clemency as of 2018. Moreover, all 197 nations we coded for at the very least make legal provision for executive clemency *or* legislative mercy of some description. Few other types of constitutional provisions have achieved such a blanket level of worldwide coverage, reflecting clemency's deep historical and contemporary ties to sovereignty itself.

It is worth considering in further detail why clemency remains popular in law, even if its use may be becoming scarcer in practice.[113] Part of the answer is undoubtedly constitutional inertia: the clemency power was once a far more useful political and legal tool than it is today, and in many jurisdictions the constitution is a difficult document to change as the state's fundamental law. A second and related explanation is that, among the newer constitutions drafted since the mid-1970s, explicit or implicit constitutional 'borrowing', thereby incorporating the clemency power of older sovereign states, is not only normal but also expected.[114] Up to the end of 2018, there were 43 newly independent or newly formed nations which had adopted new constitutions since Sebba's article was published in 1977, and strikingly, *every one* of these constitutions now contains provision for executive clemency, which suggests far more than coincidence.[115] The national constitutions that such provisions tend to be borrowed from originally incorporated the power to grant clemency as a nod to the sovereign powers of absolute monarchs, alongside the power to

112 See notes 60–63 and associated text, and Xiong, this volume.

113 Strange, 'Introduction' (n 2) 14–15; Novak, *Comparative Executive Clemency* (n 4) 2, 5; Sebba, 'The Pardoning Power' (n 2) 232–234.

114 Nelson Tebbe and Robert L Tsai, 'Constitutional Borrowing' (2009) 108 Michigan Law Review 459, 462–484; Wiktor Osiatynski, 'Paradoxes of Constitutional Borrowing' (2003) 1 International Journal of Constitutional Law 244, 244–245; Go (n 109) 90.

115 In descending order of the date of independence or formation: South Sudan; Kosovo; Serbia; Montenegro; Timor-Leste; Palau; Eritrea; Czech Republic; Slovakia; Bosnia and Herzegovina; Russia; Kazakhstan; Turkmenistan; Croatia; Armenia; Tajikistan; North Macedonia; Uzbekistan; Kyrgyzstan; Azerbaijan; Moldova; Belarus; Ukraine; Estonia; Slovenia; Georgia; Yemen; Namibia; Lithuania; Palestine; Micronesia; Marshall Islands; Saint Kitts and Nevis; Antigua and Barbuda; Belize; Vanuatu; Zimbabwe; Saint Vincent and the Grenadines; Kiribati; Saint Lucia; Dominica; Tuvalu; Solomon Islands. See further Appendix.

The Constitution of Yemen 1991 (revised 2015) does not provide a power for the president to grant executive clemency, yet pardon is still mentioned in Article 64(b)(4) (qualifications for candidates for the House of Representatives). Of these nations, Sebba nonetheless considered the constitutions of non-independent Ukraine and Zimbabwe (as Rhodesia) in his 1977 study.

wage wars, sign international treaties, maintain law and order, and punish criminals, including through the use of capital punishment.[116]

A third potential explanation is the influence of international law, in particular Article 6(4) of the ICCPR, plus related regional instruments, which mandate the 'right to seek' clemency in death penalty cases.[117] Nations which retain the death penalty in law,[118] 79 of 96 (82 per cent) of which were parties to the ICCPR by the end of 2018,[119] are mandated to allow for clemency, at least as a matter of convention, if not by constitutional or legislative provision. The most straightforward means for these states to comply with their international treaty obligations is to provide for a self-initiated clemency procedure within relevant legislation of constitutional provisions. The duty of a state to legally provide for the possibility of executive clemency in all death penalty cases (less specific than a petitioner's 'right to seek' commutation or pardon) may even have passed into customary international law, given that 94 of the 96 legally retentionist nations retain a conventional, legislative, or constitutional power for the executive to dispense post-judicial leniency for at least some capital offences.[120] Guatemala and El Salvador, which now both retain the death penalty for military offences only, remain the only global exceptions.[121]

116 Christopher Heath Wellman, 'Rights and State Punishment' (2009) 106 The Journal of Philosophy 419, 426–427; Austin Sarat and Nasser Hussain, 'On Lawful Lawlessness: George Ryan, Executive Clemency, and the Rhetoric of Sparing Life' (2004) 56 Stanford Law Review 1307, 1313; Novak, *Comparative Executive Clemency* (n 4) 17; Colin Turpin and Adam Tomkins, *British Government and the Constitution: Text and Materials* (6th edn, CUP 2007) 146, 464–468.

117 Saul Lehrfreund, 'The Impact and Importance of International Human Rights Standards: Asia in World Perspective' in Roger Hood and Surya Deva (eds), *Confronting Capital Punishment in Asia: Human Rights, Politics and Public Opinion* (OUP Oxford 2013) 42–45; ICCPR, art 6(4); UN Human Rights Committee (n 48) para 47; American Convention on Human Rights, art 4(6); African Charter on Human and Peoples' Rights, art 4; General Comment No. 3 on the African Charter on Human and Peoples' Rights: The Right to Life (art 4), para 24; Arab Charter on Human Rights, art 6.

118 Including nations which are 'retentionist', 'abolitionist in practice', and 'abolitionist for ordinary crimes' in Amnesty International's definition (Amnesty International, 'Death Sentences and Execution 2018' (2019) AI-Index ACT 50/9870/2019, 48–49; Roger Hood and Carolyn Hoyle, *The Death Penalty: A Worldwide* Perspective (5th edn, OUP 2015) 21). Such nations, even if they are not currently executing prisoners, are still bound by treaty and customary international law provisions that restrict and regulate capital punishment.

119 Amnesty International, 'Death Sentences and Execution 2018' (n 118) 48–49; 'International Covenant on Civil and Political Rights: New York, 16 December 1966' (*United Nations Treaty Collection*, 3 February 2020) <https://treaties.un.org/Pages/ViewDetails.aspx?src=TREATY&mtdsg_no=IV-4&chapter=4&clang=_en> accessed 3 February 2020.

120 Ibid.; Appendix. See also note 49.

121 See Appendix; Amnesty International, 'Death Sentences and Execution 2018' (n 118) 48; Hands Off Cain 'Database' (2019) <http://www.handsoffcain.info/ba

2. Clemency Is Still Typically Granted by the Head of State

With little change from Sebba's second major observation, in 2018 it was still the head of state that typically retained the ultimate power to reduce or abrogate criminal punishment. If the Queen of England's representative (the Governor General) is treated as the country's 'head of state' in commonwealth nations such as Australia, Canada, New Zealand, Papua New Guinea, Solomon Islands, Tuvalu, and throughout the Commonwealth Caribbean,[122] then the only sovereign countries to allocate their executive clemency power solely to an executive actor who is *not* the head of state are Colombia, Costa Rica, Marshall Islands, and Sweden. All four are countries where the Cabinet or an executive council of state makes the final decision.[123]

The present exceptions to the general rule favouring heads of state do suggest a widening divergence from Sebba's original findings, however. There now seem to be proportionally fewer *collective* final decision-makers within the national jurisdictions surveyed which retained executive clemency (a notable decline from 15 of 93 surveyed in the 1970s to 4 of 191 in 2018), and therefore a higher proportion of individual final decision-makers.[124] This change is potentially explained by the declining number of Marxist/Leninist governments and military dictatorships over time. Ironically, as more countries have become democratic,[125] clemency is now more often placed in the hands of a single decision-maker, rather than a collective body (albeit that the head of state frequently exercises the power on advice, as outlined below). Of the 15 nations utilising collective decision-making bodies within Sebba's survey, only Sweden and Costa Rica maintain a similar type of system as of 2018. Representative changes include the demise of the State Councils of Poland (1989), Burma (1988), and Bulgaria (1990), and of the military councils in Ghana (1975) and Libya (1977), each being eventually replaced by an elected president as the final decision-maker on clemency.[126]

ncadati/> accessed 21 August 2019. Both nations' constitutions provide only for legislative amnesty.

122 Relevantly: Jamaica, Belize, Grenada, Saint Kitts and Nevis, Saint Lucia, Saint Vincent and the Grenadines, Antigua and Barbuda, Bahamas, Barbados. See Appendix; Bulkan, this volume.

123 See Appendix. The Constitution of Slovakia 1992 provides, in addition to a presidential clemency power, a power to grant amnesties for misdemeanours to the government (consisting of the prime minister, deputy prime ministers and other ministers) (art 109(1), 121).

124 See Appendix and Sebba, 'The Pardoning Power' (n 2) 111–112.

125 See Freedom House, 'Freedom in the World Comparative and Historical Data: Country Status Distribution' (2018) <https://freedomhouse.org/sites/default/files/Country%20Status%20Distribution%20FIW1973-2018.xlsx> accessed on 21 August 2019, on longitudinal trends in democracy since 1973.

126 See Appendix. However, at the time of writing, the timing of the next Libyan presidential election was uncertain due to ongoing domestic conflict (Jonathan Brown, 'Arrest of Russians in Libya Raises Questions over Kremlin Election Meddling' *The National* (London, 2019)).

3. The Head of State Still (Sometimes) Receives Advice

Slightly little more than half of the national constitutions in our 2018 survey provided for the mandatory or discretionary input of a 'secondary decision maker' in all cases, beyond the primary decision-making individual or collective body. Excluding the six nations that do not have provision for executive clemency in their constitutional provisions or in any legislation or established convention, 102 of 191 jurisdictions provided for either mandatory or discretionary advice from a secondary individual body for at least the bulk of crimes or penalties eligible for clemency. Of course, the advisory and countersigning bodies listed in the Appendix are limited to those which appear in constitutional provisions, and hence there may be further advisory bodies or opportunities created by legislation or administrative regulation not included within these figures.[127] Yet in many cases, the presence of an advisory or co-signing body within a constitutional text is indicative of its importance in moderating, shaping, and even determining entirely the final clemency decision.

The longitudinal trend is that marginally fewer modern constitutions make mention of secondary decision-makers, when compared with Sebba's data from the 1970s (53 per cent versus 57 per cent). At face value, this seems to run counter to modern trends in democratic governance, whereby political power is increasingly defused among different actors rather than concentrated in the hands of an all-powerful leader or council.[128] In many jurisdictions, the clemency power has evolved into a regularised criminal justice remedy, effectively a 'final stage of appeal' befitting input from judicial, correctional, and medical personnel, rather than an extraordinary, charismatic act by the omnipotent sovereign.[129] More practically, in the United States we know that an increasing number of clemency applications throughout the twentieth century have also contributed to the rise of advisory committees as a tool to manage executive workloads.[130]

The slight decline in secondary decision-makers therefore seems counter-intuitive. Nevertheless, the lower proportion of advisers and counter-signing bodies in 2018 may have a more prosaic explanation. The apparent decline of secondary decision-makers may simply be a reflection of Sebba's concurrent reliance on legislative and other extraneous sources in addition to

127 For example, the right for victims to participate in the clemency process in Sri Lanka, Israel, and Spain. See Assistance to and Protection of Victims of Crime and Witnesses Act 2015 (Sri Lanka); Rights of Victims of Crime Law 2001 (Israel); Law 1/1988 (Spain).

128 Josep M Colomer, 'The Choice of Political Institutions' in Enriqueta Aragonès and others (eds), *The Political Economy and Democracy* (Fundación BBVA 2009) 219–220; Markus Böckenförde, Nora Hedling, and Winluck Wahiu, 'A Practical Guide to Constitution Building: The Design of the Executive Branch' (International IDEA 2011) 32. See also notes 124–125 and associated text.

129 Novak, *Comparative Executive Clemency* (n 4) 120; Novak, 'Transparency and Comparative Executive Clemency' (n 6) 827–829.

130 Abramowitz and Paget (n 5) 141.

constitutional provisions in his research. Our exclusive reliance on constitutional data in 2018 leads to attendant difficulties in comparison.[131] Notable examples are Sebba's reference to opinions from trial judges in India, and decisions of the National Offenders Rehabilitation Commission in Japan,[132] neither of which are referenced in the respective Indian and Japanese constitutions. At the very least, we can say that the numbers of secondary decision-makers in 2018 roughly match those in the 1970s. The modern numbers may even be higher, if we include legislation as well as constitutional sources.

One contemporary trend that has a much firmer grounding in the available data is that in 2018, a higher proportion of secondary decision-makers were not directly politically accountable, compared with the 1970s. In 17 of the 102 cases in 2018, advice was given by a judicial or quasi-judicial body, in two cases advice was provided by a civil servant or government department, whereas in 34 other cases a majority unelected committee provided advice or instruction on the pardon decision.[133] The combined total is 53 out of 102 (52 per cent). This is larger than the equivalent proportion of non-political secondary decision-makers in the 1970s (23 of 53, or 43 per cent). The increase is almost entirely attributable to the greater proportion of such constitutions (33 per cent) which now list unelected committees as clemency advisers, compared with Sebba's data (21 per cent).

Overall, the figures from 2018 suggest a continuation of the trend towards the 'increasing professionalisation' of the clemency power, as Sebba first described it during the 1970s.[134] As with our ambivalent findings on the expansion of secondary decision-making bodies per se, this is counterintuitive given the flourishing of democracy movements in many nations since the end of the Cold War. Over recent decades, clemency decision-making, at least on paper, has become less 'democratic' and more 'technocratic'. Non-political bodies now have an increasing sway over the power to pronounce political leniency. Nevertheless, de-politicising clemency advice to a popularly elected chief executive may provide significant benefits, allowing for a more balanced evaluation of the merits of the petitioner's case against potential societal and political costs. After following the advice of a non-political advisory body, the final decision-maker

131 Excepting those states without constitutional provision for clemency. See note 108.

132 Sebba, 'The Pardoning Power' (n 2) 91, 93.

133 Appendix. Where an unelected body (e.g. a parole board or pardons board) and an elected body (e.g. a Cabinet of ministers) *both* provide constitutional advice to the final decision-maker, we make an assumption that this is a case where the unelected body has more sway, given its more specialised membership and set of functions, plus the fact that the primary or formal decision-maker is also likely to be a ceremonial head of state. For example, we list most Commonwealth Caribbean nations as jurisdictions where the secondary decision-maker is unelected, whereas in these jurisdictions the mercy advisory body typically advises the Cabinet or a single minister, who in turn relays instructions to the governor-general as the queen's local representative. See further Bulkan, this volume.

134 Sebba, 'The Pardoning Power' (n 2) 112.

will then possess another party to 'blame' for a politically unpopular clemency grant, or refusal.[135]

4. *Types of Clemency Remain the Same*

On constitutional variations of the clemency power, some, but not all, of Sebba's observations are now out of date. Excluding the nations whose constitutions or legislation do not provide for executive clemency at all, most global constitutions now describe multiple means by which the clemency power may be exercised. Of the 191 countries listed in the Appendix, 122 identify *at least two variations* of executive leniency (64 per cent). Although Commonwealth nations typically continue to provide a detailed description of the effect of the clemency power, as Sebba suggested, non-Commonwealth member states also did so in 2018. Of the 122 countries that listed at least two forms of clemency in their constitutions in 2018, fewer than half were members of the Commonwealth.[136] Only the 77 nations with *three or more* iterations of constitutional clemency are majority Commonwealth (48 of 77, or 62 per cent).

The total count for different types of executive clemency powers in national constitutions is as follows, although we must acknowledge that the precise translation of the name of the power to English may have affected the accuracy of the results.[137] Where different countries list more than one power, we count these separately. The seven most common of the powers listed are:

- 'Pardon' simpliciter—113 references (and appearing in 59 per cent of worldwide constitutions that contain any reference to executive clemency)
- 'Remittance' or 'Remission'—62 references
- 'Commutation'—45 references
- 'Conditional Pardon'—41 references
- 'Respite' (including for an 'indefinite' or 'specified period')—39 references
- 'Free Pardon'—37 references
- 'Substitution'—34 references

While these may have been the most numerous seven categories in 2018, it is striking that Sebba identified precisely the same phrasing in the mid-1970s.[138] In other words, the most common words or phrases used to describe a multilayered executive clemency power have remained largely unchanged over the past 40 or

135 Adam M Gershowitz, 'The Diffusion of Responsibility in Capital Clemency' (2001) 17 Journal of Law and Politics 669, 711; Colgate Love (n 5) 744–747; Novak, 'Transparency and Comparative Executive Clemency' (n 6) 828–829.

136 See Appendix; Commonwealth Secretariat, 'Member Countries' (*The Commonwealth*, 2020) <https://thecommonwealth.org/member-countries> accessed 4 February 2020.

137 See note 101.

138 Sebba, 'The Pardoning Power' (n 2) 116.

more years, despite around 130 new constitutions being adopted during the same period.[139] The most obvious explanation is that newer constitutions have borrowed similar or identical terms from older constitutions, be those from former colonial powers, neighbouring jurisdictions, and indeed from previous versions of the same document. New constitutions, and especially their executive clemency provisions, are not created in a historical vacuum, but are the amalgam of existing documents. And as for *existing* constitutional provisions, those regarding clemency may not be thought of as important enough to change when constitutions undergo substantial revisions. Clemency is often considered a reserve power, which when exercised creates an exception to the rule of law and finality of the judicial process.[140] In most jurisdictions, it is not thought of as a day-to-day tool of governance.

The question then begs itself: are the clemency provisions in contemporary constitutions designed and interpreted so as to best promote modern democratic governance, or do they instead reflect now dated conceptions of the sovereign prerogative? Are a wider or distinct range of constitutional tools now required to respond to modern criminal justice dilemmas and trends, such as the return of mandatory minimum sentencing,[141] over-incarceration,[142] the expanding role of victims,[143] increasing numbers of foreign national prisoners liable to deportation,[144] DNA evidence and the rise of the 'innocence movement',[145] fiscal austerity,[146] pandemics affecting prisoners, transitional justice in post-authoritarian societies,[147] and the reduction and abolition of corporal, capital and other extreme punishments?[148] Executive

139 See Appendix.

140 Sebba, 'Clemency in Perspective' (n 1) 221; Böckenförde et al. (n 126) 34; Pascoe, 'Towards a Global Theory of Capital Clemency Incidence' (n 53) 121, 126–128; Dirk van Zyl Smit and Catherine Appleton, *Life Imprisonment: A Global Human Rights Analysis* (Harvard University Press 2019) 305.

141 Novak, *Comparative Executive Clemency* (n 4) 6; Joanna M Huang, 'Correcting Mandatory Injustice: Judicial Recommendation of Executive Clemency' (2011) 60 Duke Law Review 131, 134.

142 Rachel E Barkow, *Prisoners of Politics: Breaking the Cycle of Mass Incarceration* (Harvard University Press 2019) 81–84; Chris Barker, 'The Certainty of Punishment and the Proportionality of Incarceration' in Chris W Surprenant (ed), *Rethinking Punishment in the Era of Mass Incarceration* (Routledge 2017) 77.

143 Pascoe and Manikis (n 53) 15; James R Acker and Charles S Lanier, 'May God—Or the Governor—Have Mercy: Executive Clemency and Executions in Modern Death Penalty Systems' (2000) 36 Criminal Law Bulletin 200, 209; Novak, *Comparative Executive Clemency* (n 4) 197.

144 Catherine Bejerana Camacho, 'Immigration Matters: Governors' Powers Can Impact Deportation' *Pacific Daily News* (Guam, 8 January 2018); Peter L Markowitz and Lindsay Nash, 'Pardoning Immigrants' (2018) 93 NYU Law Review 58, 67.

145 See Cooper and Burrows, this volume; Novak and Pascoe, this volume.

146 Barkow, 'The Politics of Forgiveness' (n 5) 157.

147 Mallinder, *Amnesty, Human Rights and Political Transitions* (n 40) 4; Böckenförde et al (n 128) 34; Smailagić, this volume.

148 Sebba, 'Clemency in Perspective' (n 1) 232; Elizabeth Rapaport, 'Staying Alive: Executive Clemency, Equal Protection, and the Politics of Gender in Women' s

discretion may not be a panacea for all of these issues, but the clemency power, if drafted and interpreted in a sufficiently broad manner, provides a leniency mechanism to deal with such policy problems on a short-term and case-by-case basis. The potential benefits of providing for detailed clemency regulation in a national constitution rather than in domestic legislation include greater permanence, symbolic weight, and the possibility of constitutional review of clemency decisions in the courts.

Finally, despite the general trends identified above, it would be inaccurate to suggest that descriptions of executive clemency within global constitutions are entirely homogenous. There are numerous ways to describe the executive clemency power in English, suggesting non-linguistic explanations for the high tallies for particular terms. Indeed, the Appendix at the end of this book contains a total of 61 different terms for executive clemency, with more than half of those terms (37) appearing in only one national constitution each. Among the more unusual are powers to grant 'favour',[149] 'conditional freedom',[150] and 'partial pardon'.[151] Indeed, in 2018 Peru's was the only constitution *across the entire world* to incorporate our preferred term within this book: 'executive clemency'.[152] For political abrogation or mitigation of punishment, by far the world's most favoured English-language constitutional term is 'pardon'.

5. The Scope of the Power Typically Remains Unrestricted

Within his final category, Sebba's observations on limitations to the scope of the clemency power largely remain applicable today. Most constitutions do not contain further regulation or restriction on the scope of clemency—our count is that only about one-quarter do (45 of 191). Of these 45 cases, sometimes clemency is banned outright for certain crimes or individuals, and sometimes certain types of grants are subject to special oversight by other branches of government. For notable categories of absolute prohibitions, there are 15 different provisions in national constitutions proscribing clemency for impeachment, political crimes, or crimes by politicians or civil servants.[153] A further five

Capital Cases' (2001) 4 Buffalo Criminal Law Review 967, 1001; Pascoe, 'Towards a Global Theory of Capital Clemency Incidence' (n 53) 121.

149 Fundamental Law of Vatican City State 2000, art 19.

150 Constitution of Panama 1972, art 184(12).

151 Constitution of Finland 2000, s 105.

152 Constitution of Peru 1993, art 118(21); Constitute Project 'Peru's Constitution of 1993 with Amendments through 2009' (2019) <https://www.constituteproject.org/constitution/Peru_2009.pdf?lang=en 32> accessed 21 August 2019. See generally the above section entitled 'What is Executive Clemency?' on the use of the terms 'clemency', 'pardon', and 'commutation' throughout the book.

153 Argentina, Chile, Eritrea, Haiti, Iraq, Liberia, Malawi, Mexico, Norway, Palau, Philippines, Poland, Spain, Tonga, USA. Chile only allows the commutation of a death sentence for terrorism to life imprisonment, but otherwise does not permit clemency in cases of terrorism. See Appendix.

constitutions ban clemency in all circumstances for certain international crimes such as genocide, war crimes, or crimes against humanity.[154]

Importantly, the latter kinds of provisions were unknown at the time Sebba was conducting his research. They accord with a global trend away from impunity for human rights violators and with increasing scepticism of general amnesties by international tribunals, such as the International Criminal Court. Although there is a forceful argument that blanket amnesties are now unlawful under international law for the perpetrators of war crimes, crimes against humanity and genocide,[155] individual grants of executive clemency are not currently prohibited in these circumstances.[156] Instead, retentionist nations such as Niger and Iraq,[157] which purport to ban pardons and commutations for gross violations of human rights, clearly contravene Article 6(4) of the ICCPR, given that these bans extend to capital cases.[158]

Finally, among the various regulations and restrictions on clemency, there are special provisions for prisoners sentenced to death in 33 different countries, which is far more, proportionally, than in the 1970s, even taking into account Sebba's limited sample of worldwide jurisdictions.[159] More than half of the 2018 provisions provide for mandatory reports on the case to be provided to a mercy committee who will then directly or indirectly advise the head of state on whether or not to grant clemency.[160] The proportionally larger number of constitutions with specific death penalty provisions reflects a growing awareness among policy-makers that, in terms of punishments and their operative procedures, 'death is different'.[161] Nevertheless, in six of the 33 cases, the provisions are presently legally irrelevant, because the country itself has abolished capital punishment, at least for ordinary crimes, if not for all crimes.[162]

154 Bosnia and Herzegovina (war crimes, crimes against humanity, genocide), Ethiopia (crimes against humanity), Iraq (international crimes), Niger (imprescriptible crimes), Venezuela (offences against human rights committed by the authorities). Ethiopia permits clemency for international crimes only to commute a death sentence to life imprisonment. See Appendix, and Novak and Pascoe, this volume, for further detail on these provisions.
155 See Smailagić, this volume; Novak, *Comparative Executive Clemency* (n 4) 53–62; Mallinder, 'Amnesties and International Criminal Law' (n 40) 426–429.
156 Novak, *Comparative Executive Clemency* (n 4) 63; Mark A Drumbl, *Atrocity, Punishment and International Law* (CUP 2007) 159; Smailagić, this volume. Contrast UN Human Rights Committee, 'Concluding observations of the Human Rights Committee: Algeria' (2007) CCPR/C/DZA/CO/3, para 7.
157 Constitution of Niger 2010, art 72; Constitution of Iraq 2005, art 73(A).
158 See Death Penalty Worldwide, 'Death Penalty Database' (*Death Penalty Worldwide* 2019) <http://www.deathpenaltyworldwide.org/search.cfm> accessed 24 May 2019.
159 See note 96.
160 See Appendix.
161 *Gregg v Georgia*, 428 US 153, 188 (1976).
162 Chile (abolitionist for ordinary crimes only), Norway, Cyprus, Solomon Islands, Mauritius, Malta (the latter five nations being abolitionist for all crimes). See Amnesty International, 'Death Sentences and Execution 2018' (n 118) 48–49.

As more countries abolish capital punishment and fewer death sentences are passed in the jurisdictions that do retain,[163] these provisions will become less and less important as time goes by.[164] Indeed, from the perspective of penal parsimony, a pessimistic view on future constitutional developments holds that clemency provisions specific to death sentences will be replaced in some jurisdictions by blanket bans on clemency grants in life without parole ('LWOP') cases, as more and more nations abolish the death penalty in favour of immutable lifelong sentences.[165] The LWOP clemency bans enshrined in the laws of five US states already foreshadow potential developments at the international level.[166]

6. Summary

The preceding five subsections trace an obvious theme—despite approximately 150 national constitutions having been reinstated or having come into force since 1970, the way that clemency provisions are constitutionally drafted has remained the same in more cases than not since the time of Sebba's original research. With only six exceptions from Europe and Central America, executive clemency remains a ubiquitous inclusion within the codified constitutions of modern nation states (and further, within the laws of nation states without codified constitutions). In fact, all 197 states within our survey now make constitutional provision for *either* executive clemency or a legislative equivalent (typically referred to as 'amnesty').[167] Executive clemency's worldwide ubiquity underlines its constitutional importance and perpetuates the puzzle as to why so little comparative and empirical scholarship has appeared on the subject over the past several decades. Indeed, the data presented here confirms and strengthens our original justifications for bringing this edited collection together.

163 Amnesty International, 'Death Penalty' (2019) <https://www.amnesty.org/en/what-we-do/death-penalty/> accessed 3 December 2019. Of the 33 states with special death penalty provisions, at the end of 2018 Amnesty International further classified Swaziland, Ghana, Sri Lanka, Grenada, Zambia, and Sierra Leone as abolitionist in practice, not having conducted an execution for more than ten years and having a settled policy not to resume executions (Amnesty International, 'Death Sentences and Execution 2018' (n 118) 48–49).

164 On the assumption that no jurisdiction which has abolished the death penalty will successfully reinstate it in law. Among all abolitionist jurisdictions, this has so far proven exceedingly rare (Hood and Hoyle (n 118) 20).

165 Ibid., 482–484; Van Zyl Smit and Appleton (n 140) 305.

166 Connecticut, Georgia, Nevada, Wyoming, and Oklahoma had each banned the commutation of LWOP sentences by the end of 2015 (Novak, *Comparative Executive Clemency* (n 4) 116–117; Jing Cao, 'Commuting Life Without Parole Sentences: The Need for Reason and Justice over Politics' (SJD Dissertation, Fordham University School of Law, 2015) 29 n 176).

167 See Appendix and note 110.

Aside from the frequency with which executive clemency appears in national constitutions, modern constitutions largely mirror those from the 1970s in several important ways. First, clemency is almost always formally granted by the head of state rather than by another political body such as a Cabinet of ministers. Second, in slightly more than half of the nations under study, rather than purportedly acting alone, the head of state receives mandatory or discretionary constitutional advice on the exercise of clemency. Third, the major categories of clemency listed in national constitutions have remained uncannily consistent since the 1970s. Fourth and finally, only a minority of contemporary constitutions further regulate or restrict the clemency power beyond specifying a final decision-maker, the type or types of clemency that may be granted, and identifying any 'secondary' decision-makers.

Clemency's more novel developments, which distinguish contemporary constitutions from those that Sebba based his research on, include the relative decline of 'collective' bodies as final decision-makers, the 'increasing professionalisation' of the clemency power through non-political advisory bodies, the more expansive listing of different modes of leniency in the constitutions of non-Commonwealth nations, and the increasing popularity of clemency regulation through a) blanket bans on leniency for international crimes and b) special provisions for death penalty cases. Nonetheless, further comparison between jurisdictions on a more intimate scale, as well as empirical investigation into the practice of executive clemency, will both be required before we are able to assert that executive clemency is thoroughly understood within modern academic scholarship. The remainder of this volume goes some way towards achieving this goal.

This Collection

The preceding constitutional analysis sets the contemporary scene for our authors' contributions. This collection consists of nine chapters plus a foreword, featuring a total of 11 different authors. The book's aim is two-fold: first to update and enrich the work of Leslie Sebba on comparative executive clemency around the world, and second to analyse the *practice* of clemency in particular national contexts, particularly in the global South and the postcolonial world as understudied sites for clemency research. Building from the present chapter's global constitutional analysis, the collection's geographical coverage extends as far as continental Europe (chapters 3 and 4), Latin America (chapter 3), the Caribbean (chapter 6), and Asia (chapters 7 and 8). The volume also expands the existing US and UK clemency literature in an important new direction (chapter 5). Just as significantly, the authors consider clemency within the context of different legal traditions, namely civil law (chapters 3, 4, and 8), common law (chapters 5 and 6), socialist law (chapter 8),[168] and, of course, international law (chapter 2).

168 The contemporary legal system of the PRC can be characterised as a mixture of western civil law and socialist legal precepts (Jianfu Chen, 'Modernisation,

The collection's second defining feature, beyond comparative legal analysis, is that several chapters (in particular, chapters 3, 7, 8, and 9) also construct a political and sociological context for exercise of the clemency power. Comparing constitutional provisions on clemency tells us little about how the decision-making process works in practice, and whether clemency is an expected or exceptional outcome in a prototypical case. A more complete understanding of clemency outcomes and decision-making practices not only fills a notable gap in academic scholarship, but also has the potential to inform litigation strategies, legislative and administrative reforms, and to improve outcomes for individual prisoners.

The collection begins with several contributions that aim to account for the differences in clemency's constitutional provisions, legislation, and litigation in new contexts which have not yet been the subject of detailed comparative study. Mirroring the global focus of the present chapter 1, Sangiorgio (chapter 2) begins by interrogating the shifting international law standard on the right to seek pardon or commutation in death penalty cases, culminating with the UN Human Rights Committee's General Comment 36, adopted on 30 October 2018. Despite some recent backsliding in certain retentionist jurisdictions, Sangiorgio finds that the ICCPR's Article 6(4) 'right to seek' commutation or pardon from a death sentence must now be interpreted far more expansively, incorporating procedural safeguards to ensure transparency, fairness, and the non-discriminatory application of clemency.

Next, Arias and Kouroutakis (chapter 3) examine clemency's place in the separation of powers systems of the civil law world, through a sample of seven federal and unitary jurisdictions across continental Europe and Latin America. Complementing the present chapter's comparative constitutional law conclusions, Arias and Kouroutakis find a direct relationship between the head of state's role in the separation of powers system, and the involvement (or not) of other state organs in the decision-making process.

Moving east to the former Yugoslavia, Smailagić (chapter 4) considers the controversial role of both executive clemency and legislative amnesty in societies recently emerging from prolonged armed conflict. Smailagić notes that different countries in the Balkan region have adopted differing policies, prioritising either punishment or reconciliation, thereby reflecting the classic academic debate over transitional justice measures in post-conflict societies. Ultimately, individual commutations and pardons may prove a more flexible policy tool than legislative group amnesties in a post-conflict environment, given that the latter may contravene international law when granted for atrocity crimes.

Westernisation, and Globalisation: Legal Transplant in China' in Jorge Costa Oliveira and Paulo Cardinal (eds), *One Country, Two Systems, Three Legal Orders—Perspectives of Evolution* (Springer 2009) 92; Jingjing Liu, 'Overview of the Chinese Legal System' (2013) 1(1) ELR China Update 1, 4).

Aside from transitional justice, Cooper and Burrows (chapter 5) consider another innovative and controversial use of the executive clemency mechanism which has gained political and social traction in recent decades: clemency for innocence claims. Comparing the potential for innocence-based clemency claims in the United States and England and Wales, the authors nevertheless cast doubt on pardons as a presently viable means of correcting serious errors at the trial and appeal stages. If policy-makers adopted Cooper and Burrows' recommendations for reform, executive clemency would become a more feasible remedy in the era of 'innocence consciousness'.

Bulkan (chapter 6) also wrestles with the true purpose (mercy or error-correction) of executive clemency in common law jurisdictions, this time with a focus on the Commonwealth Caribbean. In a further call for reform, the author demands greater emphasis on public interest considerations alongside prisoner welfare in clemency decision-making, and effective and independent advisory boards as secondary decision-makers. In an echo of Cooper and Burrows' conclusions, Bulkan asserts that the most effective justice-maximising reforms are surely to be made at the judicial level, rather than in relation to the royal prerogative of mercy.

The collection's final two chapters focus on clemency in death penalty cases in Asia. India and the PRC are the world's two most populous states, and each is a notable retentionist jurisdiction that serves as a barometer for the progress of the global death penalty abolitionist movement. In both chapters, the authors identify the potential (albeit unrealised) that executive clemency possesses to mitigate the worst excesses of capital punishment, and to drive each country closer to abolition. In chapter 7, Batra uncovers the decision-making patterns relating to Indian capital clemency petitions through an impressive empirical analysis of 275 petitions, spanning six decades. Although the Indian executive utilises a well-developed series of guidelines in deciding on mercy petitions, the author finds that clemency decision-making in India is still prone to arbitrariness, politicisation, and inconsistency from one administration to the next.

The country chapters then conclude with Xiong's chapter 8. In his piece on the PRC, the author provides a disconcerting look into an authoritarian society without a functioning executive clemency mechanism, thereby underlining the arguments made elsewhere in this collection in favour of allowing for post-judicial leniency, especially in death penalty retentionist systems. Given the individual mercy regularly dispensed in imperial China, the People's Republic increasingly appears to be an aberration both within Chinese history and in relation to global procedural standards. Nevertheless, with the special amnesty procedure already present within the PRC's 1982 Constitution, relatively minor administrative changes would be required to activate it on behalf of the country's death row inmates.

The editors conclude with chapter 9, entitled 'Emerging Trends and Best Practices in Comparative Clemency', which outlines the lessons learned from the preceding eight chapters, so as to frame practical recommendations on post-judicial leniency for policy-makers around the world. Despite the vast differences among national legal systems, nearly every country in the world has some form of executive clemency procedure within its national constitution or legislation. There are shared problems that different societies experience vis-à-vis drafting clemency laws, contemplating the boundaries of judicial review, getting the decision-making process right, and determining when to exercise the clemency power itself. As one of the foremost aims of comparative scholarship in the criminal justice or constitutional law fields,[169] this volume goes some way towards providing novel policy solutions to what are common problems. Nevertheless, in this final chapter, we explicitly acknowledge the dangers of elevating some nations' approaches to executive clemency and imposing them on others. Every legal transplant or policy recommendation should be applied carefully to the local context, with respect for existing institutions and cultures.[170]

169 Antonina Bakardjieva Engelbrekt, 'Toward an Institutional Approach to Comparative Economic Law?' in Antonina Bakardjieva Engelbrekt and Joakim Nergelius (eds), *New Directions in Comparative Law* (Edward Elgar 2009) 213; Mathias Siems, *Comparative Law* (CUP 2014) 22–23.

170 Antonina Bakardjieva Engelbrekt, 'Legal and Economic Discourses on Legal Transplants: Lost in Translation?' (2015) 60 Scandinavian Studies in Law 111, 114–117; John Jupp 'Legal Transplants as Tools for Post-Conflict Criminal Law Reform: Justification and Evaluation' (2014) 3 Cambridge Journal of International and Comparative Law 381, 396; Michele Graziadei, 'Legal Transplants and the Frontiers of Legal Knowledge' (2009) 10 Theoretical Inquiries in Law 723, 726–730.

2 Clemency for Death Penalty Cases under International Law and Standards

Has the Tide Changed?

Chiara Sangiorgio

Introduction: Clemency in Capital Cases in the Context of the Development of the Right to Life

The right to seek pardon or commutation of a death sentence features prominently among the safeguards established by international human rights law to protect the rights of those facing the death penalty.[1] Understood as a mere expression of humanitarian intent from the executing state, for decades the codification and development of this right has enjoyed the overall support of the international community, in stark contrast with the intense and protracted debates on the definition of the right to life and one of its most infamous exceptions, the death penalty.

The issue of capital punishment, in fact, has occupied a contentious place in the development of the modern human rights framework since its inception.[2] In 1947, the drafters of the Universal Declaration of Human Rights were confronted early on in the process with the challenge of reconciling the abolitionist stance of some states with that of a—at the time—prevailing majority of countries that still retained this punishment, among concerns that 'the United Nations should not in any way signify approval of the death penalty'.[3] This conflict was resolved in the final text of the Declaration through the complete omission of references to the death penalty in its Article 3 on the right to life. However, the tension between the two positions has continued to affect deliberations on this topic to this day.[4]

1 International Covenant on Civil and Political Rights (1966) ('ICCPR'). See also UN Safeguards guaranteeing protection of the rights of those facing the death penalty, approved by Economic and Social Council resolution 1984/50 of 25 May 1984.

2 An analysis of the development of key international instruments on the abolition of the death penalty is included in the critical work by William Schabas, *The Abolition of the Death Penalty in International Law* (3rd edn, CUP 2002).

3 UN Economic and Social Council, 'Commission on Human Rights Drafting Committee, First Session—Summary Record of the Second Meeting' UN Doc E/CN4/AC1/SR2, 11.

4 For example, the statement of dissociation that 32 UN Member States signed following the adoption by the UN General Assembly ('UNGA') of resolution 71/

As products of the compromise between the retentionist and abolitionist factions, the instruments adopted by the international community since the Universal Declaration set out clear prohibitions and circumstances to which the use of the death penalty must be restricted under international law, while enshrining its abolitionist vision as just that—a vision, a 'desirable' outcome, to be achieved, with no timelines attached.[5]

To date, some vocal retentionist states have continued to characterise attempts to advance abolitionist initiatives in multilateral forums as efforts by some countries to infringe the right of other sovereign nations to determine the content of their criminal justice systems, thus failing to acknowledge the human rights dimensions—by definition, universal—associated with this punishment.[6]

It is in this context that the right of all those sentenced to death to seek pardon or commutation of their sentence as recognised under international human rights law assumes an additional dimension. As discussed in other chapters of this book,[7] clemency is a prerogative of the executive, exercised in an unfettered or unregulated fashion, whose outcome is subjected to little degree of scrutiny. As such, of all the safeguards put in place by international law to protect the rights of those facing the death penalty, clemency occupies a

187 of 19 December 2016 on a moratorium on the use of the death penalty. UN General Assembly, 'Note Verbale Dated 7 September 2017 from the Permanent Mission of Egypt to the United Nations Addressed to the Secretary-General' UN Doc A/71/1047.

5 ICCPR art 6(6) states that provisions in the same Article should not be used to 'prevent or delay the abolition of the death penalty'. In its General Comment No. 6 on Article 6 of the ICCPR, the Human Rights Committee—the body tasked with the interpretation of this treaty—has stated that the Article 'refers generally to abolition [of the death penalty] in terms which strongly suggest … that abolition is desirable. The Committee concludes that all measures of abolition should be considered as progress in the enjoyment of the right to life …'. Human Rights Committee, 'General Comment No. 6: The Right to Life' 27 July 1982, para 6.

6 For example, Ministry of Foreign Affairs of Singapore, 'Transcript of Minister Vivian Balakrishnan's Intervention at the High-Level Side Event at UNGA—"Moving Away from the Death Penalty: Victims and the Death Penalty"' (*Singapore Ministry of Foreign Affairs*, 2016) <https://www1.mfa.gov.sg/Newsroom/Press-Statements-Transcripts-and-Photos/2016/09/MFA-Press-Release-Transcript-of-Minister-Vivian-Balakrishnans-Intervention-at-the-HighLevel-Side-Eve> accessed 9 January 2019.

The notion of state sovereignty and its interplay with the responsibility to protect in the human rights context has been analysed in the work of scholars such as Cohen, Lloyd, Makinda, and Walker, among others. See Jean L Cohen, 'Whose Sovereignty? Empire Versus International Law' (2004) 18(3) Ethics & International Affairs 1; Lorna Lloyd, 'A Most Auspicious Beginning: The 1946 United Nations General Assembly and the Question of the Treatment of Indians in South Africa' (1990) 16(2) Review of International Studies 131; Samuel M Makinda, 'The United Nations and State Sovereignty: Mechanism for Managing International Security' (1998) 33(1) Australian Journal of Political Science 101 Neil Walker, *Sovereignty in Transition* (Bloomsbury Publishing 2003).

7 See Pascoe and Novak, this volume; Cooper and Burrows, this volume.

unique position. As the epitome of state sovereignty, clemency embodies the power to dispose of death penalty cases without interference and scrutiny by the international community.

Through an historical analysis of the development of the right to seek pardon or commutation of death sentences under international law and standards,[8] this chapter argues that for decades international human rights bodies have either omitted or declined to define how this right must be protected and promoted in practice, resulting in it being undermined or violated in several cases and countries.

This chapter contends that, with a shift in the focus among UN bodies and mechanisms on the establishment of moratoriums on the use of the death penalty, from 2007 onwards clemency procedures have acquired a new and important role as a safeguard of due process. Clemency outcomes and procedures now come under a greater level of international scrutiny, leading to significant advances in transparency, fairness and non-discrimination, as fundamental principles that should apply in the context of clemency procedures.

Finally, this chapter concludes with recommendations for further engagement by international mechanisms to ensure that clemency procedures become an effective safeguard of due process for those facing the death penalty in all countries.

The Emergence of the Right to Apply for Pardon or Commutation of a Death Sentence: 1948–1966

The early inclusion in the International Bill of Rights[9] of the right of those facing capital punishment to seek pardon or commutation of their sentence gave it unchallenged relevance within the human rights framework. The International Covenant on Civil and Political Rights, as adopted by the UN General Assembly in 1966, provides in its Article 6(4) that:

8 The standards cited in this chapter differ in their legal status. Some are provisions of treaties, which are legally binding on the states that are parties to the treaty. Others are provisions of non-treaty instruments, which are not in themselves binding, but they represent the consensus of the international community on standards to which states should conform. Some of the rights recognised in these treaties and non-treaty instruments have been recognised as rules of customary international law, which are binding on all states. International non-treaty standards cited in this chapter are the product of the work of the UN General Assembly, the UN Human Rights Council, UN treaty monitoring bodies, and UN Special Procedures with thematic mandates.

9 The International Bill of Human Rights consists of the Universal Declaration of Human Rights, the International Covenant on Economic, Social and Cultural Rights, and the International Covenant on Civil and Political Rights and its two Optional Protocols.

> Anyone sentenced to death shall have the right to seek pardon or commutation of the sentence. Amnesty, pardon or commutation of the sentence of death may be granted in all cases.

This right, however, was not included in the first draft of the treaty, as noted by Professor William Schabas.[10] When discussed by the Drafting Committee of the Commission on Human Rights in 1948, the scope of the draft article on the right to life—Article 5 at that point—was limited, in fact, to the assertion that no one must be deprived of their life and to a list of the permissible exceptions to it.[11]

It was only a year later, when the Drafting Committee began its revision of this draft article at its Fifth Session, that the right to seek clemency emerged in the text as state prerogative and humanitarian act. The representative of Chile proposed to include a new paragraph to recognise that 'Amnesty, pardon or commutation of the sentence of death may be granted in all cases'.[12] The proposal was supported by the delegate of the USSR, as it had the effect of protecting 'the individual's existence, and which was therefore of undoubted humanitarian value'. The proposal was admitted in the text with 14 votes to none, with one abstention.[13]

This very first formulation of the right to seek clemency has a dual function: it recognises the power of the state to decide on the granting of pardons, while at the same time it poses some limitations on how the state administers its power. By establishing that clemency can be granted in all cases, in fact, it is also implied that states cannot create exceptions *a priori* to limit the application of this power, for example by excluding some categories of crimes from the scope of pardons and commutations that can be granted.

A further sentence was added to the text in April 1950, when the representative of Lebanon proposed to amend the draft paragraph to read: 'A person sentenced to death shall have the right to apply for an amnesty, a pardon, or commutation of the sentence. It shall be possible in every case to grant an amnesty, a pardon or commutation of the sentence of death.'[14] In his view, the proposal aimed at acknowledging two separate concepts: it sought to proclaim, on one hand, the right to apply for leniency 'positively and without qualification'; and, on the other,

10 William Schabas, *The Abolition of the Death Penalty in International Law* (3rd edn, CUP 2002) 51.

11 Commission on Human Rights Drafting Committee, 'Second Session, Report of the Drafting Committee to the Commission on Human Rights' (1948) UN Doc E/CN4/95.

12 Commission on Human Rights Drafting Committee, 'Fifth session, Summary Record of the Ninety-Seventh Meeting' (1949) UN Doc E/CN4/SR97.

13 Ibid., 3. Belgium, Chile, China, Denmark, Egypt, France, Guatemala, India, Iran, Philippines, Ukrainian Soviet Socialist Republic, Union of Soviet Socialist Republics, United States of America, Yugoslavia voted in favour while the United Kingdom abstained at the vote.

14 Commission on Human Rights Drafting Committee, 'Sixth Session, Provisional Record of the One Hundred and Fifty-Third Meeting' (1950) UN Doc E/CN4/SR153.

the right of governments which 'were left free to grant or withhold such amnesty'[15]—effectively enshrining in the draft Covenant a right that is granted and denied entirely at the mercy of the ruler. The Lebanese amendment was adopted with the support of 13 votes, with one against.

It is critical to note that the delegation of Egypt had also suggested an amendment to this paragraph of draft Article 5, to include at the end a qualification that amnesty, pardon, or commutation may be granted 'in accordance with the procedure adopted in each country'.[16] This proposed amendment is noteworthy for several reasons. First, the wording constitutes the first attempt at including reference to the procedural dimension of the right to clemency under international law, which as discussed later in this chapter has remained for many decades only declarative. If adopted, the Egyptian addition would likely have provided an opportunity, in the years that followed, to develop a regulatory framework to delimit under international law the absolute power of states to grant or refuse amnesties, pardons, and commutations of death sentences.

Secondly, and more critically in the context of the United Nations, the text of this amendment has remained one of the most common insertions proposed by countries that retain the death penalty—among them Egypt—in opposition of international initiatives aimed at ending the use of this punishment. Such language aims at precluding international scrutiny of the promotion and protection of human rights in nation states. The proposed amendment was narrowly defeated, after 3 votes were cast in favour and 3 against, with 8 abstentions.

A year later, at the request of the representative of France, the word 'amnesty' was removed from the enunciation of the right to apply for clemency as it was:

> Not an exclusively individual right but could be exercised by groups, legal persons, and even the general public; and secondly, amnesty was a general and impersonal measure taken by legislators and applying to a whole class of facts with no special consideration for the person sentenced, a move that sealed the individualized nature of the right to apply for clemency.[17]

The final text of what became Article 6 of the ICCPR was adopted by 55 votes to none, with 17 abstentions, thereby enshrining the right to seek pardon or commutation in death penalty cases as an important element to safeguard the right to life.[18]

15 Ibid., para 18. Here, the term 'amnesty' possesses its non-legal meaning of 'leniency' or 'mercy'.
16 Commission on Human Rights, 'Draft International Covenant on Human Rights (S/1371), Egypt: Amendment to Article 5' (1950) UN Doc E/CN4/384.
17 Commission on Human Rights Drafting Committee, 'Eighth session, Summary Record of the Three Hundred and Eleventh Meeting' (1952) UN Doc E/CN4/SR309, 8.
18 UN General Assembly, 'Twelfth session – Official Records' (1957) UN Doc A/C3/SR820, para 27.

Clemency as a Critical Safeguard in Death Penalty Cases: 1967–1984

The adoption of the ICCPR also cemented under international law the tension between abolitionist and retentionist countries through its Article 6, which both contemplates the use of the death penalty in some circumstances and enshrines the desirability of its abolition. It was within this context, in the years that immediately followed 1966, that the right to apply for pardon or commutation of a death sentence began to attract renewed attention.

As an individual right interdependent with the state right to exercise its power, the seeking of clemency was an uncontroversial safeguard in capital cases for those retentionist countries opposing the codification of further restrictions to their use of the death penalty. Because of this, the right to make clemency applications (both pardons and commutations) featured prominently in early attempts by abolitionist states to resume substantive debates on the use of capital punishment at the UN General Assembly.

The first of these attempts can be traced back to 1968, when the UN General Assembly adopted a resolution asking UN Member States to ensure the respect of the 'most careful legal procedures and the greatest possible safeguards' in capital cases, including by not implementing death sentences until those facing execution have had the chance to appeal to a higher court or to petition for pardon or reprieve, and until such procedures have concluded. The resolution further asks states to consider whether such safeguards 'may not be further strengthened by the fixing of a time-limit or time-limits before the expiry of which no death sentence shall be carried out',[19] in a first, timid, attempt to spell out under international standards how clemency applications should be administered.

A subsequent resolution adopted at the 1971 session of the UN General Assembly had the significance of acknowledging for the first time the role that the right to apply for pardon or commutation can play in limiting the implementation of capital punishment, by linking these procedural rights with states' 'attitude to possible further restriction of the use of the death penalty or its total abolition'.[20] By that time, several retentionist states had already presented in reports to UN bodies their resort to clemency procedures as an indicator of their efforts to reduce the use of the death penalty.[21] Building on these developments, the 1971 resolution included a timely request for the Secretary-General to prepare a specific report on 'practices and statutory rules which may govern the right for pardon, commutation or reprieve'.

19 UN General Assembly Resolution 2393 (XXIII) on Capital punishment (26 November 1968).
20 UN General Assembly Resolution 2857 (XXVI) on Capital punishment (20 December 1971).
21 For example, Department of Economic and Social Affairs of the United Nations Secretariat, 'Capital Punishment: Developments 1961–1965' (1967).

The adoption of these instruments by the UN General Assembly also paved the way for the Economic and Social Council to take on its role as monitor of trends on the use of the death penalty and the implementation of safeguards to be observed in capital cases, leading to the preparation of reports to this aim every five years.[22] The greater scrutiny that the work of this body put on the protection of safeguards in capital cases, coupled with the growing momentum that the abolition of the death penalty was gaining internationally and within UN bodies, in turn created the space for greater enquiry into the right to seek pardon or commutation by the international community. A paper submitted to the Sixth United Nations Congress on the Prevention of Crime and the Treatment of Offenders, for example, notes how the common perception of the power of pardon—as exercised by the highest authority, without advice from the Government or other executive, judicial, or legislative body and without the knowledge of the history and behaviour of the offender, and of the nature of the offence—was not in fact met by reality in many countries.[23]

These regular assessments, however, only led to limited additions under international law and common standards that could better regulate the exercise of the power of mercy. The *Safeguards guaranteeing protection of the rights of those facing the death penalty*, adopted by the Economic and Social Council in 1984 and endorsed without a vote by the UN General Assembly later that year, reiterate the language already included in the ICCPR, reaffirming that 'Anyone sentenced to death shall have the right to seek pardon, or commutation of sentence; pardon or commutation of sentence may be granted in all cases of capital punishment'.[24] The Safeguards further set out, in paragraph 8, that executions must not be carried out when appeals or other proceedings relating to pardon or commutation of the sentence are pending, but do not further specify procedures to ensure that the exercise of the power of clemency is meaningful.

Despite the relatively restrained language used, the Safeguards made a critical contribution to the development of international law as they had the crucial effect, as noted by Schabas, 'to [likely] elevate the norms of Articles 6 and 14 of the *Civil Rights Covenant*, in death penalty cases, to the status of customary international law'.[25]

As these developments were taking place, the Human Rights Committee—the mechanism newly created by the ICCPR to interpret and monitor the implementation of the Covenant by its States Parties—also began its work. From 1977, the Human Rights Committee began to periodically review the

22 The first report covered trends for the period 1969–1973. See UN Doc E/5616 and Add.1 and Corr.1 and Corr.2.
23 Economic and Social Council, 'Sixth United Nations Congress on the Prevention of Crime and the Treatment of Offenders' (1980) UN Doc A/CONF87/9, para 43.
24 Economic and Social Council Resolution 1984/50 (25 May 1984).
25 Schabas (n 10) 168. See also William Schabas, 'International Law and Abolition of the Death Penalty' (1998) 55(3) Wash & Lee L Rev 797.

compliance of states with the treaty. In 1981, it began publishing its authoritative General Comments, interpreting individual provisions of the treaty. One year later, in 1982, the Human Rights Committee interpreted Article 6 of the ICCPR, reaffirming in this context the importance of the right to seek pardon or commutation of a death sentence but by merely referring to the language of the Article itself.[26]

By the mid-1980s the right to seek pardon or commutation in capital cases had achieved uncontested recognition under international law as a critical due process safeguard, as well as a tool to reduce the use of the death penalty. However, how this right was exercised in practice was a question, at that point, left entirely to each country to answer, outside the purview of the international community.

Status Quo and Increasing Concern: 1985–1999

The ensuing 15 years saw international law and international standards mostly maintain the status quo on the right to seek pardon or commutation of a death sentence. Notable exceptions were a landmark resolution by the Economic and Social Council in 1989, which recommended that states provide for mandatory appeals with provisions for clemency or pardon in all capital cases,[27] and the mandate of the UN Special Rapporteur on Extrajudicial, Summary or Arbitrary Executions, which through the work of its first two independent experts, Amos Wako and Bacre Waly Ndiaye, exposed the circumstances of the use of the death penalty which violated international law, including in relation to the right to seek clemency.

In 1996, for example, the Special Rapporteur suggested that states should provide in their national legislation a period of at least six months before a death sentence is implemented, to allow for a reasonable amount of time for the preparation of appeals and petitions for clemency; and that officials responsible for carrying out an execution order should be fully informed of the state of these petitions for pardon, and should not proceed with the execution if these recourses are still pending.[28]

These new elements constitute small but important additions towards safeguarding the right to seek pardon or commutation in capital cases. However, the standards set by international human rights mechanisms up to the late

26 'These rights are applicable in addition to the particular right to seek pardon or commutation of the sentence' (Human Rights Committee, 'Sixteenth Session, General Comment No. 6: Article 6 (Right to Life)' (1982) UN Doc CCPR/GEC/6630/E2, para 7).

27 Economic and Social Council Resolution 1989/64 (24 May 1989) on the Implementation of the Safeguards Guaranteeing Protection of the Rights of Those Facing the Death Penalty.

28 United Nations, 'Report by the Special Rapporteur, Mr. Bacre Waly Ndiaye, Submitted Pursuant to Commission on Human Rights Resolution 1996/74' (1996) UN Doc E/CN4/1997/60, para 117.

1990s lacked the level of detail needed to define procedures that could meaningfully and effectively guarantee this right, which has been violated or made illusory in many instances.[29] For example, at the time of writing, some retentionist countries are yet to establish clemency procedures, or regulations to give effect to the right to seek clemency. Among other examples, China remains the world's lead executioner, but famously does not have a system that allows prisoners to seek executive clemency.[30] Executions were put on hold in Guatemala in 2001[31] and Papua New Guinea in 2017[32] because of the lack of clemency procedures. In the Maldives, the presidential power to pardon was removed and shifted to the families of crime victims in 2014, to more closely accord with Islamic legal principles. Detailed regulations on how this process should be governed are yet to be defined.[33] Under Islamic Law, or the criminal codes of several states that are infused with Islamic Law principles, clemency decisions in cases of intentional murder (*qisas*) are not taken by the executive. It is the heirs or family members of the crime victim that have the power to grant full pardons, pursuant to reconciliation processes.[34]

Furthermore, several executions have been carried out in cases where petitions for clemency were still pending. In 2008, Charles Laplace became the most recent man to be hanged in the English-speaking Caribbean. It remains

29 In preparation of its 1995 quinquennial report, the Economic and Social Council asked UN Member States to submit information on their handling of clemency applications. The states that responded indicated that this safeguard guaranteed that in every country executions were on hold until all appeal, recourse, pardon, and clemency proceedings had been exhausted and the outcome communicated to the defendant and his or her legal advisers. However, the survey responses also revealed that a time limitation was present in several countries for the preparation of petitions for pardon or clemency, ranging from 3 days in Guinea to 14 in Egypt and 60 in Tonga. Economic and Social Council, 'Capital punishment and Implementation of the Safeguards Guaranteeing the Protection of the Rights of Those Facing the Death Penalty—Report of the Secretary-General' (1995) UN Doc E/1995/78, para 80.

30 Roger Hood and Carolyn Hoyle, *The Death Penalty—A Worldwide Perspective* (4th edn, OUP 2008) 258. See Xiong, this volume.

31 *Fermín Ramírez v Guatemala* (2005) IACHR Series C no 126; IHRL 1510 (Inter-American Court of Human Rights).

32 *Enforcement of Basic Rights under Section 57 of the Independent State of Papua New Guinea* (2017) PGNC 266; N6939 (National Court of Papua New Guinea).

33 Regulation No. 2014/R-33, 'Regulation on the Procedure of Investigating the Crime of Deliberately Killing a Person and Enforcing the Court-Ruled Punishment', compiled under No. 5/2008 (Police Act) and No. 14/2013 (Prison and Parole Act) of 29 April 2014. In 2019 the Human Rights Committee found that the state of Maldives had violated Article 6(4) of the International Covenant on Civil and Political Rights because of 'the lack of certainty in the law regarding the clemency process and its effectiveness'—*Hussain Humaam Ahmed v Republic of the Maldives* (2019) Comm No 2785/2016; UN Doc CCPR/C/123/D/2785/2016, para 9.9 (Human Rights Committee).

34 Daniel Pascoe and Michelle Miao, 'Victim-Perpetrator Reconciliation Agreements: What Can Muslim-Majority Jurisdictions and the PRC Learn from Each Other?' (2017) 66(4) ICLQ 963, 966–967.

unclear whether Laplace was able to prepare a clemency plea, and if so, whether it was considered by the Advisory Committee on the Prerogative of Mercy of Saint Kitts and Nevis.[35] As recently as 2016, a Nigerian national was executed in Indonesia three days after he had applied for clemency from the President, before his petition could be considered.[36] This followed the public announcement by Indonesian President Joko Widodo a year earlier that he would reject all clemency applications filed by prisoners convicted of drug-related offences,[37] thereby indicating that he would pre-judge each condemned prisoner's petition without reading it.[38]

Although the implementation of death sentences in cases where clemency petitions are still pending has become a rare occurrence, the lack of support that prisoners receive when preparing these appeals remains a more widespread concern. This is particularly relevant in countries where the legal assistance provided by the state terminates at the end of the judicial process. This can, particularly when coupled with opaque or unclear clemency processes, result in the right to seek clemency being violated. Two examples follow. Research carried out in 2008 by Amnesty International and the Legal Defence and Assistance Project highlighted that in Nigeria prisoners were asked to add their names to a list if they considered themselves eligible for commutation, meaning they had spent more than ten years under sentence of death and had a good conduct record. Prison directors then selected which names to forward to the Prison Service headquarters, who in turn prepared a list for the State and Federal Prerogative of Mercy Committees. Prisoners alleged that they had to pay prison officials to ensure their names were added to the list.[39] In Malaysia, those facing execution prepare their clemency applications with the support of prison officials, who maintain communications with the pardon authorities. The prisoners and their relatives do not know when their case will be considered by the relevant State or Federal Pardon Board, and only find out about the decision days, or even hours, before executions are carried out.[40]

35 Afua Hirsch, 'Man Hanged in Rare St Kitts Execution Had Not Exhausted Appeal Rights, Say Campaigners' *The Guardian* (23 December 2008) <www.theguardian.com/world/2008/dec/23/capital-punishment-human-rights-caribbean> accessed 13 October 2018.

36 Amnesty International, 'Four Executed, Ten Still at Risk—Urgent Action 179/16' (2016) AI-Index ASA 21/4581/2016 <www.amnesty.org/download/Documents/ASA2145812016ENGLISH.pdf> accessed 13 October 2018.

37 Australian Associated Press, 'Bali Nine: Indonesian President Rules out Clemency for Inmates on Death Row' *The Guardian* (9 December 2014) <www.theguardian.com/world/2014/dec/10/bali-nine-indonesian-president-rules-out-clemency> accessed 13 October 2018.

38 Bradley Holland, 'Clemency and Constitutional Duties in Indonesia: A Promise Made Is a Promise Kept?' (2018) 19(1) Australian Journal of Asian Law 1, 2.

39 Amnesty International and Legal Defence and Assistance Project, 'Nigeria: Waiting for the Hangman' (2008) AI-Index AFR 44/020/2008 <www.amnesty.org/download/Documents/52000/afr440202008en.pdf> accessed 13 October 2018.

40 Only in 2014 did the National Legal Aid Foundation begin a programme to provide support to prisoners seeking to apply for clemency from the ruler. This support was

Another ongoing concern remains the lack of transparency and meaningful consideration of clemency applications in capital cases, which might explain the low commutation rates in some countries. In 1998, Special Rapporteur Ndiaye expressed his dismay at the fact that in the US state of Texas the members of the parole board never met in person to discuss pending cases, instead expressing their decision on a case via telephone. Ndiaye noted how this process resulted in no recommendations for pardon to the state governor by the time of his mission to the USA a year earlier.[41] Amnesty International noted that by May 1999 the US-wide ratio of executive commutations granted to executions post 1976 was 10.6 per cent, while in Texas it was as low as 0.6 per cent.[42] More recently, in a 2018 report the organisation pointed out that no capital clemency had been granted in Florida since 1983, a period during which approximately 100 executions were carried out.[43] Similarly, in Singapore only six appeals for executive clemency have been granted since the country gained independence in 1965.[44] In Japan, no death sentences have been commuted to life imprisonment since 1975.[45]

Against this increasingly punitive backdrop, it is therefore not surprising that the momentum to further develop the right to seek pardon or commutation of

initially available only to Malaysian nationals and was later extended to all those on death row. Due to funding issues, the programme was later suspended. See Malaysian Bar, 'Speech by Steven Thiru, President, Malaysian Bar at the Opening of the Legal Year 2016 (Kuala Lumpur, 8 Jan 2016)' (*Malaysian Bar*, 2016) <www.malaysianbar.org.my/speeches/speech_by_steven_thiru_president_malaysian_bar_at_the_opening_of_the_legal_year_2016_kuala_lumpur_8_jan_2016.html> accessed 13 October 2018. More information is on file with Amnesty International and is available for consultation on request.

41 Economic and Social Council, 'Report of the Special Rapporteur on Extrajudicial, Summary or Arbitrary Executions, Mr. Bacre Waly Ndiaye, Submitted Pursuant to Commission Resolution 1997/61' (1998) UN Doc E/CN4/1998/68/Add 3, para 102.

42 Amnesty International, 'USA: Killing Without Mercy—Clemency Procedures in Texas' (1999) AI-Index AMR 51/085/1999 <www.amnesty.org/en/documents/amr51/085/1999/en/> accessed 13 October 2018. In 1976 the US Supreme Court ruled in *Gregg v Georgia* that executions could resume in the USA after nearly a decade without them (*Gregg v Georgia*, 428 U.S. 153 (1976)).

43 Amnesty International, 'Darkness Visible in the Sunshine State: The Death Penalty in Florida' (*Amnesty International*, 2018) <www.amnesty.org/en/documents/amr51/8959/2018/en/> accessed 13 October 2018.

44 Amnesty International, 'Singapore: The Death Penalty—A Hidden Toll of Executions' (2004) AI-Index ASA 36/001/2004 <www.amnesty.org/en/documents/ASA36/001/2004/en/> accessed 13 October 2018. See also Daniel Pascoe, 'Singapore and Thailand: Explaining Differences in Death Penalty Clemency' in Jianhong Liu, Max Travers, and Lennon Chang (eds), *Comparative Criminology in Asia* (Springer 2016) 167–168.

45 Daniel Pascoe, 'Towards a Global Theory of Capital Clemency Incidence' in Carol Steiker and Jordan Steiker (eds), *Comparative Capital Punishment Law* (Edward Elgar 2019) 123.

a death sentence under international law and international standards has been restored through individual cases, as the following section demonstrates.

Clemency Processes Come Under Review: 2000–2006

By the year 2000, while discussions within UN bodies on the right to seek clemency in capital cases were seemingly making few advances, the global state of the death penalty had significantly changed compared to when the issue was first debated during the preparation of the Universal Declaration on Human Rights in 1947. At the beginning of the year 2000, 74 countries had legally abolished capital punishment, an average rate of just over one per year since the United Nations were created in 1945,[46] and 108 countries were considered abolitionist in law or in practice by Amnesty International.[47] The UN, the Organization of American States and the Council of Europe had all adopted treaties on the abolition of capital punishment, while the African Commission on Human and Peoples' Rights had approved its first resolution calling for the establishment of a moratorium on executions.[48] More international organisations had taken on the abolition of the death penalty as part of their mandates. And with more recourse mechanisms and avenues available, the violations of human rights associated with the use of the death penalty were given significant exposure and litigation in capital cases before national and regional courts.

Appeals by prisoners facing execution since the early 1990s had contributed to the interpretation of international treaty provisions and the development of standards that reduced the circumstances in which the death penalty was applicable under international law, for example through the setting of time limits after which a sentence of death could no longer be implemented. While more countries moved to abolish the death penalty, some others perceived the newly established restrictions as a direct interference in their administration of criminal justice. In 1998, Jamaica and Trinidad and Tobago, for example, withdrew from the First Optional Protocol to the ICCPR and the American Convention on Human Rights, respectively. Trinidad and Tobago later withdrew and then re-acceded to the First Optional Protocol to the ICCPR, with a reservation that

46 Economic and Social Council, 'Capital Punishment and Implementation of the Safeguards Guaranteeing Protection of the Rights of Those Facing the Death Penalty' (2000) UN Doc E/2000/3.

47 Amnesty International UK, 'Amnesty International Releases Statistics on Worldwide Executions for 1999' (*Amnesty International*, 2000) <www.amnesty.org.uk/press-releases/amnesty-international-releases-statistics-worldwide-executions-1999> accessed 13 October 2018.

48 The Second Optional Protocol to the ICCPR, aiming at the abolition of the death penalty, was adopted in 1989; the Protocol on the American Convention on Human Rights to Abolish the Death Penalty in 1990; Protocol No. 13 to the European Convention on Human Rights was adopted in 2002; and African Commission on Human and Peoples' Rights resolution ACHPR/Res 42 (XXVI) was adopted in 1999.

prevents the Human Rights Committee from receiving complaints made by prisoners under sentence of death.

It is in this context that a 2000 decision by the Judicial Committee of the Privy Council ('JCPC') in London presented a new opportunity to strengthen safeguards guaranteeing the right to seek pardon or commutation of a death sentence under international law. Building on a 1983 Advisory Opinion of the Inter-American Court on Human Rights,[49] the JCPC held for the first time that to comply with their international obligations, states should exercise the prerogative of mercy 'by procedures which are fair and proper and to that end are subject to judicial review'.[50] Although the merits of clemency decisions were outside the purview of the judicial system, the process was not. The JCPC further clarified that, as the pardon application constitutes the last chance for prisoners to make their case against the execution, petitioners should have the opportunity to review the materials put forward to the pardoning board relating to their cases, including reports from international bodies, and to make their own representations, with a view to correcting or adding information as they deemed relevant. To further this aim, adequate notice of the date of the consideration of the mercy request should be given. The JCPC further clarified that there was no need for, nor the right to, an oral hearing to make such representations.[51]

The JCPC's ground-breaking decision conferred on the right to clemency a quasi-judicial status and gained immediate resonance in the jurisprudence of the Inter-American Commission on Human Rights.[52] The same, however, cannot be said for its impact on international law and standards. One month later, in fact, the Human Rights Committee considered the case of *Eversley Thompson v. St. Vincent & the Grenadines*, where Thompson was seeking a remedy against the imposition of the mandatory death penalty.[53] In its Concluding Observations, the Committee reiterated its understanding of the power to grant pardon or commutation of a death sentence as entirely a state prerogative. The Committee asserted that the consideration of the circumstances of an individual case within clemency deliberations is not a sufficient safeguard against the arbitrary deprivation of life, prohibited by Article 6.1 of the ICCPR. As an entirely discretionary prerogative of the executive, the clemency process encompasses factors that are different from those considered

49 *Advisory Opinion OC—3/83 (Restrictions to the Death Penalty)* (1983), para 55 (Inter-American Court on Human Rights).

50 *Lewis, Patrick Taylor and Anthony McLeod, Christopher Brown, Desmond Taylor and Steve Shaw v The Attorney General of Jamaica and Another (Jamaica)* (2000) UKPC 35, para 62.

51 Ibid., para 65.

52 *McKenzie v Jamaica* (2000) Case 12.023; Report No. 41/100 (Inter-American Commission on Human Rights). See also Andrew Novak, *Comparative Executive Clemency—The Constitutional Pardon Power and the Prerogative of Mercy in Global Perspective* (Routledge 2015) 46–53.

53 *Eversley Thompson v St. Vincent & the Grenadines* (2000) Comm No 806/1998; UN Doc CCPR/C/70/D/806/1998 (Human Rights Committee).

through a judicial review of the case, and as such does not offer adequate guarantees of due process when the mandatory death penalty is imposed.

In his dissenting opinion, Lord Colville pointed to the importance of the JCPC decision in *Lewis* and noted that, by holding that clemency processes are open to judicial review, the JCPC ruling gave a new dimension to the right to seek pardon or commutation of a death sentence. *Lewis* established a direct connection between paragraphs 4 and 1 of Article 6 of the ICCPR. If the Committee viewed only the judicial process as a safeguard against the arbitrary deprivation of life, Lord Colville argued that it should be the consideration of Article 6 in its entirety—with the full set of safeguards it guarantees—to determine how such violation could be prevented.

Lord Colville's dissenting view did not result in an immediate change in the jurisprudence of the Human Rights Committee. Two years later, when reviewing a complaint from Rawle Kennedy who faced execution in Trinidad and Tobago, the Committee maintained a similar position:

> [T]he wording of article 6, paragraph 4, does not prescribe a particular procedure for the modalities of the exercise of the prerogative of mercy. Accordingly, States parties retain discretion for spelling out the modalities of the exercise of the rights under article 6, paragraph 4.[54]

On many occasions the Committee has also clearly spelled out that pending pardon procedures are extraordinary remedies and as such do not count as domestic remedies precluding the Committee's consideration of a complaint, thereby relegating the remedy of clemency to a second-degree safeguard.[55] The result of doing so was inevitably that the level of scrutiny over this safeguard was also downgraded.[56]

At the opposite end of the spectrum, the 2005 decision of the Inter-American Court on Human Rights in *Fermín Ramírez v. Guatemala* enshrined procedural safeguards guaranteeing the right to apply for clemency in capital cases irrevocably under international law.[57] When interpreting Article 4.6 of the American Convention on Human Rights, this body echoed the JCPC decision and held that for the right to apply for amnesty, pardon or commutation of sentence to be respected and protected *effectively*, some procedural safeguards should be in place, including the rights to be informed of when the

54 *Rawle Kennedy v Trinidad and Tobago* (2002) Comm No. 845/1998; UN Doc CCPR/C/74/D/845/1998, para 7.4 (Human Rights Committee).

55 *Webby Chisanga v Zambia* (2005) Comm No. 1132/2002; UN Doc CCPR/C/85/D/1132/2002, para 6.3 (Human Rights Committee).

56 The only exception to this relates to the practice of pardons granted by families in reconciliation procedures under Islamic Law, which the Committee viewed as contrary to the ICCPR. Human Rights Committee, 'Concluding Observations: Yemen' (2005) UN Doc CCPR/CO/84/YEM, para 15.

57 *Fermín Ramírez v Guatemala* (2005) IACHR Series C no. 126; IHRL 1510 (Inter-American Court of Human Rights).

application would be considered; to make representations, in person or through counsel; and to receive information on the outcome within a reasonable period of time before the execution.[58]

During the same year, the former UN Commission on Human Rights in Geneva adopted a resolution calling on states to abolish the death penalty completely and, in the meantime, establish a moratorium on executions.[59] Following two failed attempts to adopt similar calls at the UNGA in 1994 and 1999, this resolution constituted a first sign that a new chapter in anti-death penalty activism in international fora was about to begin, a phase in which the right to apply for pardon or commutation would gain new prominence.

Clemency as Policy: 2007–2018

On 18 December 2007 the UN General Assembly adopted resolution 62/149 on a moratorium on the use of the death penalty—a move that was greeted by the abolitionist movement as a ground-breaking development. Supported by a cross-regional majority of states, for the first time a resolution by the main UN deliberative body with full membership made a critical call on states that still retain the death penalty to establish a moratorium on executions with a view to abolishing this punishment.

The 2007 resolution created an unequivocal link between the promotion and protection of human rights, which are universal, and the suspension of executions at international level. It challenged the perception that the death penalty is exclusively a criminal justice issue, and that, as such, decisions on capital punishment pertain solely to the authorities of the individual state. The adoption of the 2007 resolution clearly placed stopping executions within the human rights priorities of the international community.

There is no doubt that the adoption of this resolution only became possible following the progress in the global abolition of the death penalty by December 2007. However, it was also the change of focus to call for a *moratorium* on executions by several retentionist countries that led to the ground-breaking result, dispelling the perception of the resolution as an initiative enjoying support of abolitionist countries alone. As noted by Hood and Hoyle, 14 of the then 61 retentionist countries did not vote against the resolution, even if they were at that point still actively executing.[60]

58 It is worth noting that Article 4(6) of the American Convention on Human Rights also guarantees the right to apply for amnesty in addition to pardon and commutation of a death sentence, unlike the corresponding provision in the ICCPR which only confers the right to states to grant amnesties.

59 UN Commission on Human Rights Resolution 2005/59 on the Question of the Death Penalty (2005).

60 Eleven abstained (Belarus, Cameroon, Cuba, Democratic Republic of the Congo, Equatorial Guinea, Guinea, Lebanon, Lesotho, Sierra Leone, the United Arab Emirates, and Vietnam), and three voted for the resolution (Burundi, Guatemala, and Tajikistan). See Roger Hood and Carolyn Hoyle, 'Abolishing the Death

Since 2007, the UN General Assembly has gone on to adopt six further resolutions on this issue, with incremental support, including most recently in December 2018.[61] Although not legally binding, the powerful calls made by the UN General Assembly in favour of a moratorium on the use of the death penalty have carried considerable moral and political weight, and have generated a new momentum among civil society, governments, and international governmental organizations towards ending executions and abolishing the death penalty.

Among other examples of this momentum, three of the 14 retentionist countries that did not oppose the call for a moratorium in December 2007 took further legislative action. Burundi and Guinea went on to abolish the death penalty for all crimes in 2009 and 2017, respectively, whereas Guatemala became abolitionist for ordinary crimes, such as murder, in 2017. Cuba commuted all its remaining death sentences by December 2010 and stated as part of UN debates that it 'understands and respects the arguments of the international movement that advocates the abolition of or a moratorium on the death penalty'.[62] On 13 February 2014 the government of Equatorial Guinea signed a resolution which established a temporary moratorium on the application of the death penalty.[63]

Other countries also took steps to implement the calls from the UN General Assembly in their national human rights framework. In January 2010, the then President of Mongolia, Tsakhiagiin Elbegdorj, established an official moratorium on executions and announced that he would commute all death sentences by presidential pardon, a move that played a critical role in accelerating momentum towards abolition in national legislation.[64] The President of The Gambia, Adama Barrow, announced on the occasion of the 53rd anniversary of independence in February 2018 that he had established a moratorium on executions as a first step towards abolition. The Gambia became a State Party

Penalty Worldwide: The Impact of a "New Dynamic"' (2009) 38(1) Crime and Justice 1, 40.

61 UN General Assembly Resolution 63/168 (18 December 2008); UN General Assembly Resolution 65/206 (21 December 2010); UN General Assembly Resolution 67/176 (20 December 2012); UN General Assembly Resolution 69/186 (18 December 2014); UN General Assembly Resolution 71/187 (19 December 2016); UN General Assembly Resolution 73/175 (17 December 2018).

62 Human Rights Council, 'National Report Submitted in Accordance with Human Rights Council Resolution 16/21, Annex, Paragraph 5—Cuba' (2013) A/HRC/WG 6/16/CUB/1, para 98.

63 UN Human Rights Council, 'National Report Submitted in Accordance with Paragraph 5 of the Annex to Human Rights Council Resolution 16/21: Equatorial Guinea' (2014) UN Doc A/HRC/WG 6/19/GNQ/1 <www.ohchr.org/EN/HRBodies/UPR/Pages/GQSession19.aspx> accessed 27 November 2018, para 48.

64 President Tsakhia Elbegdorj, 'The Path of Democratic Mongolia Must be Clean and Bloodless' (*President of Mongolia*, 2010) <www.president.mn/eng/newsCenter/viewNews.php?newsId=122> accessed 13 October 2018.

to the Second Optional Protocol to the International Covenant on Civil and Political Rights, aiming at the abolition of the death penalty, seven months later.[65] Mass commutations of death sentences in Thailand formed the practical means through which the implementation of death sentences was suspended, at least until June 2018.[66]

The new drive for abolition triggered by the adoption of the first UNGA moratorium resolution in 2007 was also clear at global and regional level. In the past decade, 16 countries have abolished the death penalty for all crimes, whereas 20 UN Member States have ratified and three have signed the Second Optional Protocol to the International Covenant on Civil and Political Rights. The African Commission on Human and People's Rights adopted in 2008 its second resolution calling for the implementation of a moratorium on the use of the death penalty,[67] and adopted in 2015 its General Comment No. 3 on the right to life (Article 4), which states that the African Charter on Human and People's Rights does not include any provision recognising the death penalty. A new draft Protocol to the African Charter on Human and Peoples' Rights is presently awaiting consideration by the African Union. In July 2009 the Parliamentary Assembly of the Organization for Security and Cooperation in Europe adopted a resolution calling on participating states applying the death penalty to declare an immediate moratorium on executions.[68] In 2011, the Inter-American Commission on Human Rights also adopted a thematic study on the death penalty and its abolition in the Inter-American system, calling on countries that still retain the death penalty to establish a moratorium on executions.[69]

Developments in the past decade have undoubtedly marked a change in the value given to moratorium policies in the context of anti-death penalty advocacy. The unequivocal link established by the 2007 UN General Assembly resolution between the suspension of executions and the human rights framework, together with the elevation of hiatuses in the implementation of death

65 News24, 'Gambia Announces "Moratorium" on Death Penalty' (*News24*, 19 February 2018) <www.news24.com/Africa/News/gambia-announces-moratorium-on-death-penalty-20180219> accessed 13 October 2018.

66 Channel News Asia, 'Thailand Carries out First Execution since 2009' (*Channel News Asia*, 19 June 2018) <www.channelnewsasia.com/news/asia/thailand-carries-out-first-execution-since-2009-10446210> accessed 13 October 2018.

67 African Commission on Human and Peoples' Rights Resolution Calling on State Parties to Observe the Moratorium on the Death Penalty (2008) ACHPR/Res 136 (XXXXIIII) 08.

68 Parliamentary Assembly of the Organization for Security and Cooperation in Europe Resolution on a Moratorium on the Death Penalty and Towards its Abolition adopted at the Eighteenth Annual Session of the OSCE Parliamentary Assembly (2009) AS (09) D 1 E.

69 Inter-American Commission on Human Rights, 'The Death Penalty in the Inter-American System of Human Rights: From Restrictions to Abolition' (2011) OEA/Ser L/V/II; Doc 68 <www.oas.org/en/iachr/docs/pdf/deathpenalty.pdf> accessed 13 October 2018.

sentences to formal state policy, has led to new strategic directions. Activists for abolition now feel legitimized in seeking moratorium declarations through their advocacy, as much as for more permanent legal moves toward abolition.

This renewed emphasis on moratoria has conferred new attention on the right to seek clemency in capital cases, not so much as an individual right requiring procedural safeguards, but more as a collective exercise of state power to end executions and initiate abolition processes. Paradoxically, in trying to limit the use of the death penalty, abolitionist actors now place more emphasis on the often-capricious exercise of clemency by the state, appealing to the highest executive authorities for leadership in establishing moratoria. At the same time, lawyers and activists seek to bring more accountability to the equally capricious decisions to refuse to grant clemency in individual cases.[70]

A New Impetus

The renewed momentum witnessed since 2007, as described above, offered a new impetus in the work of UN bodies and mechanisms to strengthen the right to apply for pardon or commutation in capital cases. The first senior UN official to take a critical look at this right as defined under international law and standards was the then Special Rapporteur on Extrajudicial, Summary or Arbitrary Executions, Philip Alston. In his 2008 report, Alston considered the extent to which states must respect procedural safeguards to ensure the integrity of the right to seek pardon and commutation of a death sentence under Article 6(4) of the ICCPR.[71] While noting that the Article preserved the sovereign power of the state, Alston went beyond the views of the Human Rights Committee and affirmed that the right to seek clemency 'is nonetheless a part of the legal system in the broadest sense', as it serves as a final review against wrongful convictions when new evidence emerges and normal procedures cannot be reopened; as a means to take into account relevant developments that occurred after the conviction, including in relation to the rehabilitation of the offender; and to allow the executive to show mercy.

Adopting the views of the JCPC in *Lewis,* Special Rapporteur Alston further affirmed that two factors are critical to safeguard the right to seek pardon or commutation of a death sentence and the integrity of due process. The first is the provision of basic information regarding the proceedings, such as the date of consideration of the petition and notice of the decision reached. The second involves providing the opportunity to the prisoner to invoke any personal

70 Human Rights Council of the General Assembly, 'Report of the Special Rapporteur on Extrajudicial, Summary or Arbitrary Executions' (2008) UN Doc A/HRC/8/3, para 59–67.

71 Human Rights Council, 'Report of the Special Rapporteur on Extrajudicial, Summary or Arbitrary executions, Philip Alston' (2008) UN Doc A/HRC/8/3, para 59–66.

circumstances or other considerations that might appear relevant as part of their pardon application, as opposed to the reliance on written reports from the trial judge.

A further advancement in the definition of the right to seek pardon or commutation of a death sentence came from the adoption, in 2012, of the UN Principles and Guidelines on Access to Legal Aid in Criminal Justice Systems, which recommend that states introduce measures to ensure that prisoners have access to legal aid including to prepare appeals and requests for pardon, in particular when facing capital punishment.[72]

However, it was not until the adoption of resolution 71/187 by the UN General Assembly in December 2016 that the effect of this increased international scrutiny on the exercise of the power of clemency began to permeate language on clemency procedures within UN instruments. For the first time, resolution 71/187 calls on all states to 'ensure that those facing the death penalty can exercise their right to apply for pardon or commutation of their death *sentence by ensuring that clemency procedures are fair and transparent and that prompt information is provided at all stages of the process*' (emphasis added).[73] This new language is important as it establishes a direct correlation between the ability of prisoners to exercise this right and the duty on the state to ensure that the elements of fairness and transparency are defining elements of the clemency procedures. It further introduces principles that have so far more commonly been linked to judicial processes, such as fair and public disclosure in a possible indirect reference to Article 14 of the ICCPR, into the administration of the state prerogative of mercy. This is a break with the views previously held by UN bodies, identified above.

This critical advance follows two recent resolutions by the UN Human Rights Council, calling upon states that have not yet abolished the death penalty to make available information on several aspects of their use of this punishment, including 'the number of death sentences reversed, commuted on appeal or in which amnesty or pardon has been granted',[74] in an effort to increase transparency on the administration of pardons and commutations. The same language was included in UNGA resolution 71/187, adopted in December 2016, as well as in the most recent one adopted by the UNGA in December 2018, resolution 73/175.[75]

In contrast with these new advances strengthening the safeguards pertaining to the right to seek clemency, the position maintained by the Human Rights Committee on Article 6 of the ICCPR as it recently adopted its General

72 United Nations Office on Drugs and Crime, 'Guideline 6 of the Principles on Legal Aid (the UN Principles and Guidelines on Access to Legal Aid in Criminal Justice Systems)' (2012) UN Doc E/CN 15/2012/L 14/Rev 1, para 47(c).

73 UN General Assembly Resolution 71/187 (19 December 2016), para 7(f).

74 Human Rights Council Resolution 30/5 (1 October 2015) on the question of the death penalty; Human Rights Council Resolution 36/17 (29 September 2017) on the question of the death penalty.

75 UNGA Resolution 73/175 (17 December 2018), para 7(c).

Comment No. 36 remains, at first reading, somewhat narrow and conservative.[76]

The new General Comment, adopted on 30 October 2018, reaffirms the understanding of clemency as a critical safeguard of due process, but appears to limit its interpretation of the right to seek pardon or commutation in capital cases to a summary of long-established elements in the jurisprudence of the Committee, without challenging its administration as unfettered state prerogative. These elements include: ensuring that executions are not carried out before pardon applications are meaningfully considered and decided on; that states retain discretion in defining procedures relating to clemency; that no restrictions can be imposed on the categories of prisoners exercising this right; and that pardons are not consistent with the ICCPR if the victim's family plays a preponderant role in the decision. However, the draft General Comment is not entirely devoid of new features relating to clemency. The Committee specifically requests states to ensure that the pardon procedures are not 'ineffective, unnecessarily burdensome, discriminatory in nature or applied in an arbitrary manner'. Furthermore, the UN body mandates that clemency procedures 'must offer certain essential guarantees, including certainty about the processes followed and the substantive criteria applied'.

In particular, the reference to arbitrary application of clemency, as well as the request for certainty about the substantive criteria applied, mark a significant departure from the previously held views of the Committee, acknowledging that some limits and criteria ought to be imposed on an otherwise plenary state power. This line appears to be supported in the recent findings by the Committee in a case from Maldives, where the human rights body noted that:

> Article 6(4) does not prescribe a particular procedure for the exercise of the right to seek pardon or commutation, and States parties consequently retain *some* discretion in spelling out the relevant procedures. Still, such procedures should be specified in domestic legislation. Moreover, clemency procedures must not afford the families of crime victims a preponderant role in determining whether the death sentence should be carried out.[77]

The General Comment also takes note of the role of the granting of pardons and commutations in the abolitionist goal enshrined in Article 6, a possible nod to recent emphasis on clemency as policy established in some states.[78]

76 Human Rights Committee, 'General Comment No. 36 on Article 6 of the International Covenant on Civil and Political Rights, on the Right to Life' (2018) UN Doc CCPR/C/GC/36.

77 Emphasis added. See *Hussain Humaam Ahmed v Republic of the Maldives* (2019) Comm No. 2785/2016; UN Doc CCPR/C/123/D/2785/2016, para 9.9 (Human Rights Committee).

78 Ibid., para 50.

Despite the lengthy paragraph dedicated to the right to seek pardon and commutation in capital cases, the General Comment omits some important elements that could contribute to ensuring that clemency applications are meaningfully considered. States are not asked to make information on their consideration of pardon applications public, including figures on those granted and rejected; nor are they asked to divulge information on the 'substantive criteria applied' and how the merits of each application were considered against those criteria. The right to be informed promptly about the outcome of the procedure recalled by the Committee does not necessarily guarantee the prisoner the right to be informed of the reasoning for the possible rejection of their pardon application. Nor does it allow policy-makers, legal representatives, and other stakeholders in the criminal justice system access to adequate information through which to assess and improve the handling of clemency procedures. These omissions potentially perpetuate the cycle of discrimination, arbitrariness and ineffectiveness that the Committee itself aims to end.

Conclusion

The development of the right to seek pardon or commutation of a death sentence under international law and standards has been influenced greatly by the political discourse that has accompanied the evolution of the human rights framework more broadly. Sitting at the interplay between universality and sovereignty, the duality of this right—as an individual right and as a state right—has granted it substantive prominence among safeguards of due process in capital cases.

The right to seek pardon has evolved over time. As the international political context has changed, the perception of the nature of this right has also been transformed, evolving from a discretionary humanitarian act to an essential safeguard guaranteeing protection of the rights of those facing the death penalty; from an executive power to a quasi-judicial process; from unpredictable exercise of a state prerogative to official policy.[79]

Yet the limited consideration given to clemency's administration has allowed for minimal scrutiny over clemency procedures and, as a result, a lack of meaningful consideration of petitions for pardon. Repeated violations of the right to seek pardon or commutation have continued to date and concerns over arbitrariness and discrimination have tainted the use of this state prerogative in many countries. It is therefore imperative that international human rights bodies continue to define procedural standards through which clemency applications should be administered and impose closer control over the criteria that are used to guide clemency decisions. Considering the direct and growing relevance that rehabilitative processes have in the determination of pardon requests, international bodies should also consider the links that might exist between Article 6(4) of the ICCPR and its Article 10(3), which

79 See Cooper and Burrows, this volume.

clearly sets the reformation and social rehabilitation of the offender as the essential aim of the prison system.

As the human rights framework and the entire multilateral system have both come under attack following a revival of national sovereignty by certain influential countries, it is hard to predict what turn the right to seek pardon or commutation in capital cases will take next. Although, in the short term, it is likely that further development of procedural safeguards will be met with greater resistance by states retaining the death penalty, in the long term we would expect to see more and more governments resorting to clemency to establish official moratoriums on executions. This will, in turn, put greater scrutiny on state clemency practices, cementing once and for all the understanding of clemency under international law as a procedural safeguard subject to judicial review. Nevertheless, given that the global trend continues to be unequivocally in favour of abolition of the death penalty, it is highly likely that the need for clemency in capital cases will become moot in the not-too-distant future.

3 Separation of Powers and Executive Clemency in the Civil Law World

A Comparative Study

Sonsoles Arias and Antonios Kouroutakis

Introduction

Executive clemency, sometimes known as the power to pardon or the prerogative of mercy, occupies an ever-present place in modern constitutional documents around the world. However, executive clemency, which is a legal mechanism to totally or partially abrogate criminal convictions or prison sentences, or to commute fines and corresponding burdens levied on convicts, has been woven into our legal civilization since the earliest appearance of coherent legal structures. Pardon is recorded in Mosaic Law, in Greek Law, and in Roman Law.[1]

During the Middle Ages, clemency was an absolute prerogative of autocratic rulers. Nowadays, since the establishment of the principle of separation of powers, only individual pardon typically falls within the constitutional competence of the executive. General pardon, also known amnesty, typically falls within the competence of the legislature.[2]

What is the impact of the separation of powers model, another constitutional staple, on the executive clemency mechanism? Is there a correlation between different models of separation of powers (presidential, parliamentary, or semi-presidential) and executive clemency's specific institutional settings? Or, to put it differently, does the power to grant clemency carry any special weight within the balance of powers, or do different clemency models

1 William F Duker, 'The President's Power to Pardon: A Constitutional History' (1977) 18(3) William & Mary LR 475, 476.

2 See Leslie Sebba and Richard S Frase 'Amnesty and Pardon' in *Encyclopedia of Crime and Justice* (The Gale Group Inc. 2002) <https://www.encyclopedia.com/law/legal-and-political-magazines/amnesty-and-pardon> accessed 8 November 2018:

The term pardon is first found in early French law and derives from the late Latin *perdonare* ('to grant freely'), suggesting a gift bestowed by the sovereign. It has thus come to be associated with a somewhat personal concession by a head of state to the perpetrator of an offence, in mitigation or remission of the full punishment that he has merited. Amnesty, on the other hand, derives from the Greek *amnestia* ('forgetting'), and has come to be used to describe measures of a more general nature, directed to offences whose criminality is considered better forgotten.

simply fit harmoniously into the particular separation of powers system employed by each state?

This chapter aims to examine comparatively the executive clemency laws of several unitary and federal civil law systems, namely Argentina, Brazil, France, Germany, Greece, Lithuania, and Spain, and to compare and contrast different constitutional and legislative executive clemency mechanisms in correlation with specific separation of powers models.

In doing so, the chapter addresses two key questions. First, does the clemency power fall within the absolute control of the executive branch (i.e. the president) or is clemency decision-making shared amongst other executive, legislative, or judicial institutions (e.g. Cabinet ministers, parliamentary committees or judicial bodies, respectively)? Second, the chapter will test the following hypothesis: that the role of the executive decision-maker in exercising the clemency power reflects the institutional power of that executive institution within the general model of the separation of powers.

Briefly, the authors' conclusion posits that in the seven aforementioned civil law jurisdictions, an executive organ with a significant role in the constitutional separation of powers possesses the most powerful role in the clemency process vis-à-vis other governmental organs. Considering the existing comparative clemency and separation of powers literature,[3] this is not an unexpected result.

Separation of Powers and Its Evolution

The doctrine of separation of powers is a cornerstone in the foundation of modern democracies. Its roots are drawn from the manuscripts of ancient philosophers such as Aristotle.[4] However, in modern times, Montesquieu is considered foremost among the scholars who have established its dogma.[5] In theory, in each polity there are three kinds of governmental powers: legislative,

3 For example, Jody C Baumgartner and Mark H Morris, 'Presidential Power Unbound: A Comparative Look at Presidential Pardon Power' (2001) 29(2) Politics and Policy 209; Leslie Sebba, 'The Pardoning Power: A World Survey' (1977) 68(1) The Journal of Criminal Law and Criminology 83; Ruti G Teitel, *Transitional Justice* (OUP 2000); Frank J Goodnow, *Comparative Administrative Law* (Beard Books 2000); Pascoe and Novak, this volume.

4 Aristotle has remarked that: '[a]ll forms of constitution then have three factors in reference to which the good lawgiver has to consider what is expedient for each constitution; [...] Of these three factors one is, what is to be the body that deliberates about the common interests, second the one connected with the magistracies, that is, what there are to be and what matters they are to control, and what is to be the method of their election, and a third is, what is to be the judiciary'. [See Aristotle, *Politics*, 1297b–1298a].

5 As Vile accurately points out, before Montesquieu several authors discussed the idea of separation of powers, such as Locke in 1772 and Sir Humphrey Mackworth in 1701. See MJC Vile, *Constitutionalism and the Separation of Powers* (2nd edn, OUP 1967) 83.

executive, and judicial, which shall not be concentrated in the authority of the same institution. Instead, they should be separate. This distinction between institutions holding and exercising unique functions is known as the 'pure' separation of powers according to which the institutions are isolated and do not share functions.[6] However, from a functional perspective, a system of checks and balances, or, according to Madison, a limited sharing of power among the institutions is a prerequisite for good governance.[7] The perceived differences between these institutional and the functional approaches to the separation of powers may be 'blunt' or 'sharp' depending on their practical application.[8] In particular, in systems where the law-making body is institutionally independent, such as in the presidential systems, the focus is on the institutional separation of powers, while in systems where the law-making body is less independent, such as the parliamentary systems, the functional separation of powers is the focus.

Of great importance in the evaluation of each separation of powers system is the hierarchy between the separation of institutions, which is the formal approach, and the separation of functions, which is the functional approach. From the formal point of view, the extent of the institutional independence of the legislative branch from the executive and their various interactions have led to what are commonly known as parliamentary, presidential, and semi-presidential systems of government. From the functional point of view, legislative competence and institutional roles in the law-making process are significant as checks and balances. The share of functions creates more dependency and mutual controls of one institution over the others.

In practice, the separation of powers models that focus on the balance of powers between the executive and the legislature and their respective institutional settings are divided into three groups: first, in presidential models, like the US federal jurisdiction, there is a clear distinction between the executive and the legislative body. Second, there are parliamentary systems, for instance in the UK, Germany, and Spain. In such systems, the executive is dicephalic, with the head of state being clearly distinct from the legislative body. Each possesses a ceremonial and regulatory role. The head of government is a member of parliament, dependent on the confidence of the parliament, and therefore there is no clear separation between the executive and the legislative. The third major model is the semi-presidential model currently employed in France and Lithuania (of the nations under study here), where the president as head of state is elected directly by the people. The head of government is accountable to the elected president and the legislature.[9]

6 Ibid., 19.

7 Ralph Ketcham, *Selected Writings of James Madison* (Hacket Publishing 2006) 123.

8 Antonios Kouroutakis, *The Constitutional Value of Sunset Clauses* (Routledge 2017) 84.

9 A more detailed analysis about the fundamentals of each system is recorded in an academic dialogue between Bruce Ackerman, Steven G Calabresi, and Cindy

Furthermore, the separation of powers models focused on the law-making process are divided into two broad categories: the consensus model and the majoritarian model.[10] Consensus is the mode of operation in a separation of powers system where the law-making function is shared between different institutions. In contrast, there is less of a need for consensus when law-making depends on a majority in the legislature and thus the government does not in general seek agreement with the opposition in order to pass legislation. For example, consensus is an important element in law-making in the bicameral system of the US federal jurisdiction, or in the event of hung parliaments in the UK and Germany. In contrast, the majoritarian model holds sway when a single party controls the majority in the law-making body or bodies, or when the president is from the same party as the prime minister in a semi-presidential system, such as in France.

Alternatively, the separation of powers models focused on law-making may be categorised by the number of 'veto players', in other words the number of institutions with law-making power and the ability to decline the passage of a bill.[11] For example, the US has three veto players: the House, the Senate, and the president, while UK has only one veto player—Parliament. Interestingly, in France, the president has no veto power over legislation, but may veto government decrees. In Germany, some laws require the agreement of both the Bundestag and the Bundesrat and other laws require only a majority in the Bundestag. In Spain, the executive government has the ability to decline any parliamentary bill which involves an increase in appropriations or a decrease in budget revenue.[12]

In the distinction between the presidential, semi-presidential, and parliamentary models, or between majoritarian and consensus democracies, the role of political parties is a variable of paramount importance. Political parties play a significant role in channelling power from the legislative branch to the executive.[13] Hence, notwithstanding the different institutional settings, if a political party controls both branches, executive, and legislative, the outcome is that all models gain the qualities of the parliamentary system.[14] Equally, the government

Skach about the pros and cons of each model. See Bruce Ackerman, 'The New Separation of Powers' (2000) 113 Harvard Law Review 633; Steven G Calabresi, 'Virtues of Presidential Government: Why Professor Ackerman is Wrong to Prefer the German to the US Constitution' (2001) 18 Constitutional Commentary 51; Cindy Skach 'The "newest" separation of powers: Semipresidentialism' (2007) 5 International Journal of Constitutional Law 93.

10 Arend Lijphart, *Patterns of Democracy, Government Forms and Performance in Thirty-Six Countries* (Yale University Press 1999) 10.

11 George Tsebelis, *Veto Players: How Political Institutions Work* (Princeton University Press 2002).

12 Constitution of Spain 1978, s 134(6). This limitation on parliamentary activity has been very frequently used in the most recent parliamentary term (2016–2018), when the Spanish parliament's lower chamber was split along party lines.

13 Paul Craig, *Administrative Law* (7th edn, Sweet & Maxwell 2012) para 15-003.

14 Stephen Gardbaum, 'Political Parties, Voting Systems, and the Separation of Powers' (2017) 65 The American Journal of Comparative Law 229.

is in less need for consensus and the number of veto players is limited to one. By contrast, in the parliamentary model, if no political party holds a majority in the legislature, then the executive is in need of consensus and there is more than one veto player.

Finally, separation of powers models may also focus on the role of the judiciary to review the constitutionality of legislative acts, and may be categorised into three groups on this basis. Under the traditional (default) approach, courts have no power to review and strike out legislation. The judicial function is merely limited to interpreting and applying whatever laws the legislature enacts. Two examples are the UK before the adoption of the Human Rights Act in 1998, and France before the *question prioritaire de constitutionnalité* (Priority Question on Constitutionality) in 2008. The exact opposite approach authorises courts to review legislation for consistency with the constitution, and thus the courts have the power to invalidate statutes that infringe its provisions, as in the cases of the US and Germany. An intermediate or alternative approach is located in between the two aforementioned models, and allows for the courts to review the constitutionality of legislative acts without the power to strike them down. This is the position in the UK after the adoption of the Human Rights Act in 1998.[15]

Comparative Executive Clemency in Civil Law Jurisdictions

Executive clemency is a very exceptional measure, of a personal nature and generally in favour of a specific subject (as opposed to general pardon or amnesty) and is typically awarded after irrevocable conviction, that is to say, a judgment that is not amenable to legal remedy.[16] Unless the law so provides, it does not typically eliminate the conviction or stigma from the criminal process, having no retroactive effect.[17] Although the most typical forms of clemency discussed by scholars are commutations and pardons, due to their permanent effect on criminal sentences, as Pascoe has remarked 'clemency is an umbrella term for a variety of executive powers which reduce legally-imposed punishment'.[18]

15 Aileen Kavanagh, *Constitutional Review under the UK Human Rights Act* (CUP 2009) 281–292.
16 See René Lévy, 'Pardons and Amnesties as Policy Instruments in Contemporary France' (2007) 36 Crime and Justice 551, 557. See also Pascoe and Novak, this volume.
17 This means that pardon 'allows the offense to remain in judicial records and, consequently, is taken into account when passing judgment on a second offense'. See Lévy (n 16) 559.
18 Daniel Pascoe, 'The Functions of Death Penalty Clemency in Southeast Asia: Comparative Lessons for Vietnam' (*ALC Briefing Papers*, 1 December 2017) 4, 7 <https://law.unimelb.edu.au/__data/assets/pdf_file/0008/2668976/ALC-Briefing-Paper-Pascoe_EN_final.pdf> accessed 6 December 2019. Technically speaking, pardon is only one form of executive clemency. Executive clemency also includes reprieves, commutations of sentence, and remissions of fines and forfeitures. See Andrew Novak, 'Transparency and Comparative Executive Clemency: Global Lessons for Pardon Reform in the United States' (2016) 49 University of Michigan Journal of Law Reform 817, 819.

Clemency is a common constitutional feature in almost every legal system around the world.[19] From a philosophical point of view, a clemency mechanism fuses justice with leniency and mercy. In his monumental book, *Les Misérables*, Victor Hugo succinctly communicated the virtue of mercy. Hugo personified his antagonist inspector Javert as a person without a sense of pardon, with a very strict sense of legalism and incapable of compassion.[20]

Nevertheless, there exists substantial criticism on the necessity of executive clemency in the constitutional system. Derrida approaches pardon as the exception to the rule, though unwelcomed, as it 'suspends and interrupts the usual order of law'[21] while Sarat questions the compatibility of pardon with rule of law.[22] Markel argues that mercy is incompatible with and a 'failure of equal liberty under law'.[23] Sebba has argued that clemency is an 'anachronism' in a 'professionalized twentieth century scheme of criminal justice'.[24]

Further criticism has been levelled regarding the executive role and authority in exercising the pardon power in the US.[25] In particular, as Vile remarks, citing Lawson's work, initially two forms of political power were conceived: legislative power and executive power.[26] The latter was further divided into two aspects. First, the application and the operation of the laws adopted by the legislature,[27] and second, the enforcement of the law through the machinery of the courts which includes, among other tasks, 'the infliction of penalties, dispensations of judgement, suspension of execution, *and pardons*'.[28]

This threefold division of powers, closer to the current understanding between the legislature, the executive, and the judiciary, was articulated by Montesquieu, the philosopher most associated with the doctrine of separation of powers.[29] That said, as pardon was originally conceived of as a judicial function, this raises questions about when the executive should exercise such authority.

19 Pascoe and Novak, this volume; Appendix.
20 Victor Hugo, *Les Misérables* (Charles E Wilbour tr, Random House 1992).
21 Jacques Derrida, 'To Forgive: The Unforgivable and the Imprescriptable', in John Caputo, Mark Dooley, and Michael Scanlon (eds), *Questioning God* (Bloomington, 2001) 21, 26.
22 Austin Sarat, 'At the Boundaries of Law: Executive Clemency, Sovereign Prerogative, and the Dilemma of American Legality' (2005) 57 American Quarterly 611.
23 Dan Markel, 'Against Mercy' (2004) 88 Minnesota Law Review 1421.
24 Leslie Sebba, 'Clemency in Perspective' in Simha F Landau and Leslie Sebba (eds), *Criminology in Perspective: Essays in Honour of Israel Drapkin* (Lexington Books 1977) 221.
25 For an analysis of the case law on the issue see Patrick R Cowlishaw, 'The Conditional Presidential Pardon' (1975) 28 Stanford Law Review 149.
26 Vile (n 5) 61.
27 For instance, such a power will cover 'the function of the magistrates to make peace or war, send or receive embassies, establish the public security, and provide against invasions' (ibid., 95).
28 Vile (n 5) 61, emphasis added.
29 Ibid., 83.

For instance, when a new constitution was drafted for South Africa in 1996, the drafters allocated the pardon power to the president.[30] During the certification process of the new Constitution by the Constitutional Court, an objection was raised that such power violates the separation of powers principle.[31] While the Court recognised the overlap of powers and functions between the president, as a member of the executive, and the judiciary, it argued that such power has never been part of the general functions courts, and furthermore that the power to pardon is a power that is ordinarily entrusted to the head of state in many national constitutions.[32]

Interestingly, when Montesquieu refers to pardon in his seminal work ‘The Spirit of Laws’, he posits the case of imperial Persia, where no one could ask for pardon in case the king had condemned a prisoner, because this would have been seen as a challenge to the king’s legal authority.[33] However, Montesquieu proceeds to characterise pardon in monarchies as the finest exemplar of sovereignty.[34] A thorough reading of Montesquieu’s work provides us with a justification as to why pardon ought not to be exercised by the judiciary. He states that ‘it would be senseless for [a judicial decision-maker] both to make and unmake his own judgments; he would not want to contradict himself’.[35] And as Blackstone has accurately remarked: ‘it would be impolitic for the power of judging and pardoning to center in one and the same person’.[36]

Indeed, the criteria for assessing clemency petitions are often not the same as those used by the court in forming its judicial decision, since pardon primarily serves the correction and rehabilitation policy pursued by the State. However, in some cases clemency may also enhance the fairness of punishment as a further check on the judicial decision itself.[37] In its essence, executive

30 Draft Constitution South Africa 1996, s 84(2)(j):

(1) The President has the powers entrusted by the Constitution and legislation, including those necessary to perform the functions of Head of State and head of the national executive.

(2) The President is responsible for …

(j) pardoning or reprieving offenders and remitting any fines, penalties or forfeitures[.]

31 Certification of the Constitution of the Republic of South Africa, 1996 (CCT 23/96) [1996] ZACC 26; 1996 (4) SA 744 (CC); 1996 (10) BCLR 1253 (CC) (6 September 1996) para 115.

32 Certification of the Constitution of the Republic of South Africa, 1996 (CCT 23/96) [1996] ZACC 26; 1996 (4) SA 744 (CC); 1996 (10) BCLR 1253 (CC) (6 September 1996) para 117.

33 Montesquieu, *The Spirit of Laws* (Anne M Cohler, Basia Carolyn Miller and Harold Samuel Stone eds, CUP 1989) 29.

34 Ibid., 78.

35 Ibid.

36 William Blackstone, 4 *Commentaries* 397.

37 Kathleen Dean Moore, *Pardons: Justice, Mercy and the Public Interest* (OUP 1989) 89ff. For a more detailed analysis on the typology of functions that pardons serve see Mary Margaret Giannini, ‘Measured Mercy: Managing the Intersection of Executive Pardon Power and Victims’ Rights with Procedural Justice Principles’

clemency is an administrative procedure perfectly compatible with the modern understanding of checks and balances and the sharing of powers. This was exemplified in the US Supreme Court Case *Ex Parte United States* which held:

> The Constitution assigns to the legislature the power to enact laws defining crimes and fixing the degree and method of punishment, to the judiciary the power to try offenses under those laws and impose punishment within the limits and according to the methods therein provided, to the executive the power to relieve from the punishment so fixed by law and so judicially ascertained and imposed.[38]

To conclude, as Heise has pointed out, executive clemency may be thought of as an 'extrajudicial' measure with the aim, among others, of enhancing fairness and correcting deficiencies within the judicial system.[39] Concurrently, executive clemency is also a 'quasi judicial' power which is exercised by a non-judicial actor relying upon standards that resemble judicial criteria.[40] While the executive clemency power has been thoroughly examined in the United States,[41] less is known about the way it is situated in the separation of powers systems of civil law countries. The analysis below examines the constitutional and legal framework of the executive clemency power in Argentina, Brazil, France, Germany, Greece, Lithuania, and Spain.

Executive Clemency in the Civil Law World

The comparative analysis below consists of seven countries belonging to the civil law tradition,[42] namely Argentina, Brazil, France, Germany, Greece, Lithuania, and Spain.[43] Germany, Greece, and Spain each follow a parliamentary system of separation of powers, but Spain is a devolved state, whereas

(2015) 13 Ohio State Journal of Criminal Law 89 and Pascoe, 'The Functions of Death Penalty Clemency' (n 18).

38 *Ex Parte United States* 242 US 27 (1916).

39 Michael Heise, 'Mercy by the Numbers: An Empirical Analysis of Clemency and Its Structure' (2003) 89 Virginia Law Review 239, 252.

40 Moore (n 37) 77.

41 See for instance Mark J Rozell, 'President Ford's Pardon of Richard M. Nixon: Constitutional and Political Considerations' (1994) 24 Presidential Studies Quarterly 121; Harold J Krent 'Conditioning the President's Conditional Pardon Power' (2001) 89 Cal L Rev 1665; Dan Markel, 'Against Mercy' (2004) 88 Minnesota Law Review 1421; Daniel T Kobil, 'Compelling Mercy: Judicial Review and the Clemency (2012) 9 University St. Thomas Law Journal 698; Rachel E Barkow, 'Clemency and Presidential Administration of Criminal Law' (2015) 90 New York University Law Review 802.

42 About the families of law see Konrad Zweigert and Hein Kötz, *An Introduction to Comparative Law Theory and Method* (Tony Weir tr, 3rd ed, OUP 1998).

43 On comparative analysis of the executive clemency in common law countries, see Andrew Novak, *Comparative Executive Clemency: The Constitutional Pardon Power and the Prerogative of Mercy in Global Perspective* (Routledge 2015).

Germany is a federal state and Greece is a unitary state. In addition, Argentina and Brazil are examined as federal states which have adopted a presidential system of separation of powers. Finally, France and Lithuania are unitary states having a dicephalic executive, espousing the so-called semi-presidential system.

Argentina

The current version of the Constitution of Argentina was adopted in 1994. Argentina is a federal country,[44] which espouses the presidential system, according to which the president is both the head of state and the head of government.[45] The power to pardon falls within the constitutional competence of the president. According to the Constitution of Argentina, the president of the nation 'may grant pardons or commute punishments for crimes subject to federal jurisdiction, after the report of the corresponding court, except in cases of impeachment by the House of Deputies'.[46] Such power falls within the president's personal discretion, as long as the crimes concerned are prosecuted under federal law. The Constitution leaves provincial pardons to the corresponding provincial governors. Moreover, political punishment—impeachment— instituted by the House of Deputies against the president of the republic, the vice president, Cabinet ministers, or any judge of the Supreme Court is placed outside the scope of the federal power of pardon.

Nevertheless, the power of pardon is not a prerogative that is executed unilaterally by the president himself. He must follow an administrative procedure in conjunction with the judiciary since a report from the corresponding court is constitutionally mandated. Thus, both the judicial and the executive branches possess an important role within the pardon procedure.

In terms of the substance of the power, the Constitution of Argentina allows the president both to grant pardon and to commute punishments. The former implies that the president orders the non-enforcement of the sentence imposed on the convicted person. The latter authorises the president to change the punishment to another more beneficial for the convict, i.e. reducing the length of the prison sentence or commuting one punishment for another less harmful.

Argentinian Supreme Court decisions have often pointed out that a grant of presidential pardon does not equate to innocence for the crime committed, nor does it eliminate the original sentence. Instead, a presidential pardon only declares the non-enforcement of the punishment originally imposed: the non-fulfilment of the sentence. The final judgment against the perpetrator does not

44 Constitution of Argentina 1853, art 1.
45 Ibid., art 87.
46 Ibid., art 99 (5).

disappear altogether, and will be referred to in the event that the perpetrator relapses into crime, or where the victim is awarded compensation.[47]

Considering that Argentina experiences a high level of prison overcrowding, both pardons and commutations have previously been used to reduce over-population. Various human rights organisations have proposed specific clemency-based policies to improve this situation, including commuting the punishments of convicts who have served more than half of their sentences of imprisonment (if this is less than five years), and pardoning convicted persons over 60 years old, convicted pregnant women, and so forth.[48]

Moreover, pardons have been used as a transitional justice measure in Argentina. One of the most controversial examples of this policy was a series of presidential pardon measures approved by President Carlos Menem during 1989 and 1990. Around 1,200 convicted people involved in both the military government and in subversive guerrilla movements in the 1970s benefited from Menem's presidential pardons. The lingering controversy over Menem's pardons even led to their partial revocation by President Néstor Kirchner in 2003.[49]

Brazil

As with Argentina, according to the 1988 Constitution of Brazil, Brazil is a federal country[50] which follows the presidential system of separation of powers.[51] According to article 84, paragraph 12 of the Constitution of Brazil, 'the President of the Republic shall have the exclusive power to grant pardons and reduce sentences, after hearing [from] the agencies instituted by law, if necessary'.[52] Unlike Argentina, Brazil seems to grant a wider margin of

47 That is one of the most relevant differences between executive pardon and the legislative power of amnesty. Interesting analyses of *indulto* and presidential pardon in Argentina can be found in Carlos M Bidegaín, *Curso de derecho constitucional* (Abeledo-Perrot 1994) 280, and Eduardo Oteiza 'El indulto' (1989) 7337 El Derecho 1. See also a comparative approach between Argentina and the Unites States systems in William C Banks and Alejandro D Carrió, 'Presidential Systems in Stress: Emergency Powers in Argentina and the United States' (1993) 15 Michigan Journal of International Law 34.

48 See the annual reports published by the National Directorate of Criminal Policy (an administrative organ within the Ministry of Justice and Human Rights), known as *Sneep: Sistema Nacional de Estadística sobre Ejecución de la Pena* (Statistics National System on Execution of the Punishment). The last reports bring to light the recurring overpopulation problem existing in Argentina (http://www.saij.gob.ar/estadisticas-ejecucion-de-la-pena). See also Paulo Pereyra, 'El indulto y conmutación de penas como política pública para reducir la sobrepoblación penitenciaria en Argentina Experiencia en la Provincia del Chaco' (2017) Revista Pensamiento Penal 1.

49 Presidential Decrees 1002/89, 1003/89, 1004/89, 1005/89, 2741/90, 2742/90, 2745/90, 2746/90 (Argentina).

50 Constitution of Brazil 1988, art 25.

51 Ibid., art 76.

52 Ibid., art 84 (12).

discretion to the president of the republic to grant pardons, as the aforementioned consultation is not mandatory. In other words, the president can act unilaterally. However, the president may also delegate the pardon power to the Ministers of State, to the Attorney General of the Republic, or to the Advocate General of the Union, according to the sole paragraph of article 84.[53]

Despite the president's apparent plenary power to grant clemency, the role of the judiciary in the process is more active than in Argentina, as the Brazilian courts have the power to review the president's pardon decisions. For example, on 21 December 2017 when President Michel Temer issued a decree expanding the traditional Christmas pardon for non-violent prisoners who have served part of their sentence[54] so as to benefit former politicians and others convicted in a landmark corruption investigation known as *Lava Jato*, or Car Wash,[55] the Supreme Court suspended the pardon decree by issuing a temporary injunction.[56] However, a final decision on the matter is still pending.[57]

France

The Constitution of the French Fifth Republic was adopted in 1958, establishing a semi-presidential system of separation of powers. The president of the republic, who is the head of state, is directly elected by universal suffrage,[58] while the prime minister who is the head of government depends equally on the confidence of both the parliament[59] and on the confidence of the president.[60]

According to article 17, 'The President of the Republic has the right to pardon individually',[61] which implies that the president has discretion to grant pardons to individuals without sharing this authority with any other organ or having the power to delegate the granting of pardons.[62] In practice, there is no systematic pattern on how, when, and under which conditions pardons are granted in France, as the granting of pardons varies significantly from year to year.[63]

53 Ibid., art 84 [sole paragraph].
54 Presidential Decree 9246/2017 (Brazil).
55 Joe Leahy, 'Brazil Court Suspends Parts of "Christmas pardon"' *Financial Times* (28 Dec 2017).
56 Supreme Federal Court ADI 5874 (Brazil).
57 Ibid.
58 Constitution of France 1958, art 6.
59 Ibid., art 49.
60 See Sophie Boyron, *The Constitution of France; A Contextual Analysis* (Hart 2013) 59.
61 Constitution of France 1958, art 17.
62 See Lévy (n 16) 557.
63 Ibid., 566.

Germany

The Basic Law for the Federal Republic of Germany was enacted in 1949 and establishes a parliamentary democracy. The federal president is the head of state[64] and the federal chancellor is the head of government.[65] According to article 60, paragraph 2, the federal president 'shall exercise the power to pardon individual offenders on behalf of the Federation',[66] and according to paragraph 3 of the same article such power is transferable to other authorities.[67] A Federal Executive Order implements and completes the regulation of this prerogative: the 1985 Order of the Federal President on the exercise of the right of pardon of the Federation (*Anordnung des Bundespräsidenten über die Ausübung des Begnadigungsrecht des Bundes*).[68]

In the clemency provision of the Basic Law, the principle of federalism is enshrined, such that only persons convicted for so-called 'federal protection crimes' such as terrorism and treason are able to be pardoned by the federal president. In Germany, this institution is known as the right to grace or clemency (*Begnadigungsrecht*). The most remarkable element of this constitutional provision is that the power to grant clemency may be delegated. In other words, the power is transferable to the Minister of Justice. In Germany, as in most other civil law countries, the federal president has the ability both to grant pardon and to commute punishment to a specific individual. In contrast, only the federal parliament—the Bundestag and Bundesrat together—has the authority to give general amnesty to a group or a specific community.[69]

Considering that only certain crimes can be appealed from a state (i.e. provincial) court to a federal one—terrorism, 'high' treason and 'state' treason—the possibility of granting federal pardon is necessarily quite limited. One of the most controversial pardon requests of the past few decades was considered by President Köhler in 2007. Christian Klar, leader of the 'Red Army Faction' terrorist group, was condemned to a life sentence because of the murder of several people during the 1970s and 80s. After a long and fierce public debate, President Köhler decided to deny pardon to Klar. The power of the president to pardon such a crime and such a prisoner within a democracy where the rule of law (*Rechtsstaat*) prevailed was questioned at length by the media.[70]

Within Germany's federal system, the power of pardon is also enshrined at the state level and covers the vast majority of crimes, other than treason and

64 Basic Law for the Federal Republic of Germany 1949, art 54.

65 Ibid., art 63.

66 Ibid., art 60(2).

67 Ibid., art 60(3).

68 *Anordnung des Bundespräsidenten über die Ausübung des Begnadigungsrecht des Bundes* (GnadenAO), 5 October 1985.

69 Roman Herzog in: Theodore Maunz/Günter Dürig, 'Article 60' in *Grundgesetzkommentar* (Vol VI, Lieferung, 2006) 12–17. See also Ingolf Pernice in: H Dreier, 'Article 60' in *Grundgesetzkommentar* (Mohr Siebeck 2006) 1383–1386.

70 Wolfgang Kraushaar, *Die RAF und der linke Terrorismus* (Vol 2, Hamburger 2006). Also, Butz Peters, *Tödlicher Irrtum. Die Geschichte der RAF* (Argon 2004).

terrorism, as discussed above. Every *Land* (federated state in Germany) has established the executive power to pardon, generally within the relevant State Constitution.[71] The competence to grant state pardon is normally given to the State Prime Minister (*Landespräsident*).

Greece

The Constitution of Greece or the Hellenic Republic as it is formally known was adopted in 1975; it establishes a parliamentary democracy. The president is the head of state and the prime minister is the head of government.

According to article 47, paragraph 1 of the Constitution of Greece:

> The President of the Republic shall have the right, pursuant to a recommendation by the Minister of Justice and after consulting with a council composed in its majority of judges, to grant pardons, to commute or reduce sentences pronounced by the courts, and to revoke all consequences at law of sentences pronounced and served.

According to paragraph 2 of the same article, 'the President of the Republic shall have the right to grant pardon to a Minister convicted as provided in article 86, only with the consent of Parliament'.

The president can therefore use this judicial competence[72] to pardon, commute, or remit a punishment imposed by any court, on the proposal of the Minister of Justice and after receiving the opinion (but not necessarily the consent) of the Pardon Council.[73] In the case of Greece, the president does not act alone. The presidential decision requires an advisory opinion by a pardon council, and the recommendation of a designated minister. It is a power dispersed among three constitutional actors.

Pardon cases in Greece have not been systematically analysed and there is no public record containing a list of pardons granted each year. Furthermore, no pardon cases have been challenged before the courts. However, a 1989 case attracted the interest of the press, when the president of the republic refused to grant pardon to a convict despite the fact that the Cabinet was in favour.[74] Eventually, after a new president was elected in 1990, pardon was granted.

71 Constitution of Bavaria 1946, art 47 (4); Constitution of Baden-Württemberg 1953, art 52 (1) and Constitution of Hamburg 1952, art 44(1), among others.

72 Philippos K Spyropoulos and Théodore Fortsakis, *Constitutional Law in Greece* (Kluwer 2009) 93.

73 The Composition of the Pardon Committee is regulated by the Legal Decree 68/1968 (Greece), as amended by the provisions of Article 81 of the Law 4139/2013 (Greece).

74 This is the case of Christos Rousos, also known as 'Angelos'. On 7 April 1976, 19-year-old sailor Christos Rousos killed his lover Anestis Papadopoulos because, as Rousos claimed, Papadopoulos tried to push him into prostitution. Rousos' act was described as a 'crime of passion' and shocked Greek society, which for the first time was publicly confronted with homosexuality. Rousos' trial garnered immense public

Lithuania

Lithuania adopted a new Constitution in 1992 after the collapse of the Soviet Union. Lithuania is a unitary state. The president of the republic is the head of state,[75] while the head of government is the prime minister who depends on the confidence of the legislative branch, the Seimas,[76] and of the president.[77] The pardon power falls within the authority of the president. According to article 84, paragraph 23 of the 1992 Constitution, the president of the republic 'shall grant pardons to convicted persons',[78] but provides no further detail on the exercise of the power.

The Law on Administrative Proceedings adds to the basic constitutional provision by providing explicitly that administrative courts do not have jurisdiction to review acts of the president of the republic.[79] This implies that all decisions of the president to grant or to deny pardon fall outside the scope of judicial review.

The government of Lithuania explicitly endorsed this interpretation in a recently adjudicated case before the European Court of Human Rights.[80] The issue before the Court was whether life sentences imposed by the criminal courts in Lithuania without offering any genuine prospect of release violate article 3 of the European Convention on Human Rights.[81] In the course of resolving the dispute, the Court examined whether the availability of pardon has the effect of making life sentences reducible.[82] In its submissions, the Lithuanian government revealed that by September 2015, out of 12,058 pardon pleas, which had been considered by the Pardon Commission, 2,509

interest. The accused was sentenced to life imprisonment for his deed. After 14 years of detention, Rousos began a hunger strike, calling for his trial to be reopened. Later, the elected government supported the idea of pardoning Rousos for his crime. However, the president of the republic refused to sign the pardon. See 'I ipóthesi tou Khrístou Roúsou sintáraxe tin ellinikí kinonía sta téli tis dekaetías tou '70' (*Mixani toy Xronou*) <http://www.mixanitouxronou.gr/i-kopela-pou-eroteftike-ke-arravoniasti ke-ton-isoviti-christo-rouso-angelos-eno-itan-filakismenos-stin-kerkira-iche-katadika sti-gia-ton-fono-tou-erasti-tou-gia-ton-opio-ipostirixe-oti-ton-othous/> accessed 6 December 2019.

75 Constitution of Lithuania 1992, art 77.

76 Ibid., art 67 (6).

77 Ibid., art 84 (4).

78 Ibid., art 84 (23).

79 Law on Administrative Proceedings (Lithuania), art 16(2).

80 *Matiošaitis and Others v Lithuania*, 22662/13 et al., judgment 23.5.2017 (Lithuania), para 141:

> The Government admitted that, having regard to the constitutional principle of separation of powers, the courts could not influence the outcome of the examination of the pardon plea and oblige the President of the Republic to adopt a decree granting pardon. Granting pardon is one of the powers directly vested in the President by the Constitution, which no other institution may take over.

81 *Matiošaitis and Others v Lithuania*, 22662/13 et al., judgment 23.5.2017 (Lithuania).

82 Ibid.

had been granted.[83] Eventually the Court with a unanimous decision ruled that the possibility of pardon does not make life sentences reducible and therefore Lithuania violated article 3 of the ECHR.

Spain

The Constitution of Spain is a relatively recent legal document adopted in 1978, establishing a parliamentary monarchy.[84] The Spanish executive consists of two organs, the monarch as the head of state,[85] and the president of the government through the role of the prime minister as the head of government.[86] Among the monarch's constitutional competences, article 62 provides that 'it is incumbent upon the King: [...] i) To exercise the right of clemency in accordance with the law, which may not authorize general pardons'.[87]

Pardon is, therefore, a monarchical privilege that is to be exercised 'in accordance with the law'. Consequently, a law was adopted in 1988 which amended the previous—and initially 'provisional'—legal framework adopted in 1870, which is still in force today.[88] Clemency is also recognised as a royal prerogative in the Spanish Criminal Code, where pardon appears as one of the means by which criminal liability may be extinguished.[89]

According to the law of 1988, if a convicted person is considered for pardon, the convicting court that delivered the judgment shall draft a report and allow both the prosecutor and the victims of the crime to make comments on their respective opposition to the pardon.[90] Thereafter, the Minister of Justice will present all relevant documents to the Cabinet of Ministers, and if an affirmative decision is reached by the Cabinet, then a recommendation for pardon is delivered to the monarch, who will give his formal assent for the publication of a royal decree in the *Boletín Oficial del Estado* (Official State Gazette).[91]

The Spanish power to pardon, which has been used since 1241,[92] is therefore a composite administrative act requiring the initial approval of the Cabinet of Ministers and the final approval of the monarch. Interestingly, article 102 of

83 Ibid., para 138.
84 Constitution of Spain 1978, s 1(3).
85 Ibid., art 56.
86 Ibid., art 98 (1).
87 Ibid., art 62.
88 See Law 1/1988 (14 January 1988, Spain), by which the current Law (18 June 1870, Spain) is modified and updated, establishing the rules for the exercise of pardon (Ley 1/1988, 14 Enero; Ley 18 Junio 1870, de reglas para el ejercicio de la gracia de indulto).
89 Criminal Code 1995 (Spain), art 130(1)(4Ɔ).
90 Law (18 June 1870, Spain), art 24.
91 Ibid., art 30.
92 Juan Luis Jiménez and José Abreu, 'Pardon Does not Forgive Democracy: Econometrical Analysis of Pardons in Spain' (2016) 216 Review of Public Economics 81, 81.

the Constitution of Spain, which characterises pardon as a royal prerogative, prohibits the application of pardon in cases regarding the criminal liability of the prime minister and other members of government.[93] This kind of provision is seen around the world, both for impeachment proceedings and criminal charges against politicians.[94]

As in other states, the lack of transparency within the administrative procedure for pardon has been heavily criticised in Spain, in addition to the absence of detailed regulations as to the grounds for granting or rejecting pardons.[95] However, pardon is a strongly discretionary political institution. That is why there are no statistics nor public records regarding grants of executive clemency that have been issued in Spain during the democratic era, post-1978.

One of the most controversial grants of executive clemency during the democratic era in Spain (that is, post-1978) occurred during the government of José María Aznar, who was Prime Minister between 1996 and 2004. His Minister of Justice, Ángel Acebes, granted 1,333 pardons in just one day (13 December 2000). The resulting criticism was not only motivated by the considerable number of pardons granted in such a short period of time, but also by the reasons that the minister gave for the pardons—to celebrate the Holy Year declared by the Pope and the new millennium.[96] This formed the most widespread clemency measure declared by a Spanish government during the democratic era. In the years following, the power of pardon has been exercised relatively moderately in comparison with the number of pardons granted in 2000, never exceeding a total of 600 individuals pardoned per year.[97]

Executive Clemency from a Separation of Powers Perspective

The comparative analysis in this chapter has uncovered several trends regarding the interaction between the various separation of powers models and the procedures for executive clemency in the civil law world. However, the following conclusions are by no means exhaustive, as the comparative analysis in this chapter does not incorporate a complete list of countries belonging to the civil law tradition. The authors' limited choice of countries aims to represent both

93 Constitution of Spain 1978, s 102(1).

94 See Pascoe and Novak, this volume.

95 Antonio Doval País and others, 'Granting of Pardon in Spain (2000–2008)' (2011) 9 Spanish Review of Criminology Investigation 6.

96 The decision to grant clemency to 1,333 people in one day still causes debate within Spanish political life. See, for example, the recent debate in the Spanish Senate on possible changes to the existing legal framework for executive pardon (151 Senate Plenary Session, 15 April 2015, 14577).

97 This number remains high in comparison with US executive clemency. For example, President Obama granted only 212 executive pardons during his entire mandate (2009–2017), although he also granted 1,715 commutations (Rachel E Barkow and Mark Osler, 'Designed to Fail: The President's Deference to the Department of Justice in Advancing Criminal Justice Reform' (2017) 59(2) William & Mary Law Review 387, 437 n 241).

the different models of separation of powers and different geographical regions, including Europe, Eastern Europe, and Latin America.

The first observable trend is that the structure of the clemency decision-making process depends on the precise separation of powers model adopted. In parliamentary systems, although the pardon power is formally allocated to the head of state, president, or monarch, such power is usually subject to a well-defined procedure according to which the judicial branch participates with an advisory opinion, while the elected government via a designated minister or ministers (for example the Minister of Justice or the Cabinet as a whole) has the ultimate power to determine the outcome of the process.

On the other hand, in presidential and in semi-presidential systems, as in the cases of Lithuania, France, and Brazil, the president is permitted to act alone on his or her individual discretion in dispensing or refusing clemency. Only in Argentina does the president collaborate with members of the judiciary, namely with the court that delivered the decision.

In substance, the pardon power is entrusted to the head of state in almost all constitutional systems.[98] In presidential and in semi-presidential systems, the head of state acts unilaterally and exclusively and possesses the power to initiate the pardon process and to affirm the final decision. On the other hand, in parliamentary systems, the clemency power is exercised collectively, alongside government ministers or judicial bodies. In parliamentary systems, this implies that it is in fact the head of state who possesses a veto power in the pardon process, whereas other institutional bodies like the Cabinet may have initiated the process. Interestingly, the power of pardon may be subject to delegation, regardless the separation of powers model, as with the cases of Brazil, France, and Germany.

Furthermore, the principle of federalism, in other words, the vertical separation of powers[99] between central and decentralised authorities, is enshrined in certain constitutions.[100] In federal civil law systems, the pardon is materially limited by federalism. This trend appears both in parliamentary systems like Germany and in presidential systems like Argentina.

Finally, on the role of the courts, it is noteworthy that with the exception of the ongoing case in Brazil, in the civil law nations under study there is no legal provision either based on formal legislation or on substantive litigation enabling the review and challenge of pardon procedures and outcomes. The most probable explanation is legal and constitutional convention. Indeed, from a separation of powers point of view, it would be paradoxical if pardon decisions (which purportedly act as a check on judicial power) were also checked by the judiciary. From a separation of powers perspective, the

98 See Pascoe and Novak, this volume.

99 On the vertical separation of powers, see Victoria Nourse, 'The Vertical Separation of Powers' (1999) 49(3) Duke Law Journal 749.

100 Likewise, for clemency in countries belonging to the common law tradition, see Novak, *Comparative Executive Clemency* (n 43) 81.

executive ought to exercise complete discretion on matters of prerogative, whereas the courts may not review the administrative process either on formal or on substantive grounds.

Conclusions

The modern power to grant clemency falls within executive competence. This has precipitated criticism, as clemency is, in its very nature, a judicial function. However, in reality, commutations and pardons reflect the exercise of a quasi-judicial and quasi-executive power. Social and political factors, rather than judicial criteria, are often taken into account as part of the executive's decision-making.

This chapter has addressed two questions: first, whether the clemency power falls within the absolute control of the executive branch (i.e. the president) or whether it is a function shared with other executive, legislative, or judicial institutions (i.e. Cabinet ministers, parliamentary committees, or judicial bodies, respectively); and second, the chapter has tested the following assumption—that the role of the executive decision-maker in exercising the clemency power reflects the actual institutional power of that executive institution within the general model of the separation of powers.

An analysis of the constitutional framework of a number of countries belonging to the civil law legal tradition has revealed the following: in parliamentary systems where the popular legitimacy of the head of state is limited, the pardon power is more often shared between different institutions, such as the Cabinet, the judiciary, or even a specially constituted clemency committee. Sharing the clemency power between different democratic institutions adds to its democratic legitimacy.

On the other hand, in presidential and semi-presidential systems, where the legitimacy of the head of state is greater due to popular vote, the head of state's role in the pardon process is absolute. Here, an executive organ with a significant role in the constitutional separation of powers possesses the most powerful role in the clemency process vis-à-vis other governmental organs.

These are the authors' preliminary observations regarding the prevailing trends in executive clemency provisions in different civil law countries. Further comparative analysis may test these ideas over a more exhaustive list of civil law countries in the future.

4 Rethinking Amnesty and Clemency in Countries in Transition

A Comparative Analysis of Laws and Practices in Countries of the Former Yugoslavia

Nedžad Smailagić

Introduction

Should crimes and defendants be subject to acts of clemency by the state? Should crimes be forgotten, victims ignored? Should the usual rules and standards be applied to perpetrators of war crimes and other serious human rights violations, i.e. should 'extraordinary crimes' be processed and sanctioned by 'ordinary punishment'?[1] Based on the comparative legal framework of the countries of the former Yugoslavia, this chapter explores what role clemency laws and practices should play in striking a balance between justice and fairness in societies in transition and, more generally, in liberal societies.

Clemency is a generic term denoting the application of mercy or leniency in the context of a state's response to criminal offending, usually at the post-sentencing stage.[2] In this context, various entry points into the conversation around clemency exist, each with equal levels of legitimacy. From the *criminal law* point of view, acts of clemency, usually in the form of amnesty or pardon, extinguish or terminate a criminal sanction, with or without extinguishing the conviction itself.[3] While the determination of a defendant's guilt and the imposition of criminal sanctions are prerogatives of judicial authorities, here the author defines the power to grant clemency as being co-located within the non-judicial branches, namely, the legislative and executive branches of government.[4] From the

1 Cf. Mark Drumbl, *Atrocity, Punishment and International Law* (CUP 2007) 1ff.

2 *Black's Law Dictionary* (9th edn, 2009) 288; Hélène Ruiz-Fabri, Gabriele Della Morte, and Elisabeth Lambert Abdelgawad, 'Les institutions de clémence (amnistie, grâce, prescription) en droit international et droit constitutionnel comparé' (2015) 28(1) Archives de politique criminelle 237.

3 Jean Pradel, *Droit pénal comparé* (4th edn, Dalloz 2016) 700ff; Petar Novoselec, *Opći dio kaznenog prava* (3rd edn, Pravni fakultet Sveučilišta u Zagrebu 2009) 50ff.

4 Nikola Srzentić, Aleksandar Stajić, and Ljubiša Lazarević, *Krivično pravo Socijalističke Federativne Republike Jugoslavije—Opšti deo* (15th edn, Savremena administracija 1988) 476; André Laingui, 'Aspects historiques: La phase exécutoire du procès pénal en droit comparé' (1990) 61(3–4) Revue internationale de droit

criminal justice policy point of view, acts of clemency are regarded as tools for realising crime control policy or for remedying past miscarriages of justice, as there is at least a theoretical possibility of convicting an innocent person.[5] In exceptional circumstances, shifts in criminal justice policy, especially in the context of wider social and economic changes, may favour resorting to acts of clemency.[6] Furthermore, the *international legal dimension* of clemency surfaced as of the second half of twentieth century, with the rise of human rights treaties and further development of international humanitarian and criminal law. Of particular importance, in this context, is the tendency to prohibit amnesties in cases involving allegations of genocide, crimes against humanity or war crimes.[7]

Given this background, this chapter provides a comparative analysis of the normative framework and practices of executive and legislative clemency in countries experiencing a post-conflict transition period, namely the countries of the former Socialist Federal Republic of Yugoslavia ('SFRY'), which consist of Slovenia, Croatia, Bosnia and Herzegovina ('BiH'), Serbia, Montenegro, North Macedonia, and Kosovo. Since declaring their independence over the past 30 years,[8] these states have undergone different processes of transition, including conflicts with mass atrocities committed during 1991–1995 in BiH and Croatia, during 1998–1999 in Kosovo, and the 2001 insurgency in the Republic of North Macedonia.

As part of the overall international response to the 1991–1995 conflict, the UN Security Council, acting under Chapter VII of the UN Charter, established the International Criminal Tribunal for the former Yugoslavia ('ICTY') with the task to investigate, prosecute, and adjudicate cases involving

pénal 371. See also Pascoe and Novak, this volume, on definitions of the term 'clemency'.

5 Srzentić, Stajić, and Lazarević (n 4) 477.

6 See e.g., Zoran Stojanović, *Krivično pravo—opšti deo* (16th edn, Pravna knjiga 2009) 327ff.

7 See John Dugard, 'Dealing with Crimes of a Past Regime. Is Amnesty Still an Option?' (1999) 12(4) Leiden Journal of International Law 1001. See also Josepha Close, *Amnesty, Serious Crimes and International Law* (Routledge 2019) on the customary international law position here.

8 In 1991, Slovenia, Croatia, and North Macedonia declared independence from SFRY following referendums that largely supported the independence of those countries. In addition, following an independence referendum held on 29 February and 1 March 1992, on 3 March 1992, BiH also declared independence. SFRY, officially called the Federal Republic of Yugoslavia (FRY), continued to exist with Serbia and Montenegro as its member states until 2003, and until the declaration independence of Montenegro in 2006, as the State Union of Serbia and Montenegro. On 17 February 2008, Kosovo, one of two autonomous regions in Serbia, unilaterally declared its independence from Serbia. As of August 2019, Kosovo's independence had been recognised by 114 states, although it is not a member state of the United Nations (Agata Palickova, '15 countries, and counting, revoke recognition of Kosovo Serbia says' (*EURACTIV*, 27 August 2019) <https://www.euractiv.com/section/enlargement/news/15-countries-and-counting-revoke-recognition-of-kosovo-serbia-says/> accessed 9 December 2019).

allegations of crimes of genocide, crimes against humanity, violations of laws and customs of war, and war crimes.[9] The conflict, experienced differently by each country involved, conditioned later political and economic development in the post-conflict period. While some countries became members of the European Union, such as Slovenia and Croatia, others are still struggling towards defining their status in terms of statehood and independence, such as Kosovo.[10] Following adoption of amendments to its constitution, North Macedonia ended a decades-long naming dispute with Greece, one of its neighbouring countries.[11] All of these factors have affected crime trends, as well as national criminal justice policies. Once part of a single legal system,[12] these seven states now possess their own systems with different stages and directions of development. While still retaining their civil law legal systems, each of the countries mentioned above underwent extensive transition processes which affected their institutional framework, substantive and procedural laws, as well as their laws on the execution of criminal sanctions. Each have attempted to bring their own system in line with the requirements of the rule of law and international standards, most notably applicable universal and regional human rights treaties.[13]

In order to analyse the applicable legal and policy framework, acts of clemency are differentiated below according to the branch of government deciding upon such leniency, namely the legislature or the executive. As a form of

9 UN Security Council, 'The International Tribunal for the Prosecution of Persons Responsible for Serious Violations of International Humanitarian Law Committed in the Territory of the Former Yugoslavia Since 1991' UNSC Res 827 (25 May 1993) UN Doc S/RES/827.

10 While the International Court of Justice held that declaration of independence of Kosovo did not violate international law, the issue is still politically disputed between the Serbian and Kosovar governments. See *Accordance with International Law of the Unilateral Declaration of Independence in Respect of Kosovo* (Advisory Opinion) [2010] ICJ Rep 403.

11 On 11 January 2019, the Parliament of the Republic of Macedonia adopted a set of amendments to the Constitution changing the country's official name to North Macedonia. See, *Предлогот на амандманите XXXIII, XXXIV, XXXV и XXXVI на Уставот на Република Македонија* (Government of the Republic of Macedonia, 12 December 2018) <https://www.sobranie.mk/materialdetails.nspx?materialId=c6733ea5-eb58-46ec-9221-c86dfbbfa5cf> accessed 5 February 2019.

12 Given its federal nature, SFRY legislation included federal laws and legislation of states and autonomous provinces (i.e. Kosovo and Vojvodina). The 1976 SFRY Criminal Code provided for amnesties and pardons as clemency mechanisms. The 1974 SFRY Constitution vested the power of granting amnesty to the Federal Chamber of the SFRY Assembly (art 285(14)) and to the SFRY presidency the power to grant pardons (art 315(9)) for crimes prescribed in the SFRY Criminal Code. Meanwhile, state/autonomous province assemblies and presidencies were vested with similar powers for crimes prescribed in state/autonomous province legislation.

13 For an overview, see Alenka Šelih, 'Crime and Crime Control in Transition Countries' in Alenka Šelih and Aleš Završnik (eds), *Crime and Transition in Central and Eastern Europe* (Springer 2013) 15ff.

legislative clemency, amnesties are analysed in Part II in general terms, with an emphasis on the use of this mechanism in the context of dealing with crime committed during civil and international conflict. Pardon, as a form of executive clemency, is considered one of the discretionary prerogatives vested in the executive government, usually the head of state. In this context, the legislative framework as well as the conditions under which pardons are granted are discussed in Part III, again with an emphasis on atrocity crimes.

Legislative Mercy: Amnesty for Past Wrongdoing

Amnesty, stemming from the Greek word *amnestia* (forgetting), is an act of clemency extended by a legislative body, usually a parliament, issued with the aim of pardoning a group or a class of individuals for certain types of crimes.[14] As the state has the authority to define crimes, the same authority empowers the state to extinguish criminal responsibility or a criminal sanction imposed as the result of a final and binding conviction by a court.[15] Within this part, section 1, below, demonstrates that the adoption of amnesty laws in the former Yugoslavia in the aftermath of conflict generally mirrors binding international law, by extending amnesty only to ordinary crimes committed during conflict. However, section 2, below, describes a concerning and widely criticized approach that was taken in North Macedonia by the National Parliament and the Constitutional Court to extend amnesty to cases that involved allegations of core international crimes.

Legal Framework and Criminal Justice Policy Considerations in a Transitional Context

The power to grant amnesties is a prerogative vested in the legislative branch in all of the countries under analysis, either through constitutional provisions, applicable legislation, or both. While some national constitutions explicitly vest such power in the legislature, namely in Croatia,[16] Serbia,[17] Montenegro,[18] North Macedonia,[19] and partially in BiH,[20] in the remaining former Yugoslav

14 *Black's Law Dictionary* (n 2) 99.

15 See Pradel (n 3) 703.

16 Constitution of the Republic of Croatia, Official Gazette (OG) of the Republic of Croatia nos 56/90, 135/97, 8/98, 113/00, 124/00, 28/01, 41/01, 55/01, 76/10, 85/10, 05/14, art 81(1)(12).

17 Constitution of the Republic of Serbia, OG of the Republic of Serbia no 98/06 of 10 November 2006, art 105(1)(1).

18 Constitution of Montenegro, OG of Montenegro nos 1/07, 38/13, art 82(1)(16).

19 Constitution of the Republic of Macedonia, OG of the Republic of Macedonia no 52/91 of 22 November 1991, art 68(1)(18).

20 Only the Constitution of the Entity of Republika Srpska explicitly provides its parliament the power to grant amnesty (Constitution of Republika Srpska, OG of RS nos 21/92-Consolidated Version, 28/94, 8/96, 13/96, 15/96, 16/96, 21/

republics the prerogative is instead defined in legislation. In the case of BiH, given its complex constitutional structure and criminal justice system,[21] state,[22] entity,[23] and cantonal parliaments[24] each have the power to grant amnesty. In addition, the Brčko District Assembly may grant amnesties for crimes defined under the Criminal Code of Brčko District.[25] In all cases, amnesty is granted in the form of a specific law.

As to their scope, amnesties may be given for certain crimes, or for certain criminal sanctions, regardless of the crime committed.[26] While, in theory, the effects of an amnesty should be wholly defined by the specific amnesty act, and not in general terms through legislation,[27] according to general legislative provisions in the countries under analysis, persons affected by amnesty may:[28]

a *Be released from criminal prosecution.* Depending on the timing of the amnesty, the law may terminate ongoing proceedings or may impose a statutory bar for initiation of proceedings in the future.
b *Be released from serving the punishment.* Release can be partial or full, depending on conditions set forth by the amnesty act.
c Have their *criminal sanction substituted by a less severe one.*

96, 21/02, 26/02, 30/02, 31/02, 69/02, 31/03, 98/03, 115/05, 117/05, art 70(10)).

21 Beyond the state level, BiH consists of two entities—the 'Federation of BiH' and the 'Republika Srpska', plus the 'Brčko District' as a specific unit of self-government, each with its own government consisting of legislative, executive, and judicial branches. (Constitution of BiH; UNGA, 'General Framework Agreement for Peace in Bosnia and Herzegovina' (30 November 1995) UN Doc A/50/79C (GFAP BiH), annex 4, art I).
22 Criminal Code of BiH (CC BiH), OG of BiH nos 3/03, 37/03, 54/04, 61/04, 30/05, 53/06, 55/06, 8/10, 47/14, 22/15, 40/15, art 118.
23 Criminal Code of Federation of BiH (CC FBiH), OG of FBiH nos 36/03, 37/03, 21/04, 69/04, 18/05, 42/10, 42/11, 59/14, 76/14, art 122; Constitution of Republika Srpska, art 70, para 10.
24 Cantons are administrative units in the Federation of BiH whose parliaments, as legislative bodies, may grant amnesty for crimes defined by cantonal laws (CC BiH, art 122(2)).
25 Criminal Code of Brčko District of BiH (CC BD BiH), OG of Brčko District nos 33/13—Consolidated Version, 26/16, 13/17, art 122(2).
26 Stojanović (n 6) 328.
27 Novoselec (n 3) 511.
28 Stojanovic (n 6) 328; Criminal Code of Slovenia (CC Slo), OG of the Republic of Slovenia nos 50/12—Official Consolidated Version, 54/15, 6/16, 27/17, art 96; CC BiH, art 118(1); CC FBiH, art 122(1); Criminal Code of Republika Srpska (CC RS), OG of Republika Srpska nos 64/17 of 13 July 2017, art 100; CC BD BiH, art 122(1); Criminal Code of Serbia (CCSerb), OG of the Republic of Serbia nos 85/05, 88/05, 107/05, 72/09, 111/09, 121/12, 104/13, 108/14, 94/16, art 109(1); Criminal Code of Montenegro (CC MN), OG of the Republic Montenegro nos 70/03, 13/04, 47/06 and the OG of Montenegro nos 40/08, 25/10, 32/11, 40/13, 56/13, art 131(1); Criminal Code of Macedonia (CC NM), OG of the Republic of Macedonia no 37/96 of 6 August 1996, art 113.

d *Have their conviction deleted from the register*, i.e. from the record of prior convictions including those which, according to legislation, may normally not be subject of deletion.
e *Have the legal consequences of the final and binding conviction suspended.*

The need to grant amnesties depends on the principles and approaches guiding the respective national criminal justice policy.[29] The *conditions* under which amnesty will be given also depend on these principles, as well as the needs within the given system, but may not contravene either national or binding international law. Most often, amnesty is motivated by political reasons and is usually applied after major sociopolitical changes, or in the aftermath of international or civil conflicts or wide-scale riots.[30] In the context of social and political changes, such was the case in countries of the former Yugoslavia, where resorting to amnesty has been a common trend since 1990. As the following overview illustrates, countries of the former Yugoslavia typically passed amnesty legislation extending to ordinary crimes only, to the exclusion of atrocity crimes.

Slovenia. On 22 November 2001, the Slovenian parliament (*Državni zbor Republike Slovenije*) passed the Amnesty Act[31] of general character, according to which one quarter of the final and binding sentence of imprisonment was forgiven for all defendants who were convicted before the Slovenian courts but who had not yet started serving their sentence. The amnesty also removed one fifth of the prison sentence of defendants who were already serving their sentence (art 1). The amnesty's benefits were not extended to defendants convicted of, among others, crimes against humanity and values protected under international law, as well as to defendants still at large (art 2).

Croatia. In Croatia, several amnesty acts related to the conflict were passed by the Croatian parliament (*Hrvatski sabor*) from 1990 onwards. The first Amnesty Act was passed on 26 September 1990 and allowed for the reduction of one quarter of the sentence for all defendants then serving their sentences.[32] This act was superseded by the Act on Amnesty for Crimes Committed during Armed Conflicts and the War against Croatia,[33] passed on 25 September 1992, according to which amnesty from criminal prosecution and trial was granted to perpetrators of criminal offences committed during the armed conflict from 17 August

29 Željko Horvatić, Davor Derenčinović, and Leo Cvitanović, *Kazneno pravo. Opći dio 2: kazneno djelo i kaznenopravne sankcije* (Pravni fakultet Sveučilišta u Zagrebu 2017) 289.
30 Martha Minow, *Between Vengeance and Forgiveness* (Beacon Press 1998) 28; Louise Mallinder, *Amnesty, Human Rights and Political Transitions. Bridging the Peace and Justice Divide* (Hart Publishing 2008) 29ff; Ruti G Teitel, *Tranziciona pravda* (Fabrika knjiga 2014) 79ff.
31 *Amnesty Act*, OG of the Republic of Slovenia no 97/01 of 4 December 2001 (ZA-1).
32 Novoselec (n 3) 512.
33 Act on Amnesty from Criminal Prosecution and Trial for Crimes Committed During the Armed Conflict and During the War against the Republic of Croatia, OG of the Republic of Croatia No 58/92 of 25 September 1992.

1990 onwards (art 1). This act was later amended with regard to its temporal application, by providing that the period covered extends to 10 May 1995.[34] Finally, in 1996, the Croatian parliament passed a comprehensive General Amnesty Act ('1996 GAA'),[35] according to which general amnesty from criminal prosecution and trial was extended to the perpetrators of criminal offences committed during 'aggression, armed rebellion or armed conflicts and in connection with aggression, armed rebellion and conflicts in the Republic of Croatia' (art 1 (1)) committed between 17 August 1990 and 23 August 1996 (art 1(3)). This act specifically provided that amnesty does not extend to the perpetrators of grave breaches of humanitarian law, such as crimes of genocide, all types of war crimes as well as violations of laws and customs of war and warfare (art 3(1)).

Bosnia and Herzegovina. Granting amnesty constituted an important step in the peace-building process and the post-conflict recovery in BiH. The adoption of amnesty-related legislation was a requirement under the General Framework Agreement for Peace in Bosnia and Herzegovina ('GFAP BiH')[36] in order to strengthen the return of refugees and displaced persons.[37] Given the complex constitutional structure of BiH, four different amnesty acts were adopted in order to implement this requirement. At the state level, on 12 February 1996, the Parliament of the Republic of BiH (*Skupština Republike Bosne i Hercegovine*) adopted the Amnesty Act ('AA RBiH')[38] pursuant to which amnesty from prosecution and trial was granted to perpetrators of criminal offences against the social order and security of BiH, as well as to perpetrators of criminal offences against the Army of BiH (art 1). In addition, amnesty was granted to perpetrators of some specific criminal offences, such as unlawful possession of weapons or desertion from the army (art 2). Similar acts were passed in both the Federation of Bosnia and Herzegovina and the Republika Srpska,[39] and, following its establishment, in the Brčko District of BiH.[40]

34 Act Amending the Act on Amnesty from Criminal Prosecution and Trial for Crimes Committed During the Armed Conflict and During the War against the Republic of Croatia, OG of the Republic of Croatia no 39/95 of 9 June 1995, art 1.

35 General Amnesty Act, OG of the Republic of Croatia no 80/96 of 27 September 1996.

36 GFAP BiH, Annex 7, art VI.

37 'Any returning refugee or displaced person charged with a crime, other than a serious violation of international humanitarian law as defined in the Statute of the International Tribunal for the Former Yugoslavia since January 1, 1991 or a common crime unrelated to the conflict, shall upon return enjoy an amnesty. In no case shall charges for crimes be imposed for political or other inappropriate reasons or to circumvent the application of the amnesty' (GFAP BiH, annex 7, art VI).

38 Amnesty Act, OG of the Republic of BiH no 6/96 of 23 February 1996.

39 The Amnesty Act of the Federation of BiH was adopted by the Constituent Assembly of the Federation of BiH (*Ustavotvorna skupština Federacije BiH*) on 15 January 1995 (See Amnesty Act, OG of the Federation of BiH No 2/95 of 11 February 1995). Furthermore, on 19 June 1996 an Amnesty Act was adopted by National Assembly of RS (*Narodna skupština Republike Srpske*), the parliament of the other entity in BiH (see Amnesty Act, OG of RS no 13/96 of 26 June 1996).

40 On 19 June 2001, the Assembly of the Brčko District BiH (*Skupština Brčko Distrikta BiH*) passed its own Amnesty Act. This act was amended in 2007 to reflect

Serbia and *Montenegro*. In this overview, Serbia and Montenegro will be presented jointly, as both countries were part of the Federal Republic of Yugoslavia between 1992 and 2003 ('FRY') and later of the State Union of Serbia and Montenegro (2003–2006). The National Assembly of FRY (*Narodna skupština Savezne Republike Jugoslavije*) adopted the Amnesty Act in 1996.[41] This original Amnesty Act was incomplete, since it covered only cases of failure to respond to military call-ups and those who fled abroad before 14 December 1995, as concluded by GFAP BiH (art 1).[42] Thereafter, in 2001, a new Amnesty Act[43] was adopted, according to which amnesty was extended to criminal offences against the military in the period from 27 April 1992 to 2000.[44] Of particular importance is the subsequent 2002 Amnesty Act, according to which amnesty was granted for criminal offences committed during the insurgency in southern Serbia by the Albanian ethnic community in three southern municipalities: Preševo, Medveđa, and Bujanovac, from 1 January 1999 to 31 May 2011.[45]

Following the dissolution of the State Union on 3 June 2006, Serbia and Montenegro proceeded to pass separate amnesty acts. In Serbia, two separate amnesty acts were adopted in 2006[46] and 2010,[47] which addressed the then widespread problem of diversion from military duty. In 2012, the Serbian National Assembly (*Narodna skupština Srbije*) passed a final Amnesty Act according to which prison sentences were reduced by a quarter or a half.[48] This act does not extend to criminal offences punishable by long-term imprisonment or, for example, crimes against humanity and other crimes against international law (art 2 (1)). In 2013, the Parliament of Montenegro (*Skupština Crne Gore*) passed its own Amnesty Act,[49] which provided for a revocation of one quarter of an imposed final and binding sentence (art 1) for all prisoners. However, under art 3(1) of this law, no amnesty was granted to individuals convicted for war crimes against the civilian population or for war crimes against prisoners of war.

reforms passed in the criminal justice sector. See Amnesty Act, OG of Brčko District BiH no 10/01; act amending the Amnesty Act, OG of Brčko District BiH no 19/07.

41 Amnesty Act, OG of FRY no 28/96 of 21 June 1996.

42 Biljana Kovacevic-Vuco, 'The Balkans: Deserters as Victims in War and Peace' (*Žene u crnom*, 1999) <http://zeneucrnom.org/index.php?option=com_content&task=view&id=118&Itemid=16&lang=en> accessed 27 August 2018.

43 Amnesty Act, OG of FRY no 9/01 of 2 March 2001.

44 At the state level, Serbia passed an Amnesty Act in 2001 according to which final and binding sentences were reduced from 15 to 25 per cent. See Amnesty Act, OG of the Republic of Serbia no 10/01 of 14 February 2001.

45 Amnesty Act, OG of FRY no 37/02 of 3 July 2002.

46 Amnesty Act, OG of the Republic of Serbia no 33/06 of 3 July 2006.

47 Amnesty Act, OG of the Republic of Serbia no 18/10 of 26 March 2010.

48 Amnesty Act, OG of the Republic of Serbia no 107/12 of 9 November 2012.

49 Act on Amnesty of Individuals Convicted for Crimes by Laws of Montenegro and of Individuals Convicted by Foreign Courts and Serving Sentence in Montenegro, OG of Montenegro no 39/13 of 7 August 2013.

North Macedonia. In 2002, the Macedonian Parliament (*Собрание на Република Македонија*) adopted the Amnesty Act,[50] whose interpretation and application, as the author will demonstrate in the next section, generated much controversy within the country and abroad. Under art 1(1) of the Amnesty Act, amnesty is granted from criminal prosecution and trial to all persons against whom there is reasonable suspicion of perpetration of a criminal act during the conflict that took place from 1 January to 26 September 2001. However, benefits of this act do not extend to persons under suspicion of having committed atrocity crimes during the 2001 insurgency.[51]

Kosovo. On 11 July 2013, as a part of the European Union-led political dialogue between Serbia and Kosovo,[52] the Assembly of Kosovo (*Kuvendi i Kosovës*) adopted an Amnesty Act[53] granting complete exemption of criminal prosecution and execution of punishment of perpetrators for crimes committed before 20 June 2013 (art 2 (1)). Amnesty, as provided in this law, does not extend to offenders who either committed criminal offences against international actors and international security forces in Kosovo, or to acts that constitute a grave breach of international humanitarian law, or to criminal offences that resulted in a grievous bodily injury or death (art 4). The Amnesty Act was controversial due to its questionable legality, wide scope of crimes for which amnesty was granted, and its vagueness.[54] As of August 2018, a draft Law on Amnesty was pending before the Assembly of Kosovo, which would provide amnesty for crimes related to unlawful possession of weapons, and obstruction of official persons in their performance of official duties.[55] This draft law also forms part of the ongoing political dialogue between Serbia and Kosovo.

50 Amnesty Act, OG of the Republic of Macedonia no 18/2002 of 8 March 2002.

51 Article 1(4) of the Amnesty Act 2002 (North Macedonia) provides for a clear exclusion of the benefits of the act to individuals against whom there are allegations of having committed crimes under the subject matter jurisdiction of the ICTY, namely the crimes of genocide, crimes against humanity, war crimes and violations of laws, and customs of war.

52 Strategic Communications Division, 'EU Facilitated Dialogue for the Normalisation of Relations Between Belgrade and Pristina' (*European Union External Action*, 15 June 2016) <https://eeas.europa.eu/diplomatic-network/eu-facilitated-dialogue-belgrade-pristina-relations/349/dialogue-between-belgrade-and-pristina_en> accessed 27 August 2018.

53 Law No. 04/L-209 on Amnesty, OG of the Republic of Kosovo no 39/13 of 19 September 2013.

54 Arlinda Rrustemi and Moritz Baumgärtel, 'Shooting in the Dark: Evaluating Kosovo's Amnesty Law and the Role of International Actors' (2014) 6(2) Hague Journal on the Rule of Law 115.

55 Assembly of the Republic of Kosovo, 'Explanatory Memorandum of the Draft law on Amnesty, Draft Law No. 06/L-047 on Amnesty' (*Assembly of the Republic of Kosovo*, 20 March 2018) <http://ligjet.assembly-kosova.org/Uploads/Data/Documents/47memorandumishpjegues_syPGpMkx2V.pdf> accessed 27 August 2018.

Amnesty and Atrocity Crimes: Opposing Tendencies in Croatia and North Macedonia

Amnesty practices in the countries of the former Yugoslavia have moved in two opposite directions. While the legislation in place typically reflects international standards, amnesty practice, on the other hand, exhibits inconsistencies that raise concerns in terms of international law. In attempting to strike a balance between the rule of law, justice, peacebuilding, and political expediency, can impunity for atrocity crimes through the application of amnesties ever be acceptable?

Contrary to contemporary international law standards, a brief look into the history of individual responsibility under international law would suggest that amnesties were often considered and practised as then-legitimate responses to mass human rights abuses, including for those abuses that amounted to atrocity crimes, i.e. the crime of genocide, crimes against humanity, and war crimes.[56] However, the development of international law, most notably international criminal law, human rights law, and humanitarian law in the post-World War II era, has led to the outlawing, to a degree, of amnesty for atrocity crimes and other abuses of human rights. This tendency is evident on several levels: first, through the *widespread adoption of applicable conventions* that impose obligations to investigate, prosecute, and penalise atrocity crimes in domestic law;[57] second, through the *emerging practice of international and hybrid criminal courts*, which excludes amnesties as a bar from

56 See e.g., Stephen R Rather, Jason S Abrams, and James L Bischof, *Accountability for Human Rights Atrocities in International Law—Beyond the Nuremberg Legacy* (Oxford University Press 2009) 7ff; Antonio Cassese, *International Criminal Law* (Oxford University Press 2003) 5.

57 Under the Genocide Convention, states are obliged to criminalise genocide in domestic law (Art V) as well as to put to trial all persons charged with genocide (Convention on the Prevention and Punishment of the Crime of Genocide (adopted 9 December 1948, entered into force 12 January 1951) 78 UNTS 277, art VI). In addition, the 1949 Geneva Conventions require states to either investigate or extradite for grave breaches of conventions (Geneva Convention for the Amelioration of the Condition of the Wounded and Sick in Armed Forces in the Field of 12 August 1949 (adopted 12 August 1949, entered into force 21 October 1950) 75 UNTS 31, art 49); Geneva Convention for the Amelioration of the Condition of Wounded, Sick and Shipwrecked Members of Armed Forces at Sea of 12 August 1949 (adopted 12 August 1949, entered into force 21 October 1950) 75 UNTS 85, art 50; Geneva Convention Relative to the Treatment of Prisoners of War of 12 August 1949 (adopted 12 August 1949, entered into force 21 October 1950) 75 UNTS 136, art 129–131; Geneva Convention Relative to the Protection of Civilian Persons in Time of War of 12 August 1949 (adopted 12 August 1949, entered into force 21 October 1950) 75 UNTS 287, art 146–148. Under the UN Convention on Torture, Member States are also required to criminalise torture in domestic law as well as to investigate and prosecute allegations of it (Convention against Torture and Other Cruel, Inhuman or Degrading Treatment or Punishment (adopted 10 December 1984, entered into force 16 June 1987) 1465 UNTS 85, art 4–14).

prosecution in cases involving allegations of atrocity crimes. In the Furundžija decision, the ICTY held that granting amnesty for situations amounting to torture contravenes peremptory norms of international law. Such amnesties cannot gain international legal recognition;[58] and third, through *institutional mechanisms for the protection of human rights*. The UN Human Rights Committee has stated that:

> [A]mnesties are generally incompatible with the duty of States to investigate such acts; to guarantee freedom from such acts within their jurisdiction; and to ensure that they do not occur in the future. States may not deprive individuals of the right to an effective remedy, including compensation and such full rehabilitation as may be possible.[59]

In addition, the European Court of Human Rights (ECtHR) has taken the same view, as is discussed in further detail below. Based on the foregoing, failure to fulfil either a negative or positive obligation under binding international law standards invokes state responsibility before existing universal or regional human rights mechanisms.

In the case of Croatia, the issue of amnesty has been raised in the context of the double jeopardy clause within the European Convention on Human Rights ('ECHR') before the European Court of Human Rights ('ECtHR'). *Marguš v Croatia* is a case affirming the importance of criminal proceedings and sentencing enforcement over earlier amnesty schemes. By contrast, the privileges of North Macedonia's 2001 Amnesty Act have instead been extended to individuals under suspicion of committing war crimes.

Justice over Impunity: Marguš v Croatia

The case of *Marguš v Croatia*[60] concerns the conviction of the applicant, who was a commander in the Croatian army, of war crimes against a civilian population in 1991. The ECtHR was asked to decide whether the crimes the applicant had been convicted of were the same as those which had been the subject of proceedings terminated in 1997 via the application of Croatia's 1996 GAA. The legal issue in the case concerned the double jeopardy clause under Article 4 of Protocol 7 of the ECHR.

Initially, the applicant was indicted by the Croatian authorities for multiple murders and the infliction of bodily injuries as ordinary crimes that occurred in November 1991 in Osijek. Following enactment of the aforementioned 1996 GAA, on 24 June 1997, the Osijek County Court terminated the proceedings.

58 *Prosecutor v Furundžija* (Judgment) ICTY-95–17/1-T (10 December 1998), para 155.
59 UNCHR, 'CCPR General Comment No. 20: Article 7 (Prohibition of Torture, or Other Cruel, Inhuman or Degrading Treatment or Punishment)' (10 March 1992) UN Doc A/44/40.
60 *Marguš v Croatia* App no 4455/10 (ECtHR, 27 May 2014).

This decision was subsequently overturned by the Supreme Court of Croatia, following the prosecutor's request for protection of legality as an extraordinary remedy, on the grounds that the case fell outside the scope of GAA. The Supreme Court upheld the prosecutor's motion and ruled that the decision of Osijek County Court violated the GAA. In doing so, the Supreme Court ruled that a direct and significant connection between the criminal offence in question and the wider aggression, armed rebellion, or armed conflict must exist in order to consider applicability of the 1996 GAA.[61] In 2006, the applicant was charged with war crimes against civilians for the same events, and in 2007 found guilty and sentenced to 14 years' imprisonment by the Osijek County Court. The Supreme Court upheld the County Court's ruling on guilt, but increased the imprisonment sentence to 15 years. In 2009, the Constitutional Court of Croatia dismissed the defendant's constitutional complaint, following which an application was lodged with the ECtHR alleging a violation of the right to fair trial and the right not to be punished twice.

The ECtHR found that the double jeopardy principle under Article 4 of Protocol 7 to the ECHR is not applicable in the context of amnesty for acts which amount to allegations of war crimes. The ECtHR's stance reflects the modern view whereby amnesties are considered unacceptable as they are incompatible with the ECHR obligation of states to prosecute and punish grave breaches of fundamental human rights (para 139).[62] In this regard, the court held that by bringing a fresh indictment against the applicant and convicting him of war crimes against the civilian population, the Croatian authorities acted in compliance with the procedural obligations enshrined within the meaning of Articles 2 and 3 of the ECHR, and in a manner consistent with the requirements and recommendations of the abovementioned international mechanisms and instruments (para 140).

Impunity over Justice: Amnesty Law of North Macedonia

As a part of the 2001 Ohrid Agreement,[63] which ended the internal conflict between the North Macedonia government and the ethnic Albanian community, the Parliament of North Macedonia passed the Amnesty Act in 2002. Concerns were raised as to whether the Amnesty Act was applicable to conflict-related cases returned from the ICTY to the Macedonian judiciary for further processing. While the case of Boškoski and Tarčulovski, which involved the

61 Case no K-94/07 (Supreme Court of Croatia, 19 September 2007). See also note 35 and associated text.

62 See e.g., William Schabas, *The European Convention on Human Rights: A Commentary* (Oxford University Press 2015) 67.

63 Organization for Security and Co-operation in Europe, 'Framework Agreement Concluded at Ohrid (North Macedonia) and Signed at Skopje (North Macedonia) on 13 August 2001' (*Organization for Security and Co-operation in Europe*, 13 August 2001) <https://www.osce.org/skopje/100622?download=true> accessed 12 May 2018.

Minister of Interior and the inspector of the unit providing security for the president, was tried on the merits before the ICTY,[64] four cases relating to four separate events were returned to the North Macedonian authorities for further investigation and possible prosecution.[65]

While the 2002 Amnesty Act initially reflected international legal standards, later events and political and legal developments in the Macedonian Parliament and the Macedonian Constitutional Court have barred further processing of the four transferred cases, thus leading to ongoing impunity. Namely, on 19 June 2011, the Macedonian Parliament adopted an Authentic Interpretation of Article 1 of the 2002 Amnesty Act, whereby it extended the benefits of that act to all cases relating to the 2001 conflict, including those returned from the ICTY to the North Macedonian judiciary.[66] On 31 October 2012, the Macedonian Constitutional Court dismissed the motion for constitutional review of the Authentic Interpretation.[67] Thus, proceedings in the four pending cases were terminated as the scope of the 2002 Amnesty Act was extended to cover those cases.

This stance was fiercely debated and was criticised mainly by international organisations and human rights activists. In the view of the Commissioner for Human Rights of the Council of Europe, this development dealt 'a serious blow to the ongoing efforts towards achieving justice in the region'.[68] Furthermore, in view of Amnesty International, the Macedonian Parliament's Authentic Interpretation is 'inconsistent with international law and will leave the victims and their relatives without access to justice'.[69]

64 See *Prosecutor v Boškoski & Tarčulovski* (Appeals Judgment) ICTY-04–82 (19 May 2010).
65 See Marija Risteska and Kristina Miševa, 'The Application of International Law in Macedonia' in Siniša Rodin and Tamara Perišin (eds), *Judicial Application of International Law in Southeast Europe* (Springer 2015) 214.
66 Authentic Interpretation of Article 1 of the Amnesty Act (Official Gazette of the Republic of Macedonia no 18/2002), OG of Macedonia no 99/2011 of 22 July 2011. Authentic interpretation denotes the interpretation of a document delivered by its drafter. It is most commonly employed by a legislator where specific provisions are subject to incorrect or diversified interpretation in practice. See *Black's Law Dictionary* (n 2) 824; Teodor Antić, 'Vjerodostojno tumačenje zakona' (2015) 36(1) Zbornik Pravnog fakulteta Sveučilišta u Rijeci 623.
67 Constitutional Court of Macedonia, Decision of 31 October 2011, Case No 158/2011.
68 Commissioner for Human Rights, *Post-war Justice and Durable Peace in the Former Yugoslavia: Issue Paper by the Council of Europe Commissioner for Human Rights* (Council of Europe Publishing 2012) 17. See also Council of Europe Commissioner for Human Rights, 'Report by Nils Muižnieks, Council of Europe Commissioner for Human Rights, Following His Visit to "the former Yugoslav Republic of Macedonia" from 26 to 29 November 2012' (*Council of Europe Commission for Human Rights*, 9 April 2013) 4, 12–13 <https://rm.coe.int/16806db8a1> accessed 27 August 2018.
69 Sinisa Jakov Marusic and Maryrose Fison, 'Amnesty International Calls for Justice for Macedonians' (*Balkan Insight*, 2 September 2011) <http://www.balkaninsight.com/en/article/macedonia-slammed-over-controversial-amnesty> accessed 27 August 2018.

Outlook and Perspectives

While amnesty legislation in the countries under analysis generally tends to satisfy existing international standards by, among other features, forbidding amnesty for cases involving allegations of atrocity crimes, the preceding overview demonstrates the inconsistent application of post-conflict amnesties across the countries of the former Yugoslavia. Macedonia's 2002 Amnesty Law, whose application was extended to all cases referred by the ICTY for processing at national level, is a concerning example in the fight against impunity for atrocity crimes. By comparison, within Croatian law and practice, as evidenced by the 2014 ECtHR case of *Marguš v Croatia*, the importance of criminal proceedings and sentencing enforcement has outweighed earlier amnesty schemes.

Executive Clemency: Individual Pardons

This section addresses the legislative framework relating to pardons, as just one example of executive clemency, albeit with a specific emphasis on atrocity crimes. For the purposes of this chapter, pardon denotes 'an act or an instance of officially nullifying punishment or other legal consequences of a crime'.[70] Compared with amnesties, pardon as a form of clemency is a prerogative of the executive branch and may be bestowed upon an individual defendant.[71] Given its long history and role during the earliest ages as an act of mercy by a ruler towards defendants, despite its near ubiquity in national constitutional provisions,[72] pardon is arguably a 'living fossil' within contemporary criminal law.[73] In *An Essay on Crimes and Punishments* (1764), Beccaria fiercely criticised the very idea of extrajudicial pardon by stating that as punishments become more mild, clemency and pardon are less necessary.[74] As Pradel notes, in common law countries,

70 *Black's Law Dictionary* (n 2) 1221; cf. Ruiz-Fabri, Della Morte, and Lambert Abdelgawad (n 2) 237, 245; Andrew Novak, 'Pardon Power', *Max Planck Encyclopedia of Comparative Constitutional Law* (February 2016) para 1–3 <http://oxcon.ouplaw.com/view/10.1093/law:mpeccol/law-mpeccol-e405> accessed 7 February 2019. As such, the author's definition of 'pardon' incorporates both commutations and releases from prison—see further Pascoe and Novak, this volume, on clemency terminology.

71 Horvatić, Derenčinović, and Cvitanović (n 29) 290.

72 See further Pascoe and Novak, this volume.

73 Anita Kurtović, 'Pomilovanje u kaznenom pravosuđu (u povodu novoga Zakona o pomilovanju)' (2003) 10(2) Hrvatski ljetopis za kazneno pravo i praksu 479, 487; Dušica Miladinović-Stefanović, 'Istorijski razvoj ustanove pomilovanja—sa posebnim osvrtom na pravo Srbije od perioda srednjeg veka do 1929. godine' (2008) 52(1) Zbornik radova Pravnog fakulteta u Nišu 165, 166; Leslie Sebba, 'Clemency in Perspective' in Simha F Landau and Leslie Sebba (eds), *Criminology in Perspective: Essays in Honour of Israel Drapkin* (Lexington Books 1977) 221–222.

74 Furthermore, when discussing the attributes of 'the perfect legislation', Beccaria suggested that clemency should be excluded as punishments 'would be mild, and

pardon was once widely used to mitigate the severity of criminal law.[75] However, should pardon have a specific role in the criminal justice policies of countries in transition? Are there any constitutional, legislative, and practical pardon trends in the countries of the former Yugoslavia? This section will touch briefly on these issues.

Overview of Constitutional and Legislative Rules on Pardon

Authority. As a rule, the power to grant pardon is denoted as one of prerogatives of heads of state within all former Yugoslavian countries. This prerogative is of either constitutional[76] or legal character.[77] The Constitutions of North Macedonia and Kosovo limit presidential pardons by providing that such power may only be exercised in accordance with the law.[78] With regard to BiH, two specific characteristics arise as a result of its complex constitutional structure. First, there are a wider scope of organs with constitutional or legal power which may grant pardon. In addition to the Presidency of BiH as the nation's collective head of state,[79] the pardon power may be exercised by

the proceedings in criminal cases regular and expeditious'. In addition, in his view '[t]he prince in pardoning gives up the public security in favour of an individual, and, by his ill-judged benevolence, proclaims a public act of impunity' (Cesare Beccaria, *An Essay on Crimes and Punishments* (John Exshaw 1767) 132).

75 Until the nineteenth century, when the UK Parliament started to pass criminal law statutes, pardon was often used to mitigate the severity of criminal common law (Pradel (n 3) 702). See also Samuel T Morison, 'The Politics of Grace: On the Moral Justification of Executive Clemency' (2005) 9(1) Buffalo Criminal Law Review 2005, 2ff.

76 Constitution of the Republic of Slovenia, OG of the Republic of Slovenia nos 33/91-I, 42/97—UZS68, 66/00—UZ80, 24/03—UZ3a, 47, 68, 69/04—UZ14, 69/04—UZ43, 69/04—UZ50, 68/06—UZ121, 140, 143, 47/13—UZ148, 47/13—UZ90, 97, 99 and 75/16—UZ70a, art 107(1); Constitution of the Republic of Croatia, art 98(1); Constitution of the Republic of Serbia, art 97(2), 112(7); Constitution of Montenegro, art 95(1)(9); Constitution of the Republic of Macedonia, art 84(1)(10); Constitution of the Republic of Kosovo, art 84(1)(29).

77 The Presidency of BiH may pardon individuals who: (i) were convicted and sentenced by the Court of Bosnia and Herzegovina or by any other domestic court to which proceedings were transferred by the decision of the Court of Bosnia and Herzegovina; (ii) are serving a sentence in Bosnia and Herzegovina on the basis of final judgment rendered by a foreign court; (iii) are suffering legal consequences of criminal convictions. See Pardon Act (PA BiH), OG of BiH no 93/05 of 30 December 2005, art 2.

78 Constitution of the Republic of Macedonia, art 84(1)(10); Constitution of the Republic of Kosovo, art 84(1)(29).

79 Following the adoption of the Criminal Code of BiH in 2003, as part of extensive reforms of the Bosnian-Herzegovinian criminal justice system, the Parliamentary Assembly of BiH also adopted pardon legislation. See Pardon Act (PA BiH), OG of BiH no 93/05 of 30 December 2005.

the heads of two entities within BiH which do not have the character of a state: the Federation of Bosnia and Herzegovina and the Republika Srpska,[80] as well as by the Mayor of the Brčko District of BiH,[81] all falling under the executive branch of government. Each actor may only pardon crimes committed within the physical jurisdiction concerned. Second, until 2015 a certain degree of cooperation between the entity president and two vice presidents was required in the Federation of Bosnia and Herzegovina.[82] While the pardon power is the exclusive constitutional prerogative of the entity president,[83] since 1996 the implementing legislation has provided for an additional requirement for the entity president either to seek the prior consent of two vice presidents,[84] or to consult them prior to making final decisions on pardon.[85] The constitutionality of this requirement was challenged before the Constitutional Court of the Federation of BiH, which held that this provision of the 2009 Pardon Act contravened the entity Constitution as the latter vests exclusive power to grant pardons to the entity president without any specific constitutional requirement to conduct consultations with vice presidents.[86] Under the 2015 amendments to the 2009 Pardon Act, such mandatory consultations are no longer a legal requirement for the entity president.[87]

Scope and effect. Existing comparative reviews demonstrate differences regarding the scope and effect of pardons.[88] The same general observation is relevant in context of the countries under analysis. It is common ground that a pardon may have an effect on the sentence of an individual already subject to a final court judgment. First, pardon may serve as the basis for full or partial release from serving the sentence. In case the execution of sentence has not been initiated, the pardon bars its execution. In addition, pardon may

80 Constitution of the Federation of BiH, OG of Federation of BiH no 1/94 of 21 July 1994, art 7(VI); Constitution of RS, art 80(1)(5).
81 Pardon Act (PA BD BiH), OG of Brčko District of BiH no 13/07, art 2.
82 The entity president is the head of the executive within the entity. The president has two vice presidents who come from different constituent peoples. See Constitution of the Federation of BiH, art IV.B.1.1.
83 Constitution of the Federation of BiH, art IV.B.3.7.a(VI).
84 Pardon Act (1996 PA FBiH), OG of Federation of BiH nos 9/96 of 30 June 1996 and 14/97 of 16 June 1997, art 2.
85 Pardon Act (2009 PA FBiH), OG of Federation of BiH no 22/09 of 6 April 2009, art 2.
86 *Judgment U-34/10* (Constitutional Court of the Federation of Bosnia and Herzegovina, 8 October 2013), OG of the Federation of BiH no 3/14 of 15 January 2014, 55.
87 Act on Amendments of the PA FBiH, OG of the Federation of BiH no 91/15 of 27 November 2015.
88 See e.g., Leslie Sebba, 'The Pardoning Power—A World Survey' (1977) 68(1) The Journal of Criminal Law and Criminology 116ff; Andrew Novak, *Comparative Executive Clemency: The Constitutional Pardon Power and the Prerogative of Mercy in Global Perspective* (Routledge 2015).

affect both a principal and an accessory sentence, as well as a sentence of juvenile imprisonment.[89]

The second form of pardon (sometimes labelled a 'commutation') occurs where a less severe criminal sanction or a suspended sentence is substituted in place of the initial punishment. Substitution of a criminal sanction in this context means the imposition of a different type of criminal sanction, e.g. a sentence of imprisonment being substituted by a fine. In that context, substitution leads to a release from serving the remainder of the original sentence.

The third type of pardon leads to the rehabilitation of the offender, that is the deletion of the offender from the record of prior convictions, including those which, according to legislation, may not otherwise be subject of deletion. The fourth and final type of pardon may simply suspend the legal consequences of a final and binding conviction.[90]

Different states approach in different ways the question of whether pardon bars the initiation of proceedings in future. While in some countries pardon may amount to abolition, such as in Slovenia,[91] Serbia,[92] Montenegro,[93] and North Macedonia,[94] the Croatian, Bosnian-Herzegovinian and Kosovar legislation does not provide for such possibility. Such legislative developments represent a departure from the former Yugoslav legislation under which pardon did represent a bar from future criminal prosecution.[95]

Statutory conditions and limitations. The legislation passed in the countries under analysis generally does not provide for substantive restrictions on pardons. The most notable exception is the Kosovar legislation. Law No. 03/L-101 on Pardon ('LP Kos')[96] explicitly stipulates that pardon is the president's prerogative but is not to be issued as a 'routine remedy, but [instead as] a seldom-used tool to reward extraordinary displays of character and conduct or to address serious humanitarian concerns' (art 1(1)). Additionally, LP Kos provides for general criteria to be taken into consideration, which relate to gravity of the crime for which the defendant was convicted, the risk of recidivism, the existence of genuine repentance, and the defendant's good behaviour (art 5(2)).

89 Miloš Babić, Ljiljana Filipović, Ivanka Marković, and Zdravko Rajić, *Komentari krivičnih/kaznenih zakona u Bosni i Hercegovini* (Council of Europe, 2005) 451.
90 CC Slo, art 97(1); CC BiH, art 119(1); CC FBiH, art 123(1); CC RS, art 101(1); CC Serb, art 110(1); CC MN, art 131(1); CC NM, art 114(1); Code No. 04/L-082 – Criminal Code of Kosovo (CC Kos), art 112(1) <http://www.assembly-kosova.org/common/docs/ligjet/Criminal%20Code.pdf> accessed 27 August 2018.
91 CC Slo, art 97(1).
92 CC Serb, art 110(1).
93 CC MN, art 131(1).
94 CC NM, art 114(1).
95 CC SFRY, art 102(1); Srzentić, Stajić, and Lazarević (n 4) 480.
96 Law No. 03/L-101 on Pardon (LP Kos) <http://www.assembly-kosova.org/common/docs/ligjet/2008_03-L-101_en.pdf> accessed 27 August 2018.

Other national legislation also stipulates that if a sentence of long-term or life imprisonment is imposed, pardon may only be considered or granted pursuant to certain limitations. In BiH, a partial pardon may be granted after the defendant has served two-thirds of a term of imprisonment of up to 20 years[97] or after serving three-fifths[98] of a sentence of long-term imprisonment, while in Croatia a partial pardon may be granted after serving a minimum of ten years in prison.[99] The Slovenian legislation stipulates that the sentence of life imprisonment, in the case of pardon, may be substituted by imprisonment of between 25 and 30 years.[100] Specific national laws on pardon outline pardon procedures in all the countries under analysis.[101]

Pardoning Atrocity Crimes: Policies and Practices

Of particular importance here are the possibilities, requirements, and procedures for pardons in case of atrocity crimes. International law imposes an obligation on states to investigate serious violations of human rights.[102] This issue is acutely important in the context of those countries in which cases involving allegations of atrocity crimes were or are still being investigated, prosecuted and tried before the courts, which is the case with the countries under analysis. Pardons for these kinds of defendants are very much a live issue in the countries of the former Yugoslavia.

In the context of countries under analysis, two opposing tendencies are noticeable. To one side are countries whose legislation provides for limitations on pardon as a form of clemency for atrocity crimes, namely BiH, Kosovo, and Slovenia. The BiH legislation prohibits pardons being granted to defendants convicted of genocide, crimes against humanity, and war crimes.[103] A similar provision exists in the Kosovo legislation, it being formulated more broadly by excluding pardon for defendants convicted of international crimes.[104] The Slovenian legislation specifically excludes the possibility of granting pardon to defendants sentenced by the International Criminal Court.[105] To the other

97 See e.g., CC RS, art 101.
98 See e.g., CC BiH, art 42b; CC FBiH, art 43b(3); CC BD BiH, art 43(3).
99 PA Cro, art 5(4).
100 Pardon Act (PA Slo), OG of the Republic of Slovenia no 23/05, art 98(2).
101 PA Slo; Pardon Act (PA Cro), OG of the Republic of Croatia no 175/03; PA BiH; Pardon Act (PA FBiH), OG of Federation of BiH no 22/09 of 6 April 2009; Pardon Act (PA RS), OG of Republika Srpska no 34/06; Pardon Act (PA BD BiH), OG of Brčko District of BiH no 13/07; Pardon Act (PA Serb), OG of the Republic of Serbia no 49/95 of 24 November 1995; Pardon Act (PA MN), OG of Montenegro no 31/12 of 15 June 2012; Pardon Act (PA NM), OG of the Republic of Macedonia no 20/93; 12/09; LP Kos.
102 Novak (n 87) 60.
103 PA BiH, art 3; PA FBiH, art 3; PA RS, art 3; PA BD BiH, art 3.
104 PA Kos, art 4(5).
105 PA Slo, art 1(3).

side are countries whose legislation does not explicitly provide for such limitations, including Croatia, Serbia, Montenegro, and North Macedonia.

While the possibility of granting pardons for atrocity crimes is explicitly excluded under the applicable legislation in BiH, as noted above, this legislative prohibition has not prevented discussions and initiatives favouring this possibility. The two most recent government initiatives to this effect were proposed in 2013[106] and 2017,[107] each being openly criticised by the political opposition, international organisations and the NGO sector.[108] The 2017 initiative purported to provide defendants convicted of atrocity crimes the opportunity to file a petition for pardon after serving three-fifths of their sentence.[109]

International monitoring mechanisms such as the UN Committee on Enforced Disappearances have also raised concern in this context. In a 2016 report, the Committee explicitly recommended that the BiH government 'withdraw the proposal to amend the Law on Pardon of Bosnia and Herzegovina and ensure that the extreme seriousness of acts of enforced disappearance is taken into account when contemplating the possibility of granting pardon'.[110]

Outlook and Perspectives

The two contrasting legislative approaches to pardoning individuals convicted of atrocity crimes as part of a broader regional conflict indicate the need for a harmonised regional pardoning policy in respect of such crimes. There is no international legal obligation on the states under analysis to harmonise their legislation, limiting the possibility of pardoning these offenders. However, this course of action, at least on the level of policy, is important from a transitional

106 Amer Jahic, 'War Crimes on the Way to Being Pardoned' (*Detector*, 28 November 2018) <http://detektor.ba/en/war-crimes-on-the-way-to-being-pardoned/> accessed 28 October 2018; Council of Ministers of BiH, Zaključci 72. sjednice Vijeća ministara Bosne i Hercegovine (*Council of Ministers of BiH*, 28 November 2013) <http://vijeceministara.gov.ba/saopstenja/sjednice/zakljucci_sa_sjednica/default.aspx?id=16119&langTag=hr-HR> accessed 28 October 2018.

107 *Draft of Act Amending the Pardon Act of Bosnia and Herzegovina* (Council of Ministers of BiH, 18 April 2017), on file with the author.

108 Initiative for monitoring of the European integration of BiH, 'Reaction: Pardoning War Criminals is Unacceptable' (*Initiative for monitoring of the European integration of BiH*, 19 April 2017) <http://eu-monitoring.ba/en/reaction-pardoning-war-criminals-is-unacceptable/> accessed 28 October 2018; TRIAL International, 'Nedopustivo/Pomilovanje ratnih zločinaca' (*TRIAL BiH*, 21 April 2017) <https://trial.ba/?utm_content=&utm_source=facebook&utm_campaign=social&utm_medium=TRIAL+u+Bosni+i+Hercegovini&cat=3> accessed 28 October 2018.

109 *Draft of Act Amending the Pardon Act of Bosnia and Herzegovina* (n 105) art 3.

110 Committee on Enforced Disappearances, 'Concluding observations on the report submitted by Bosnia and Herzegovina under article 29(1) of the Convention' (3 November 2916) UN Doc CED/C/BIH/CO/1.

justice point of view. Generally speaking, pardons are limited by few legislative restrictions. Each nation under analysis affords its executive decision-maker a wide legal margin of appreciation, thus resulting in divergent practices across national borders and even within federal jurisdictions in the former Yugoslavia.

Conclusion

Once part of a single legal system, the countries of the former Yugoslavia have developed independent legislative frameworks and practices related to amnesty and pardon as instruments of mercy. In these countries, executive clemency practice must be understood in the context of executive clemency's relationship with the legislative amnesty power. Following the end of conflict in the former Yugoslavia, a considerable number of amnesty laws were adopted. Inevitably, allegations amounting to atrocity crimes were considered in the context of these laws, which led to inconsistent and opposing practices, particularly in Croatia and North Macedonia. This chapter identifies North Macedonia's 2002 Amnesty Act, whose application was extended to all cases returned from the ICTY, as a concerning example in the fight against impunity for atrocity crimes. By comparison, within Croatian law and practice, as evidenced by the 2014 case of *Marguš v Croatia* before the ECtHR, the importance of criminal proceedings and sentencing enforcement has outweighed earlier amnesty schemes.

A similar tendency is noticeable in relation to individual pardons. While some pieces of legislation are silent as to whether the perpetrators of atrocity crimes may be considered for pardon, legislative initiatives in other countries explicitly aim at extending the possibility of pardon despite explicit legal prohibitions, such as is the case of BiH. Different legislative approaches and initiatives to pardons for atrocity crimes call, at the very minimum, for a transnational harmonisation of policy, given the sensitivity of the issue in these countries and the regional dimension. In sum, in addition to timely and effective investigation, prosecution and adjudication of past atrocity crimes by the judiciaries of countries in transition, it is equally important to pass mercy-related legislation which closes the impunity gap for such crimes and adheres to rule of law principles.

5 Remedying Wrongful Conviction

Comparisons between the Royal Prerogative of Mercy in England and Wales and Clemency in the USA

Sarah L Cooper and Hannah Burrows

Introduction

The problem of wrongful conviction is 'present around the world'.[1] This situation has motivated stakeholders to consider ways to prevent, identify, correct, and atone for wrongful conviction. Such deliberation has led to an increased understanding about how criminal justice systems, including those established in the United States of America ('USA') and England and Wales ('E&W'), produce wrongful convictions. In both jurisdictions, individuals, groups, and institutions have emerged to pursue wrongful conviction-focused research, litigation, and reform. There is now a growing catalogue of information about the scale of wrongful conviction in both jurisdictions, and a sizeable body of research about common causes of wrongful conviction. The practices of relevant actors, including lawyers, judges, jurors, experts, law enforcement, and forensic scientists, have also been scrutinised in order to further understand how they might contribute to wrongful conviction, as have the procedures and institutions in which they work to investigate, trial, and appeal cases. These efforts have led to both localised and systemic reform agendas, and the identification of further avenues for research.[2]

1 Miranda Jolicoeur, 'International Perspectives on Wrongful Convictions: Workshop Report' (*US Department of Justice*, September 2010) <https://www.ncjrs.gov/pdffiles1/nij/234631.pdf> accessed 24 January 2019.

2 For relevant literature on the USA, see Sarah L Cooper, *Controversies in Innocence Cases in America* (1st edn, Ashgate Publishing 2014); Brandon Garrett, *Convicting the Innocent: Where Criminal Prosecutions Go Wrong* (Harvard University Press 2011); 'Innocence Project' (*Innocent Project*, 2019) <https://www.innocenceproject.org> accessed 6 July 2018. For E&W, see Sam Poyser, Angus Nurse, and Rebecca Milne, *Miscarriages of Justice: Causes, Consequences and Remedies—Key Themes in Policing* (1st edn, Policy Press 2018); Michael Naughton, *The Innocent and the Criminal Justice System: A Sociological Analysis of Miscarriages of Justice* (Palgrave 2013); Samuel Hammond, *The Criminal Cases Review Commission: An Effective Addition to the Criminal Appeals Process?* (LAP LAMBERT Academic Publishing 2017).

One area that is particularly ripe for research in relation to wrongful convictions is the clemency/pardon power.[3] Rooted in notions of mercy and forgiveness,[4] this power allows the state to relieve lawbreakers from punishment, yet maintain the effectiveness of the law. Naturally, a conceptual tension pervades the exercise of clemency/pardon to remedy wrongful conviction, as illustrated by a famous exchange that took place during the reign of King Richard II, a prolific user of the pardon power in fourteenth century England:

> Thomas Arundel: For what reasons am I standing here accused? I have been pardoned twice by the King.
> John of Gaunt: Those pardons have been revoked, traitor!
> Thomas Arundel: Truly, you lie. I was never traitor.
> John of Gaunt: Then why did you seek a pardon?[5]

Arundel and Gaunt's exchange underscores the point that, conceptually, the clemency/pardon power should be used where there is something to forgive. But what if—because the convicted is innocent, there is—in fact—nothing to forgive? If clemency/pardon is a 'cutting back' on the state's legal right to punish criminals, what happens when the right to punish does not exist in the first place, because the convict is innocent?

These are difficult questions. Still, the idea that clemency/pardon has a corrective function has long existed. Aristotle, for example, said, '[clemency] is a correction where the law is defective owing to its universality'.[6] Presently, the clemency/pardon power is inextricably bound with error correction in both the USA and E&W, with both jurisdictions promoting the power as a remedy for wrongful conviction. In 1993, the United States Supreme Court ('SCOTUS') declared clemency the 'fail safe'[7] of the American criminal justice system, and the 'historic remedy for preventing miscarriages of justice'.[8] This ruling thrust clemency into each state's mechanics for correcting error.[9] Only months later, in 1994, the High Court of England and Wales stated, 'The prerogative of mercy ... is now a constitutional safeguard against mistakes',[10]

3 The authors use the term 'clemency' to refer to mercy frameworks in the USA, and use the term 'pardon' as a shorthand to refer to the royal prerogative of mercy in E&W.
4 Sarah L Cooper and Daniel Gough, 'The Controversy of Clemency and Innocence in America' (2014) 51 Cal W L Rev 55, 58–61.
5 The Narcisist, *The History of England* (June 2014) <https://thehistoryofengland.co.uk/2014/06/22/128-the-narcisist/> accessed 8 July 2018; see also Bryan Bevan, *Henry IV* (Palgrave Macmillan 1994) 45.
6 Aristotle, *The Ethics of Aristotle* (Alexander Grant ed, John W Parker & Son 1857) 27–28.
7 *Herrera v Collins* 506 US 390, 415.
8 Ibid., 412.
9 Cooper and Gough (n 4) 71.
10 *R v Secretary of State for the Home Department Ex p Bentley* [1994] QB 349, 365.

and that 'pardon should be reserved for cases where it can be established that the convicted person was morally and technically innocent'.[11] Subsequently, the Criminal Cases Review Commission (CCRC), the body responsible for investigating miscarriages of justice in England, Wales, and Northern Ireland,[12] was given the power to refer cases (with reasons) to the Secretary of State so that he or she could consider the exercise of the prerogative of mercy.[13]

In the light of an ever-growing 'innocence consciousness' worldwide, this chapter provides a compact comparative review of the relationship between wrongful conviction and the clemency/pardon power in the USA and E&W. The first section outlines current clemency/pardon frameworks in both jurisdictions. The second explores common themes across both jurisdictions, namely (1) eligibility and standards of proof; (2) transparency and reviewability; and (3) political will. It concludes that both jurisdictions encounter similar challenges when utilising the clemency/pardon power to correct error, and offers five ideas for fostering better practice in both jurisdictions.

Current Frameworks

Throughout history, the clemency/pardon power has vested in various actors, including God, the Greek *Ecclesia*, Julius Caesar, and the Roman Empire. In England, the power has vested in monarchs, the clergy, parliamentarians, and, more recently, government ministers. In the USA, combinations of legislatures, executives, and administrative boards have exercised (and continue to exercise) the clemency power.[14] This section summarises current frameworks in the USA and E&W.

USA Frameworks

In the USA, clemency covers various mechanisms that executives can use to remit the consequences of a crime,[15] including pardons, reprieves, commutations, and remissions of fines or restitution.[16]

Article II of the United States Constitution provides for federal executive clemency, stating that '[The President] shall have Power to grant Reprieves and Pardons for Offenses against the United States, except in Cases of

11 Ibid., 364E.
12 Criminal Cases Review Commission, 'Criminal Cases Review Commission' <https://ccrc.gov.uk/> accessed 8 July 2018.
13 Criminal Appeal Act 1995 ('CAA 1995'), s 16(2).
14 Cooper and Gough (n 4) 58–73.
15 Molly Clayton, 'Forgiving the Unforgivable: Reinvigorating the Use of Executive Clemency in Capital Cases' (2013) 54 Boston College Law Review 751, 754.
16 Kathleen Ridolfi and Seth Gordon, 'Gubernatorial Clemency Powers: Justice or Mercy' [2009] Northern California Innocence Project Scholarship <https://digitalcommons.law.scu.edu/ncipscholarship/3/> accessed 3 June 2020.

Impeachment.'[17] Article II thereby grants the president sole discretion over the application of the clemency power in federal criminal offences, and is one of the broadest powers constitutionally granted to him.[18] Reprieves allow the president to commute an existing sentence, but keep intact the legal finding of guilt. Pardons, however, allow the president to remove the legal effects of a conviction.[19] The Department of Justice (DOJ) and, specifically, the Office of the Pardon Attorney (OPA) support the president in his exercise of executive clemency.[20] All requests are directed to the Pardon Attorney for 'review, investigation and preparation of the Department's recommendation to the President'.[21] When applying for executive clemency, there are detailed standards and procedures for applicants to follow.[22]

At state level, the application of the clemency power differs from state to state.[23] Some states vest the power solely in the governor, whereas others invest the power solely in an administrative board.[24] Administrative boards comprise varying degrees of diversity. Some boards bring together members with experience in a variety of professions, such as teaching, medicine, law enforcement, parole, social work, and criminal defence.[25] Other boards are more overtly state aligned, including boards entirely made up of state officials, or with most members having experience in state-aligned departments.[26] In some states, administrative boards share the clemency power with the governor. In such structures, some states require the governor to receive a recommendation for clemency from the relevant administrative board before he or she can act; whereas others provide for boards to make non-binding recommendations to the governor.[27]

The lack of uniformity across US clemency proceedings can be attributed to limited 'statutory or administrative standards governing use of the power'.[28] However, all clemency proceedings are considered to have an

17 Constitution of the US 1789, art 2(2)(1).
18 James Pfiffner, 'Pardon Power' (*The Heritage Guide to the Constitution*, 2017) <https://www.heritage.org/constitution/#!/articles/2/essays/89/pardon-power> accessed 7 July 2018.
19 Ibid.
20 Office of the Pardon Attorney, 'About the Office' (*The United States Department of Justice*, February 2017) <https://www.justice.gov/pardon/about-office> accessed 8 July 2018.
21 Ibid.
22 Office of the Pardon Attorney, 'Clemency Forms and Instructions' (*The United States Department of Justice*, June 2018) <https://www.justice.gov/pardon/clemency-forms-instructions> accessed 8 July 2018. See also note 20.
23 Sarah L Cooper, 'The State Clemency Power and Innocence Claims: The Influence of Finality and its Implications for Innocents' [2015] Charlotte Law Review 51, 95–96.
24 Ibid.
25 Ibid, 98–100.
26 Ibid.
27 Cooper (n 23) 95–96.
28 Daniel Kobil, 'The Quality of Mercy Strained: Wresting the Pardoning Power from the King' (1991) 69 Texas Law Review 569, 605.

error correction function. In 1993, in *Herrera,* SCOTUS stated that clemency proceedings are the 'failsafe' of the US criminal justice system,[29] and are the appropriate forum for remedying wrongful conviction.[30] Despite this, SCOTUS subsequently ruled in *Ohio Adult Parole Authority v Woodard*[31] that only minimal due process protections attach to clemency proceedings,[32] outlawing, for instance, decisions made using a 'coin toss'.[33] This standard has generally been interpreted narrowly by US courts.[34] As Heise puts it, 'lower federal courts have taken [*Woodard*'s] "procedural minimalism" approach to heart'.[35]

Cooper has previously questioned the effectiveness of current US clemency frameworks to address wrongful conviction claims in the USA; making observations about how limited transparency, high standards for eligibility and proof, imbalanced board compositions, and a lack of bespoke procedures, might hinder the bringing and articulation of wrongful conviction-based applications.[36] She has also suggested that courts should broaden their interpretation of *Woodard*'s minimal due process standard in order to facilitate relief in appropriate cases.[37] This chapter situates Cooper's previous consideration of these issues within a comparative discussion of the royal prerogative of mercy in E&W.

Frameworks in England and Wales

In E&W, the pardon power has long been associated with the monarch,[38] and is known as the 'royal prerogative of mercy'.[39] Presently, the power lies in the hands of the Justice Secretary, a government minister and elected politician.[40] The Justice Secretary recommends cases deserving of pardon to the monarch for approval.[41] It is, therefore, a relief mechanism outside of the judicial

29 *Herrera* (n 7) 415.
30 Ibid., 417: 'History shows that the traditional remedy for claims of innocence based on new evidence … has been executive clemency'.
31 *Ohio Adult Parole Authority v Woodard* 523 US 272.
32 Ibid., 289 (O'Connor J, concurring).
33 Ibid.: '[j]udicial intervention might, for example, be warranted in the face of a scheme whereby a state official flipped a coin to determine whether to grant clemency, or in a case where the State arbitrarily denied a prisoner any access to its clemency process'.
34 Cooper (n 23) 63–81.
35 Michael Heise, 'The Death of Death Row Clemency and the Evolving Politics of Unequal Grace' (2015) 66(5) Alabama Law Review 949, 966.
36 Cooper and Gough (n 4); Cooper (n 23).
37 ibid.
38 Helen Lacey, *The Royal Pardon: Access to Mercy in Fourteenth-Century England* (York Medieval Press 2009).
39 *Bentley* (n 10) 357.
40 *R (Shields) v Secretary of State for Justice* [2010] QB 150, 156.
41 Ministry of Justice and The Rt Hon Chris Grayling MP, 'Royal Pardon for WW2 Code-Breaker Dr. Alan Turing' (*Gov.uk*, 24 December 2013) <https://www.gov.

process.[42] Two types of pardon exist in E&W, namely a 'free pardon' and a 'conditional pardon'.[43] A free pardon relieves the recipient from all penalties associated with the conviction. It does not, however, quash a conviction, which, constitutionally, can only be done by the courts.[44] A conditional pardon is rarely used,[45] and generally substitutes a lesser sentence.[46]

Seeking a pardon under the royal prerogative is one of three relief avenues a wrongly convicted individual can take in E&W. The other two options, are, first, lodging an appeal within the criminal court system, and, second, making an application to the Criminal Cases Review Commission ('CCRC'). Since April 1908,[47] anyone convicted of an indictable offence has had the possibility of lodging an appeal against his conviction (or sentence) at the Court of Appeal (Criminal Division).[48] The test applied by the Court of Appeal is whether the conviction is unsafe.[49] Factual innocence is not a standalone ground of appeal. If this appeal fails, the applicant may apply to the UK Supreme Court ('UKSC'), whose jurisdiction is limited to cases that raise matters of public importance.[50] If the UKSC does not grant leave or dismisses the appeal, the applicant has exhausted all of their traditional remedies within the legal system. After exhausting these legal remedies, he or she may apply to the CCRC, although in theory a pardon can be sought from the Justice Secretary at any time.[51]

uk/government/news/royal-pardon-for-ww2-code-breaker-dr-alan-turing> accessed 8 July 2018.

42 Note that the power was previously exercised by the Home Secretary but was transferred to the Justice Secretary (Lord Faulks, 'Prerogative of Mercy: Written question – HL2637' (*UK Parliament*, 18 November 2014) <https://www.parliament.uk/business/publications/written-questions-answers-statements/written-question/Lords/2014-11-04/HL2637> accessed 9 December 2019).

43 A conditional pardon was generally used to substitute a prison sentence for a death sentence. Note there also exists the concept of a remission, where part of a penalty is remitted. This is rarely used. Indeed, no records exist of a remission being granted in the last 20 years (ibid).

44 *R v Foster* [1985] QB 115, 130.

45 David Malone and Christopher Snell, 'The Royal Prerogative of Mercy' [2015] Law Society Gazette <https://www.lawgazette.co.uk/practice-points/the-royal-prerogative-of-mercy/5052062.article> accessed 8 July 2018.

46 *Bentley* (n 10) 357. The term 'commutation' is usually employed for this purpose. See Pascoe and Novak, this volume.

47 Criminal Appeal Act 1907, s 23. Prior to this, the opportunity to appeal in the Court of Crown Cases Reserved was entirely discretionary and only on points of law.

48 Those convicted of less serious offences in the Magistrates Court, known as summary offences, can appeal to the Crown Court.

49 Criminal Appeal Act 1968, s 2.

50 The Supreme Court, 'Role of the Supreme Court' (*The Supreme Court*, 2019) <https://www.supremecourt.uk/about/role-of-the-supreme-court.html> accessed 9 December 2019.

51 Jennifer Schweppe, 'Pardon Me: The Contemporary Application of the Prerogative of Mercy' (2013) 49 Irish Jurist 211, 217–218. Although in theory a

Following numerous high profile miscarriages of justice,[52] the CCRC was set up in 1995 to 'investigate possible miscarriages of justice in England, Wales, and Northern Ireland'.[53] If there is new evidence or a new legal argument that was not available during the applicant's trial, the CCRC may refer the case to the Court of Appeal.[54] The test applied by the CCRC in determining whether to refer is whether there is a 'real possibility' that the relevant outcome would have been different if the jury had the opportunity to consider the new evidence or argument.[55] If a referral to the Court of Appeal is not appropriate, however, the CCRC may refer the case to the Justice Secretary, recommending pardon.[56] The CCRC will set out its reasons for this conclusion,[57] and the Justice Secretary 'shall, in considering whether so to recommend, treat the Commission's statement as conclusive of the matter referred'.[58] There are no published guidelines about how this decision is made.[59] Referral to the Justice Secretary may be the only option available to the CCRC in some instances, because, for example, referral to the Court of Appeal is not possible due to relevant evidence being inadmissible or the Court of Appeal lacks appellate jurisdiction over the case.[60]

pardon is possible at any stage, in practice the Justice Secretary needs to satisfy him or herself of the moral and technical innocence of the applicant and prefers to see the full legal record examining all technical and evidential issues in the case.

52 Afua Hirsch, 'Last resort: How the Criminal Cases Review Commission Works' (*The Guardian*, 5 May 2009) <https://www.theguardian.com/uk/2009/may/05/criminal-cases-review-commission> accessed 8 July 2018.

53 Criminal Cases Review Commission, 'Who We Are' (*Criminal Cases Review Commission*) <https://ccrc.gov.uk/about-us/who-we-are/> accessed 8 July 2018.

54 The CCRC's power to refer the case for a fresh appeal is a statutory power and, if referred, the Court of Appeal must hear the appeal.

55 CAA 1995, s 13(1)(a).

56 Criminal Cases Review Commission, 'What We Do' (*Criminal Cases Review Commission*) <https://ccrc.gov.uk/about-us/what-we-do/> accessed 8 July 2018.

57 CAA 1995, s 16(2).

58 Ibid., s 16(1).

59 That the authors could identify.

60 *Bentley* (n 10) 358. Notably, between April 1997 and December 2017, the CCRC only referred a total of 636 matters to the Court of Appeal out of 23,150 applications received. Of those referred, the majority of convictions or sentences have been overturned at the Court of Appeal (421 out of 629 appeals heard), giving the CCRC a high success rate of 66.9 per cent. See Criminal Cases Review Commission (n 56).

Notably, in E&W, the CCRC referral approach has been successful in helping to relieve miscarriages of justice. The CCRC is able to independently investigate cases and utilise a more inquisitorial approach. This provides a level of transparency and independently verified detail that is generally absent in a mercy petition to the Justice Secretary. The CCRC does not, however, have the power to 'declare' innocence. In E&W, only a court process can do that, which is why—save through a future, significant system overhaul—any error-correcting mechanism in E&W must include a role for the judicial system.

Following unsuccessful applications through both the traditional appellate and CCRC processes, an application to the Justice Secretary for pardon is the only remaining option. As the Privy Council famously stated, 'Mercy is not the subject of legal rights. It begins where legal rights end.'[61] Although a pardon application can be made at any time, the Justice Secretary may defer any consideration of the application until one or both of the two processes outlined above are complete. Ultimately, the Justice Secretary must approach pardon applications carefully, so as not to improperly usurp the constitutional function of the Court of Appeal.[62] The Justice Secretary may also refer the case back to the CCRC for advice on the exercise of the pardon power.[63]

There is limited information about how the modern pardon power is exercised in E&W. It is known to be a power used sparingly, with only two recorded instances of free pardons being granted in the last 20 years.[64] However, what is known is that the royal prerogative of mercy is a power subject to judicial review.[65] Naturally, the pardon power is exercised within the mindset of central government decision-making, with the criteria used to exercise the power once termed 'as long as the Chancellor's foot'.[66] Following *Bentley*, however, it is accepted that—to obtain a pardon—applicants must demonstrate that they are 'morally and technically innocent'.[67]

With these current frameworks in mind, the second section explores common themes in the tensions that emerge in both the USA and E&W with regard to the exercise of the clemency/pardon power to remedy wrongful conviction.

Common Themes of Analysis

The common themes explored in this section are: (1) eligibility and standards of proof; (2) transparency and reviewability; and (3) political will. Within each theme, the authors provide a flavour of the kinds of issues that might present challenges for the use of the clemency/pardon power to relieve wrongful conviction in the USA and E&W.

61 *de Freitas v Benny* [1976] AC 239, 247 per Lord Diplock.
62 Schweppe (n 51) 218.
63 CAA 1995, s 16.
64 It has seemingly only been exercised recently in 2009 (Dr Alan Turing) and in 2014 (Michael Shields). Prior to this, the only posthumous free pardon was granted to Timothy Evans in 1966. See Simon Hughes, 'Prerogative of Mercy: Written Question—221301' (*UK Parliament*, 20 January 2015) <https://www.parliament.uk/business/publications/written-questions-answers-statements/written-question/Commons/2015-01-20/221301/> accessed 8 July 2018.
65 *Bentley* (n 10) 363.
66 Ibid., 353–366 (Watkins LJ).
67 *Shields* (n 40); *R v James Hanratty (Deceased)* [2002] EWCA Crim 1141.

Eligibility and Standards of Proof

Applicants in both the USA and E&W must, first, be eligible to apply for clemency/pardon. Second, they must satisfy the relevant procedure's standard of proof. A common theme across the USA and E&W is the presence of challenging standards during these early stages.

In both jurisdictions, there is a general need to exhaust other legal remedies before applying.[68] Austin Sarat, for example, describes clemency in the USA as 'the court of last resort'.[69] Although individuals in E&W can apply to the Justice Secretary at any time, he or she appears reluctant to consider an application absent the applicant having utilised the appellate process, or the CCRC referring the case to the Ministry of Justice.[70] The main government services website underscores the narrow application of the pardon power, stating 'pardon is only normally granted when the person is innocent of the offence and where a request has been made by someone with a vested interest such as a family member'.[71] Further, the courts have determined an applicant's innocence must be both moral *and* technical.[72]

In the USA, on the other hand, reluctance towards granting innocence-based applications is evident. The practical approach of some states underscores the rarity of a clemency grant on the basis of innocence. Georgia,[73] Virginia,[74] and Wisconsin[75] provide examples of this. High eligibility thresholds are also evident across the USA. For instance, qualification criteria examples include the need for applicants to purchase an application form;[76] serve certain

68 For the USA, see *Herrera* (n 7) 412 ('historic remedy for preventing miscarriages of justice where judicial process has been exhausted'); for E&W, see *Shields* (n 40) para 23, 25.

69 Austin Sarat, 'Memorializing Miscarriages of Justice: Clemency Petitions in the Killing State' (2008) 42 Law & Society Review 183, 185.

70 This is evident from the few pardons granted, and more generally in *Shields* (n 40).

71 Ministry of Justice and The Rt Hon Chris Grayling MP (n 41).

72 *Bentley* (n 10).

73 Georgia State Board of Pardons and Paroles, 'Annual Report 2006' (*Georgia State Board of Pardons and Paroles*, 2006) <https://web.archive.org/web/20170130205836/http://pap.georgia.gov/sites/pap.georgia.gov/files/Annual_Reports/06Annual_Report.pdf> accessed 30 January 2019: 'A pardon can be granted in two instances. The first, and the most rare, is if an individual proves his or her complete innocence of the crime for which he or she was convicted.'

74 Kelly Thomasson, 'Absolute Pardons' (*Secretary of the Commonwealth)* <https://www.commonwealth.virginia.gov/judicial-system/pardons/absolute-pardons/> accessed 6 July 2018: 'An absolute pardon may be granted when the Governor is convinced that the petitioner is innocent of the charge for which he or she was convicted … Absolute pardons are rarely granted.'

75 State of Wisconsin: Office of the Governor, 'Application for Executive Clemency' (*recordgone.com*) <http://www.recordgone.com/templates/default/pdf/Wisconsin-Pardon-Application.pdf> accessed 27 January 2019: 'Executive clemency is an extraordinary measure and is rarely granted'.

76 For example, see Pennsylvania's procedure: Pennsylvania Board of Pardons, 'How to Obtain an Application' (*PA.gov*) <https://web.archive.org/web/

portions of their sentence before being able to apply;[77] and being subject to disqualification criteria, such as being precluded from the application procedure if they have certain 'marks' on their institutional record,[78] or if their conviction is based on a guilty plea.[79]

In both the USA and E&W, eligible applicants must satisfy certain standards to obtain relief. These standards can be demanding, reflected in their phrasing. Various US states showcase such practice. Examples include Washington (requiring 'extraordinary cases');[80] South Dakota (requiring applicants to show 'substantial evidence' indicating a miscarriage of justice);[81] Tennessee (also requiring 'clear and convincing evidence' that the applicant 'didn't commit the crime');[82] Connecticut (requiring applicants to 'describe and submit evidence of specific extraordinary circumstances or specific exemplary conduct supporting the request for clemency');[83] and Wisconsin (requiring the need for clemency be 'significant and documented').[84] These are high burdens to satisfy, and, interestingly, not burdens shared by other applicants requesting other forms of clemency in these states.

The phrasing of the standard in E&W also reflects a high burden. The current standard is that the applicant be 'morally and technically innocent of the crime.'[85] The interpretation of this standard is particularly challenging. For instance, the standard—as conceived in *Bentley*—is silent on whether moral and technical innocence should be judged on *current* standards of criminal liability and procedure, or by the standards of the past (i.e., those that existed *at the time of the conviction*).

20180621042812/http://www.bop.pa.gov/Purchase-an-Application/Pages/How-to-Obtain-an-Application.aspx> accessed 9 December 2019.

77 Cooper and Gough (n 4) 85–86.

78 Ibid. Procedures that require minimum serves for eligibility showcase the conceptual tension between clemency/pardon and innocence. Clemency typically applies when there is something to forgive—and the requirement of minimum serves is a way of re-enforcing that—through requiring the applicant to be subject to punishment (for a certain amount of time) for their crime. However, in reality, the right to punish arguably does not apply because the applicant is innocent. Disqualifications such as guilty pleas are also particularly troublesome for innocents, as evidence shows innocent people do admit to crimes they have not committed.

79 Ibid.

80 Revised Code of Washington s 9.94A.885.

81 South Dakota Administrative Rules, rule 17:60:05:12.

82 2010 Tenessee Code, 40–27–109; 'Application for Exoneration' (*State of Tennessee Board of Paroles*) <https://www.tn.gov/content/dam/tn/boardofparole/documents/BOP_Exoneration_Application-BP_0247.pdf> accessed 8 July 2018.

83 State of Connecticut Board of Pardons and Paroles, 'Information and Instructions for New Clemency Form' (*CT.gov*, 2019) <www.ct.gov/bopp/cwp/view.asp?A=4331&Q=508208> accessed 8 July 2018.

84 State of Wisconsin: Office of the Governor, 'Application for Executive Clemency' (*recordclearing.org*) <http://www.recordclearing.org/wp-content/forms/Wisconsin-Pardon-Application.pdf> accessed 8 July 2018.

85 *Bentley* (n 10) 356.

This question of which temporal standards apply is important. If a person was properly convicted of a criminal offence in the past because it was perceived as conduct warranting criminal liability, but that conduct is no longer considered to be criminal presently due to society's evolving moral compass, can he or she realistically seek pardon via the Justice Secretary? Although the Court of Appeal determined in the case of James Hanratty[86] that it *could* look at how changes in standards affect appeals against convictions (and did so in that case in relation to procedural developments),[87] the Court also cautioned that 'there had to be exceptional circumstances to justify the expenditure of resources on [a large scale], including the Court of Appeal, on a case of this age' (the case dated back to 1961).[88]

Despite the Court of Appeal's preparedness to consider changing standards in a procedural context, other cases—most infamously that of Dr Alan Turing—have demonstrated inclinations towards favouring standards of the past. Turing—the great Enigma-solving World War II Hero—was convicted in E&W of the offence of 'gross indecency' because of his homosexuality in 1952. Turing committed suicide in 1954, following his punishment of chemical castration.[89] In 2009, long after laws criminalising homosexuality were abolished, Turing received a formal apology from Prime Minister Gordon Brown for the mistakes of previous governments.[90] However, a pardon was not forthcoming. The exercise of the pardon power was seemingly to be considered through the lens of the 1950s, a time when Turing's conduct was generally perceived as morally and technically criminal. As Crispin Blunt has commented, a long-standing policy of government was not to exercise the royal prerogative of mercy where a person was 'correctly convicted under the laws that existed at the time'.[91] The more accepting standards of the twenty-first century were not immediately seized upon. Turing was eventually posthumously pardoned in 2013.[92]

The demand for both moral *and* technical innocence by the E&W standard is also challenging. A line of case law from the Court of Appeal (arising from CCRC referrals including *Bentley*, *Hanratty*, and *Shields*)—although not

86 *Hanratty* (n 67). For example, in *Hanratty*, the Court of Appeal were prepared to consider that Hanratty, suspected of rape and murder in 1961, did not receive the benefit of procedural safeguards presently in place for people suspected of crime.

87 Ibid., para 95.

88 Ibid., para 215.

89 'Alan Turing's Homosexual Court Files go on Display' (*BBC*, 23 September 2016) <https://web.archive.org/web/20180731092511/https://www.bbc.co.uk/news/uk-england-manchester-37443639> accessed 30 January 2019.

90 Gordon Brown, 'Gordon Brown: I'm Proud to Say Sorry to a Real War Hero' (*The Telegraph*, 10 September 2009) <https://www.telegraph.co.uk/news/politics/gordon-brown/6170112/Gordon-Brown-Im-proud-to-say-sorry-to-a-real-war-hero.html> accessed 8 July 2018.

91 HC Deb 27 June 2012, vol 547, cols 126WH-127WH.

92 'Royal pardon for Code-Breaker Alan Turing' (*BBC*, 24 December 2013) <https://www.bbc.co.uk/news/technology-25495315> accessed 8 July 2018.

directly concerned with the pardon power—is instructive to interpreting this standard. This is because it informs debate on the meaning of 'innocence' in E&W.

An example is the case of Ruth Ellis, who was executed in 1955, and the last woman to be hanged in the UK. Ellis killed her lover in a 'jealous rage',[93] and did not appeal her murder conviction or death sentence.[94] Her family, however, sought posthumous relief for her. The CCRC referred Ellis's case to the Court of Appeal in 2003, where it was argued that Ellis had suffered from 'battered wife syndrome' and—in light of current law—should have her murder conviction substituted with manslaughter.[95] This is because Ellis would have been able to—under current law—avail herself of the defences of provocation and/or diminished responsibility.[96] At the time of Ellis's crime, provocation was narrowly construed and diminished responsibility did not exist.[97] However, the Court of Appeal rejected the referral and was unconvinced of Ellis's innocence in spite of what could be modern-day technical innocence of murder. The Court felt it was not in the interests of justice to engage in a hypothetical discussion about whether a jury today would reach a different conclusion on new psychiatric evidence about domestic abuse and was forthright in its refusal to engage with arguments about whether Ellis should have been spared execution.[98] Kay LJ called the case 'without merit'[99] compared to others, and cited *Hanratty's* case.[100] Kay LJ demonstrated particular concerns about using limited resources to unpick cases like Ellis's.[101]

93 'Crowd Outside Prison Appeals for Mrs Ellis' (*The Guardian*, 13 July 2009) <https://www.theguardian.com/theguardian/2009/jul/13/from-archive-ruth-ellis-hanging> accessed 8 July 2018.
94 *Ruth Ellis v R* [2003] EWCA Crim 3556, para 90.
95 Ibid.
96 Ibid, para 38, 51.
97 Diminished responsibility was not introduced until two years after the events in Ellis's case took place, with the passing of the Homicide Act 1957.
98 *Ellis* (n 94) para 89.
99 Ibid., para 89.
100 Ibid., para 90: 'This case is, therefore, quite different from a case like [Hanratty] where the issue was whether a wholly innocent person had been convicted of murder. A wrong on that scale, if it had occurred, might even today be a matter for general public concern, but in this case there was no question that Mrs Ellis was other than the killer and the only issue was the precise crime of which she was guilty.
101 Ibid., para 90: 'If we had not been obliged to consider her case we would perhaps in the time available have dealt with 8 to 12 other cases, the majority of which would have involved people who were said to be wrongly in custody. The Court of Appeal's workload is an ever-increasing one and recent legislation will add substantially to that load. Parliament may wish to consider whether going back many years into history to re-examine a case of this kind is a use that ought to be made of the limited resources that are available. The exercise of the CCRC's discretion in deciding whether to refer cases is one that is a frequent source of challenge by way of Judicial Review and it may be that an express power to consider

The general reluctance—in both jurisdictions—to broadly approach the application of the clemency/pardon power is not wholly surprising. The post-conviction relief arena is primarily driven by a need to safeguard both finality interests (such as preserving state resources) and institutional settlement (such as jury verdicts).[102]

Transparency and Reviewability

This sub-section considers issues related to the transparency of the relevant clemency/pardon power processes (i.e., the level of information known about the relevant process and associated decision-making), and the extent to which pardons are reviewable by the judiciary.

In E&W, details about how and why the pardon power is exercised are limited. There is no statutory requirement to maintain records of free pardons.[103] Likewise, there is little known about conditional pardons or remissions. As with free pardons, there was no requirement to maintain records of conditional pardons or remissions of sentence prior to 1 February 2013 and none have been recorded since that date.[104] Media reports are sometimes able to provide information. For example, media reports exist about the infamous remissions granted to 'drug barons' John Haase and Paul Bennett by the Home Secretary in 1996. Haase and Bennett, media reported, 'conned two royal pardons out of the highest powers in the land'.[105]

factors of this kind would enable the CCRC to take into account more readily the public interest in making its decision.'

102 Sarah L Cooper, 'Forensic Science Identification Evidence: Tensions Between Law and Science' [2016] J Philosophy Sci & L 1, 15–16; Andrew Chongseh Kim, 'Beyond Finality: How Making Criminal Judgments Less Final Can Further the "Interests of Finality"' [2013] Utah L Rev 561, 563 (preventing error, increasing certainty, and improving the quality of representation); Carrie Sperling, 'When Finality and Innocence Collide' in Sarah L Cooper (ed), *Controversies in Innocence Cases in America* (Ashgate 2014), 139, 144.

103 Ministry of Justice and The Rt Hon Chris Grayling MP (n 41).

104 Conditional pardons are no longer deemed necessary since the abolition of the death penalty, as they were used to remove the sentence of death rather than the fact of conviction. Condition pardon was last used posthumously, 40 years post execution, in the case of Derek Bentley.

105 Graham Johnson and Mark Townsend, 'How Drug Barons Won Royal Pardon in Jail Con' (*The Guardian*, 23 November 2008) <https://www.theguardian.com/uk/2008/nov/23/drug-barons-haase-bennett> accessed 9 December 2019; John Haase, Graham Johnson, and Mark Townsend, 'My Shock at Seeing John Haase on the Door at Pub' (*The Liverpool Echo*, 15 October 2008) <https://www.liverpoolecho.co.uk/news/liverpool-news/shock-seeing-john-haase-door-3469758> accessed 9 December 2019; Peter Kilfoyle, 'MR. John Hasse and MR. Paul Bennett—in the House of Commons at 8:06 pm on 25th November 2008' (*TheyWorkForYou*, 25 November 2008) <https://www.theyworkforyou.com/debates/?id=2008-11-25b.693.0> accessed 12 October 2018.

With limited information and records, it is difficult to determine both the frequency of the exercise of the royal prerogative of mercy, and the reasons behind decision-making. The Justice Secretary's policy is not formally promulgated, with the only widely known policy being that pardon is for cases of moral and technical innocence. Successive ministers have applied this standard in recent decades,[106] and the approach has been confirmed in government responses to applications for judicial review,[107] and in parliamentary debates.[108] Beyond this, the most extensive articulation about the substance of the power exists in the High Court's decision in *Bentley*.[109] In that case, the Court determined that the relevant minister could not fetter his discretion by employing a strict pardon policy, but must rather consider cases individually.[110] This reflects a comment by former Home Secretary, Herbert Gladstone, who said 'hard and fast rules' were undesirable, with 'numerous considerations—the motive, the degree of premeditation or deliberation, the amount of provocation, the state of mind … character and antecedents … and many other [factors]' being worthy of consideration.[111] Ultimately, the exercise of the power in E&W is dependent on the mindset of government. As such, it is susceptible to periodic change.

Transparency is further limited in the context of published reasoning. The Justice Secretary is not required to publish reasons for his/her decision to accept or reject a pardon application, although reasons have been published on occasion.[112] Again, there is limited information about reasoning, but the ruling in *Shields*[113] provides an example of where a Justice Secretary was considered wrong in his reasoning to not consider pardon. Shields was convicted of

106 *Bentley* (n 10) 352.
107 *Shields* (n 40).
108 HC Deb (n 91).
109 Bentley was hanged for capital murder in 1953. Bentley (19) and CC (16) were found trespassing at a warehouse by a police officer. The police officer was fatally shot, and evidence suggested Bentley was not the shooter. Bentley, however, was said to have shouted 'let him have it, Chris!' as the police officer approached the pair. There was a dispute about the interpretation of this phrase, and whether Bentley said it to encourage his accomplice to surrender the weapon or shoot it. At trial, the co-defendant, owing to his age, was sentenced to imprisonment and Bentley to death. Bentley's sister campaigned for Bentley to be pardoned on the basis that his death sentence was not proportionate to his crime. The Home Secretary (who, at the time, was responsible for considering the royal prerogative of mercy) declined to issue a free pardon for the murder conviction as he was not satisfied of Bentley's moral and technical innocence, although he did grant a conditional pardon in respect of the sentence of death (Com Deb 21 May 2004, vol 421, col 1281).
110 *Bentley* (n 10) 351F (argument on behalf of the applicant).
111 HC Deb 11 April 1907, vol 172, col 366.
112 *Shields* (n 40) para 8.
113 Ibid.

attempted murder in Bulgaria. His appeals in Bulgaria were unsuccessful despite conflicting evidence. In response to a referral from the CCRC, the Justice Secretary reasoned that he did not have jurisdiction to consider a pardon for Shields due to international law obligations, and the need for the UK to respect the competence of the Bulgarian legal process.[114] The Court of Appeal concluded the Justice Secretary did have the power to consider pardon on the basis the Justice Secretary was wrong in law to think international obligations precluded consideration of a pardon; remitting the decision back to him.[115] The narrow point of *Shields* is that if—due to an erroneous interpretation of law—a Justice Secretary refuses to consider a pardon application, his or her actions can be considered unlawful. However, it would be permissible if he or she refused consideration on the basis of a belief that the case did not meet the relevant criteria. Ultimately, *Shields* underscores a point previously made by the Privy Council that the pardon power is a matter solely in the discretion of the sovereign, and that a person has 'no legal right to have his case considered by the Home Secretary [now Justice Secretary] in connection with the exercise of the prerogative of mercy'.[116]

In E&W, *Bentley* first recognised that 'some aspects of the Royal Prerogative are amenable to the judicial process'.[117] *Shields* affirmed this. What standard applies to this review, however, depends on the nature of the complaint.[118] The general standard of review for decisions of government ministers is 'Wednesbury unreasonableness'.[119] This standard considers whether the decision taken by a public authority, such as the Justice Secretary, was so unreasonable that no reasonable authority could have come to it.[120] This standard is relatively deferential, and would typically be used for challenges based on illegality or irrationality. If the complaint alleges a human rights breach, the applicable standard is one of proportionality, namely whether the state's interference was proportional to achieving the relevant legitimate aim.[121] If the complaint involves a discernible promise made directly to the applicant, upon which the applicant has relied to his or her detriment, that is to say a legitimate expectation that is recognised in English public law, the standard of review is different yet again.[122]

114 Ibid., 352.
115 *Shields* (n 40).
116 *de Freitas* (n 61) 247.
117 *Bentley* (n 10) 363.
118 The intricacies of judicial review in E&W are complex, comprising numerous different grounds for review and different standards of review. For a useful overview, see Michael Fordham QC, *Judicial Review Handbook* (6th edn, Hart Publishing 2012).
119 *Associated Provincial Picture Houses Limited v Wednesbury Corporation* [1948] 1 KB 223.
120 Ibid., 234.
121 *R v Ministry of Defence, ex parte Smith* [1996] QB 517.
122 *R v North and East Devon Health Authority, ex parte Coughlan* [2001] QB 215.

In the USA, similar limitations in terms of transparency and appellate review exist. The transparency of state procedures can be hampered by a lack of substantive published reasoning, a lack of record-keeping, and broad confidentiality rules. For instance, some states do not require decision-makers to publish reasons for their clemency decisions, whereas others publish bare outcomes, but do not embellish with reasons. In some states, grants of clemency attract the publication of reasons, but rejections do not.[123] There are also examples of a lack of general record-keeping,[124] and confidentiality rules 'can extend to internal processes, decision-making, inmate files, board member deliberations, and bespoke reports about applicants'.[125] Although maintaining certain levels of confidentiality is important to protect the privacy of participants, and to encourage candid and informed discussion and decision-making, it can also shield irrational decision-making and/or other forms of abuse of process from public view. Considering the error-correction function clemency proceedings have, these transparency issues can combine to 'shield the inadequate assessment of innocence claims from appropriate scrutiny'.[126] This is troublesome given clemency's 'unique and critical functions'.[127] The power's application should be 'clear, evenhanded, and transparent'.[128] The meaningful publication of reasons, in particular, would allow scrutiny of whether a clemency decision is principled, reasonable, and fair.[129] Transparency can—in effect—act as an antiseptic.[130]

With regard to appellate review, Heise considers that clemency proceedings do not 'readily lend themselves to judicial supervision or review'.[131] In *Woodard*, SCOTUS determined clemency proceedings to be outside of the trial and adjudicatory process, and, thus, not 'the business of courts'.[132] As Chief Justice Rehnquist wrote, 'pardon and commutation decisions have not traditionally been the business of courts; as such, they are rarely, if ever, appropriate subjects for judicial review'.[133] Despite this, a majority of justices agreed in *Woodard* that minimal procedural due process protections attach to clemency proceedings.[134] Justice O'Connor reasoned, '[j]udicial intervention might, for

123 Cooper and Gough (n 4) 74–78.
124 Ibid., 79–81.
125 Cooper (n 23) 97.
126 Ibid., 98.
127 Heise (n 35) 987.
128 Ibid.
129 Kathleen Dean Moore, 'Pardon for Good and Sufficient Reasons' (1993) 27 University of Richmond Law Review 281, 281.
130 Leona D Jochnowitz, 'Public Access to State Clemency Petitions' (2008) 44 Criminal Law Bulletin 176, 176.
131 Heise (n 35) 965–966.
132 *Woodard* (n 31) 284 (quoting *Connecticut Bd. of Pardons v Dumschat* 452 US 458 (1981), 464).
133 Ibid., 276 (quoting *Connecticut Bd. of Pardons v Dumschat* 452 US 458 (1981), 464).
134 Ibid., 272–288.

example, be warranted in the face of a scheme whereby a state official flipped a coin to determine whether to grant clemency, or in a case where the State arbitrarily denied a prisoner any access to its clemency process'.[135] Justice Stevens concurred, commenting that the constitution could not properly tolerate clemency processes 'infected by bribery, personal or political animosity, or the deliberate fabrication of false evidence'.[136]

Subsequently, applicants have alleged breaches of *Woodard*'s minimal due process standard in various ways.[137] This includes arguments that state proceedings: do not adequately facilitate access to and/or the assessment of potentially exculpatory evidence[138] or assist with the preparation of clemency applications;[139] comprise procedural inadequacies (such as a lack of notice, hearings, transparency, and compliance with state imposed procedures);[140] and involve state officials who have engaged in inappropriate conduct[141] and/or lack impartiality.[142] These claims have largely been rejected, with courts taking a very narrow approach towards what constitutes a breach of minimal due process.[143] As courts themselves have observed, presenting a successful claim is a 'steep hill to climb'[144] and it is a 'rare case that presents a successful due process challenge to clemency procedures'.[145]

That said, there are a few examples of judicial sensitivity to *Woodard*-based challenges (though they do not typically go hand in hand with a successful claim). This includes where there has been active interference by the state with a prisoner's access to the clemency system;[146] non-compliance with state law, regulations and/or policy pertaining to clemency proceedings by a state

135 Ibid., 289 (O'Connor J, concurring).
136 Ibid., 290–291 (Stevens J, concurring in part and dissenting in part).
137 Cooper and Gough (n 4) 95–109; Cooper (n 23) 63–74.
138 For example, *McKithen v Brown* [2008] 565 F Supp. 2d 440 (US).
139 For example, *Turner v Epps* [2012] 460 F App'x 322, 330 (US); *Lewis v State Dept. of Corrections* (07/28/2006) sp-6030, 139 P3d 1266, 1268–69 (Alaska, US); *Baze v Parker* 632 F.3d 338, 342 (6th Cir. 2010) (US).
140 For example, *Faulder v Texas Bd. of Pardons & Paroles* 178 F.3d 343 (1999) (US); *Faulder v Texas Board of Pardons & Paroles* 527 US 1017 (1999); *Kormondy v Scott* 135 S. Ct. 1028 (Mem) (US); *Fugate v Georgia Board of Pardons & Paroles* 536 US 980 (US); *Lee v Hutchinson* 137 S. Ct. 1623 (Mem) (US); *Lee v Hutchinson* 854 F.3d 978 (US); *Sepulvado v La. Board of Pardons & Parole* 171 Fed App'x 470, 2006 WL 707024 (US).
141 For example, *Parker v State Bd. of Pardons & Paroles* 275 F.3d 1032 (US), and *Gilreath v State Bd. of Pardons & Paroles* 273 F.3d 932 (US).
142 For example, *Gardner v Garner* 383 Fed App'x 722 (US), 724; *Duvall v Keating* 162 F.3d 1058 (US), 1060; *Anderson v Davis* 279 F.3d 674 (US), 675; *Link v Nixon* 562 US 1209, 79 USLW 3474 (US), 1; *Roll v Carnaham* 225 F.3d 1016 (US), 1017; *Bacon v Lee* 549 S.E. 2d 840 (US), 849; *Schad v Brewer* 732 F.3d 946 (US).
143 Cooper (n 23) 82 ('challenges to *Woodard*'s minimal due process standard seldom trigger judicial intervention despite the exposure of troublesome practices').
144 *Lee v Hutchinson* 854 F.3d 978 (US), 981.
145 *Noel v Norris* 336 F.3d 648 (US), 649.
146 *Young v Hayes* 218 F.3d 850 (US), 851.

authority;[147] a denial of access to an 'updated' clemency consideration;[148] use or reliance upon admittedly false information, or a 'fundamentally flawed' decision-making process;[149] and/or a lack of judicial interrogation of a decision-maker's overt bias.[150] Ultimately, however, it is clear that *Woodard's* requirements really are minimal.[151] The courts' general approach is to lightly scrutinise clemency proceedings, and require the states to provide limited procedural substance. Considering the purported error-corrective function of clemency in the USA, this is troubling. A broader approach to *Woodard* would arguably be more appropriate.

Political Will

As the pardon/clemency power is exercised by elected and/or nominated state officials, it has an inherently political nature. This has long been the case. For example, early English monarchs granted pardons in exchange for funds, and to build armies.[152] In the USA—in the early years of the Republic—clemency was used to ease the fall-out from unpopular increases in federal taxation and the centralisation of power.[153] As Cooper has previously concluded:

> [P]olitical expediency appears to be the traditional, primary function of clemency … [the] clemency power has never truly been a power of legal significance, but rather one controlled by the need for political expedience. Clemency decisions are vulnerable to political pressures and agendas, both of which can trump goals concerned with justice and accuracy.[154]

The tradition of exercising pardon/clemency for political expediency rather than error correction can, to some extent, explain the struggles (as explored

147 *Lee* (n 144) 986. Kelly, Circuit Judge dissenting: 'I conclude that the lack of notice in combination with the other statutory violations—such as the shortened period to prepare applications, the reduction in the hearing time, and the impossibility that the Governor could act on the recommendation of a grant of clemency in the time allotted—create a significant possibility that the appellants can succeed in showing that the procedure followed in rendering their clemency decisions was wholly arbitrary.'

148 *Mann v Palmer* 713 F.3d 1306 (US), 1318.

149 *Fugate v Bd. of Pardons & Paroles* 536 US 980, 123 S. Ct. 15 (Mem) (US), 2.

150 *Parker v State Bd. Of Pardons & Paroles* 275 F.3d 1032 (US), 1034 and 1037 (Special concurrence of Circuit Judge Barkett).

151 Heise (n 35) 966 ('Lower federal courts have taken [*Woodard*'s] "procedural minimalism" approach to heart').

152 Stanley Grupp, 'Some Historical Aspects of the Pardon in England' (1963) 7 The American Journal of Legal History 51, 59.

153 Cooper and Gough (n 4) 65; PS Ruckman Jr, 'Policy as an Indicator of "Original Understanding": Executive Clemency in the Early Republic (1789–1817)' (*Rock Valley College*, 2018) <http://www.rvc.cc.il.us/faclink/pruckman/pardoncharts/Paper7.pdf> accessed 7 July 2018.

154 Cooper (n 23) 94.

above) encountered by systems trying to use it as an error-correction tool. Simply put, the power was not built to—at least primarily—shoulder a corrective justice function.[155]

One particular anxiety about the political nature of pardon/clemency in E&W and USA is that, due to concerns about political ramifications, decision-makers can be overly cautious about exercising the power. In E&W, the Alan Turing pardon saga reflects such caution. As aforementioned, despite Turing's heroic achievements and the general ill feeling about how he was criminalised for his homosexuality, Turing's posthumous pardon was not straightforward. In fact, Parliament debated the political merits of pardoning him.[156] Even when a pardon was provided, the Justice Secretary underscored its rarity, stating: 'uniquely on this occasion a pardon has been issued without [the moral and technical innocence] requirement having been met, reflecting the exceptional nature of Alan Turing's achievements'.[157] Lord Quirk pointed out the absurdity of needing to debate a pardon for Turing, saying:

> None of us in this debate can do more than merely outline the vast amount which the world at large owes to this young man. No one can remotely guess how much more we would have owed to him if he had become an old man. I end by noting something surely perverse, if constitutionally sound enough, about this Bill. It would grant Alan a pardon, when surely all of us would far prefer to receive a pardon from him.[158]

Notably, thousands of men have since been pardoned under the so-called 'Turing's Law'.[159] Still, similar frictions recently emerged in relation to whether the Suffragettes should be posthumously pardoned for convictions

155 Ibid., 55.

156 HC Deb (n 91); HL Deb 19 July 2013, vol 747.

157 Steven Swinford, 'Alan Turing Granted Royal Pardon by the Queen' (*The Telegraph*, 24 December 2013) <https://www.telegraph.co.uk/history/world-war-two/10536246/Alan-Turing-granted-Royal-pardon-by-the-Queen.html> accessed 8 July 2018.

158 Cooper (n 23).

159 Owen Bowcott, 'UK Issues Posthumous Pardons for Thousands of Gay Men' (*The Guardian*, 31 January 2017) <https://www.theguardian.com/world/2017/jan/31/uk-issues-posthumous-pardons-thousands-gay-men-alan-turing-law> accessed 8 July 2018; Ministry of Justice and Sam Gyimah, 'Thousands Pardoned under "Turing's Law"' (*Gov.uk*, 31 January 2017) <https://www.gov.uk/government/news/thousands-officially-pardoned-under-turings-law> accessed 9 December 2019.

Mass pardons are not unknown. The Armed Forces Act 2006, for example, granted pardons to 306 men from around the British Empire who were executed for several offences including 'cowardice' during WWI.

stemming from their protests against women being denied the right to vote.[160] The issue was debated in Parliament without a definitive conclusion.[161]

In the USA, cautious decision-making is evident at both federal and state levels. Federal administrations have placed restrictions on clemency applications,[162] and there has been a noticeable trend toward presidents employing the federal clemency power sparingly.[163] However, President Obama engaged in a 'clemency initiative' in efforts to relieve drug crime offenders from harsh sentences,[164] and provided a record number of pardons towards the end of his presidency.[165] Since taking office, President Trump has engaged in controversial use of the federal clemency power too,[166] including a meeting with celebrity Kim Kardashian West to discuss the case of Alice Marie Johnson, whose sentence he later commuted.[167] Reports in July 2018 noted President Trump had 'pardoned slightly fewer people than most recent presidents at this stage of a presidency',[168] and his pardon practices have been labelled as 'heavily politicised'.[169]

At the state level, use of the clemency power can stall political careers. As Kobil explains, 'more common than outright removal from office is the toll that the exercise of the clemency power has taken on the political careers of various governors, which in turn has affected the way in which the clemency

160 Kate McCann, 'Amber Rudd Agrees to Consider Pardons for Jailed Suffragettes as UK marks 100th anniversary of right to vote' (*The Telegraph*, 6 February 2018) <https://www.telegraph.co.uk/news/2018/02/05/suffragettes-jailed-should-pardoned-100th-anniversary-right/> accessed 8 July 2018.

161 HC Deb 6 February 2018, vol 635.

162 Charles Clark, 'Reagan Parsimonious in Use of Pardon Power' (1984) 42 Cong. Q. 2878, 2878.

163 Cooper (n 23) 92–93.

164 Gregory Korte, 'Obama Grants 78 Pre-Christmas Pardons in Last-Minute Clemency Push (*USA Today*, 19 December 2016) <https://eu.usatoday.com/story/news/politics/2016/12/19/obama-grants-78-pre-christmas-pardons/95615810/> accessed 7 July 2018; Rachel E Barkow and Mark Osler, 'Designed to Fail: The President's Deference to the Department of Justice in Advancing Criminal Justice Reform' (2017) 59(2) William & Mary Law Review 387, 434–438.

165 Ibid.

166 Julia Carrie Wong and Lauren Gambino, 'Donald Trump Pardons Joe Arpaio, Former Sheriff Convicted in Racial Profiling Case' (*The Guardian*, 26 August 2017) <https://www.theguardian.com/us-news/2017/aug/25/donald-trump-joe-arpaio-pardon-arizona-sheriff> accessed 7 July 2018.

167 Clark Mindock, 'Trump Commutes Life Sentence for Alice Johnson after Kim Kardashian White House Visit' (*The Independent*, 6 June 2018) <https://www.independent.co.uk/news/world/americas/us-politics/alice-johnson-kim-kardashian-trump-white-house-visit-commutes-sentence-a8386601.html> accessed 29 October 2018.

168 Sam Wolfson, 'What Can We Learn from the People Trump has Pardoned So Far?' (*The Guardian*, 10 July 2018) <https://www.theguardian.com/us-news/2018/jun/07/trump-presidential-pardons-mueller-investigation> accessed 29 October 2018.

169 Ibid.

power has been used'.[170] Governors continue to find their exercising of clemency being used against them in election campaigns,[171] and feel political pressures interfere with their decision-making.[172] There is evidence that the use of administrative boards can provide some protection against these pressures. As Novak has written:

> Research from the United States suggests that an impartial committee, operating under regulated procedures and insulated from politics, is more likely to grant routine pardons than an elected official acting alone … the most frequent clemency grants occur in states with independent pardons boards.[173]

Caution is also evident from the practice of decision-makers in both jurisdictions to defer to the competence of the courts. For example, in E&W, the Justice Secretary is unlikely to grant a pardon where the case has been examined (and rejected) by the courts. In *Shields*, it was said that if legal redress in the Court of Appeal failed, 'the Secretary of State would not—leaving aside the case of Timothy Evans—now consider granting a pardon on the ground the Court of Appeal (Criminal Division) reached a wrong decision on the material before it'.[174] The Court further commented that 'in neither case could the Secretary of State conclude that the prisoner was morally and technically innocent without usurping the constitutional function of the courts'.[175] In the USA, Texas, for example, allows pardons when there is evidence of actual innocence or where a court has determined the person is innocent. However, to consider a pardon for innocence, the Texas Board of Pardons and Paroles requires either evidence of actual innocence from at least two trial officials, or else findings of fact and conclusions of law indicating actual innocence from a district judge.[176] Appellate court decisions have also urged clemency boards not to second-guess trial court determinations. For example, in *Corliss v Pennsylvania Board of Pardons & Parole*,[177] Corliss challenged the Board's decision to deny him parole, alleging that, in light of exculpatory DNA evidence, the denial violated his constitutional rights. The court rejected his

170 Kobil (n 28) 607.
171 Austin Sarat, *Mercy on Trial: What It Means to Stop an Execution* (Princeton University Press 2005) 66–68.
172 Cooper (n 23) 90–91 (noting, for example, former California Governor Pat Brown, who stated that political pressures had affected his decision-making).
173 Andrew Novak, 'Transparency and Comparative Executive Clemency: Global Lessons for Pardon Reform in the United States' (2016) 49 University of Michigan Journal of Law Reform 817, 828.
174 *Shields* (n 40) para 161.
175 Ibid.
176 'What Is a Pardon for Innocence?' (*Texas Board of Pardon and Paroles*, 13 February 2017) <http://www.tdcj.state.tx.us/bpp/exec_clem/Pardon_for_Innocence.html> accessed 8 July 2018.
177 *Corliss v Pennsylvania Board of Probation & Parole* (2006) WL 2927270.

claim, stating that Corliss had presented no basis for his conclusion that DNA evidence proved his innocence; the fact that the trial court properly rejected the DNA evidence as inconclusive illustrated that Corliss's claim was meritless.[178] As Pettys has commented:

> Once a court declares that the … standard [for review] has not been met, a governor fearful of controversy may find it irresistibly tempting to take cover behind the court's declaration … It certainly would not be the first time that a governor presented with a difficult clemency petition has sought shelter behind a court's refusal to grant the prisoner's request for relief.[179]

Conclusion

This chapter has explored the error-correction function of the clemency and pardon power, respectively, in the USA and E&W. In both jurisdictions, the power can be (and, in the view of the authors, it should be) employed to remedy wrongful conviction, but it is evident that both systems encounter significant challenges when exercising the power in this way. These challenges include high eligibility thresholds, with particularly demanding standards of proof; limited transparency at key junctures of proceedings, particularly with regard to the reasoning involved in decision-making; and the unavoidable influence of politics on decision-makers. A key thread that runs through all these challenges is the conceptual and practical challenges associated with defining, proving, and determining wrongful convictions within systems that naturally place value on safeguarding institutional settlement and finality interests.

The authors consider that the following ideas can contribute to forging better practices in both the USA and E&W (and, perhaps, beyond), when it comes to using the clemency/pardon power to remedy wrongful conviction. First, decision-makers should be supported to be better able to identify and evaluate innocence claims. This could be through standardised training or the use of expert advisors, for example. There is a significant body of research available about the causes of wrongful conviction, and decision-makers should be enabled to access, understand, and apply it. Second, efforts must be made to enhance transparency throughout clemency/pardon procedures. This includes requiring decision-makers to publish reasons for their decisions to accept and reject applications, and implementing mandatory record-keeping systems. Third, common-sense approaches to eligibility should be implemented. For instance, applicants should not be required to demonstrate rarity, uniqueness, or the extraordinary, in order to be eligible for relief. There is little

178 Ibid., 4.

179 Todd E Pettys, 'Killing Roger Coleman: Habeas, Finality, and the Innocence Gap' (2007) 48 William & Mary Law Review 2313, 2361.

clarity about what these terms demand. Moreover, such standards are counter-intuitive to existing knowledge about the broad presence of the causes of wrongful conviction. Procedures should be based on the ability of applicants to make meaningful and evidence-based representations that can satisfy achievable and sensible standards of proof, without prescriptions that are unrelated to the substance of their claims, such as the need to serve a minimum sentence before applying. Fourth, courts need a more pragmatic approach to interpreting relevant legal standards in each jurisdiction. In the USA, *Woodard*'s due process protection standard is seemingly too narrow, and, thus, unable to protect against even the most obvious procedural concerns. In E&W, *Bentley*'s requirement that applicant be both morally *and* technically innocent is evidently problematic, particularly in terms of the temporal lens to be applied by decision-makers.

Our final and most fundamental suggestion is that stakeholders—including clemency/pardon decision-makers, lawyers, scholars, law and policy-makers, and the public—collectively consider how society and legal systems view error. Legal systems are charged with maintaining public order and confidence. Naturally, therefore, concerns exist about how the error-correction function of the pardon/clemency power can undermine rational and established procedures and decision-making (such as those associated with trial judges, lawyers, jurors, and appellate courts), as well as finality interests, which include preventing frivolous claims, and safeguarding public resources. The error-correction function of pardon/clemency can—ultimately—publicly legitimise system errors, and, thus, threaten public order and confidence in our legal systems. Our suggestion is that stakeholders consider how systems and actors can become more comfortable with error, and, as a consequence, feel more empowered to support error-correction mechanisms, such as pardon/clemency. The authors consider that enabling stakeholders to become more comfortable with the reality that legal systems can and do generate error and, therefore, require embedded error-correction mechanisms, could ultimately lead to an increase in public order and confidence in our legal systems.

With growing concerns about the problem of wrongful conviction across both the USA and E&W, and the role envisaged for clemency and the prerogative of mercy in contributing to limiting that problem respectively, generating further conversations and research about the challenges explored in this chapter would be a worthwhile exercise for all interested stakeholders.

6 Mercy Litigation in the Commonwealth Caribbean

Arif Bulkan

Background and Statutory Framework

Executive clemency in the Caribbean, more commonly referred to as the exercise of mercy, is a specie of the royal prerogative that has survived in all of the former British colonies. At common law this power emerged in response to the draconian nature of criminal liability, in which capital offences proliferated and defences were limited. The results of that combination were harsh and unforgiving, and royal intervention helped to blunt its worst excesses.[1] Regarded as an 'act of grace', this power was dispensed by the sovereign like any other prerogative power, that is in her personal discretion.[2] It remained in this form long after the 1688 Revolution, and not until the mid-nineteenth century did it become constrained by the convention that it would be exercised on the advice of a member of the executive government, usually one of the Secretaries of State.[3] Today, the responsibility is that of the Justice Secretary, and the Crown is no longer personally involved in the dispensation of mercy.[4]

The genesis of this power contributed to some of its most problematic characteristics, such as its personal, discretionary, and secretive nature. Convenient to decision-makers, these enduring qualities have attracted both public disaffection and scholarly critique. The latter includes a rich literature interrogating the traditional non-reviewability of the power, in contrast to the benefits of transparency in decision-making. Of note is the closely reasoned analysis of BV Harris, which exposes the flaws of initial judicial reluctance to review an exercise of the prerogative and provides a model by which to assess

1 *R v Secretary of State for the Home Department, ex parte Bentley* [1993] 4 LRC 15, 20.

2 *De Freitas v Benny* (1975) 27 WIR 318, 322 (Lord Diplock).

3 *R v Secretary of State for the Home Department, ex parte Bentley* (n 1) 20.

4 Lord Faulks, 'Prerogative of Mercy: Written question – HL2637' (*UK Parliament*, 18 November 2014) <https://www.parliament.uk/business/publications/written-questions-answers-statements/written-question/Lords/2014-11-04/HL2637> accessed 9 December 2019; Hilaire Barnett, *Constitutional and Administrative Law* (9th edn, Routledge 2011) 101.

the appropriateness of its justiciability.[5] Others have pointedly assessed the dangers of unchecked executive discretion, noting its tendency to produce not just arbitrariness but 'self-dealing' and political manipulation.[6] In a meticulously researched analysis, Rob Turrell describes the arbitrariness that often accompanied the exercise of mercy, no doubt as a result of the wide discretion attendant on the power.[7] Drawing on examples from the grant of mercy in England, Canada, and South Africa, Turrell reveals how factors such as race and class played an outsized role in the award of mercy.

These insights are equally applicable to the Anglophone Caribbean, where the British framework was reproduced faithfully and inevitably led to the same fissures. Given the centrality and importance of the prerogative to the criminal justice system, these deficiencies spawned extensive litigation. However, the existing literature regarding the Caribbean has tended to focus on specific cases, invariably concerned with issues of justiciability or how this has intersected with concerns around certainty and predictability.[8] This chapter proposes to build on these approaches by undertaking a more comprehensive analysis. It examines not just the pervasive issue of justiciability, but also the gaps in procedure and substantive concerns regarding constitutionality, with the aim of providing a holistic view of the operation of the prerogative in the Caribbean. While statistics on usage would have provided a definitive base from which to commence, these were unavailable precisely because of the secrecy and bureaucracy that continue to surround the power.[9] Nonetheless, any potential limits to the discussion are hopefully balanced by the voluminous jurisprudence generated by this issue, which provides diverse

5 BV Harris, 'Judicial Review, Justiciability and the Prerogative of Mercy' (2003) 62 Camb Law J 631.
6 Andrew Novak, 'Transparency and Comparative Executive Clemency: Global Lessons for Pardon Reform in the US' (2016) 49 U Mich JL Reform 817; Minhazul Islam, 'Judicially Reviewing the President's Prerogative of Mercy: A Comparative Study' (2012) 7 Bangladesh Research Publications Journal 257.
7 Rob Turrell, 'It's a Mystery: The Royal Prerogative of Mercy in England, Canada and South Africa' (2000) 4(1) Crime, History & Societies 83.
8 David Pannick, 'Tempering Justice with Mercy' (1996) 4 PL 557; Louis Blom-Cooper, 'Justice and Mercy in the Caribbean' [1997] Crim LR 116; Christopher Gelber, '*Reckley (No. 2)* and the Prerogative of Mercy: Act of Grace or Constitutional Safeguard?' (1997) 60 MLR 572; Ivan Hare, 'Prerogative and Precedent: The Privy Council on Death Row' (2001) 60(1) Camb LJ 1; Dennis Morrison, 'The Judicial Committee of the Privy Council and the Death Penalty in the Commonwealth Caribbean: Studies in Judicial Activism' (2006) 30 Nova Law Review 403.
9 Part of the challenge of research in the Caribbean is the widely dispersed nature of individual countries. Thus, attempts to obtain information by correspondence in several territories were simply ignored. But even in places where access to bureaucrats was managed, notably in Guyana and Trinidad and Tobago, a plethora of obstacles were encountered—such as the reluctance of public servants to reveal information without the permission of superiors (the latter not accessible), claims that clemency statistics are not kept, and even the suggestion from one officer that the information be obtained by consulting old newspapers. No individual consulted was willing to divulge how decisions were taken, and ultimately it is the

experiences for close analysis. Accordingly, it is the body of case law and, to a lesser extent, publicly reported accounts of the exercise of the power, that inform this discussion.

Constitutions across the Commonwealth Caribbean all codified the power of executive clemency, yet despite its inclusion as part of the written law it is still (with only one exception)[10] referred to as the 'Prerogative of Mercy'. The constitutional scheme is fairly standard across the region, though as highlighted herein there are a few localised variations of note. Generally, this scheme covers three matters: one, a description of the specific terms of the power; two, the creation of an advisory body on mercy; and three, details as to the role and functions of that advisory body. As made clear by Lord Diplock in *de Freitas v Benny*,[11] the constitutional scheme was meant to capture both the law and practice governing the Prerogative of Mercy as it existed in the UK. Inevitably, however, the transition from unwritten British practice to codified text in Commonwealth Caribbean constitutions had both intended and unanticipated effects on the nature and scope of the power. In the nebulous space it ended up occupying—somewhere between historical personal discretion and modern constitutional requirement—its most persistent and complex ambiguities have flourished.

Regarding the first of the constitutional provisions, in the three Republics of Dominica, Guyana, and Trinidad and Tobago the power is exercisable by the president as head of state; elsewhere it is vested in the Governor-General who exercises it 'in Her Majesty's name and on Her Majesty's behalf'. The actual power is extensive, conferring on the head of state a broad discretion to do any of the following: grant a free (unconditional) or conditional pardon; delay the execution of any punishment, whether for a specified period or even indefinitely; substitute a less severe punishment; and finally, remit the whole or part of any punishment imposed for any offence whatever.[12] In Guyana and Trinidad and Tobago, the president can also pardon for criminal activity *before* charge.[13] This is not a personal power, for in exercising it the head of state (with only one exception) must act in conformity with advice from a specified

facts revealed in litigation, buttressed by newspaper reports, that provide the background for this discussion.

10 In Trinidad and Tobago it is the 'power of pardon': Constitution of Trinidad and Tobago 1976, s 87–88.

11 *De Freitas v Benny* (n 2) 323.

12 Constitution of Antigua and Barbuda 1981, s 84(1)(a)–(d); Constitution of the Bahamas 1973, s 90(1)(a)–(d); Constitution of Barbados 1966, s 78(1)(a)–(d); Constitution of Belize 1981, s 52(1)(a)–(d); Constitution of Dominica 1978, s 73 (1)(a)–(d); Constitution of Grenada 1973, s 72(1)(a)–(d); Constitution of Guyana 1980, s 188(1)(a)–(d); Constitution of Jamaica 1962, s 90(1)(a)–(d); Constitution of Saint Kitts and Nevis 1983, s 66(1)(a)–(d); Constitution of Saint Lucia 1978, s 74(1)(a)–(d); Constitution of Saint Vincent and the Grenadines 1979, s 65(1)(a)–(d); Constitution of Trinidad and Tobago 1976, s 87(2)(a)–(d).

13 Constitution of Guyana 1980, art 188(1)(a); Constitution of Trinidad and Tobago 1976, s 87(1).

minister or, in some instances, an executive body known as the 'Privy Council'.[14] The sole exception is Guyana, where uniquely the president—in whose office is merged the roles of both head of state and head of government—need only 'consult' with the designated minister.[15]

The body established to provide advice on the exercise of mercy is called either an Advisory Committee/Council or Privy Council. The specific composition of this entity varies, but generally it includes the minister designated to advise the head of state on the exercise of the power along with several other members as appointed by the head of state.[16] Invariably, the designated minister functions as the chair of the body, though in some instances it is the Governor-General who performs this role. The assumption has routinely been that the persons named to sit on this body will be 'distinguished citizens',[17] and in Belize the constitution actually dictates that members of the Advisory Council must be 'persons of integrity and high national standing'.[18] The term of membership is generally left up to the Governor-General when making the appointment, though a few countries prescribe both disqualifying conditions and outline circumstances in which membership may be rescinded.[19] In Guyana alone appointments to the Advisory Council are limited to a short period of three years.[20] More importantly, except for Belize,[21] the constitutions are generally silent on the procedure to be adopted by this body in discharging its functions, leaving it up to them to formulate their own guidelines.[22]

14 Constitution of Antigua and Barbuda 1981, s 84(2); Constitution of the Bahamas 1973, s 90(2); Constitution of Barbados 1966, s 78(2); Constitution of Belize 1981, s 52(2); Constitution of Dominica 1978, s 73(2); Constitution of Grenada 1973, s 72(2); Constitution of Jamaica 1962, s 90(2); Constitution of Saint Kitts and Nevis 1983, s 66(2); Constitution of Saint Lucia 1978, s 74(2); Constitution of Saint Vincent and the Grenadines 1979, s 65(2); Constitution of Trinidad and Tobago 1976, s 87(3).
15 Constitution of Guyana 1980, art 188(2).
16 Constitution of Antigua and Barbuda 1981, s 85(a)–(d); Constitution of the Bahamas 1973, s 91(a)–(c); Constitution of Barbados 1966, s 76(1); Constitution of Belize 1981, s 54(1); Constitution of Dominica 1978, s 74(1)(a)–(c); Constitution of Grenada 1973, s 73(1)(a)–(d); Constitution of Guyana 1980, s 189(1)(a)–(d); Constitution of Jamaica 1962, s 82(1); Constitution of Saint Kitts and Nevis 1983, s 67(1)(a)–(c); Constitution of Saint Lucia 1978, s 75(1)(a)–(d); Constitution of Saint Vincent and the Grenadines 1979, s 66(1)(a)–(c); Constitution of Trinidad and Tobago 1976, s 88(a)–(d).
17 *Reckley v Minister of Public Safety and Immigration (No 2)* [1996] AC 527, [18] (Lord Goff).
18 Constitution of Belize 1981, s 54(2).
19 Constitution of Dominica 1978, s 74(2)(a), 74(2)(b); Constitution of Grenada 1973, s 73(2); Constitution of Guyana 1980, s 189(2); Constitution of Saint Kitts and Nevis 1983, s 87(2); Constitution of Saint Lucia 1978, s 75(2); Constitution of Saint Vincent and the Grenadines 1979, s 66(2).
20 Constitution of Guyana 1980, s 189(3).
21 Constitution of Belize 1981, s 54.
22 Constitution of Antigua and Barbuda 1981, s 86(4); Constitution of the Bahamas 1973, s 92(4); Constitution of Barbados 1966, s 77(3); Constitution of Dominica

The third matter addressed in the constitutional scheme of mercy is the post-conviction process to be followed in relation to persons sentenced to death. Largely, this mirrors what formerly applied in England, commencing with a written report from the trial judge that must be furnished to the advisory body along with such other information, whether from the case or elsewhere, as deemed relevant by the designated minister. Armed with these reports or other information, the advisory body is required to meet in all capital punishment cases and then provide its advice to the designated minister.[23] In the majority of countries, the minister need not follow this advice.[24] But even though its advice may be non-binding, the committee's raison d'être was said to be that of a 'safeguard', given that ouster clauses simultaneously protected (or purported to protect) the minister's power from review.[25] In non-capital cases, the designated minister may, but is not required to, consult with this body before advising the head of state on the exercise of mercy.

Given mercy's role in mitigating the harshness of criminal liability, distinguishing it from the substantive criminal justice process is a challenge. Lord Bingham attempted to do so in the following terms:

> The administration of justice involves the determination of what punishment a transgressor deserves, the fixing of the appropriate sentence for the crime. The grant of mercy involves the determination that a transgressor need not suffer the punishment he deserves, that the appropriate sentence may for some reason be remitted.[26]

But this was perhaps clearer in theory, for in practice clemency has long been thrust into a more substantial role—as a constitutional safeguard,[27] to correct

1978, s 74(4); Constitution of Grenada 1973, s 73(4); Constitution of Guyana 1980, s 190(3); Constitution of Jamaica 1962, s 88(3); Constitution of Saint Kitts and Nevis 1983, s 67(4); Constitution of Saint Lucia 1978, s 75(4); Constitution of Saint Vincent and the Grenadines 1979, s 66(4); Constitution of Trinidad and Tobago 1976, s 89(4).

23 Constitution of Antigua and Barbuda 1981, s 86(1); Constitution of the Bahamas 1973, s 92(1); Constitution of Barbados 1966, s 78(3); Constitution of Belize 1981, s 53; Constitution of Dominica 1978, s 75(1); Constitution of Grenada 1973, s 74 (1); Constitution of Guyana 1980, s 190(1); Constitution of Jamaica 1962, s 91(1); Constitution of Saint Kitts and Nevis 1983, s 68(1); Constitution of Saint Lucia 1978, s 76; Constitution of Saint Vincent and the Grenadines 1979, s 67(1); Constitution of Trinidad and Tobago 1976, s 89(1).

24 Constitution of Antigua and Barbuda 1981, s 86(3); Constitution of the Bahamas 1973, s 92(3); Constitution of Dominica 1978, s 75(1); Constitution of Grenada 1973, s 74(1); Constitution of Guyana 1980, s 190(1); Constitution of Saint Kitts and Nevis 1983, s 68(1); Constitution of Saint Vincent and the Grenadines 1979, s 67(1); Constitution of Trinidad and Tobago 1976, s 89(3).

25 *Reckley v Minister of Public Safety and Immigration* (n 17) 18.

26 *Reyes v the Queen* (2002) 60 WIR 42, [44].

27 *Halsbury's Laws of England* (4th edn) vol 8(2), [824].

mistakes[28] or even function as a 'safety net' for those wrongly convicted.[29] Indeed, under international human rights law, the availability of mercy—at least for persons sentenced to death—is a guaranteed right, with Article 6(4) of the International Covenant on Civil and Political Rights expressly providing that 'Anyone sentenced to death shall have the right to seek pardon or commutation of the sentence'.[30]

Likewise, the widely acknowledged reality in the Commonwealth Caribbean, where until recently the penalty for murder was a mandatory sentence of death,[31] is that the prerogative of mercy functioned to sift out the worst of the worst cases deserving of execution.[32] And it is this evolved understanding of the prerogative which highlights a noticeable slippage between the characterisation of mercy and its application. If it functions to cure wrongful convictions or to individualise punishment, that sounds remarkably like the administration of justice as described by Lord Bingham. It hardly needs saying that it should not be left to uncertain, discretionary processes vested in the hands of an executive office-holder to vindicate innocence or ensure fairness, least of all where the punishment is irrevocable. Where mercy shoulders such an enormous responsibility, it would seem that an executive power has strayed far from its appropriate constitutional function. It is on these issues, along with the procedural dimension of the power, that this chapter will focus.

Justiciability

A direct consequence of its exalted pedigree and its historically personal, discretionary nature is that the grant (or not) of mercy has traditionally been unaccountable, even unreviewable, by the courts. For centuries, common law orthodoxy was that the courts could merely inquire into the existence and extent of prerogative powers, but not into the manner of their exercise,[33] and

28 *Thomas v Baptiste* (1999) 54 WIR 387, [2002] 2 AC 1, 3 WLR 249.
29 *Burt v Governor-General* [1993] 4 LRC 1, 9.
30 International Covenant on Civil and Political Rights (1976) 999 UNTS 171. See further Sangiorgio, this volume.
31 In the Commonwealth Caribbean, the death penalty now remains mandatory for murder only in Trinidad and Tobago. In Guyana, the mandatory feature in relation to convictions for murder was substantially restricted to certain categories of killing in 2010: Criminal Law (Offences) (Amendment) Act 2010 and it was subsequently extended in 2015 to a limited extent for 'acts of terrorism' which result in death: see Anti-Terrorism and Terrorist Related Activities Act 2015, No 15 of 2015, s 3(1)(a). In Barbados, the mandatory feature of the death penalty for murder was declared unconstitutional and struck down by the CCJ in 2018: *Nervais and Severin v the Queen* [2018] CCJ 19 (AJ). Everywhere else in the Caribbean, the mandatory death penalty was dismantled by the PC in a remarkable series of cases between 2002 and 2004 that struck down the mandatory aspect alone as a violation of the constitutional prohibition against inhuman and degrading punishments.
32 *Yasseen and Thomas v Attorney General* (1996) 62 WIR 98, 117–118.
33 Thomas Poole, 'UK-The Royal Prerogative' (2010) 8 ICON 146, 148; Barnett (n 4) 107.

it was not until 1984 that the House of Lords broke decisively with this tradition.[34] Common law non-justiciability was embraced by courts in the Caribbean. In the post-colonial period, one of the first cases to consider this issue was *de Freitas v Benny*,[35] where a condemned prisoner in Trinidad and Tobago sought access to the material furnished by the designated minister to the Advisory Committee on Mercy as well as the right to be heard by that Committee. It was argued that the Committee's functions were quasi-judicial in nature, so that any failure to grant those rights to the prisoner would contravene the rules of natural justice and infringe his right not to be deprived of life except by due process of law guaranteed under s 1(a) of the Constitution. The challenge was unsuccessful at every level. The Judicial Committee of the Privy Council ('PC'), Trinidad's final appellate court, held that the exercise of the prerogative of mercy is an executive act not subject to review or control by the courts. Further, the grant of mercy was purely discretionary, and the constitutional provisions to this effect did not vest the prisoner with any rights.

Delivering the judgment of the PC, Lord Diplock likened the exercise of mercy under the Constitution to what existed in England at common law, where it was in the personal discretion of the sovereign.[36] Lord Diplock added his now infamous assessment of the power, declaring that 'mercy is not the subject of legal rights. It begins where legal rights end.'[37] Under the practice that applied in the UK, a convicted person had no right to the consideration of his case by the Home Secretary, much less to see any of the information relied upon by the relevant officials in advising the sovereign. The same restrictions were held to apply in Trinidad and Tobago, even though the power and procedures around the granting of mercy had been codified in the country's supreme law. The PC noted, but dismissed, the requirement that in all capital cases the minister was obliged to consult with an Advisory Committee before tendering advice to the head of state on commutation. In its view, the fact that the minister did not have to follow any advice reinforced the discretionary nature of the power.

In hindsight, the weaknesses of this reasoning seem manifest, yet its authority endured for decades. It was reaffirmed as late as 1996 in *Reckley v Minister of Public Safety and Immigration (No 2)*,[38] an appeal from the Bahamas where virtually identical constitutional provisions on the prerogative of mercy were considered. There, the PC reiterated that the prerogative was a purely personal discretion vested in the minister, zeroing in on the point previously made by Lord Diplock that the minister was not bound to follow the advice of the Advisory Committee. Lord Goff added that this Committee would be constituted by 'men and women of distinction, whose presence, and

34 *CCSU v Minister for the Civil Service* [1985] LRC (Const) 948; [1985] AC 374.
35 *De Freitas v Benny* (n 2).
36 Ibid., 322.
37 Ibid.
38 *Reckley v Minister of Public Safety and Immigration* (n 17).

contribution, at the heart of the process will ensure that the condemned man's case is given, and is seen by citizens to be given, full and fair consideration'.[39] As such, there was no need for a supervisory role by the courts.

But even as the PC was clinging to this position in its overseas jurisdictions, elsewhere the need for accountability was gradually being acknowledged. In 1992, the Court of Appeal of New Zealand held that since the prerogative of mercy had come to play such an important role in the criminal justice system, it 'would be disposed to favour any form of increased judicial review that could help to prevent [injustices]'.[40] In that case there was no evidence to suggest that the common law safeguards had failed to protect the applicant, but in principle the court would exercise this power if necessary.

In so holding, New Zealand's court of appeal was building upon a foundation already laid by the English House of Lords. Earlier, in the landmark GCHQ case challenging Margaret Thatcher's use of a prerogative power to terminate the union membership rights of civil service employees working at the Government Communications Headquarters, the House of Lords unanimously held that powers exercised directly under the prerogative were not automatically immune from judicial review because of their source.[41] If the subject matter of a prerogative power is justiciable then the exercise of the power is open to judicial review in the same way as any statutory power. In his judgment Lord Roskill pointed to the artificiality of likening prerogative powers in modern times to absolute monarchical acts, given that they are performed by the sovereign on the advice of, and will be carried out by, the sovereign's ministers currently in power. In other words, such acts were really acts of the executive government, and to 'talk of that act as the act of the sovereign savours of the archaism of past centuries.'[42] Ironically, in that judgment Lord Roskill thought that certain prerogative powers, including the prerogative of mercy, would remain immune from judicial review—but this obiter proved unable to forestall further reform.

Almost a decade later, in *R v SSHD, ex parte Bentley*,[43] the *CCSU* principle of reviewability was extended to the prerogative of mercy. In *Bentley* the applicant had been campaigning for years to obtain a posthumous pardon for her brother, who had been executed for the murder of a police officer while the principal who carried out the shooting was spared the death penalty on account of his age. The Home Secretary refused to recommend a free pardon on the ground that the applicant's brother was technically guilty, but on the applicant's challenge, the Court of Appeal held that he had erred by failing to recognise that other forms of pardon were possible. Squarely confronting Lord Roskill's view in *CCSU* that the prerogative of mercy might be unreviewable,

39 Ibid., para 21.
40 *Burt* (n 29) 13.
41 *CCSU* (n 34).
42 Ibid., 1033 (Lord Roskill).
43 *R v Secretary of State for the Home Department, ex parte Bentley* (n 1).

Watkins LJ dismissed this as obiter and relied upon the subject matter of the power—as 'an important feature of [the] criminal justice system'—to underscore its amenability to scrutiny.[44]

These developments set the stage for the dismantling of *de Freitas*. The cocoon it had wrapped around the prerogative was first stripped off by the Guyana Court of Appeal,[45] which at the time was the final court for the country, in a decision cited by the Privy Council[46] when it too finally overruled *de Freitas*. Following suit and completing the picture in 2006 was the ruling of the Caribbean Court of Justice ('CCJ'),[47] this being the newly inaugurated appellate court set up by CARICOM heads of government and which was meant to replace the Privy Council as the apex court for the Anglophone Caribbean.[48] In all these decisions the historic immunity from review enjoyed by the prerogative of mercy was rejected, including in Barbados whose Constitution contained an ouster clause shielding the Barbados Privy Council from judicial inquiry into the performance of its functions.[49] Of interest in the respective judgments are the rationales proffered for departing from Lord Diplock's stance, particularly insofar as these frankly assessed the modern function of mercy.

Lord Diplock's argument that the constitutional scheme in Trinidad and Tobago merely reflected UK practice received the most unceremonious treatment in the Guyana Court of Appeal. Fitzpatrick JA thundered brusquely that:

> Guyana as a constitutional Republic should not adopt the same reverential attitude to the prerogative. Republics have, or should have, little truck with royal grace and favour which are founded in the arbitrary will of kings. And republican courts should be guided by republican principles.[50]

Consistently with this approach, Fitzpatrick JA finely dissected Lord Diplock's description of the power of mercy as a *personal discretion* of the sovereign. Adverting to the developments wrought by the *CCSU* case, Fitzpatrick JA noted that this power was now delineated in a written constitution. It had long been the case that once legislated, a prerogative power became subsumed by or

44 Ibid., 25–6.
45 *Yasseen* (n 32).
46 *Lewis and others v AG of Jamaica* (2000) 57 WIR 275.
47 *Joseph and Boyce v AG of Barbados* (2006) 69 WIR 104.
48 The CCJ was established on 14 February 2001 by the Agreement Establishing the Caribbean Court of Justice and inaugurated in 2005 with original jurisdiction in Caribbean Community law and final appellate jurisdiction for the region: *Revised Treaty of Chaguaramas Establishing the Caribbean Community, Including the CARICOM Single Market and Economy* (adopted 5 Jul 2001, in force 1 Jan 2006) 2259 UNTS 293. At the time of writing in 2018, its appellate jurisdiction is accepted only by Barbados, Belize, Dominica, and Guyana; the remaining countries continue to use the Privy Council as their final appellate court.
49 Constitution of Barbados 1966, s 77(4).
50 *Yasseen* (n 32) 15.

in the statute;[51] *a fortiori*, the scheme governing mercy could hardly be protected by sovereign immunity now that it was constitutionalised.[52] Indeed, only the year before *Yaseen* was decided, Georges CJ, another respected Caribbean jurist, observed as much in the Belize Court of Appeal, emphasising that the modern scope of the power was not coterminous with its historic form.[53] Obviously, now that the prerogative was delineated in a written, foundational instrument, it could hardly have survived in all its autocratic, imperial breadth.

By now, the writing was on the wall. Only a few years after upholding *de Freitas* in *Reckley (No 2)*, the PC revisited the issue in *Lewis v AG of Jamaica*.[54] There, it gave full force to the distinction between source and subject matter of a prerogative power that it had itself propounded long before. On behalf of the majority, Lord Slynn disparaged characterisations of the power as a personal one, firmly asserting that '*the act of clemency is to be seen as part of the whole constitutional process* of conviction, sentence and the carrying out of the sentence'.[55]

Of possibly even greater significance than the break with a fiction of a time long past was the renewed examination given to Lord Diplock's view on the distinction between mercy and legal rights, which had been so influential at one time. Multiple cases had already acknowledged that decisions tainted by errors of procedure would be reviewable;[56] in *Yaseen*, Fitzpatrick JA developed this theme by reference to the consequential function served by mercy. He pointed out that the procedure operates as a 'safety net' for those wrongly convicted and not just merely as a matter of grace, which accentuated the need for fair play.[57] Crucially, justiciability was concerned with procedure and not substance, for 'the manner in which it is exercised may pollute the decision itself'.[58]

In *Lewis* the majority continued this trend, noting that while 'on the merits there is no legal right to mercy, there is not the clear-cut distinction as to procedural matters between mercy and legal rights which Lord Diplock's aphorism that mercy begins where legal rights end might indicate'.[59] It was this need to ensure procedural fidelity and overall fair play that justified the ability of courts to review an exercise of the prerogative. In the CCJ, de la Bastide P and Saunders J, who delivered the leading judgment, grappled with this frontally, asserting that:

51 *AG v De Keyser's Royal Hotel* [1920] AC 508.
52 *Yasseen* (n 32) 116.
53 *Lauriano v AG* (1995) 47 WIR 74.
54 *Lewis* (n 46).
55 Ibid., 294, emphasis added.
56 For example, *R v Secretary of State for the Home Department, ex parte Bentley* (n 1).
57 *Yasseen* (n 32) 117.
58 Ibid.
59 *Lewis* (n 46) 293.

> Rooted though they be in language and literature, conceptual differences between mercy and justice cannot justify denying to a man under sentence of death, an enforceable right to have the decision whether he is to live or die arrived at by a procedure which is fair.[60]

The cumulative effect of these decisions was thus to remove all previous doubt as to justiciability of the prerogative power of mercy. Given the sensitive nature of the subject matter involved, no longer would its exercise be treated as the insulated, untouchable discretion of the head of state. Instead, it could be subject to judicial scrutiny to ensure that the procedures surrounding its exercise were fair. That said, however, the rationale of judicial review has not always been consistently articulated, which leaves some potential for much greater judicial activism than was probably contemplated. Indeed, there are statements in several of these very decisions which suggest a far more expansive basis for review. In *Bentley*, for example, Watkins LJ suggested that if the Home Secretary has been motivated in his decision by some personal status of the petitioner—identifying 'sex, race or religion'[61] as problematic bases—that would entitle the courts to interfere with his or her decision. Such a review, if conducted, would clearly go beyond mere procedure and involve scrutiny of the merits. In *Lewis*, Lord Slynn also dropped hints in this direction, warning that if the decision of the Jamaican Privy Council was taken in an 'arbitrary or perverse way (on the throw of a dice or on the basis of a convicted man's hairstyle) or is otherwise arrived at in an improper, unreasonable way' that would be grounds for judicial interference. Lord Slynn added that if the decision-making body were to be 'unconsciously biased', that too would provide grounds for intervention.[62] And in the CCJ, de la Bastide P and Saunders J in their joint judgment made reference to the need for compliance with the fundamental rights guaranteed in the constitution, though admittedly in the context of procedural propriety.[63]

These various examples tread a very fine line, insofar as scrutiny of the reasons for which a committee came to a decision necessarily involves scrutiny of its merits. It is entirely possible that this creeping jurisdiction asserted by courts is motivated by an understanding, however inchoate and unarticulated, that the power and responsibility of granting mercy as vested in the executive involves the dispensation of justice, a function which it is entirely ill-equipped (and constitutionally forbidden) to perform. This subject is taken up in the final section of this chapter.

60 *Joseph and Boyce* (n 47) para 39.
61 *R v Secretary of State for the Home Department, ex parte Bentley* (n 1) 26.
62 *Lewis* (n 46) 293.
63 *Joseph and Boyce* (n 47) [41].

The Processes around Pardon

In *Joseph and Boyce*, the leading judgment in the Caribbean Court of Justice noted that:

> Whether [a condemned person] is or is not ultimately put to death by the State depends, not just on the substantive exercise of the prerogative of mercy, but also on the procedures governing and leading up to its exercise. The quality and nature of the advice given to the Governor-General bear a direct relationship to the quality and nature of the process followed by the [Barbados Privy Council] in coming to its decision.[64]

In spite of the obvious logic of this position, the various Commonwealth Caribbean constitutions are largely silent on the procedures to be followed by advisory bodies, or for that matter even by the ultimate decision-maker. Aside from establishing advisory bodies and specifying how they are to be composed, the only other matter provided for is whether the advice they proffer is binding or not. As to procedure, the brevity of the Trinidad and Tobago provision is typical:

> Where an offender has been sentenced to death by any court for an offence … the Minister shall cause a written report of the case from the trial judge, together with such other information derived from the record of the case or elsewhere as the Minister may require, to be taken into consideration at a meeting of the Advisory Committee.[65]

Lack of legislative guidance in this regard has meant that across the region these bodies have struggled in carrying out their functions and, crucially, in striking the appropriate balance while doing so. The battle over judicial review of the ultimate grant of pardon, described above, was fought over two procedural matters, namely whether a condemned person has the right to see the judge's report and other information furnished to the committee and whether that person could make representations to it. In *de Freitas*, the PC answered both these questions in the negative, based on UK practice and the fact that the advisory committee in Trinidad and Tobago 'remains a purely consultative body without any decision-making power'.[66] When they reaffirmed this position two decades later in *Reckley (No 2)*, the PC made heavy weather of the 'distinguished' composition of the Advisory Committee and the fact that it would give every case 'full and fair consideration'.[67] Lord Goff expressed supreme confidence that if material favourable to the condemned man was not placed before them, those 'men and women of distinction' who

64 Ibid., [31].
65 Constitution of Trinidad and Tobago 1976, s 89(1).
66 *De Freitas v Benny* (n 2).
67 *Reckley v Minister of Public Safety and Immigration* (n 17) [18]–[21].

make up the Advisory Committee would inquire into this omission.[68] However, in eventually repudiating this stance in *Lewis*, the PC acknowledged that previous UK practice was irrelevant, particularly in light of increasing judicial recognition of the importance of following the rules of natural justice and fair play. The majority judgment accepted that there were 'compelling reasons' why *de Freitas* should be reversed—not only would this be the last chance of a condemned person to ensure that procedures are properly followed before execution, but the material furnished at the instance of the state could conceivably be incomplete, false, or even biased.[69] This outcome reflected the long overdue recognition of a well-established, mundane principle—simply, that process matters.

As remarkable as the concessions in *Lewis* were, in particular the realisation that skewed material could find its way before the committee, the ruling only addressed one aspect of the process. Even as many of the cases began to acknowledge the need for procedural propriety, they did not presume to dictate specifics. This left open a host of other questions surrounding the committees' work. How would hearings be conducted and would there be any ethical constraints? How soon after conviction should they be held? What period of notice, if any, would be given to the condemned person? Most importantly, would criteria be published to inform how the committees would be guided in their deliberations? The PC felt that the nature of their membership and insulation from the executive meant that they could be trusted to do the right thing,[70] but the not inconsiderable amount of litigation generated over the committees' work would show that to have been an overly sanguine view. As David Pannick QC frankly observed: 'the judges of the Privy Council well understand from their regular diet of capital cases from the Caribbean [that] there is no cause for complacency about the reasonableness and propriety of government action in this context'.[71] The issues discussed at greater length below, which concern various aspects of government action alluded to by Pannick, are useful not only because of what they say about reasonableness and propriety, but also because of the insight they provide into the sincerity of those involved and ultimate value of the process.

Timelines and Processes for Hearings

One pivotal aspect of the committees' work relates to the timelines followed by them. Their central function is to meet and consider the case of each person sentenced to death prior to advising the relevant minister whether that sentence should be carried out. The one thing dictated by law is that this process is mandatory in all capital cases. Yet, procedural irregularities of some

68 Ibid., [21].
69 *Lewis* (n 46) 292–293.
70 *Reckley v Minister of Public Safety and Immigration* (n 17) [21].
71 Pannick (n 8) 559.

magnitude have occurred in a succession of cases from across the region, enough for one to question, at a minimum, the judgment of the bodies involved. Time and again in multiple locations, advisory bodies have met even though legal processes surrounding the convictions had not yet been exhausted. Admittedly, many of these concerned international legal processes,[72] for which the necessity of waiting was vigorously contested and remained an uncertain obligation even after repeated judicial challenges. However, in some extraordinary cases, it would appear that advisory bodies met even before *domestic* appeals had been completed. In *Lewis*, for example, which dealt conjointly with several appeals, the first-named appellant (Neville Lewis) was convicted on 14 October 1994 and sentenced to death. His appeal against conviction was dismissed on 31 July 1995 and on 13 February 1996 the Jamaican Privy Council ('JPC') refused to recommend that the prerogative of mercy be exercised in his favour. But it was not until 2 May 1996 that he was refused special leave to appeal by the PC. This chronology means that the JPC met as constitutionally required and considered Lewis' case, declining to recommend mercy, even though at the time it did so in February 1996, his case had not yet been heard by Jamaica's final appellate court, the Privy Council. The substantive appeal was ultimately unsuccessful, but that fact is irrelevant as the JPC had no way of knowing this outcome in advance.

Similarly, Jeffrey Joseph and Lennox Boyce, the condemned men at the centre of the appeal heard by the CCJ in 2006,[73] had been convicted on 2 February 2001 and their appeals were dismissed by the Court of Appeal of Barbados on 27 March 2002. While their appeals to the PC were pending,[74] the Barbados Privy Council ('BPC') notified the men that it intended to meet pursuant to its obligations under s 78 of the Constitution of Barbados. The BPC met on the 24 June 2002 and advised against commutation, and two days later death warrants were read to the men. Bizarrely, all this took place even though their appeal was not heard by the PC for another two years, with the decision only given on 7 July 2004! Although both Joseph and Boyce filed applications to the Inter-American Commission on Human Rights on 3 September 2004, ten days later the BPC met again, recommending for the second time that the death sentences be carried out. Accordingly, death warrants were read to them again on 15 September 2004. Thus, as did its Jamaican counterpart, the advisory body in Barbados met and deliberated on the case of two convicted persons, even though the domestic criminal process was still ongoing.

Having fought for and obtained the right to make representations to the committee did not necessarily guarantee fair treatment of convicted persons. In

72 *Fisher v Minister of Public Safety and Immigration (No 2)* (1998) 53 WIR 27; *Higgs and Mitchell v Minister of National Security* (1999) 55 WIR 10; *Joseph and Boyce* (n 47); *Lewis* (n 46); *Thomas v Baptiste* (n 28).

73 *Joseph and Boyce* (n 47).

74 At that time, the CCJ had not yet come into existence.

the Trinidad and Tobago decision *Dottin et al. v Commissioner of Prisons*,[75] it was revealed that a letter was issued by the Mercy Committee on Pardon on Friday 10 June 2005 informing the four applicants that their cases would be considered on the following Monday, 13 June. In other words, the condemned men were given less than three days' notice—over a weekend no less—to prepare for the hearing that would help determine whether they would live or die. Compounding the abrupt notification was the fact that only a few days before it was sent, the Attorney General had declared in Parliament that the government intended to hang every person on death row if granted that opportunity. In strong language, he continued saying that 'the State will, cognizant with the rule of law, do everything within its power to pursue the sentence of death in relation to every person on death row'. In Trinidad and Tobago, the Attorney General is a member of the Mercy Committee, so it is difficult to dismiss a connection between his statement in Parliament and the summoning of the committee very shortly thereafter. Accordingly, the four men quickly moved to the court and obtained a conservatory order prohibiting their execution pending the determination of their challenge to the proposed hearing. On the substantive complaint, Rajkumar J held that the process commenced by the Advisory Committee was tainted both by the announcement in Parliament as well as the truncated timelines initially stipulated. Significantly, the judge added that these events suggested that the outcome of the process was preordained.

The procedures followed by advisory bodies in the above examples suggest a degree of disregard for petitioners, a bias probably rooted in attitudes about crime and punishment in strongly retentionist states. Although it might seem trivial, the facts as recounted in one Bahamian appeal give some pause. In *Reckley (No 2)*, it was revealed that on 8 May 1992 lawyers acting for the petitioner wrote to the Advisory Committee in the Bahamas, drawing its attention to certain features of the petitioner's case. They received no acknowledgement of the receipt of that letter, nor answer to it.[76] Even if at the time the law was that a condemned person had no right to make representations to the advisory body in keeping with British practice, the failure even to treat the request with courtesy is an insight into the mindset the committee, and hinting at the vulnerability of condemned persons in this process.

In these various instances, the prematurity of meeting and advising on mercy, or the transparent attempts to frustrate petitioners' right of participation by unrealistic periods of notice, suggest a rush to judgment, or worse, the robotic performance of a charade. Time and again, it was only through express judicial intervention that the error of such haste was exposed. In upholding the obligation of the advisory bodies to wait on the completion of the local and international processes before meeting, or by insisting that prisoners be given

75 *Dottin and others v Rougier (Commissioner of Prisons) and others* TT (2010) HC 12.

76 *Reckley v Minister of Public Safety and Immigration* (n 17) 11.

reasonable notice, courts were simply mandating a process consistent with elementary principles of natural justice. That ought to have been obvious to any fair-minded body without the need for litigation.

Bias

There are other cases which contribute to a suspicion that despite the elaborate nature of the post-conviction processes, advisory bodies could be approaching their role in a perfunctory manner. In *Yaseen*,[77] for example, the condemned men had sought judicial review because when the Advisory Council was eventually constituted to consider their cases, its chairman happened to be their former defence counsel. The Attorney General ('AG') was the minister designated to chair the Advisory Council on the Prerogative of Mercy, and it was therefore his constitutional duty to advise the president whether to commute the sentence of death.[78] What had happened here was that between the time of the conviction of the appellants and the sitting of the Council there had been a change of government in Guyana, and the appellants' defence counsel had become the country's AG. At the meeting of the council held to consider the appellants' petitions the AG took his place as chairman, though he claimed not to have taken any part in the deliberations. After the council concluded its processes, the AG duly advised the president of the Council's position and, in accordance with art 190(1) of the Constitution of Guyana, also expressed to the president his own deliberate opinion on the case. The president thereupon directed that the law should take its course. In other words, the sentences would not be commuted and the men would have to be executed.

In a challenge to the propriety of the AG's conduct in this case, the Court of Appeal of Guyana unsurprisingly held that in acting as the chairman of the Advisory Council, the AG had behaved improperly since that placed him in a position of conflict between his duty of confidentiality to his (former) clients and his loyalty and the consequent need for frankness to another (in this case, the president). That impropriety was exacerbated when he expressed his opinion to the president; as a result of these multiple errors the court vacated the decision of the president not to commute the sentences.

The outrageous facts in *Yaseen* are admittedly exceptional, but insofar as they raised the possibility of bias it is by no means an isolated case. In *August v R*,[79] a case dealing with the constitutionality of statutory punishments in Belize, one of the issues that arose involved the Belize Advisory Council (Procedure) Rules ('BAC Rules'), which set out the procedure for the exercise of the prerogative of mercy by the Governor-General. The appellant's claim was that insofar as these rules did not define what constituted the 'special or exceptional circumstances' which would entitle persons convicted

77 *Yasseen* (n 32).
78 Constitution of Guyana 1980, art 188(2).
79 *August v R* (2016) 89 WIR 201.

of non-capital offences to have their petitions for mercy heard by the Governor-General, they were unfair. Unusually, and explosively one might add, a current member of the BAC executed two affidavits in which she deposed that based on the results of a search she had caused to conduct, she believed that the BAC had *never* recommended to the Governor-General that the sentence of life imprisonment be remitted for any convicted prisoner serving a life term. This member also deposed that the Council had no clear understanding of the meaning of the term 'special or exceptional circumstances'. The Court of Appeal of Belize held that the mandatory nature of a sentence of life imprisonment for murder, without the possibility of parole, violated the constitutional guarantees of both the right to a fair trial and protection from inhuman and degrading treatment; further, the prerogative of mercy, since it was exercised by the executive, could not cure any constitutional breach in the sentencing process. Significantly, however, it relied on the evidence to find that in any event, the appellant did not have a *real* possibility of release by an exercise of prerogative of mercy. The safeguard of application to the BAC was therefore not sufficient, in law or in its operation, to save a disproportionate sentence. There is no way to view that judicial assessment of the elaborate clemency procedure as anything other than bleak.

The Lack of Substantive Criteria

Of all the issues surrounding process, the one that has the greatest potential of impacting on the exercise of the prerogative of mercy is the complete absence of criteria to guide either the advisory committee or the designated minister in assessing individual cases. The significance of this omission is heightened when considered against the breadth of the power of mercy constitutionally vested in the head of state. As pointed out above, the president or Governor-General, as the case may be, is empowered to grant any of a range of types of reprieve in relation to criminal offenders. Thus, the fact that there are no guidelines at any stage of the process, whether by the advisory committee, the designated minister or even by the head of state, is an acute gap. Inevitably, that gap has had consequences.

In Barbados, for instance, the excessive zeal displayed by the BPC in carrying out its functions, as recounted in the *Joseph and Boyce* case, was discussed above as possibly reflecting some bias against commutation on the part of the advisory body. But the facts of the case reveal another dimension—one that calls into question their competence. The condemned men were only two of four participants in an attack on the victim which led to his death. Though they were charged with murder, prior to trial the prosecution had offered to reduce the charge to manslaughter if they pleaded guilty. Two of the participants accepted the plea bargain and were each sentenced to 12 years' imprisonment, whereas Joseph and Boyce opted to take their chances at trial. That turned out to be a miscalculation as they were both convicted as charged and thus given the mandatory sentence of death. Given that the prosecution had at one time been prepared to accept a plea of guilty to manslaughter, however, the inflexible stance towards execution subsequently adopted by the BPC defies explanation. In the CCJ, Wit J alluded to the incongruity of the prosecution seeking to execute the men whose lives they had initially offered to spare, adding that the costs of the trial were not a sufficient reason to justify such disproportionality in the sentencing of those who accepted the plea bargain and those who did not.[80] While incompetence may be too harsh an assessment of the role played by the BPC, a committee guided by objectives of sentencing and principles of equity and proportionality might have come to a more rational conclusion. A dispassionate examination of the facts of this case would have readily revealed the manifest 'disproportionality and unreasonableness' of seeking ultimate vengeance in relation to two participants, while another two of equal culpability in the same common enterprise would be free men in less than a decade.

Incompetence in the performance of their functions is only one hazard of the absence of criteria; an obviously more problematic one is outright bias or the misuse of the power to advance partisan or personal objectives. This possibility has repeatedly been canvassed in Guyana, where the dispensation of mercy by successive presidents across different political administrations has been shrouded in mystery and controversy. After a change of government in May 2015, for example, the incoming president used the occasion of his accession to office to pardon a whopping number of 60 prisoners. These were all young (between 18 and 25 years of age), non-violent offenders, who were pardoned unconditionally on the president's belief that youths ought to be in school and not jails.[81] But despite its noble motivation, the blanket pardon caused considerable consternation, so much so that the president did not make it an annual practice as he first promised.

Of equal concern was the lack of transparency that shrouded the May 2015 pardons. The former AG, by then an opposition member of Parliament, publicly called for the names of those pardoned to be disclosed along with details of the offences they had committed, the time they spent incarcerated, and the process and criteria relied upon by the president in exercising this power. His appeals elicited no response, and even the questions he tabled in Parliament were disallowed by the Speaker on the dubious ground that they were abusive.[82] The Guyana Bar Association ('GBA') in a rare public commentary, cited its own concerns, which included reference to the plethora of

80 *Joseph and Boyce* (n 47) [5].
81 'Granger Announces Pardon for 60 Non-Violent Youth Offenders' (*Stabroek News*, 26 May 2015) <https://www.stabroeknews.com/2015/news/guyana/05/26/granger-announces-pardons-for-60-non-violent-youth-offenders/> accessed 14 November 2018.
82 Denis Chabrol, 'House Speaker Dumps PPP Questions on Pardoning of Prisoners—Jagdeo' (*Demerara Waves*, 1 June 2016) <http://demerarawaves.com/2016/06/01/house-speaker-dumps-ppp-questions-on-pardoning-of-prisoners-jagdeo/> accessed 14 November 2018.

sentencing laws that would have allowed courts to impose non-custodial sentences at the time of conviction. The GBA argued for transparency in the granting of pardons, deploring the failure to consider victims' perspectives in the process leading up to the grant, or to articulate a plan that would address the factors contributing to youth offending instead of circumventing judicial processes by pardoning them *after* they had committed crimes.[83] However, save for the explanation as to the desirability of education instead of incarceration, neither the president nor any member of his Cabinet provided any details as to process or criteria in the choice of prisoners who were pardoned.

The grand gesture of a mass pardon at the time of accession to office is suspiciously reminiscent of the magnanimity often displayed by newly inaugurated monarchs. Admittedly, not only did the president have a broad power to pardon, but based on his terse explanation he may have exercised his discretion rationally and for defensible reasons. Still, as Novak has observed, secrecy fosters arbitrariness and misuse of the power,[84] which has been the critique on several previous occasions. Indeed, shortly before the 2015 national election that led to the change of government in Guyana, the then outgoing president pardoned a prisoner who, 21 years earlier, had murdered a nine-year-old boy in the course of a kidnapping for ransom.[85] In a country inured to violent crime, this callous murder of an innocent attracted inordinate public interest all through the trial and subsequent conviction. Two decades later, the pardon reopened the trauma and was swiftly condemned, including by the parents of the murdered child. Given the brutal and merciless nature of the killing, there was no obvious explanation for the president's pardon, particularly when it subsequently came to light that there were other condemned prisoners who had spent much longer periods incarcerated than the man pardoned. In the complete absence of any explanation from the executive, rumours of an improper motivation, including that of some personal, familial connection, surfaced. Whether true or not, it is precisely the combination of unfettered discretion and lack of transparency that facilitates the corrupt exercise of this power. In still yet another case from Guyana, a previous president had pre-emptively pardoned two prisoners, both opposition activists, for sedition and treason charges (neither had been convicted at the time).[86] Given the criticism that had followed upon charging political opponents, their subsequent pardons

83 'Presidential Pardon and Transparency' (*Stabroek News*, 8 October 2015) <https://www.stabroeknews.com/2015/features/10/08/presidential-pardon-and-transparency/> accessed 14 November 2018.

84 Novak (n 6) 838.

85 'Former President Pardons Child Killer Ravindra Deo' (*Kaieteur News*, 17 May 2015) <https://www.kaieteurnewsonline.com/2015/05/17/former-president-pardons-child-killer-ravindra-deo/> accessed 14 November 2018.

86 'Treason Accused Pardoned' (*BBC News*, 28 August 2007) <http://www.bbc.co.uk/caribbean/news/story/2007/08/070828_benschopnew.shtml> accessed 14 November 2018; 'Jagdeo Pardons Bynoe' (*Stabroek News*, 2 December 2008) <https://www.stabroeknews.com/2008/news/guyana/12/02/jagdeo-pardons-bynoe/> accessed 14 November 2018.

(one after spending five years in jail on remand) smacked more of cold political calculus rather than the benevolent grant of mercy.

In these questionable exercises of discretion, such uses of the pardon power in Guyana are not unique, as Turrell's research, mentioned above, demonstrates. To avoid such abuses the courts in India have formulated comprehensive criteria, which take into account the interests and perspectives of all stakeholders, to guide the exercise of the discretion.[87] In light of the controversies that inevitably attend use of the prerogative, not to mention the litigation that frequently results, it is clear that Caribbean jurisdictions could benefit from the Indian example.

The Prerogative and Separation of Powers

One issue of persistent doubt regarding the prerogative of mercy is its uneasy place in a constitutional scheme that purports to subscribe to separated powers among different branches of government.[88] Conventional wisdom has traditionally been that Caribbean constitutions respect the separation of powers, and when in the post-independence era the doctrine was first applied in *Hinds v AG*,[89] Lord Diplock articulated an expansive definition of its meaning. In his view, the absence of a textual base for the doctrine in the constitutions did 'not prevent the legislative, the executive and the judicial powers of the new state being exercisable *exclusively* by the legislature, by the executive and by the judicature respectively'.[90] While this was greeted with some scepticism as being exaggerated,[91] its relevance to the independence of the judicial function has never been doubted. The separation between the exercise of judicial powers on the one hand and legislative and executive powers on the other is regarded as total or effectively so. Such separation, based on the rule of law, was described by Lord Steyn as 'a characteristic feature of democracies'.[92] That said, however, Caribbean courts have struggled to rationalise this strict position with respect to mandatory sentences and their relationship to the exercise of executive mercy.

This constitutional dilemma was first frontally raised in a pair of cases from Barbados and Trinidad and Tobago, decided by the PC in 2004: *Boyce* and *Matthew*.[93] In both cases, the argument was that the mandatory death penalty

87 Islam (n 6) 264. See further Batra, this volume.
88 See Arias and Kouroutakis, this volume.
89 *Hinds v AG* (1975) 24 WIR 326, [1976] 1 All ER 353.
90 Ibid., 331, emphasis added. Compare Pascoe and Novak, this volume.
91 Owen Hood Phillips, 'A Constitutional Myth: Separation of Powers' (1977) 93 LQR 11; Ralph Carnegie, 'Floreat the Westminster Model? A Commonwealth Caribbean Perspective' (1996) 6 Carib LR 1.
92 *R (Anderson) v Secretary of State for the Home Department* [2002] 3 WLR 1800, [50].
93 *Boyce v R* (2004) 64 WIR 37 and *Charles Matthew v the State* (2004) 64 WIR 412.

combined with the exercise of the constitutional power of mercy by the head of state infringed the principle of separation of powers. It was premised on the reality that the law did not envisage that everyone sentenced to death would actually be executed, with that actual determination being made by the executive branch. In the case of Barbados, the function was that of the BPC which advised on the commutation, while in Trinidad and Tobago it was that of the president acting on the advice of a designated minister. Since neither of these entities forms part of the judiciary, the actual punishment involved an illegitimate exercise of the judicial function by the executive. In neither appeal did this argument succeed. The PC held that since the mercy power was set out in the constitutions themselves, combined with the fact that the mandatory death penalty was preserved by a savings clause, there was no room for a finding of unconstitutionality. Lord Hoffman for the majority in *Boyce* thought that the separation of powers is simply 'a pithy description of how the constitution works'; the principle could not be invoked to invalidate the provision for executive clemency since it was itself contained in the Constitution.[94]

As a matter of strict constitutional theory, the PC may have been right in the limited scope placed on the doctrine of separation of powers. But in taking this approach with the actual case before them, the constitutional dilemma in issue was elided. First, the mandatory death penalty was contained in ordinary law and not the constitution. Even though it was preserved by savings clauses in both constitutions, those clauses immunise existing laws only against bills of rights' challenges, and are impotent in the face of implicit constitutional principles such as the separation of powers.[95] More crucially, however, was the scant attention paid to the problem of an outsized executive role in sentencing, which represented the crux of the dispute.[96]

In *Hinds*, the Caribbean *locus classicus* on this subject, the PC carefully insulated the judicial role of sentencing from executive interference. *Hinds* involved a challenge to legislation passed to address rising levels of crime in Jamaica, in particular gun violence. As part of the scheme instituted by the act, a new court called a 'Gun Court' was created to try all firearm and related offences. For certain specified offences, the Gun Court was required to impose a mandatory sentence of detention at hard labour, from which the convicted person could only be discharged at the direction of the Governor-General acting in accordance with the advice of a Review Board, a non-judicial body established by the act. The PC invalidated these provisions related to the mandatory sentence on the basis that they violated the separation of powers implicit in the Jamaican Constitution by transferring a judicial function to the executive. As a non-judicial body, the Review Board could not constitutionally exercise any discretion to determine the severity of the punishment to be

94 Ibid., para 70.
95 *DPP v Mollison* (2003) 64 WIR 140.
96 Tracy Robinson, Arif Bulkan and Adrian Saunders, *Fundamentals of Caribbean Constitutional Law* (Sweet & Maxwell 2015) 339–341.

inflicted upon an individual member of a class of offenders—which was the effect of the legislative scheme. That too was precisely the scenario involved in the *Boyce* and *Matthew* cases. There, the sentencing function was only nominally vested in the court, for the sentence of death was automatic on conviction for murder. Effectively, as the appellants pointed out, the real discretion was entrusted to the executive, which through the prerogative of mercy actually decided whether a convicted person would be executed or not. Looking beyond form to substance, such a pivotal executive role in sentencing should have been caught (and invalidated) by *Hinds*.

One of the difficulties with the *Boyce/Matthew* reasoning is how studiously it avoided any examination of the substantial role of the prerogative of mercy in individualising sentences. Even though multiple courts have acknowledged the impact of mercy in the sentencing process—particularly in those countries that retained the mandatory death penalty—the view taken has been to treat this as a safeguard, or 'safety valve' and not to interrogate the incongruity (if not outright unconstitutionality) of an executive body being entrusted with the power to individualise sentences.[97] No doubt because of lingering dissatisfaction with the manner in which this issue has been determined, it continues to be litigated in the Caribbean.

In *Lendore and others v AG*,[98] a challenge to the use of the presidential prerogative *en masse* to commute the sentences of a substantial number of condemned men[99] who could no longer be executed because of unreasonable delay reignited these very concerns. Commutation was exercised in large batches, without distinction between the different members in each group. The first group received conditional pardons and their death sentences were commuted to life imprisonment with hard labour for the rest of their natural lives, while the sentences of those in the second group were commuted to 75 years' imprisonment with hard labour. The appellants challenged the substituted sentences attached as conditions to the grants of pardon on multiple grounds, including the recurring one that it involved the unconstitutional exercise of a judicial function by the executive. They were unsuccessful at every stage, save for the sole concession of the Court of Appeal, upheld by the PC, that the men should have been allowed to make representations before the power of pardon was exercised. Accordingly, the appropriate sentences for each had to be reconsidered—but by the president and not the High Court, as urged by the appellants.

Arguing that the presidential commutation (done to stave off an inevitable finding that they could not be executed since they were all on death row for too long) amounted to a re-sentencing, the appellants urged that they were

97 *Yasseen* (n 32) 118; *Joseph and Boyce* (n 47) [31]; *Reckley v Minister of Public Safety and Immigration* (n 17) [19].
98 *Lendore and others v AG* [2017] UKPC 25, [2017] 5 LRC 369, 1 WLR 3369.
99 Acting under the power conferred on him under the Constitution of Trinidad and Tobago 1976, s 87(2).

entitled to a *judicial* substitution of their sentences. The PC disagreed, making the irrelevant distinction that the original sentences were not unlawful, but that it had instead become unlawful to carry them out. The PC added that the fact that the appellants had become entitled to constitutional relief precluding the implementation of the original death sentences did not exclude the power of pardon. On the contrary, if the power of pardon was exercised, that itself relieved the convicted person of the threat of unconstitutional execution.

As to the concerns raised regarding the propriety of this procedure in light of separation of powers, the PC fell back on the previous *Boyce/Matthew* reasoning. Since the scheme governing pardons was set out in the Constitution of Trinidad and Tobago itself, the court had no power to go behind it on the basis of 'some higher norm of legal theory' and treat a section of the Constitution itself as unconstitutional.[100] The PC further rejected the argument that executive clemency was part of the sentencing process, holding that it constituted a separate power which fell to be exercised independently of sentencing. Although the power of pardon was not ordinarily part of a process of vindicating constitutional rights, there was no impediment to using it in this way, as was done for all the appellants.[101]

Even on the most generous view the PC entangled itself with this reasoning, which is impossible to reconcile with the position it has otherwise taken regarding the sacrosanct nature of the judicial function. In the first place, the fatalistic *Boyce/Matthew* position that what the constitution says is final does not always prevail, and the PC has previously shown itself willing to disregard constitutional ouster clauses or otherwise go behind explicit language to uphold its powers of review and/or arrive at some other result.[102] Nonetheless, acceptance of the executive power of pardon should not mean its *exercise* can never be questioned, and it is the arbitrariness of the PC's position on this issue that is indefensible. Since *Hinds* there has been no shortage of authority that the judicial function, which covers the power of sentencing, is sacrosanct.

In *Anderson*,[103] for example, the House of Lords found that the power entrusted to the Secretary of State to fix a tariff determining the actual period of imprisonment to be served by persons receiving a mandatory sentence of life imprisonment to be incompatible with the right to a fair hearing in the European Convention on Human Rights. In language espousing very similar reasoning to that of the PC in *Lendore*, counsel for the crown in *Anderson* drew a distinction between the mandatory sentence imposed by the court and the tariff fixed by the Home Secretary. The former constituted the punishment, he

100 *Lendore* (n 98) [16].
101 Ibid., [19]–[20].
102 Tracy Robinson, 'Our Inherent Constitution' in David Berry and Tracy Robinson (eds), *Transitions in Caribbean Law: Law-making, Constitutionalism and the Convergence of National and International Law* (Caribbean Law Publishing 2013) 248, 249–251.
103 *R (Anderson)* (n 92).

argued, while the latter was a mere 'administrative procedure'. Describing the argument as 'fragile', Lord Steyn emphasised the reality that the court's view had no bearing on the actual sentence to be served by a person, whereas it was the Home Secretary's tariff which had definite legal consequences. He concluded bluntly: 'a decision fixing the tariff in an individual case is unquestionably a decision about the level of punishment which is appropriate. Mellifluous words cannot hide this reality.'[104]

In its cases originating from the Caribbean, the PC has never satisfactorily explained how the combination of a mandatory sentence combined with executive discretion does not represent executive trespass on a purely judicial function. In *Boyce* and *Matthew*, the solution would have been to strike down the mandatory aspect of the sentence as incompatible with the separation of powers, a course they had taken before. In *Lendore*, even if the appellants had at one time been lawfully sentenced, the subsequent exercise of the power of pardon was nonetheless questionable, for its effect was to confer on the president the sole discretion regarding the sentence each prisoner would individually serve, an unquestionably judicial function.

More than a decade before *Lendore*, Lord Bingham had stated in *Reyes*:

> While the [PC] would be the first to acknowledge the importance of the role which the constitution has conferred on the Advisory Council, it is clear that such a non-judicial body cannot decide what is the appropriate measure of punishment to be visited on a defendant for the crime he has committed.[105]

This caution presumably applies not just to the role of the advisory body in advising on the dispensation of mercy, but ultimately to the role of the head of state in granting mercy, especially in the context of mandatory sentences. Where executive clemency is relied upon routinely as a cure for inadequacies of the criminal justice system, its use would seem to have expanded beyond that of an *exceptional*, extra-judicial measure to temper justice.[106] That surely calls into question its constitutionality, given prevailing understandings of the separation of powers principle.

Conclusion

Framers of Caribbean constitutions clearly expected that by constitutionalising British mercy practice, they were providing a safeguard within the criminal justice system. But that practice was itself imperfect, and the unconstrained

104 Ibid., [52].
105 *Reyes* (n 26) [47].
106 See further Daniel Pascoe, 'Towards a global theory of capital clemency incidence' in Carol S Steiker and Jordan M Steiker, *Comparative Capital Punishment* (Edward Elgar 2019) 128–129.

discretion retained by heads of state to dispense mercy was compounded by weak or non-existent procedures. The fraught history of how advisory bodies have functioned demonstrates and reinforces these concerns. In the perfunctory manner in which they have often carried out their operations and the disregard sometimes shown to condemned persons, it is not speculative to wonder whether this process is ultimately mere window-dressing. Additionally, the possibility of bias has been not just sub-text but an inescapable reality underlying many exercises of the power. Overall, the wide discretion entrusted to the executive in this regard, combined with the veil of secrecy over its actual use, are key concerns of the current constitutional scheme. Questionable grants of mercy clearly indicate the need to mandate consideration of multiple perspectives in advance of the exercise of this power. The focus on the welfare of the prisoners, a common and albeit laudable rationale, should not eclipse other valid public interests. Those legitimately include the nature and prevalence of the offence in question and, as the controversial pardon of a child killer in Guyana agonisingly demonstrated, the perspectives of victims as well.

This last dimension of the use of the prerogative arises partly because of the risk that mercy could be utilised to address deficits in the criminal justice system. There is indeed a long tradition of the prerogative serving to temper the harshest effects of pure justice. However, that presupposes justice to have been done in the first place, and the power ought not to be normalised to the extent where it is relied upon to fulfil such eminently judicial functions as that of individualising punishments. While judicial review has been instrumental in correcting some of the procedural imbalances, it remains a discretionary remedy available only after the fact, if at all. Clearly, not only do the above shortcomings need to be addressed, but some containment of the discretion—whether by way of limits on the power or criteria to guide its exercise—is necessary.

7 Secret Jurisprudence

Decision-Making on Capital Clemency Petitions in India

Bikramjeet Batra

Introduction

Despite operating at the intersection of law, governance, and realpolitik, little is known about clemency petitions in capital cases in India. While news of the rejection of individual petitions is widely covered in the media, internal guidelines on clemency decision-making remained a secret and even the process of deciding clemency petitions was not well known until recently. Occasional glimpses into the murkiness of clemency decision-making have usually only been possible in the rare instances where constitutional challenges involving clemency petitions were heard in the Supreme Court.

This chapter is based on a study of Indian Ministry of Home Affairs files relating to over 275 clemency petitions filed by death row inmates between 1947 and 2006.[1] The individual files included complete minutes, summaries, and file-notings of various civil servants, ministers, and presidents involved in decision-making in each of the mercy petitions.[2] Based on this information, this chapter examines the internal guidelines that have been used for decision-making on clemency petitions in India, as well some factors beyond the

1 This chapter relies on a selection of archived mercy petition files dating from 1947 to 1949, and 1953 to 1971, as well as contemporary petitions from 1981 to 2006. The author conducted archival research at the National Archives of India ('NAI') in 2007 and 2018. Contemporary petitions were sourced in the same year via Right to Information ('RTI') applications and follow-up inspection of files at the Ministry of Home Affairs ('MHA'), New Delhi. This research was conducted as part of a visiting fellowship at the Centre of Study of Law and Governance at Jawaharlal Nehru University, New Delhi. See further Bikram Batra, '"Court" of Last Resort: A Study of Constitutional Clemency for Capital Crimes in India' (2009) Centre for the Study of Law and Governance, Jawaharlal Nehru University, New Delhi Working Paper CSLG/WP/11 <https://www.jnu.ac.in/sites/default/files/u63/11-Court%20%28Bikram%29.pdf> accessed 24 February 2019.

2 While the size of the sample is significant (275 petitions), the information is skewed to the extent that most of the archived petitions were those *accepted* for commutation. As per the MHA-Judicial Division 'Retention Schedule' for mercy petitions, rejected mercy petitions are destroyed after ten years. With respect to petitions from 1981–2006, which were files sought directly from the MHA, only 26 of the 76 mercy petitions disposed were available for inspection.

guidelines which have influenced the executive. In addition, the chapter briefly examines the role played by individual actors—presidents, ministers, and key civil servants—in creating the internal, largely secret 'jurisprudence' on clemency decision-making in capital cases.

Clemency Law and Policy

Article 72(1) of the Constitution of India 1950 gives the president 'the power to grant pardons, reprieves, respites or remissions of punishment or to suspend, remit or commute the sentence of any person convicted of any offence … (c) Where the sentence is a sentence of death'.[3] These powers are concurrent with those of governor in their respective states.[4] Although the mercy powers of the president and governors extend to other sentences too, this chapter focuses on the constitutional powers of the president of India with respect to death sentences.

Given the nature of the office, the president of India is bound by the advice of the Cabinet.[5] Generally the decision on a mercy petition is arrived at within the Ministry of Home Affairs ('MHA'): a memorandum is prepared by a junior official in the MHA, and on the basis of that memorandum, a Joint Secretary or an Additional Secretary recommends a decision to commute the death sentence or reject the mercy petition. The case is then considered by the Minister of Home Affairs who makes the final recommendation, on behalf of the Cabinet of Ministers, to the president. The Constitution of India allows the president one opportunity to return the recommendation for the decision to be reviewed.[6] If no change is made on review, the president is bound by the recommendation.

3 In addition, the executive has similar powers of clemency prescribed by the Indian Penal Code and the Code of Criminal Procedure: see Indian Penal Code 1860 ss 54–55 and Code of Criminal Procedure 1973 (India) ss 432–433A. These provisions do not appear to have been used in commuting death sentences after independence in 1947. Article 72(2) of the Constitution of India 1950 also allows the military hierarchy to exercise clemency powers with respect to those sentenced by a court martial.

4 See Articles 161 and 72(3) of the Constitution of India 1950. In practice, the initial mercy petition is sent to the Governor of the State, and then sent to the president only when rejected. Where the governor grants clemency, the president does not have the power to overturn the decision or sit in appeal against it. As per internal ministry rules, where the president has rejected a mercy petition, a subsequent mercy petition should not be admitted by the governor. Instead it should be sent by the State Government to the Central Government. See letter dated 20 July 1967 from Under Secretary MHA to Secretary, Home Department Punjab reiterating a similar instruction in a previous letter dated 6 March 1950 (File no. MHA (Judicial-III), 32/1/67, NAI).

5 *Maru Ram v Union of India and others* (1981) 1 SCC 107.

6 Proviso to Article 74(1), Constitution of India 1950.

Internal Guidelines

Some aspects of clemency in India are relatively uncontested: clemency proceedings are completely distinct from judicial proceedings;[7] and the executive has a wide scope to examine a range of factors in making the eventual decision. However what factors could or should be taken into account in the decision-making in clemency petitions has long remained a subject of controversy. The extensive discussion within the executive that has led to these positions has rarely been revealed publicly.

The earliest principles of decision-making appear in an 1873 noting by Lord Hobhouse of the colonial home department that read as follows:

> The principles on which the prerogative of mercy should be exercised may be then briefly summarized. First, if the quality of the case is such that from a moral point of view the offence is not so grave as it is from the legal point; secondly, if fresh evidence not procurable for the trial is brought forward to throw doubt on a sentence which cannot be judicially reviewed; thirdly, if those who tried the case differ among themselves or on subsequent reflection felt doubt enough to ask that their decision may be reviewed.[8]

In 1923, the then Viceroy and Governor General, the Earl of Reading, expanded the scope of clemency decision-making by stressing that the executive would not only be entitled but was 'indeed bound to take into full and anxious consideration matters which would be excluded in a court of law and could not there receive the same kind of analysis and attention.'[9] He noted that while 'impossible to lay down any definite rules' for the disposal of mercy petitions, the following were adopted as 'general guides':

> In particular, the primary aspect in which such cases should be in the first instance be considered should be the object of determining whether there are grounds of an exceptional nature, connected either with the personality of the accused (such as age, sex or mental deficiency) or with the facts of the case (such as provocation or other extenuating circumstances) or otherwise, to justify suspension, remission or commutation. If, in the course of the examination of the case in this aspect, any grave and serious doubts arise on the question of guilt, this question should be fully examined.[10]

7 *KM Nanavati v The State of Bombay*, AIR 1961 SC 112.
8 Dated 9 September 1873 in *Regina v Nha Loogyee*, excerpted in File no. Home (Judicial) 373/1923, NAI.
9 Order of Governor General in Council, 10 August 1923, File No. Home (Judicial) 373/1923, NAI.
10 File no. Home (Judicial) 373/1923, NAI.

The 1923 order remained the mainstay for clemency decision-making over the next few decades, including after independence in 1947.[11] In 1962, when the Law Commission of India was examining the question of abolition of the death penalty, they sought information from the MHA on the principles followed in dealing with mercy petitions. Noting that they were 'well understood', the MHA stated that the principles fell 'broadly into the following grounds, [namely] age, sex, mental deficiency, grave or sudden provocation, absence of motive, and premeditation. There are other grounds which are also taken into consideration i.e. inadequacy of evidence, long delays in investigation and trial, fixation of responsibility in "gang murders", difference of opinion in a two-Judge bench, necessitating reference to a third Judge of the High Court etc. Apart from these, the case is considered, examined and disposed of on its own merits.'[12]

Eventually, the 1873 note, the 1923 order, and the 'well understood' principles were distilled by the MHA into formal 'Guidelines for dealing with mercy petitions' for internal decision-making.[13] The guidelines provide the following general grounds when clemency is justified on special consideration:

> I. Personality of the accused (such as age, sex or mental deficiency) or the circumstances of the case (such as provocation or other similar justification);
> II. Cases in which the Appellate court has expressed its doubt as to the reliability of the evidence and has nevertheless decided on conviction;
> III. Cases where it is alleged that fresh evidence is obtainable mainly with a view to seeing whether fresh enquiry is justified;
> IV. Where the High Court has reversed on appeal an acquittal by the Session Judge or has on appeal enhanced the sentence.

The Guidelines further note, 'in the course of years, various Home Ministers have also contributed to enlarge the field of considerations.' These are:

> V. Difference of opinions in a bench of two judges necessitating reference to a third judge of the High Court;

11 Batra '"Court" of last resort' (n 1) 6–16.

12 Letter to Shri SK Hirachandani, Secretary of Law Commission dated 6 July 1962, File no. MHA (Judicial-II) 19/61/62, NAI.

13 These guidelines featured prominently in decision-making in the 1980s, but similar guidelines appear to have been followed in the previous decades as well. A copy of the guidelines was sent by the Ministry of Home Affairs to the Ministry of Law and Justice in response to request dated 20 June 2006 by Satish Chandra, Additional Government Counsel, seeking guidelines on decision-making in mercy petitions. A copy of this communication is available tagged with the Mercy Petition of Kheraj Ram s/o Cheema Ram, File no. 14/4/2003—JC, MHA, New Delhi.

VI. Consideration of evidence in fixation of responsibility in gang murder cases;

VII. Long delays in investigation and trial etc.[14]

The latest version of the guidelines which remain in force presently has the same seven points.[15] However, when information on the guidelines was sought in Parliament in 2006, the MHA response refused to even acknowledge their existence:

> No specific guidelines can be framed for examining the mercy petitions as the power under Article 72 of the Constitution is of the widest amplitude, can contemplate myriad kinds and categories of cases with facts and situations varying from case to case. However, the broad guidelines generally considered while examining the mercy petitions are personality of the accused such as age, sex or mental deficiency or circumstances of the case, conduct of the offender, medical abnormality falling short of legal insanity and so on.[16]

The Supreme Court and the Guidelines Question

The question of mercy guidelines has often come before the Supreme Court of India. In 1980 in its judgment in *Maru Ram*, the constitutional bench of the apex court observed that '[t]he proper thing to do' would be for the executive 'to make rules for its own guidance in the exercise of the [clemency] powers keeping, of course, a large residuary power to meet special situations or sudden developments'.[17] Another subsequent judgment, however, suggested that this view was *obiter dicta*, particularly as clemency was not the main subject matter in the case.[18]

The first head-on engagement on the issue came when a condemned prisoner in the *Billa–Ranga* case challenged the rejection by the president of his mercy petition taking the plea of arbitrariness and the absence of any guidelines. The writ petition was admitted by the Supreme Court, which noted, '[w]e do not know whether the Government of India has formulated any uniform standard or guidelines by which the exercise of the constitutional power under Article

14 The guidelines also make reference to a particular decision taken by the Cabinet of Ministers in its meeting on 7 September 1976 to divide s 302 of the Indian Penal Code 1860 into two grades of murders—only one of which would be punishable by death. The Cabinet policy provided that, until legislation to amend was cleared by Parliament, this division should also be considered in clemency decisions. Although the bill lapsed in Parliament and the policy was subsequently revoked, the classification may have however remained a factor in decision-making until much later.

15 Minute by AK Jain, Joint Secretary—HR J1, dated 29 June 2004 in Mercy Petition of Dhananjoy Chatterjee, File no. 4/3/94—MP, MHA.

16 Rajya Sabha Unstarred Question no. 815, answered on 29 November 2006.

17 *Maru Ram* (n 5).

18 *Ashok Kumar alias Golu v Union of India and others,* AIR 1991 SC 1792.

72 is intended to be or is in fact governed.'[19] After seeking an explanation from the state on the existing guidelines, the court mysteriously changed its mind. At the next hearing it noted:

> The question as regards the scope of the power of the President … to commute a sentence of death into a lesser sentence may have to await examination on an appropriate occasion. This clearly is not that occasion because in so far as this case is concerned, whatever be the guidelines observed for the exercise of the power conferred by article 72, the only sentence which can possibly be imposed upon the petitioner is that of death and no circumstances exist for interference with that sentence … we are quite clear that not even the most liberal use of his mercy jurisdiction could have persuaded the President to interfere with the sentence of death imposed upon the petitioner.[20]

The Court's U-turn was controversial, probably influenced by the risk of public outrage over interfering in the infamous case.[21] Its next engagement with the issue of guidelines was in another controversial case. In *Kehar Singh*, the judges rejected the plea that to prevent an arbitrary exercise of power under Article 72, the court should draw up a set of guidelines regulating the exercise of executive clemency. The Supreme Court asserted that there was 'sufficient indication' in the terms of the power, the history and case law and no further guidelines were required. They further added:

> Power under Article 72 is of the widest amplitude, can contemplate a myriad kinds and categories of cases with facts and situations varying from case to case in which the merits and reasons of State may be profoundly assisted by prevailing occasion and passing time. And it is of great significance that the function itself enjoys high status in the constitutional scheme.[22]

This view was reiterated in *Epuru Sudhakar*.[23] Throughout this period of nearly 25 years, the existence of the MHA guidelines remained a secret.

19 *Kuljeet Singh Alias Ranga v Lt. Governor, Delhi and Anr*, AIR 1981 SC 2339.
20 *Kuljit Singh Alias Ranga v Lt. Governor of Delhi and Ors*, AIR 1982 SC 774.
21 As the jurist Hormasji Maneckji Seervai pointed out, all the facts were known to the court when it admitted the petition (Hormasji Maneckji Seervai, *Constitutional Law of India* (4th edn, Universal Law Publishing 2005) 2108). Billa and Ranga were subsequently executed on 31 January 1982.
22 *Kehar Singh and Anr. v Union Of India and Anr*, AIR 1989 SC 653.
23 *Epuru Sudhakar and Anr. v Govt. of Andhra Pradesh and Ors*, AIR 2006 SC 3385. In this case, the amicus curiae appointed by the court suggested that, considering the frequency of clemency petitions and the present political scenario, it would be appropriate for the Supreme Court to lay down guidelines so that there would be no scope to misuse the power.

After sustained engagement with delayed disposal of mercy petitions through much of the 1980s, and again in the past decade,[24] some judges of the court appear to have lost patience with the executive. In January 2014, the MHA guidelines were included in full in the landmark *Shatrughan Chauhan* judgment of the Supreme Court. Curiously, even though the MHA guidelines were annexed to written submissions by one of the petitioners, the Supreme Court judgment specifically avoided referring to them as guidelines—preferring instead to call them 'certain criteria in the form of [a] circular' laid down by the Union Government.[25] Furthermore, the judgment also recommended adding an eighth guideline, namely 'consideration of the delay that may have occurred in disposal of a mercy petition'.[26]

Additional Factors in Decision-Making

Amongst the more vocal critics of the MHA guidelines was Dr APJ Abdul Kalam who, while president of India in 2005, is reported to have requested consideration of additional factors during the decision-making process on capital clemency petitions. These included examining sociological aspects; humanist and compassionate grounds in each case (e.g. the age of the convict and his physical and mental condition); the risk of recidivism following commutation, and the financial liabilities of the convict's family.[27] It is unclear whether there was any internal debate on the then president's views. Publicly, the MHA claims no knowledge of this communication.[28] Yet, while the MHA may not wish to acknowledge the Kalam communication, it is clear from a study of archived petitions that some of the above factors—and others—have commonly influenced clemency decision-making.

24 Bikramjeet Batra, 'Don't be Cruel: The "Death Row Phenomenon" and India's "Delay" Jurisprudence' in Roger Hood and Surya Deva (eds), *Confronting Capital Punishment in Asia: Human Rights, Politics and Public Opinion* (OUP 2014) 297–303.

25 *Shatrughan Chauhan v Union of India* (2014) 3 SCC 1, para 48. The guidelines—with their correct name—were also subsequently included in a Gauhati High Court judgment of 23 December 2015: *Holiram Bordoloi v The Union of India*, WP (Crl) No. 5 of 2014, para 8.

26 *Shatrughan Chauhan* (2014) 3 SCC 1, para 49.

27 V Venkatesan, 'Death Penalty: A Presidential Dilemma' (2005) 22(23) Frontline <https://frontline.thehindu.com/static/html/fl2223/stories/20051118002005000.htm> accessed 11 December 2019.

28 Himanshi Dhawan, 'No information on Kalam's Letter on Mercy Pleas, Home Ministry Says' (*The Times of India*, 2013) <https://timesofindia.indiatimes.com/india/No-information-on-Kalams-letter-on-mercy-pleas-home-ministry-says/articleshow/25285925.cms> accessed 22 October 2018.

Factors Relating to Evidence

Despite the wide scope of mercy proceedings, the Indian executive has long argued that it should not become an additional Court of Appeal.[29] The existing guidelines also suggest that matters of evidence are only taken up where judges expressed some concern about the evidence (Guideline II) or disagreed amongst themselves (Guideline V); in specific cases where fresh evidence was claimed (Guideline III); or where an individual's precise role in a gang murder had to be determined (Guideline VI). In practice, however, the executive has commuted a large number of sentences on grounds of inadequate or unsatisfactory evidence even when the judges themselves were convinced about the suitability of the evidence. These reasons have ranged from 'absence of direct evidence'[30] to 'defects in the evidence'.[31] In a number of cases the executive has commuted the sentence on the grounds that the evidence left some scope for doubt or did not show 'cent per cent' (100 per cent) reliability.[32] In a rare case, the death sentence of one prisoner was even commuted to a ten-year sentence, rather than to life imprisonment, as typically done due to the infirmities of evidence.[33]

The discussion on evidence in mercy petitions has often extended to minute particular details. Sentences have been commuted upon the executive being dissatisfied with the particular evidence presented in a case. In a petition filed by Jit Singh, the sentence was commuted, as the executive believed it would be risky to send a person to the gallows only on the basis of 'oral evidence of a

29 Such concerns were raised as long ago as 1873 by Lord Hobhouse, who warned: 'but to use the prerogative of mercy for the practical erection of an additional Court of Appeal is, as I think, to abuse it'. See File no. Home (Judicial) 373/1923, NAI.

30 Petition of Lila Singh s/o Chittar Singh, File no. MHA (Judicial-1) 32/64/65, NAI.

31 Petition of Sundararajan, File no. MHA (Judicial-1) 32/31/62, NAI. See also 'Evidence is not clear' in Petition of Raja Ram, File no. MHA (Judicial-1) 32/102/57, NAI; 'Evidence is not strong-miscarriage of justice' in Petition of Sarana, File no. MHA (Judicial-1) 32/67/61, NAI; 'Unsatisfactory state of the evidence' in Petition of Debi Singh, File no. MHA (Judicial-1) 32/44/61, NAI; 'Infirmities in evidence' in Petition of Jang Bahadur, File no. MHA (Judicial-1) 32/39/61, NAI.

32 Petition of Manickam, File no. MHA (Judicial-1) 32/2/62, NAI. Other similar reasons include 'Many holes in the evidence' in Petition of Joseph Thomas, File no. MHA (Judicial-1) 32/186/61, NAI; 'Circumstantial evidence not without holes' in Petition of Dhakkan, File no. MHA (Judicial-1) 32/185/61, NAI; 'Generally poor evidence' in Mercy Petition of Subramaniam, File no. MHA (Judicial-1) 32/172/61, NAI.

33 Mercy Petition of Babu, File no. MHA (Judicial-1), 32/64/62, NAI. In another case, the MHA had recommended a complete remission of the sentence but this was not assented to by President Prasad who instead decided to only commute the death sentence. See Mercy Petition of Darbara Singh, File no. MHA (Judicial-1) 32/14/56, NAI.

stereotyped nature'.[34] Other reasons have ranged from the inconsistencies in dying declarations[35] and the scope for witness coaching, to contradiction in witness testimonies and a lack of independence in testimony.[36] In one case, the executive even found fault with the evidence from the post-mortem, concluding that it did not support the time of death claimed by the prosecution and therefore removing a vital link from the chain or circumstances found against the condemned prisoner.[37] Even where the executive has not been able to find fault with the evidence on record in a particular case, it has still commuted a sentence 'by way of abundant caution'.[38] In a few cases, the executive has even gone so far as to conclude that the evidence on record does not show the real facts of the case, thereby *presuming* other reasons for the offence.[39]

Legal Defence

Although as per existing law, all persons accused of murder and other heinous offences are provided free legal counsel by the state, concerns have been raised about the adequacy and competence of legal-aid lawyers.[40] The lack of adequate legal defence has not been sufficiently considered as a mitigating circumstance by Indian courts, even in capital cases. In such a context, it is welcome that despite this not being mentioned in the guidelines, the competence and adequacy of the legal defence has been a key factor for commutation of sentences in several cases.

In a case where a man killed his wife (and their son), suspecting her of infidelity, the civil servants noted that the defence case was not properly thought of, and a wrong defence was made on the petitioner's behalf.[41] This resulted in the

34 Mercy Petition of Jit Singh s/o Bachan Singh etc, File no. MHA (Judicial-1) 32/163/61, NAI.
35 Mercy Petition of Augusthy Augusthy @ Kunjukunju, File no. MHA (Judicial-1) 32/181/59, NAI.
36 Mercy Petition of Mahabir s/o Jagannath, File no. MHA (Judicial-1) 32/121/59, NAI.
37 Mercy Petition of Batahu Sahani, File no. MHA (Judicial-1) 32/177/57, NAI. The MHA notings argued that the undigested food found in the stomach of the victim during the post-mortem showed a later death than what the prosecution claimed.
38 Mercy Petition of Punugupati Venkatramiah etc, File no. MHA (Judicial-1) 32/177/61, NAI.
39 Mercy Petition of Natarajan s/o Ganapathy Goundan, File no. MHA (Judicial-1) 32/25/62, NAI; Mercy Petition of Ram Singh, File no. MHA (Judicial-1) 32/1/58, NAI, and Mercy Petition of Thiruram Chucklian, File no. MHA (Judicial-1) 32/191/57, NAI.
40 See Amnesty International India and People's Union for Civil Liberties (Tamil Nadu & Puducherry), 'Lethal Lottery: The Death Penalty in India, New Delhi' (*Amnesty International*, May 2008) 134–150 <https://www.amnesty.org/download/Documents/52000/asa200072008eng.pdf> accessed 11 December 2019.
41 Mercy Petition of 'Haridas Ramdas @ Abdul Rashid Abdul Rehman', File no. MHA (Judicial-1) 32/96/58, NAI.

petitioner being found guilty by the court, despite strong comments on the inadequate defence of the petitioner. The Minister of State for Home Affairs, also finding that witnesses for the prosecution were not even properly cross-examined, recommended commutation of the sentence, noting that he was 'amazed at the utter incompetency of the defence put forward on behalf of the petitioner'.[42] Furthermore, in a number of other cases, the poor legal defence available to the prisoner led to a later commutation.[43] In addition to the defence, commutations have also been granted where the role of other institutions including the prosecution and the High Court has been suspect.[44]

Broad Political Situation

Lord Reading's Order in Council laying down factors to be considered in decision-making on clemency petitions was based largely on the notes prepared by his Home Member WH Hailey. However, Hailey's note of 28 May 1923 also noted that the factors discussed:

> Do not and cannot of course apply to cases in which there are special or political considerations. I refer to instances of the type of the Amritsar appeals, the Katarpur appeals in the past and Chauri Chaura appeals when they come up to us. These must be considered partly in view of their political implications; indeed as a rule such cases are settled only after circulation in council.[45]

It is thus clear that 'political cases' were treated distinctly, and the regular criterion was not applied to them.

There are no similar references in available post-independence MHA documents, but it is undeniable that political considerations are a factor in determining mercy in some cases. In one of the early prominent cases soon after the formation of Gujarat state, the petitioner who had killed his wife over a dowry dispute had his sentence commuted by the president. Although officially this was done citing concerns about the lack of proof of the motive, another factor that appeared to have influenced the decision was the nearly 1,500 petitions

42 Noting by BN Datar dated 11 November 1958, 'Haridas Ramdas @ Abdul Rashid Abdul Rehman', File no. MHA (Judicial-1) 32/96/58, NAI.

43 Mercy Petition of Hazara Singh s/o Sunder Singh, File no. MHA (Judicial-1) 32/66/58, NAI; Mercy Petition of Anthoni Vannan, File no. MHA (Judicial-1) 32/49/58, NAI; Mercy Petition of Sita Ram s/o Dhara Singh, File no. MHA (Judicial-1) 32/36/56, NAI; Mercy Petition of Parthasarathy Chettiar, File no. MHA (Judicial-1) 32/111/53, NAI.

44 'Evidence of Prosecution suffers from manipulation' in Mercy Petition of Raja Ram, File no. MHA (Judicial-1) 32/102/57, NAI. The High Court judgment was effectively a 'special pleading' in mercy Petition of Banshi Munda, File no. MHA (Judicial) 32/80/54, NAI.

45 Minute by WH Hailey dated 28 May 1923, File No. Home (Judicial) 373/1923, NAI.

sent by persons across Gujarat pleading for mercy in the case. Most of the petitioners saw the death sentence as an affront to the new Gujarat state and identity.[46] A more obvious case was that of Sukha and Jinda (the assassins of former Chief of Army Staff General Vaidya) where the Maharashtra Government left the decision to the Central Government given that the petition raised 'political issues relating to developments in Punjab'.[47] In another high-profile case relating to the assassination of Indira Gandhi, the then Prime Minister, the initial noting in the mercy petitions stated that given the circumstances of the case, 'the question of grant of clemency in this case hardly arises'.[48] This was a case where the broader political circumstances completely swept aside serious concerns of inadequate evidence with respect to the petitioner, Kehar Singh.[49]

General Security Considerations

Similar to broad political considerations are general security considerations, seeing that the courts do not typically enter this domain in their own disposition of the case. The potential impact on law and order has often been taken into account as a factor by the executive in the decision-making process. In the case of Sawai Singh, the petition was rejected since the victim was a policeman and commutation 'would not be in the interests of maintaining the morale of the police'.[50] The notings in Sawai Singh's file made reference to the general 'law and order' situations in the state—this was also a factor in recommending rejection in other cases.[51] In a case from Punjab in 1956, President Prasad observed the prevalence of continuing family feuds in the state. He therefore warned, '[w]e have therefore to look into such cases coming from the Punjab with a view also to the effect that the decision in the

46 Mercy Petition of Dinubhai Bhimbhai Desai, File no. MHA (Judicial-1) 32/136/60, NAI.

47 Letter from Secretary, Maharashtra Home Dept to Secretary, MHA dated 24 Aug 1992 in Mercy Petition of Sukhdev Singh @ Sukha and Harjinder Singh @ Jinda, File no. 9/2/92—Judl. (MP), MHA.

48 See Note by PS Ananthanarayanan, US (Judl) dated 15 October 1988, Mercy Petition of Satwant Singh and Kehar Singh, File. no. 9/4/88—Judl, MHA. There was hardly any real discussion on clemency in the MHA and Cabinet and virtually none on the (lack of) evidence against Kehar Singh. Even in the second round of decision making (required as per the direction of the Supreme Court), despite the involvement of the Solicitor General, the summary prepared by the MHA did not enter into issues of evidence.

49 For a sharp and detailed analysis of the inadequate evidence and the case in general, see Seervai (n 21) 1206–1233.

50 Mercy Petition of Sawai Singh, File no. 9/5/85—Judl, MHA.

51 Manipur's law and order situation was referred to by Secretary, Manipur Administration in Mercy Petition of Pukhrambam Jugeshwar Singh, File no. MHA (Judicial-1) 32/131/62, NAI; the law and order situation was also discussed in the Mercy Petition of Suraj Ahir, File no. MHA (Judicial-1) 32/195/61, NAI.

particular case under review may have on the people concerned and their likely conduct in the future'.[52]

Extinction of the Family Line

Continuation of the 'family line' is one of the more curious factors that have influenced the executive to commute death sentences. This appears to have come about as early as 1956 when the sentence of Angrez Singh was commuted 'with a view to saving the family from virtual extinction'.[53] In another case, where one brother murdered his parents, the executive commuted the sentence to avoid 'magnifying the loss' of the remaining brothers,[54] while in yet another, a husband who killed his wife had his death sentence commuted to prevent the children from becoming guardian-less.[55] The eventuality of an old man becoming 'sonless' was sufficient to commute the sentence in a fourth case.[56] Although it is arguable that these are cases where clemency proceedings have been closely attuned to the individual circumstances of petitioners, clemency to continue the family line can become an outright lottery, for example in a case where two brothers killed their parents. One brother's death sentence was commuted to life while the other was hanged, despite playing identical roles in the murder.[57]

Identity of the Victim

Although appearing to be a vital consideration in practice, this is one factor that is rarely mentioned on the record. A notable exception was a case where the Home Minister of then Madras State sought the rejection of a mercy petition as the victim was the mother of one of the Deputy Directors of Education in the State 'and the case had created a lot of excitement locally'.[58] In two other cases, victims' surviving family members played a vital role. In the petition filed by Parmatma Saran, a letter from the father of the victim in favour of mercy played a major role in the executive's decision to commute the

52 See handwritten note by President Prasad dated 27 May 1956 in Mercy Petition of Santa Singh, File no. MHA (Judicial-1) 32/65/56, NAI. See also Mercy Petition of Bagh Singh, File no. MHA (Judicial) 32/45/56, NAI.
53 Mercy Petition of Bagh Singh. ibid.
54 Mercy Petition of Koola Boyan, File no. MHA (Judicial-1) 32/87/61, NAI.
55 Mercy Petition of Pukhrambam Jugeshwar Singh (n 51).
56 Mercy Petition of Nasib Chand s/o Jai Ram, File no. MHA (Judicial-1) 32/121/58, NAI.
57 Mercy Petition of Bharwad Mepa Dana, File no. MHA (Judicial-1) 32/7/60, NAI.
58 See Mercy Petition of Subramanian (n 32); The petition was rejected by the Governor of Madras, but it was commuted by the president largely on grounds of insufficient evidence.

sentence,[59] while in proceedings relating to Dhananjoy Chatterjee, a letter from the father of the victim asking for the rejection of the petition and the execution of the accused was relied upon by the MHA in recommending rejection in its summary for the Home Minister.[60]

Ad-hoc Policies and Personal Views

Some ad-hoc policies also appear to have developed, although apparently limited to specific time periods. In a petition soon after independence, Home Minister VJ Patel noted:

> I am inclined to take a less severe view of offences arising out of these disputes over agricultural property, particularly where monetary transactions are involved. It is impossible for us to appreciate the feelings of a poor villager when he is deprived of his land and other agricultural property, as a result of transactions to which we might attach both moral and legal value, but which he can only view from the point of view of exploitation and usurpation.[61]

Although this view was followed as ad-hoc policy, it did not last long. By 1956 the MHA found no extenuating circumstances in a case where murders took place in an agricultural dispute.[62]

Next, in a 1962 case of murder by the victim's 31 year old brother over a property dispute, the minister had observed, 'in such cases, where there is positive refusal on the part of a member of a family of such a nature as to drive the other member thereof to desperation, it is our practice to treat it as constituting some element of mitigation.'[63] Although this kind of case may also be treated as provocation in Guideline I, the situation becomes more complicated when mitigation is afforded after the prisoner was a 'wronged' party in some form.[64] A broad formulation of 'wronged' can also became a guise for personal views to be brought in. This is evident in numerous cases from the 1950s,

59 Mercy Petition of Parmatma Saran s/o Kailash Chandra, File no. MHA (Judicial-1) 32/183/61, NAI.
60 See, for instance, the minutes dated 28 June 2004 by YK Baweja, Deputy Secretary in Mercy Petition of Dhananjoy Chatterjee, MHA (n 15).
61 Note by VJ Patel, Home Minister dated 5 September 1948 in Mercy Petition of Tirthu Singh, File no. MHA (Judicial) 20/93/48, NAI. In another case dated 11 April 1949, Patel recommended commutation 'in accordance with our previous attitude over such disputes on agricultural property' (Mercy Petition of Kanchan Mahton, File no. MHA (Judicial) 20/39/49, NAI).
62 Minute by Gulzar Singh, Under Secretary, in Mercy Petition of Harpal s/o Ram Singh, File no. MHA (Judicial-1) 32/37/56, NAI.
63 Minister of State for Home Affairs BN Datar dated 24 June 1962 in Mercy Petition of Abdul Hafiz s/o Salimullah, File no. MHA (Judicial-1) 32/18/62, NAI.
64 'When it is possible to believe that both the parties were wrong in the interests of justice or humanity, it would not be proper to send this young man of

when the then Minister of State for Home Affairs BN Datar commuted the sentence of many men sentenced to death for the murder of their wives, on the presumption that for a man to have taken such an extreme step, he *must* have been wronged.[65]

Lastly, in a large number of cases *absence of pre-meditation* and/or *lack of motive* were considered grounds for clemency, but these can also be read as being part of the 'circumstances of the case' mentioned in Guideline I.[66] A notion of '*parity*'—similar punishment to those with similar roles—has also been oft raised in many petitions, but this factor may also be read within Guideline I.[67]

The Role of the Individual Presidents

Although Indian presidents cannot make independent decisions on mercy petitions as they are bound by the recommendation of the Cabinet, they can play a significant role in determining the final decision. An exhaustive analysis of the way in which various presidents have exercised these powers is beyond the scope of this chapter.[68] However, it is nonetheless important to touch briefly upon the past role played by India's presidents, as the particular views, skills, and experience of the individuals holding that office form an important factor influencing mercy petition decision-making.

The first President—Rajendra Prasad (1950–1962)—was a trained lawyer and was able to significantly influence decisions on mercy petitions without overstepping his powers. Although his personal views on capital punishment are not publicly known, it is clear that he did not disagree when the ministers recommended commutation.[69] Prasad put his legal expertise to sound use where the Cabinet recommended rejection, but he had concerns about

impecunious habits to the gallows' (BN Datar, noting dated 22 December 1961 in Mercy Petition of Pokkiri, File no. MHA (Judicial-1) 32/181/61, NAI).

65 See Mercy Petition of Pannady, File no. MHA (Judicial-1) 32/6/56, NAI; Mercy Petition of Kiran Singh, File no. MHA (Judicial-1) 32/29/58, NAI; Mercy Petition of Sadhu Singh, File no. MHA (Judicial-1) 32/157/61, NAI; Mercy Petition of Chiraunji Lal, File no. MHA (Judicial-1) 32/41/61, NAI; Mercy Petition of Eswaran, File no. MHA (Judicial-1) 32/53/61, NAI.

66 It currently only refers to circumstances 'such as provocation or other similar justification'.

67 See e.g. Mercy Petition of Baladin s/o Nand Ram, File no. MHA (Judicial-1) 32/5/56, NAI; Mercy Petition of Santa Singh s/o Pal Singh, File no. MHA (Judicial-1) 32/65/56, NAI; Mercy Petition of Merhe Singh s/o Bachchu Singh, File no. MHA (Judicial-1) 32/1/59, NAI.

68 For details, see Batra, '"Court" of Last Resort' (n 1) 58–80.

69 After accepting the commutation, Prasad adds in his own handwriting, 'I do not ordinarily express my opinion contrary to that of the HM [Home Minister], particularly when the recommendation is for commutation of death sentence, as imprisonment for life which is given in substitution is a serious enough sentence'. See Mercy Petition of Ramu Khirappa Patil, File no. MHA (Judicial-1) 32/125/57, NAI.

culpability and role of the petitioner, often recommending reconsideration of such petitions.[70] Holding the office for the first 12 years of the Republic, President Prasad made the clemency system fairer and more credible. His rigorous analysis stretched the limited powers available to the presidency and asserted his moral authority over the Cabinet. Moreover, his propriety avoided embarrassing confrontations with the ministers. President Prasad undoubtedly made the task easier for his successors. His immediate successor—Sarvapalli Radhakrishnan (1962–1967)—had a clear abolitionist position.[71] Nonetheless, he does not appear to have used clemency powers to further this view.[72] While he actively continued the tradition of asking the ministers to reconsider their rejection of a number of petitions where he believed the decision ought to be changed, unlike his predecessor, he did not concern himself with the finer details of the law.[73]

In his brief stay in the office, President Zakir Hussain (1967–1969) also appears to have continued the trend toward seeking reconsideration from the minister. Hussain adopted a style similar to Radhakrishnan, relying often on the Secretary to the President to make the requisite notings, rather than doing so himself.[74] He even allowed regular public audiences where, amongst other citizens, family members of petitioners could also meet with the president.[75] Under Hussain and in the early years of the VV Giri presidency (1969–1974), a large number of petitions were commuted because of the Mahatma Gandhi birth centenary amnesty decision of the government.[76] Petitions from the

70 Mercy Petition of Baba Narain Das, File no. MHA (Judicial-1), 32/14/61, NAI; Mercy Petition of Iswar Dutt, File no. MHA (Judicial-1) 32/202/60, NAI; Mercy Petition of Kaloo, File no. MHA (Judicial-1) 32/14/58, NAI and Mercy Petition of Pakkirasami Nadar, File no. MHA (Judicial-1) 32/7/56, NAI.

71 See letter dated 21 May 1962 from President Radhakrishnan to Prime Minister Nehru; Nehru's reply to the president dated 22 May 1962 and the president's response dated 23 May 1962; PM Nehru's letters to the Home Minister dated 22 May 1962 and 25 May 1962, in File no. MHA (Judicial-II) 19/61/62, NAI.

72 His biographer suggests that throughout his five years in office, President Radhakrishnan rarely rejected a petition for mercy (Sarvepalli Gopal, *Radhakrishnan: A Biography* (Unwin Hyman 1989) 309). This does not appear to be correct, however, since Radhakrishnan rejected 112 petitions in 1963 and rejected 128 in 1964.

73 Unlike Dr Prasad who usually made his own notings, Radhakrishnan tended to either speak informally with the minister or send memos prepared by the Secretary to the President when required.

74 Noting by Nagendra Singh, Secretary to President, dated 27 April 1967 in Mercy Petition of Chinnappan, File no. MHA (Judicial-1) 32/99/66, NAI, which merely states, 'President would like the case to be reviewed.'

75 Mercy petitions of Chajju etc, File no. MHA (Judicial-III), 32/96/67, NAI.

76 As per the Cabinet meeting on 12 November 1968, all persons under sentence of death as of that day would have their sentences commuted. This decision was communicated to the State Governments via Circular Letter no. 35–2-68 J III dated 17 November 1968. See Mercy Petition of Shamrao s/o Apparao Chavan, File no. MHA (Judicial-B) 32/6/71, NAI.

tenure of Fakruddin Ali Ahmed (1974–1977) and N Sanjiva Reddy (1977–1982) were not available in the National Archives of India.[77]

Thereafter, decision-making on clemency petitions appears to have virtually come to a halt in the early 1980s. This was probably the result of the ongoing debate on capital punishment in the Supreme Court that also led to occasional stays on executions and death sentences, as well as delays within the MHA.[78] A large backlog of clemency petitions was eventually finalised in 1983–1984, during the tenure of President Giani Zail Singh (1982–1987). Unfortunately, none of these files are accessible and it is unclear what particular role the president played in the decision-making during this period.

By the time President Zail Singh left office, there was again a backlog of mercy petitions to be addressed by the MHA. President Venkataraman's tenure (1987–1992) saw 39 petitions disposed. Sentences were commuted in only five cases—four on the grounds of delay.[79] President Venkataraman personally supported capital punishment; even his interventions on delayed mercy petitions were not on humanitarian grounds but because delay ensured that the executive had little choice but to commute the sentence.[80] Venkataraman's tenure also saw the unprecedented event of a president sending back petitions for review where the minister had suggested commutation of the capital sentence.[81] It was also during President Venkataraman's tenure that the Kehar Singh clemency fiasco seriously damaged the moral standing of the presidency.[82] Following Venkataraman, President SD Sharma's tenure (1992–1997) saw 14 petitions decided. In all the petitions available for analysis, President SD Sharma did little more than sign the rejection order sent to him.[83]

No executions took place in the tenure of President KR Narayanan (1997–2002). While opposed to the death penalty in principle, he did nonetheless reject one petition. However, in that case, the Cabinet, in an extraordinary step, stayed

77 See note 1.
78 See Batra 'Don't be Cruel' (n 24) 297.
79 CK Banker (May 1988), Harbhajan Singh (July 1988), Nana Bhai Chormole (June 1988) and Daya Ram (August 1989). The only commutation on merits was Lok Pal Singh (July 1988). See MHA RTI reply (14 December 2007), on file with author (note 1).
80 In his autobiography, President Venkataraman also refers to the note he addressed to the Prime Minister on the same subject. In the note he states that 'delay in deciding mercy petitions not only inflicts mental torture on the convicts but also compels decision in favour of commutation, even where a penalty of death is otherwise warranted'. See Ramaswamy Venkataraman, *My Presidential Years* (Harper Collins 1994) 158.
81 Mercy Petition of Sawai Singh, File no. 9/5/85—Judl, MHA; Mercy Petition of Lok Pal Singh, File no. 9/7/85—Judl, MHA.
82 Seervai agreed with Justice Tarkunde's statement that even a dog could not be hanged on the evidence against Kehar Singh (Seervai (n 21) 1206–1233).
83 Nearly half of the 14 cases adjudicated upon by SD Sharma were inspected in the MHA while researching this study. Notes and details on file with the author. See note 1.

the execution.[84] President Narayanan also took the unusual step of not taking a decision on a number of mercy petitions. By the end of his tenure, several petitions still remained pending. While an uncommon step, this was certainly constitutional—a predecessor had done similarly with a piece of legislation.[85] A similar tactic was also adopted by his successor APJ Abdul Kalam (2002–2007), another reported opponent of the death penalty. However, an execution nonetheless took place in 2004,[86] and there is no indication in the executed man's mercy petition files that President Kalam asked the MHA to reconsider the recommendation. In a speech in October 2005, President Kalam questioned why only the poor ended up on death row.[87] He reportedly also raised this issue with the MHA and sought a review of pending mercy petitions.[88]

In recent years, Presidents Pratibha Patil (2007–2012), Pranab Mukherjee (2012–2017), and the current incumbent Ram Nath Kovind (2017–) appear to have stopped the practice of keeping mercy petitions pending, particularly following the Supreme Court's intervention in this matter.[89] Many petitions were therefore commuted during President Patil's tenure and President Mukherjee's tenure saw three executions carried out (in 2012, 2013, and 2015). However, mercy petition files and records relating to this period of the presidency have not yet been archived or otherwise made available to researchers.[90]

84 The death sentence of Govindasamy was eventually commuted by President Patil in November 2009: 'Report Card of Union Ministry of Home Affairs for November 2009' (*Press Information Bureau, Government of India*, 1 December 2009) <http://pibmumbai.gov.in/scripts/detail.asp?releaseId=E2009PR1364> accessed 22 October 2018.

85 Fali S Nariman, 'The Silences in Our Constitutional Law' (2006) 2 SCC (Jour) 15.

86 President Kalam is reported to have met Attorney General Milon Banerjee on 6 July 2004. See 'Dhananjoy Case: Kalam Consults Attorney General' (*The Hindu*, 7 July 2004) <https://www.thehindu.com/2004/07/07/stories/2004070703551200.htm> accessed 5 March 2019.

87 'Why Only Poor on Death Row?' (*The Times of India*, 18 October 2005) <https://timesofindia.indiatimes.com/city/delhi/Why-only-poor-on-death-row/articleshow/1266015.cms?> accessed 5 March 2019.

88 Venkatesan, 'Death Penalty' (n 27); another report notes, 'officials familiar with the correspondence say the files came back in three bulky bundles. The president had carefully catalogued the cases and given suggestions on possible remedial and rehabilitation methods the Home Ministry could adopt. Kalam is understood to have named specific convicts who had crossed 75, or belonged to the poorest strata of society, or for whom there was no scope of recidivism.' See 'Beg Your Pardon, Mr President?' (*The Indian Express*, 23 October 2005) <http://archive.indianexpress.com/oldStory/80547/> accessed 6 March 2019.

89 In a decision in January 2014, a three-judge bench of the Supreme Court ruled that excessive delay in carrying out the death sentence was an essential mitigating factor in a plea for commutation. See *Shatrughan Chauhan v Union of India* (2014) 3 SCC 1.

90 See note 1.

Conclusion

Unlike judicial proceedings, clemency proceedings are closed, with no 'reasoned judgment' published. The jurisprudence of the clemency process is thus largely secret. Despite the gaps and the inherent limitations of the sources relied upon in this chapter, the available material shows that several factors beyond those mentioned in the guidelines have influenced the eventual disposition of clemency petitions. Such an approach to decision-making, where the 'on the ground' situation often overrides the findings of the courts, makes clemency an invaluable resource, not only for academic research but also for abolitionists or those supporting specific commutation campaigns. In particular, while the executive may wish to assert a lack of precedent value among clemency decisions,[91] clemency outcomes attaining informal precedential status is arguably inevitable, particularly given the growing involvement of the Supreme Court in examining clemency decisions.

From a due process perspective, there is good news. As this chapter demonstrates, in practice, the executive has evolved a higher threshold for evidence of guilt in its mercy jurisprudence. This is a welcome development. The failures of the Indian criminal justice system—even in capital cases—are well documented.[92] Concerns in previous cases include fabricated or manipulated evidence, the use of confessions obtained by torture, and regular errors in the appreciation of evidence. In such a context, examination of evidence in mercy proceedings adds another welcome layer of protection.

Nevertheless, the mercy jurisprudence of the executive also demonstrates significant arbitrariness, perhaps unsurprising for such a closed and secretive process. For example, despite a general practice of not executing elderly persons, a condemned prisoner aged 75 has previously been refused clemency. In another case where a 65-year-old was executed in 1991, the issue of age was not even discussed during the deliberations on clemency.[93] A further example involves two cases with similar facts decided in the same year—the executive presumed some mental disturbance for one accused, while refusing to even consider it in the latter.[94]

91 Note by JA Kalyanakrishnan, Home Secretary, dated 19 December 1988 in the Kehar Singh case (note 48). The note stated, 'decisions in cases of mercy can have no precedent and will be unique in every case. To this extent it is a subjective value judgment which has to be exercised every time.'

92 See Amnesty International India and People's Union for Civil Liberties (Tamil Nadu & Puducherry) (n 40) 95–134.

93 Mercy Petition of Ajodhya, File no. MHA (Judicial-1) 32/16/61, NAI; Mercy Petition of Nataraya Gounder and Nattuthurai @ Natarayan, File no. 9/2/88—Judl (MP), MHA.

94 In Shiv Dayal's case (File no. MHA (Judicial-1), 32/25/56, NAI) the petitioner was a 50-year-old man who had killed his own cousin and his infant son. While the minister agreed that petitioner was not technically of unsound mind, he observed 'I am constrained to believe that the petitioner's mind had not been working in a normal order. It is impossible to believe that a person would act in the manner that the petitioner did even towards his own kith and kin except on the

The role of the individual view of the minister or other officials is also evident in the rare cases where, due to a change in personnel mid-way through the decision-making process, the previous recommendation is invariably reversed.[95] In a number of cases, where executions had not been carried out after the rejection, prisoners have been able to secure commutations via a second mercy petition with a new official in place.[96] The background, personal views, and personalities of the president also invariably contribute to different results.

The risk of politicisation of clemency powers is even higher in cases where questions of 'national security' are raised. The execution in 1984 of Mohammed Maqbool Butt, the founder and former leader of the separatist Jammu and Kashmir Liberation Front is an apt illustration. His petition, pending for seven years, was rejected after the abduction and killing of an Indian diplomat in Britain by the 'Kashmir Liberation Army' which sought the release of Butt in return for the diplomat.[97] Similarly, despite there being many relevant concerns raised in petitions filed by the Kashmiri militant Mohammad Afzal or by others on his behalf (i.e. unreliable evidence, quality of legal defence; and broader political implications in Kashmir),[98] no further departmental investigation or inquiry was announced.[99] Mohammad Afzal was executed in 2013.

Arbitrariness and discrimination in decision-making is arguably a human fallibility, and the abolition of capital punishment is the only way to completely prevent miscarriages of justice leading to unlawful executions. In the meantime—while the death penalty remains a part of the law in India—it is vital that the executive continues to consider a wide range of factors in clemency

assumption that he was working under the strain of a great excitation or perturbance that made him cease to be a human being.' However, in the case of Sukhbir (File no. MHA (Judicial-1) 32/31/56, NAI), where the petitioner had killed his own two children, the minister did not even consider his mental health, noting instead: 'a man who, in a gust of rage and emotion murders his own children, is not entitled to any clemency'.

95 Mercy Petition of Ram Charan, File no. MHA (Judicial-1) 32/70/62, NAI; Mercy Petition of Randhir Singh, File no. MHA (Judicial-1) 32/154/63, NAI.

96 See, for example, Mercy Petition of Ramsahai, File no. MHA (Judicial-1) 32/27/66, NAI. This is one of 14 similar petitions over the years.

97 'Death Penalty: Political Bias' (*Economic and Political Weekly*, 14 October 1989) <https://www.epw.in/journal/1989/41/uncategorised/death-penalty-political-bias.html> accessed 6 March 2019. Curiously, there is no reference whatsoever to any clemency proceedings in Butt's case in the MHA lists.

98 V Venkatesan, 'Mercy Guidelines' (2009 26(7)) Frontline <https://frontline.thehindu.com/static/html/fl2607/stories/20090410260703400.htm> accessed 6 March 2019.

99 In a number of previous mercy cases, both state and central governments saw fit to seek fresh inquiries from various government departments. In at least three cases in the 1960s, such re-investigations at the mercy stage led to commutation. See Mercy Petition of Avtar Singh s/o Sohan Singh, File no. MHA (Judicial-1) 32/199/61, NAI; Mercy Petition of Baij Nath Puri chela Shankar Puri, File no. MGA (Judicial-1) 32/122/63, NAI; Mercy Petition of Har Charan s/o Chandrabhal, File no. MHA (Judicial-1) 32/61/67, NAI.

decision-making. To combat arbitrariness, rejections of mercy petitions ought to require a reasoned decision and should be subject to regular oversight by the Supreme Court. A right to challenge the rejection of a mercy petition in the Supreme Court may be the best solution. Such an approach would be consistent with the right to life with dignity enshrined in the Constitution of India,[100] by ensuring that no condemned prisoner would be disadvantaged by the secret jurisprudence of the clemency process, which this chapter has brought to public attention.

100 Constitution of India 1950, art 21.

8 Executive Clemency in Capital Cases

Inadequate Laws and Inactive Practice in Contemporary China

Moulin Xiong

Introduction

On 15 November 2016, Jia Jinglong was executed in Shijiazhuang City, Hebei Province, despite a group of concerned scholars and citizens having requested executive clemency. This execution triggered public discussion over whether or not the People's Republic of China ('PRC') should reintroduce a mercy law applicable to capital cases. Jia, aged 29, had used a nail gun to kill 55-year-old village chief He Jianhua on 19 February 2015, after he ordered the demolition of Jia's house in May 2013.[1] Shijiazhuang Intermediate Court convicted Jia of murder and sentenced him to the death penalty with immediate execution. In justifying its death sentence, the court declared Jia's crime to be heinous and cited the public rage that his unforgivable offences caused.[2] After Hebei Provincial Higher Court rejected Jia's first appeal, the apex-level Supreme People's Court ('SPC') upheld his death sentence through the death penalty review process and affirmed the execution order.

In the weeks before Jia's execution, a number of professors and lawyers signed a joint letter addressed to SPC Chief Justice Zhou Qiang asking that Jia's life be spared, based on the idea that the legality of the house demolition was itself problematic.[3] One of the most famous voices included in these protests was that of Professor He Haibo (何海波), an expert on constitutional law affiliated with Tsinghua University's law school, who argued that Jia should

1 Stephen McDonell, 'Jia Jinglong: Chinese Villager Executed Despite Campaign' (*BBC News*, 15 November 2016) <www.bbc.com/news/world-asia-china-37985339> accessed 12 October 2017.

2 Hua Xuan, 'When Murder Meets Demolition: An Investigation of the Jia Jinglong Case (dangxuean yu chaiqian zaici jiaozhi)' *Southern Weekly* (Guangzhou, 11 November 2016) <www.infzm.com/content/120749> accessed 5 May 2018.

3 Zhang Zhenglei, 'Approval of the Death Penalty for Jia Jinglong's Murder Causes Controversy: Family Applies for Temporary Stay of Execution' (Jia Jinglong sharen an hezhun sixing yingfa Zhengyi, jiashu shenqing lingchang tingzhi zhixing)' *Kankanews* (Shanghai, 23 October 2016) <www.kankanews.com/a/2016-10-23/0037735582.shtml> accessed 15 November 2018.

not be executed, given the faults of the government's forcible house demolition policy.[4] Jia Jinglong's older sister also petitioned the SPC in an attempt to stop his execution,[5] while citizen Li Wei (李蔚) also launched an online petition addressed to the Standing Committee of the National People's Congress ('SCNPC') calling for executive clemency.[6]

Jia Jinglong's execution merely forms the tip of a proverbial iceberg of cases for which executive clemency has been requested in recent years, all of which ended in execution. Few criminal justice topics are as important as the death penalty in China, given the huge numbers of executions over the past several decades, particularly when China's punitive practice is compared with that of other death penalty retentionist states. It is high time we asked whether the Chinese state is ready to start considering executive clemency petitions for condemned inmates. However, the official answer is: simply not yet. Despite frequent requests for executive clemency in capital cases by death row inmates, family members, and concerned citizens, there is currently no possibility of sparing offenders' lives through amnesty, commutation, or pardon in contemporary China.

China's current legal system only makes use of special amnesty (特赦 *teshe*), provided for in the 1982 PRC Constitution (Articles 67 and 80), the 1997 Criminal Law (Article 65), and the 2012 Criminal Procedure Law (Article 15). During the history of the People's Republic, special amnesties have been applied en masse to the perpetrators of particular crimes, such as war criminals, as well as to elderly and juvenile prisoners. However, neither individual commutation nor individual pardon has been used in Chinese capital cases since 1949. Historically, another type of mercy, general amnesty (大赦 *dashe*), was the only form of post-judicial leniency included in the first PRC Constitution in 1954; only the National People's Congress (全国人民代表大会, hereinafter 'NPC') had the power to grant it.[7] Nevertheless, general amnesty was never used in practice, and was removed from the 1975 PRC Constitution altogether.[8] Despite the various

4 He Haibo, 'Tsinghua Law Professor: Jia Jinglong Should not be Killed (Jia Jinglong shi bugai sha de)' (*Xinlang Pinglun*, 23 October 2016) <http://news.sina.com.cn/pl/2016-10-23/doc-ifxwztrt0175510.shtml> accessed 8 May 2018.

5 Xue Rongmin, 'An Urgent Application to Suspend Jia Jinglong's Execution (Jia Jinglong guyi sharen an sixing tingzhi zhixing de jinji shenqing)' (*Weibo*, 21 October 2016) <https://weibo.com/ttarticle/p/show?id=2309404033155559515465> accessed 10 May 2018.

6 Du Xiansheng, 'Raise Your Voice in Support of Jia Jinglong's Fight for Executive Clemency (wei Jia Jinglong zhengqu teshe, qing fachu nide shengying)' (*xici.net*, 25 October 2016) <www.xici.net/d234991075.htm> accessed 10 May 2018; Liu Shengqian, 'The Supreme People's Court's Approval of Jia Jinglong's Death Sentence Ignites Controversy (zuigaofa hezhun jiajinglong sixing xuanqi yuqing fengbo)' *Sohu news* (18 November 2016) <http://news.sohu.com/20161108/n472649569.shtml> accessed 11 May 2018.

7 Constitution of the PRC 1954, art 27(12).

8 Liu Renwen, 'The Perfection of China's Pardon System (woguo shemian zhidu de wanshan)' (2014) 4 Science of Law (falyv kexue) 152, 155.

constitutional amendments that took place between 1975 and 2018, general amnesty has never again been included in China's constitutional scheme.[9]

Special amnesty, on the other hand, has been issued on several occasions since 1949. Prior to the implementation of the eighth special amnesty in 2015, covering juvenile offenders who committed minor offences and older offenders who had been incarcerated for lengthy periods, seven special amnesties had been granted primarily to war criminals convicted of non-capital offences.[10] Although it is widely accepted that executive clemency has never been issued to death row prisoners in China,[11] no constitution since 1949 has explicitly *prohibited* executive clemency (either individually or collectively) via general or special amnesty for death row prisoners.

In this chapter, the author examines the legal and political explanations for the practical absence of executive clemency in PRC capital cases, by means of special amnesty or otherwise. The author does not attempt to detail the long history of executive clemency in imperial China, but rather, describes the legal development of mercy law, practice, and related social concern in the People's Republic era. The author concludes the chapter by discussing the urgent necessity to activate executive clemency practice in contemporary China, in order to control execution numbers and to avoid wrongful executions.

Amnesty Law in Contemporary China

On 5 October 1998, China signed the International Covenant on Civil and Political Rights ('ICCPR') through representative Qing Huasun, China's ambassador to the United Nations. Nevertheless, the SCNPC never proceeded to ratify the Covenant, meaning that the ICCPR does not yet bind China in international law.[12] In Article 6(4), the ICCPR states that 'Anyone sentenced to death shall have the right to seek pardon or commutation of the sentence. Amnesty, pardon or commutation of the sentence of death may be granted in all cases'. Therefore, pursuant to international law, some clemency appeals in capital cases might be acceded to if China were to ratify the ICCPR in the future. This remains a hypothetical, however, and the unratified ICCPR may be one of the key reasons why informal requests for executive clemency have so far been invariably rejected.

9 Ibid.
10 Li Shouwei, 'Discussing the Eighth Special Amnesty in China (shenxing xueqiu: jiedu woguo dibaci tese)' (2016) 1 China Law Review (zhongguo falyv pinglun) 29, 30–31.
11 Fan Wen, 'Protecting the Right to Request Mercy for Death Row Inmates Sentenced to Immediate Execution (lun sixing liji zhixing fan shemian qingqiuquan zhi baozhang)' (2015) 5 Criminal Science (zhongguo xingshifa zazhi) 20, 23–33.
12 Siyan Sun, 'The Understanding and Interpretation of the ICCPR in the Context of China's Possible Ratification' (2007) 6 Chinese Journal of International Law 17, 18; Daniel Pascoe and Michelle Miao, 'Victim Perpetrator Reconciliation Agreements: What Can Muslim-Majority Jurisdictions and the PRC Learn From Each Other?' (2017) 66 ICLQ 963, 975.

It is in this context that the author introduces China's special amnesty law. The primary international law concern is that special amnesty does not provide for specific application procedures.[13] When PRC law does mention special amnesty, it does not address how defendants and family members might engage the amnesty process, but instead introduces other regulations. The constitutional laws mentioning amnesty introduce the SCNPC's authority over special amnesty and the president's power to issue special amnesty orders, while the criminal law and criminal procedure legislation covering amnesty only mention recidivism and special amnesty's effect on ongoing criminal proceedings.

Constitutional Law

The PRC's first constitution was promulgated in 1954. To date, this has been China's only constitution to mention both general amnesty and special amnesty. Article 27 of the 1954 Constitution declared that 'The National People's Congress exercises the following functions and powers: [...] (12) to decide on the granting of general amnesty'. Article 31 declared that 'The Standing Committee of the National People's Congress exercises the following functions and powers: [...] (15) special amnesty'. Article 40 declared that 'The President of the People's Republic of China, in pursuance of decisions of the National People's Congress and its Standing Committee, promulgates orders of general amnesty and special amnesty'.[14] Thereafter, the 1975 Constitution did not mention amnesty at all, omitting all references to general amnesty and special amnesty.[15]

On 15 March 1978, the NPC passed a new constitution, which likewise did not include general amnesty but which did reinstate special amnesty in Article 25, which declares that 'The Standing Committee of the National People's Congress exercises the following functions and powers: [...] (11) special amnesty'.[16] In July 1979, further constitutional amendments were passed by the NPC, but these did not affect the special amnesty power contained within the 1978 document.[17]

The current constitutional regulations regarding special amnesty are provided for in the 1982 Constitution, as amended in 2018. Article 67 states that 'The Standing Committee of the National People's Congress exercises the

13 Liu (n 8) 154; Chang Ning, 'Death Row Pardons in Moderation (sixing shemian shidu tanxi)' (2008) 3 Law Science Magazine (faxue zazhi) 113, 115.
14 Constitution of the PRC 1954, art 40. See Pascoe and Novak, this volume, on clemency terminology in the PRC context.
15 Constitution of the PRC 1975. See further Pascoe and Novak, this volume, on Sebba's interpretation of the 1975 Constitution's provisions.
16 Constitution of the PRC 1978, art 25(11).
17 Resolution to Amend Certain Articles of the Constitution of the People's Republic of China (guanyu xiugai 'zhonghua renmin gongheguo xianfa' ruogan guiding de jueyi), 1 July 1979.

following functions and powers: [...] (18) to decide on the granting of special amnesty'. Article 80 of the 1982 Constitution further states that 'The President of the People's Republic of China, in pursuance of decisions of the National People's Congress and its Standing Committee, promulgates orders of special amnesty'.[18] Since 1982, these substantive provisions have remained unaltered, despite the 1982 Constitution's five subsequent amendments (1988, 1993, 1999, 2004, 2018). The only differences in this context between the 1954 Constitution and the 1982 Constitution plus its subsequent amendments is the fact that 'general amnesty' has been removed from Chinese constitutional law altogether.

Criminal Law

Articles 65 and 66 of the current Chinese Criminal Law mention amnesty in the context of the regulation of recidivists, following the earlier version of the Criminal Law enacted in 1979.[19] Article 65 of the present version states that:

> If a criminal commits another crime punishable by fixed-term imprisonment or a heavier penalty within five years after serving his sentence of not less than fixed-term imprisonment or [after] receiving an amnesty (赦 *she)* or exemption (免 *mian*), he is a recidivist and shall be given a heavier punishment.[20]

Article 66 states that any 'criminal endangering national security [who] commits the same crime again at any time after serving his sentence or [after] receiving an amnesty or exemption shall be dealt with as a recidivist'.[21]

Nevertheless, nothing in the present Criminal Law further regulates special amnesty procedures, let alone describes what penalty should be rendered to criminals after special amnesty is applied. Considering the wording of the previous eight special amnesty decrees, amnesty generally means to exempt the recipient from prosecution or to free the recipient from imprisonment. However, the Criminal Law itself does not contain any article indicating whether offenders should be pardoned or whether their sentences should be commuted from heavier to lighter punishments. In the case of death sentences, for instance, whether special amnesty has the effect of pardoning the offence altogether or instead operates to commute the sentence to death with suspension, to life imprisonment, or to fixed-term imprisonment is unclear.

Thus, it is safe to say that the current Chinese Criminal Law does not at all envisage collective amnesty, individual pardon, or individual commutation of

18 Constitution of the PRC 1982, art 80.
19 Criminal Law of the PRC 1997, art 65–66; Criminal Law of the PRC 1979, art 61–62.
20 Criminal Law of the PRC 1997, art 65.
21 Criminal Law of the PRC 1997, art 66.

sentences for criminals on death row, even if it might contemplate mercy for lesser offenders. For capital prisoners condemned at the Provincial High Court stage, there is only one effective strategy to remain alive, namely concentrating all efforts on avoiding the confirmation of the death sentence with immediate execution during the SPC review stage. Once the SPC approves the death penalty with immediate execution, there are effectively no legal means of saving the offender's life. The absence of legal provisions regarding executive clemency is the critical reason why the effort to save Jia Jinglong failed. Within the current legal climate in China, those given death sentences are doomed to be executed.

Criminal Procedure Law

Article 15 of the current Criminal Procedure Law of China (2012) mentions that special amnesty brings criminal proceedings to an end, replicating a provision within the original version passed in 1979.[22] Article 15 states:

> In any of the following circumstances, no criminal responsibility shall be investigated; if investigation has already been undertaken, the case shall be dismissed, or prosecution shall not be initiated, or the handling shall be terminated, or innocence shall be declared: … (3) *if an exemption of criminal punishment has been granted in a special amnesty decree.*[23]

This was and is a unique article regarding the criminal procedures surrounding special amnesty. No other articles in the 2012 Criminal Procedure Law mention anything about mercy.

Given that the Criminal Procedure Law serves as a guideline for all judicial behaviour, there are thus many procedural problems regarding applications for special amnesty, including the question of how judicial organs or other authorities should transfer clemency petitions to the SCNPC as the final decision-maker. In practice, the absence of relevant procedural articles in the Criminal Procedure Law hinders the use of executive clemency altogether. The Criminal Procedure Law does not provide any systematic guidance on how to apply, when to apply, and who can apply for executive clemency. This lack of legislative guidance explains why Jia Jinglong's older sister applied for special amnesty directly to the SPC, and why citizen Li Wei, who had no familial relationship with Jia, could issue to the SCNPC a collection of signatures petitioning for special amnesty.

22 Criminal Procedure Law of PRC 1979, art 11(3).
23 Criminal Procedure Law of PRC 2012, art 15, emphasis added.

Summary

To summarise, I conclude that Chinese law allows for special amnesty, albeit on a superficial basis. The amnesty power rests with the central authority, as self-exercised by the SCNPC and signed into law by the president. By contrast, specific regulations regarding when, who, and how to apply for special amnesty are absent. It is doubtful whether Chinese law allows individual applications for special amnesty, including from prisoners sentenced to death.

Nevertheless, the Chinese government has passed eight unilateral special amnesty orders over the past half-century. These orders were issued by the central government itself, hence no individual applications were granted or rejected. Members of the public do not understand how and why the SCNPC decides to collectively pardon criminals, and how and why the president signs the special amnesty decree.

Thus, regarding the failure of the executive clemency requests submitted by Jia Jinglong's sister and by Li Wei, fault does not lie with the justices of the SPC. There is no proof that the justices were unwilling to be merciful, but at the same time, they presumably did not know how to respond to requests beyond their judicial power. Even if any of the justices had been willing to save Jia's life, there was no procedural way to do so.

It is not my wish to comment on whether China's death penalty laws meet the minimum requirement regarding the 'right to seek' pardons or commutations as enunciated by the ICCPR, but the absence of any executive clemency for death row prisoners over the PRC's history is good evidence from which to draw a conclusion.[24] At the very least, I believe that what China needs is a detailed amnesty law, specifying a bottom-up (自下而上 *zixia ershang*) application procedure so that individuals may directly petition the government for special amnesty. Mine is far from the first scholarly call for legal reform on special amnesty. For example, a group of scholars from the China University of Political Science and Law in Beijing has petitioned the SCNPC to add an article regarding special amnesty into the draft amendment of the Criminal Procedure Law.[25] In addition, Professor Liu Renwen has proposed new amnesty legislation so as to clarify the application procedure and ensure that it complies with the ICCPR.[26]

24 See further Novak and Pascoe, this volume, on the PRC's position with respect to ICCPR art 6(4).

25 Zhang Yuan, 'Experts and Scholars Recommend that Criminal Procedure Law Offers Death Row Offenders the Right to Apply for Executive Clemency (zhuanjia xuezhe jianyi xingsufa ying fuyu sixingfan shenqing teshe quan)' (*news.china.com.cn*, 11 December 2011) <http://www.china.com.cn/news/law/2011-12/01/content_24047492.htm> accessed 13 March 2018.

26 Mei Shuang, 'Criminal Jurists Recommend Implementation of Mercy Law (xingfa xuejia jianyi zhiding shemianfa)' (*News.163*, 23 July 2014) <http://news.163.com/14/0723/20/A1S8LN2T00014Q4P.html> accessed 1 May 2018; Liu Renwen, 'Recent Reforms and Prospects in China' in Roger Hood and Surya

Special Amnesty 1959–2015

On 17 September 1959, Chairman Liu Shaoqi issued the first order of special amnesty in the PRC's history. The amnesty pardoned certain war criminals, counter-revolutionaries, and ordinary prisoners. It was granted to commemorate the tenth anniversary of the founding of the PRC and the country's accomplishments since its establishment in 1949. By 1975, following seven separate rounds of special amnesty, China had freed a total of 554 Kuomintang war criminals.[27] In addition, 1,062 Japanese war criminals were freed from prison in 1956 by various acts of mercy such as early release, parole, and exemption from prosecution.[28] The sentences of the offenders pardoned in the first seven special amnesty orders ranged from, at the upper end, those who were originally sentenced to suspended death sentences but whose sentences had already been commuted to lesser punishments after two years' imprisonment, through to prisoners originally sentenced to life imprisonment and fixed-term sentences of imprisonment.[29] Most amnesty recipients were initially serving fixed-term sentences or life sentences. Notably, the first seven special amnesties did not benefit any prisoners sentenced to the death penalty with immediate execution.[30]

Deva (eds), *Confronting Capital Punishment in Asia: Human Rights, Politics, and Public Opinion* (OUP 2013) 118–122.

27 Hou Puwen, 'Special Amnesty for 554 Kuomintang Civil War Criminals (Teshe 554 ming guomingdang zhanfan shimo)' (2011) 3 Wan Qing 43, 44.

28 Zhuo Aiping and Wang Yonggui. 'Zhou Enlai and the Japanese War Criminals Pardoned in 1956 (Zhou Enlai yu 1956 nian kuanshi riben zhanfan)' (2005) 5 Hong Guangjiao 46, 47–48; Zhang Xibo, *The Criminal Law History of the People's Republic of China* (zhonghua renmin gongheguo xingfashi) (People's Security University of China Press 1998) 500; Sui Shuying, 'The Trial and Release of Japanese War Criminals in China in 1950s (20 shiji wushi niandai zhongguo dui riben zhanfan de shenpan yu shifang)' (2006) 4 Journal of Yantai University 459, 460.

29 Fan (n 11) 26–34; Ren Dawang, 'The Seven Orders of Special Amnesty in History, a List of the Pardoned Criminals, and the PRC's Special Amnesty Orders (1959–1975) (lishi shang de qici teseling, teshe renyuan mingdan, zhonghua renmin gongheguo tesheling)' (*Lvfawang*, 25 August 2015) <http://www.88148.com/Info/201508251O778.html#n1> accessed 12 February 2019.

30 In China, since the 1950s there have existed two types of death sentences: the death penalty with immediate execution and the suspended death penalty. The former refers to a death sentence designed to kill the offender, whereas the latter offers a commutation to a lesser penalty given meritorious behaviour. The commuted penalty is either life imprisonment, or a fixed-term sentence of 15 years (prior to 1979), 15–20 years (between 1980 and 2011), or 25 years (since 2011).

According to the first six (1959–1966) Special Amnesty Orders, before becoming eligible for special amnesty, war criminals had to serve at least ten years in prison. Hence, prisoners who had originally been sentenced to the suspended death penalty had to already have their death sentences reduced to life imprisonment or a fixed term sentence some years beforehand in order to fall within the terms of the Special Amnesty Order. See Fan (n 11) 25–26; Xiong Moulin, 'The Death Penalty after the Restoration of Centralized Review: An Empirical Study of Capital Sentencing' in Liang Bin and Lu Hong (eds) *Death Penalty in China: Policy, Practice,*

The eighth special amnesty was granted by the SCNPC and signed by President Xi Jinping on 29 August 2015, before the national commemoration of the 70th anniversary of the end of World War II. Four types of criminals benefited: (a) offenders who had fought against the Japanese invasion and in the Chinese Civil War against the Kuomintang; (b) offenders who had participated in wars to safeguard national sovereignty, security, and territorial integrity after 1949, with the exception of those found guilty of serious crimes and repeat offenders; (c) offenders aged 75 or above, and those with severe physical disabilities; (d) juvenile offenders who had committed crimes while under the age of 18 and had received a maximum sentence of three years in prison, or had less than a year left to serve, with the exception of those convicted of serious crimes or narcotics offences. The official statistics confirmed by Chief Justice Zhou Qiang stated that 31,527 prisoners were released from prison in 2015, pursuant to this order for special amnesty.[31]

Despite these eight special amnesty decrees, not a single death row prisoner has been released or has had his or her sentence converted to a lesser punishment.[32] Within the first eight decrees the offenders pardoned and released were mainly those sentenced to fixed-term imprisonment, plus a select few sentenced to the death penalty with suspension or to life imprisonment, rather than those condemned to death with immediate execution.[33] For nascent communist China, the most important missions were to reunify Taiwan with the mainland, to legitimise the state's authority, and to stabilise China's sovereignty worldwide. As a result, the earliest PRC governments granted special amnesty to demonstrate state accomplishments, to provide socialist education, and to engender national harmony.[34] As policymaker, the Central Government decided that the purpose of holding war

and Reform (Columbia University Press 2016) 218–219; Michelle Miao, 'Two Years between Life and Death: A Critical Analysis of the Suspended Death Penalty in China' (2016) 45 International Journal of Law, Crime and Justice 26, 28–29.

31 '31527 Criminals Pardoned; Most are Minors (31527 ren huo teshe daduoshu wei weichengnian fan)' *Beijing News* (26 January 2016) <http://epaper.bjnews.com.cn/html/2016-01/26/content_620440.htm?div=-1> accessed 2 January 2018.

A ninth Special Amnesty was recently promulgated in June 2019 to celebrate the 70th anniversary of the founding of the PRC. Again, no death row prisoners were eligible for pardon or commutation ('NPCSC Grants Amnesty to Convicts to Mark 70th P.R.C. Founding Anniversary' (*NPC Observer*, 30 June 2019) <https://npcobserver.com/2019/06/30/npcsc-grants-amnesty-to-convicts-to-mark-70th-p-r-c-founding-anniversary/> accessed 12 December 2019).

32 See also note 31.

33 Life imprisonment in the PRC is not meant to incarcerate the prisoner until death. According to the Criminal Law of the PRC 1997, art 81, and the state's earlier policy on life imprisonment, an offender may have the right to apply for parole under certain circumstances, following a minimum period of incarceration of 13 years (Fan (n 11) 26–31).

34 Hou (n 27) 44; Wang Yongqing. 'Special Amnesty for Kuomintang War Criminals (teshe guomingdang zhanfan shimo)' (2002) 11 Dang Shi Bo Lan 37, 38–40; Yi Hua, 'The Search for a Special Amnesty That Will Peacefully Unite China

crimes trials was not necessarily to enforce deadly punishment. Therefore, none of those convicted were sentenced to death, and moreover, no Japanese war criminals were even sentenced to life imprisonment. In his speech on the 'Ten Relationships' (论十大关系 *lun shida guanxi*), Chairman Mao Zedong stated that no Civil War criminals should be killed, neither Emperor Pu Yi nor the Nationalist agent and general Kang Ze, nor others, in order to prevent further reprisal killings.[35] This political instruction was rooted in the goals of reunifying Taiwan by persuading escaped individuals to return to Mainland China, and salvaging Sino-Japanese relations after the Korean War in the 1950s.[36]

With the Communist victory over the Kuomintang during the Chinese Civil War, reunifying Taiwan with mainland China became the PRC's main foreign policy challenge. PRC politicians recognised that killing Civil War criminals would not prove helpful in reunifying Taiwan.[37] For example, Premier Zhou Enlai stated that 'killing has only a negative effect rather than a positive effect on the Taiwan issue, as it makes them nervous by thinking of their fate'.[38] As a result, none of the Civil War criminals tried in court were ever sentenced to death, though most of them originally believed that their punishment would be execution. Instead, the Civil War detainees were punished with suspended death sentences, or life imprisonment, but never with capital punishment with immediate execution.[39] For example, in October 1951 Cai Shengsan was sentenced to the death penalty with suspended execution in Shangrao, Jiangxi Province, given that the leader of the local Public Security Bureau wished to spare his life. Cai's suspended death sentence was commuted to life imprisonment in 1953, and after serving 25 years, Cai

(zhengqu heping tongyi zuguo de teshe xingdong)' (2001) 11 Liang An Guan Xi 50, 51–52.

35 Zhang (n 28) 511; Zhang Yawen, 'Interviewing Cai Shengshan, the Last KMT War Criminal (fang guomindang zuihou yiming zhanfan Cai Shengsan)' <https://web.archive.org/web/20180104182920/http://blog.sina.com.cn/s/blog_4c396b5e0102wnai.html> accessed 12 December 2019.

36 Hyon Joo Yoo, 'China's Friendly Offensive toward Japan in the 1950s: The Theory of Wedge Strategies and International Relations' (2015) 39 Asian Perspectives 1, 12–13.

37 Wang (n 34) 38; Hou (n 27) 43–44; Yi (n 34) 50–51.

38 Ibid.

39 The academic literature disputes whether any Chinese Civil War captives were ever sentenced to death. I argue that there were no death sentences judicially imposed, because of the absence of formal trial processes. However, in his book, Jin Yuan asserts that six Civil War convicts were sentenced to death with immediate execution and ten Civil War convicts were sentenced to the suspended death penalty by local authorities. In 1956, these prisoners were sent to Fushun War Criminals Correction Centre. See Jin Yuan, *Special Destiny, Reminiscences from the War Criminal Management Office (Qiyuan Yige zhanfan guanli suozhang de huiyi)* (Chinese People's Liberation Army Publishing House 1999) 243.

was pardoned from Fushun War Correction Centre on 19 March 1975.[40] According to the 1959 special amnesty decree, sentences of death with suspension, life imprisonment, and fixed-term prison sentences were all pardonable. Cai's suspended death sentence which resulted in eventual pardon is one of many such cases.[41]

Aside from Civil War captives, Zhou Enlai also instructed the Minister of Public Security Luo Ruiqing (罗瑞卿) and the Minister of Justice Shi Liang (史良) to incarcerate Japanese and Manchurian war criminals, to ensure that none escaped or died in captivity, and to ensure that they would not be sentenced to death in future.[42] Premier Zhou gave instructions that neither death sentences nor life imprisonment were to be given to Japanese war criminals, and that their fixed terms of imprisonment were to be as short as possible.[43] Consequently, 45 notorious Japanese war criminals tried in China were each sentenced to fixed-term imprisonment of not more than 20 years, despite the fact that most of them had ordered or participated in killings of the elderly, women, and children in China.[44] The PRC's policy proved extremely lenient, when compared with the Nationalist government's sentencing of 149 war criminals to death with immediate execution between December 1945 and December 1947, followed by the actual execution of 145 of these convicts prior to 1949.[45]

Given the nature of executive clemency as post-judicial leniency awarded by political authorities, the suspended death sentence should not technically be regarded as a form of executive clemency itself, but instead as a trial sentence imposed in the courtroom. However, the sentencing of war criminals to fixed terms of imprisonment and to suspended death sentences directly followed instructions from PRC leaders Mao Zedong and Zhou Enlai that no one should be killed in the aftermath of the Chinese Civil War and the Second World War. These pre-directed sentences may be considered as a form of official mercy, but as mentioned were not acts of executive clemency, formally speaking. This is perhaps the fundamental reason why recent PRC governments have not granted clemency to offenders sentenced to death: no political leader wants to be the first to approve

40 'Cai Shengsan, The Last Kuomintang Civil War Criminal (Cai Shengsan, zuihoude guomindang zhanfan)' (*iqiyi*) 23:47~26:25 <www.iqiyi.com/v_19rrj5sz6k.html> accessed 12 December 2017.

41 Special Amnesty Order of the Chairman of the People's Republic of China (zhonghua renmin gongheguo zhuxi teshe ling), 17 September 1959.

42 Yin Jiamin, 'Why New China Pardoned High-level War Criminals (xin zhongguo weihe teshe gaoji zhanfan)' (2015) 18 Leaders Articles (lingdao wencui) 81, 82.

43 Jin (n 39) 200–201; Zhang (n 28) 504–505; Wang Junyan, *The Japanese War Criminals Tried in Secret (riben zhanfan shenpan miwen)* (The Chinese Overseas Publishing House 1995) 413–416.

44 Wang (n 43) 418–474; Justin Jacobs, 'Preparing the People for Mass Clemency: The 1956 War Crime Trials in Shengyang and Taiyuan' (2011) 205 The China Quarterly 152, 153.

45 Liu Tong, 'How the Courts of China tried Japanese War Criminals (minguo fating ruhe shenpan riben zhanfan)' (2014) 3 Tongzhou Gongjin 56.

legal mercy in capital cases. It therefore appears that a desire not to break with political tradition may be impeding mercy reform in China.

Legally speaking, China used executive clemency only for non-capital cases during the first eight special amnesties, yet Chinese political leaders undoubtedly exercised a parallel form of mercy in capital cases, sparing war criminals' lives through extra-legal political instructions. The critical difference between the legal and extra-legal measures concerns the relative stage of the criminal justice process during which the offenders are pardoned. The 'legal' form of mercy occurs after conviction and sentencing, whereas the 'extra-legal' form is based on political orders given before trial, in a society without effective judicial independence.

In this respect, the absence of any executive clemency for capital cases within the first eight special amnesties reflects the absence of the rule of law in the early PRC era and the dominant culture of administrative rule by political leaders. The largely administrative rule exercised during the first 30 years after 1949 can be partially attributed to the new communist regime abolishing the Six Laws (六法全书 *liufa quanshu*) used in the prior Nationalist era.[46] As noted, China's current practice is reflective of its past history. If the war criminals had been formally reprieved after conviction and capital sentencing, rather than by political instruction before any sentence had been handed down, it is likely that executive clemency for death row prisoners would now exist in contemporary China, through the constitutional mechanism of special amnesty.

Examining the Absence of Executive Clemency

Historically, executive clemency was used in China as far back as the Western Zhou Dynasty, founded in 1046 BC, through to the Qing Dynasty, ending in AD 1911.[47] Imperial decrees were used to spare death row prisoners in almost every dynasty.[48] Prior to the founding of the PRC in 1949, executive clemency in capital cases could also be found in the Republic of China, ruled by the Kuomintang. For instance, Zhou Fohai, a traitor to both the Chinese Communist Party and the Kuomintang, was first sentenced to death for treason by the Capital High Court in Nanjing under the Nationalist government. His sentence was upheld by the Supreme Court in 1946. Nevertheless, Nationalist leader Chiang Kai-shek commuted Zhou's death sentence to life imprisonment on 26 March 1947 after Zhou's wife interceded on his behalf.[49] Thereafter,

46 Xiong Xianjue. 'The Origins and Impressions of Abolishing Six Laws (Feichu liufa quanshu de yuanyou ji yingxiang)' (2007) 3 Yanhuang Chunqiu 10, 11.

47 Brian E McKnight, *The Quality of Mercy: Amnesties and Traditional Chinese Justice* (University Press of Hawaii 1981) 112–127; Tan Qiu, 'Ancient Mercy in China (woguo gudai de dashe)' (2015) 34 Zhengfu Fazhi 54.

48 McKnight (n 47) 112; Børge Bakken, 'China, A Punitive Society?' (2011) 6 Asian Journal of Criminology 33, 38.

49 Ma Li, 'The Unknown Story Why Chiang Kai Shek Pardoned Zhou Fohai (Jiang Jieshi teshe Zhou Fohai neimu)' (2014) 10 Dangan Jiyi 40, 42.

since the foundation of Communist China in 1949, although thousands of war criminals have been freed by special amnesty within non-death penalty cases, no capital prisoner's sentence has ever been commuted after conviction.

Within the following subsections, I offer several plausible explanations for the lack of a functioning executive clemency petition system in contemporary China, based upon available documentary evidence. Nevertheless, the true reasons for China's dearth of clemency regulations and grants may never be known.

Tradition

In ancient China there existed diverse and complex post-conviction mercy systems to abrogate execution by means of imperial decree, including monetary redemption (赎), release from prison, and commutation to exile (流).[50] Nevertheless, not every prisoner had the opportunity to obtain clemency from the emperor and, moreover, some heinous crimes were not pardonable at all. For instance, the famous principle of 'no mercy for ten heinous crimes' (十恶不赦 *shie bushe*), formulated long ago during the Sui Dynasty (隋朝) (AD 581 to 618), was still in use in recent centuries.[51] This rule provided that offenders who committed heinous crimes including treason, killing elders, murdering more than three people, and so forth, would never be pardoned, thereby reflecting ancient political, retributive, and ethical values. In this way, arguably contemporary criminal law in the PRC continues to reflect traditional culture.

Article 48 of Criminal Law of the People's Republic of China, revised in 1997, stipulates that the death penalty shall only be applied to criminals who have committed extremely serious crimes.[52] Moreover, the term 'extremely serious crimes' (罪行极其严重 *zuixing jiqiyanzhong*) is similar to the equivalent 'most heinous crimes' (罪大恶极 *zuida keji*) found in Article 43 of the 1979 Criminal Law of the People's Republic of China. Despite no reference being made within the present criminal law legislation to the principle of 'no mercy for ten heinous crimes', the very fact that capital punishment is practised in the first place implies that the relevant offenders have committed the most heinous crimes known to Chinese law. Given that the death sentence is already reserved for 'extremely serious crimes' or previously the 'most heinous' crimes, PRC officials remain loathe to commute or pardon the sentences of capital prisoners, given the historical influence of an anti-mercy culture regarding such crimes.

50 Cang Hai, 'Which Methods were used to Commute Death Sentences in the Criminal Law of Ancient China? (zhongguo gudai xingfa zhong *jiansi* you naxie changshi)' (2015) 23 Zhengfu Fazhi 16, 17.

51 The ten heinous crimes were rebellion against authority (谋反), destroying imperial ancestral temples (谋大逆), treason (谋判), rebellion against feudal ethics (恶逆), brutality 不道), disrespect (大不敬), to be unfilial (不孝), to be disharmonious (不睦), immorality (不义), and incest (内乱).

52 Criminal Law of the PRC 1997, art 48.

The most problematic issue here is that current criminal law legislation does not determine whether a crime is extremely serious or not. Some crimes punishable by the death penalty in Chinese criminal law may not be extremely serious in comparative perspective. For example, drug transporting, regulated by Article 347 of the Criminal Law 1997, should arguably not be punishable by death, when compared with the more serious offences of smuggling, manufacturing, and selling drugs. Moreover, even serious drug offences are not as heinous as homicide. Even some murders, such as that committed by Jia Jinglong, which caused the death of only one victim, are less heinous than others.

Connecting the phrases 'serious crimes' and 'heinous crimes', I suggest that imperial China's anti-mercy culture may be one influence on the absence of executive clemency for capital crimes in contemporary China. However, there are also enormous societal differences between modern China and imperial China. Modern, global values do not regard some of the crimes denoted as 'heinous' in ancient China as heinous today. Likewise, in contemporary China, there is no reason why enlightened citizens should not support executive clemency as a form of legal mercy.

Equality

Hu Yunteng, one of the most influential judges of the SPC, commented in the context of the eighth special amnesty in 2015 that 'for a long time, the special amnesty [has been] so sensitive that the inappropriateness of usage would incur doubt and criticism'.[53] As Hu recognised, opposition to special amnesty in China is, in fact, extremely common.

A common concern of critics is that judicial authority should not be overridden by special amnesty, which would serve to undermine the deterrent effect of criminal punishment and would undermine the rule of law.[54] This is because amnesty entertains the illusion that convicted criminals can receive lenient punishment or can escape punishment altogether. Amnesty also increases the risk of corrupt practices. As Bakken acknowledges, the term 'mercy' has acquired a negative connotation within modern Chinese vocabulary, in large part due to the slogan: 'To show mercy to the enemy is to show cruelty to the masses' (对敌人仁慈就是对人民残忍 *dui diren renci jiushi dui renmin canren*).[55]

53 Jiang Anjie, 'Member of the Supreme People's Court Law Review Commission: Re-Implement the Amnesty System to Follow the Trend of Modern Times (zuigaofa shenweihui zhuanzhi weiyuan: chongqi teshe zhidu shunying shidai chaoliu)' *Xinhua News* (Beijing, 9 September 2015) <http://www.chinanews.com/sh/2015/09-02/7503448.shtml> accessed 10 March 2018.

54 Yin Jianfeng, 'The Misunderstanding and Reinterpretation of Special Pardon in the New Era (xin shiqi teshe de renshi wudu jiqi xiaojie)' (2016) 1 Cognition and Practice 27, 28.

55 Bakken (n 48) 40.

On the other hand, proponents of a revival of post-judicial mercy contend that the use of pardons and commutations in China can help restore balance, given the inconsistencies inherent within the modern Chinese criminal justice system. The ability of clemency to promote balanced punishment is supported by former SPC chief justice Xiao Yang: 'I agree [with the] research on amnesty rules … fully demonstrating [that] the pardon system will certainly have enormously positive impacts on creating a harmonious and stable social environment, and enhancing the internal unity of the people'.[56]

As noted above, proposals to include a right to seek clemency in PRC law have so far not succeeded. Nevertheless, the potential benefits of more frequent amnesties have been discussed at length by scholars. Several scholars have proposed an amnesty scheme to lessen future corruption. Granting amnesty to corrupt officials would wipe the slate clean, leading to incorruptible and honest political performance in the future. He Jiahong, a leading and respected legal scholar based at Renmin Law School, recently warned that China must pardon two million corrupt officials to avoid falling into a 'vicious cycle' of sleaze that could ultimately lead to the government's collapse.[57] However, such a widespread use of the special amnesty power would presumably prove difficult for the public to accept. An earlier survey conducted in Hunan province by Li Yongzhong, a leading professor in anti-corruption research, found that over 90 per cent of respondents opposed pardoning corrupted officials.[58]

I am inclined to believe that the dominant judicial philosophy of equality in socialist China plays a significant role in the absence of clemency in capital cases in China, although here, my argument relies more on speculation than on hard evidence. Despite clemency's promotion by Xiao Yang, a former president of the SPC and noted legalist,[59] the absence of executive clemency in capital cases demonstrates that the opponents of clemency presently have the upper hand. At the core of opposition to clemency in capital cases is a concern regarding inequality, whereby the rich and powerful possess the possibility of being spared while the poor are invariably executed. In the view of clemency's opponents, executive clemency runs the risk of benefiting only rich and privileged individuals, which was a significant feature of the imperial criminal justice system. For example, the leading mass media publications are opposed to granting clemency to white collar criminals, in part because of the fact that

56 Wang Shu, 'Suspended for 40 Years, Why Restore Special Pardon Now? (Chenfeng 40 nian weihe xianzai chongqi tese)' *Beijing News* (24 August 2015) <www.bjnews.com.cn/news/2015/08/24/375387.html> accessed 8 April 2018.

57 Tom Phillips, 'China must Pardon Corrupt Officials, Says Author Dubbed China's John Grisham' *The Telegraph* (London, 15 March 2015) <www.telegraph.co.uk/news/worldnews/asia/china/11473630/China-must-pardon-corrupt-officials-says-author-dubbed-Chinas-John-Grisham.html> accessed 4 April 2018.

58 Yang Jiang, 'Is It Legitimate to Pardon Corrupt Officials? (teshe tanguan kebu kexing)' (2015) 16 Xinmin Weekly (xinmin zhoukan) 52.

59 Wang (n 56).

they are affluent and privileged.[60] With the concern that those who would benefit would overwhelmingly consist of influential individuals, the PRC government insists on a socialist equilibrium with the punishment system. As a result, no death row prisoner may seek mitigation, no matter who they are.

According to the 1982 Constitution, decisions regarding special amnesty are made by the SCNPC by democratic vote, rather than by local justice administrations. The risk of corruption is therefore reduced. Personally, I have confidence that executive clemency for capital cases will be revived in the near future, once the Chinese public begin to observe that mercy is not a threat to legalism and the rule of law. Furthermore, the risk of unequal justice, as the downside of selective mercy, is controllable via proper legal procedures. If the law establishes a set of transparent and practical guidelines to steer individuals' applications, then death row inmates, their relatives, and the public will know precisely what to expect. But if the government does not allow executive clemency at all, every death row prisoner will be executed without exception, and the public concern for disadvantaged individuals will persist, as with the regrettable case of Jia Jinglong. Even if some privileged offenders are wrongfully saved via executive clemency, 'unjustifiably' sparing life is undoubtedly preferable to wrongful execution.

Retribution

Moving on from corruption-related crimes, to which the death penalty is applied less frequently than for violent and drug-related crimes in contemporary China,[61] the reasons for reinstituting a functioning executive clemency regime become more controversial. Although the limited academic literature does not provide concrete evidence of public opinion regarding mercy for capital crimes, retribution is a key lens through which we may examine the reasons for public concern.

The talionic maxim of 'an eye for an eye and a tooth for a tooth' (以眼还眼，以牙还牙 *yiyan huanyan, yiya huanya*) is reflected in criminal justice policy and social culture in both modern and historical China. Although the Confucian concept of mercy existed in imperial China, retribution and revenge also form a core part of Chinese judicial philosophy and are deeply embedded in the whole of Chinese history.[62] In contemporary China, most members of the public believe it just and legitimate to execute criminals who commit severe crimes such as homicide.[63] Given that the majority of death sentences are

60 Shuang Die, 'Why Offer Special Pardon to the Rich? (pingshenme yao teshe furen)' (2003) 9 New West (xin xibu) 71.

61 Xiong (n 30) 226–230.

62 Børge Bakken, 'The Culture of Revenge and the Power of Politics: A Comparative Attempt to Explain the Punitive' (2008) 1 Journal of Power 169, 174–180.

63 Mo Hongxian and Zeng Yan, 'An Empirical Study of the Practice and Policy of China's Death Penalty: An Investigative Interview with Legal Practice (zhongguo sixing shiyong wenti shizheng yanjiu: dui jing e falv shiwujie de

passed on those who commit violent crimes causing victims' deaths, thereby 'paying with life for killing' (杀人偿命 *sharen changming*), death sentences based upon retribution and revenge are seen as forming an acceptable standard of punishment. In particular, the Chinese public tend to support the execution of a murderer who kills using brutal methods and in aggravated circumstances, or a murderer who kills two or more victims. Regarding the brutality of Jia Jinglong's murder, one of the judges of the SPC explained that the critical reason why Jia had to be executed was that he killed his victim, the deputy village chief, in such severely aggravated circumstances:

> In order to carry out the murder, Jia Jinglong made preparations for nearly two years, carefully planning the murder, including preparing murder weapons, choosing the time and place of the murder, [thereby] reflecting a deep and subjective malignancy … By deliberately choosing to commit crimes during the Spring Festival, the crime scene and the social impact are particularly bad. The Spring Festival is the most important and most traditional festival for Chinese people, and Jia Jinglong deliberately chose the Lunar New Year's Day [for the murder] … nearly a thousand men, women and children [were present], causing great panic and indignation among the villagers, and causing serious social impact … At the first instance trial, hundreds of villagers in Beigaoying Village made a joint petition to the court, strongly demanding that the court uphold justice and severely punish Jia Jinglong according to law.[64]

Xiong Zhenglin's execution forms another example. Xiong was responsible for multiple victims' deaths, and thus had no chance of receiving judicial leniency. On 9 February 2009, at Suizhou Intermediate Court, while on trial for the murder of seven adults and one baby, Xiong suddenly said to the judge 'I beg for special amnesty'.[65] In a letter of application, he subsequently wrote 'this year is the 60th anniversary of the founding of the PRC, will our [Communist] party and government grant clemency [to me]? I would appreciate it if you

tiaocha fangtan)' (2009) 3 Journal of Henan Administrative Institute of Politics and Law (henansheng zhengfa guanli ganbu xueyuan xuebao) 14, 15–16; Zhang Ning, 'Public Opinion and the Death Penalty Debate in China' (2010) 1 China Perspectives 85, 95.

64 Ni Zijian, 'The Supreme Court Removes Doubts about Jia Jinglong's Case: Why Should He Be Executed? (zuigao fayuan shiyi Jia Jingling an zhenxiang: ta weihe zui gai chusi)' (*news.sina.com.cn* 19 November 2016) <http://news.sina.com.cn/o/2016-11-16/doc-ifxxsfip4896849.shtml> accessed 20 April 2018.

65 Zhu Chunxian, 'Murderer Applies for Special Pardon on China's 60th National Day, Lawyers Prepare to Call for Signatures Nationwide (guoqing 60 nian sharenfan shenqing teshe lvshi ni tian quanguo zheng qianming)' *Legal Weekly* (Fazhi zhoubao) (Changsha, 27 February 2009) <http://news.sohu.com/20090227/n262512358.shtml> accessed 11 January 2018.

could leave me with my life'.[66] Inevitably, Xiong's petition was rejected, and he was executed after the SPC approved his death sentence.

Executive clemency has become all but impossible for the perpetrators of heinous crimes such as murder, in part due to the influence of a traditional culture favouring retribution. As a result, hundreds of thousands of murderers have been executed without exception in contemporary China. I am not arguing that executing a murderer is inherently wrong, nor do I sympathise with offenders who kill their victims. But what I really ask is why we must kill thousands of citizens in such a revengeful, retributive manner? If the Chinese legal system and political authorities showed compassion to offenders through executive clemency, there might be less killing in the future and more sympathy for victims.

Deterrence

In China, executing prisoners sentenced to death is regarded as a very important means by which to deter crime. Although no direct evidence exists, there is a very strong belief in the deterrent effect of the death penalty among the Chinese public and PRC policy-makers. Dominant in contemporary China is the belief that the execution of death sentences deters potential criminals from committing severe crimes, and maintains social order and safety. This view is encapsulated by the phrase 'killing the chicken to scare the monkey' (杀鸡给猴看 *shaji geihou kan*), which has been mentioned in a variety of official speeches and documents.[67] For example, in 1983 Deng Xiaoping asked Liu Fuzhi, the Minister of Public Security, to kill dozens of criminals (必须杀一批 *bixu sha yipi*) in order to increase social order by deterring would-be criminals. This subsequently became known as the 'strike hard (严打 *yanda*)' policy.[68] As a result, 24,000 criminals were sentenced to death and executed among 861,000 individuals convicted of criminal offences over a 12-month period thereafter.[69] Despite the PRC's more lenient criminal justice policy and decreasing number of executions over the past

66 Yang Tao, 'The Special Pardon System from the Perspective of Xiong Zhenlin's Case (cong Xiong Zhenlin de shenqing kan teshe zhidu)' *Beijing Youth Daily* (Beijing, 8 February 2009) <http://www.jcrb.com/pinglun/jrkd/200902/t20090220_181615.html> accessed 10 January 2018.

67 Bakken (n 62) 172.

68 He Libo, '1983: How the Party Decided on the "Strike Hard" Campaign (1983: Dangzhongyang juece yanda shimo)' (2008)17 Prosecutorial View (jiancha fengyun) 66, 67; Sue Trevaskes, *Policing Serious Crime in China: From 'Strike Hard' to 'Kill Fewer'* (Routledge 2010) 55–57; Sue Trevaskes, *The Death Penalty in Contemporary China* (Palgrave Macmillan 2012) 1–2.

69 Ma Qibing and Chen Wenbing, *Forty Years under The Communist Party of China 1949–1989 (zhongguo gongchandang zhizheng sishi nian 1949–1989)* (The CPC History Publishing House (Zhongguo dangshi chubanshe) 1989) 525; Kuo-Hsing Hsieh, *The Exclusionary Rule of Evidence: Comparative Analysis and Proposals for Reform* (Routledge 2014) 143.

decade,[70] the deterrent justification blocking the exercise of executive clemency remains unchanged for violent crimes.

Harsh punishment is also regarded as a vital criminal justice strategy to deter participation in drug dealing and trafficking in China. To increase the deterrent effect of harsh punishments, mass education campaigns have concurrently been run to help raise awareness among the populace.[71] Article 347 of the Criminal Law 1997 sets a very low minimum weight threshold punishable by the death penalty for smuggling, trafficking, transporting, or manufacturing heroin (50 grams). Although the SPC death sentence review process has interpreted the quantity of heroin required for a death sentence with immediate execution as in excess of 600g,[72] this more lenient criterion has not prevented the execution of large numbers of drug dealers in China. In recent years, China has witnessed a sharp increase in the numbers of drug abusers and drug dealers,[73] and as a result, drug crime has become a major contributor to death sentence totals, now ranked second behind murder in terms of capital crimes.[74] Given the fact that most drugs on the Chinese market are smuggled from overseas, including from South America, Southeast Asia, and so forth,[75] the threat of execution for drug mules is regarded as a critical means of deterring transnational drug crime. The Chinese state's preference for harsh punishments as a deterrent mechanism explains why several mercy applications have failed to save foreign drug mules. All legal and extra-legal calls for commutation have thus far been rejected by the Chinese government.[76] Overall, although the steadily

70 On the decline in PRC executions since 2002, see Dui Hua Foundation, 'Death Penalty Reform' (*Dui Hua*, 2019) <https://duihua.org/resources/death-penalty-reform/> accessed 12 December 2019.

71 Ko-lin Qin and Sheldon X Zhang, *The Chinese Heroin Trade: Cross-Border Drug Trafficking in Southeast Asia and Beyond* (NYU Press 2015) 220–246.

72 Lin Qiang, 'Chief Gao Guijun of the 5th Criminal Division of the Supreme Court: Issues in Applying the Death Penalty in Drug Cases (zuigaoyuan xingwuting tingzhang Gao Guijun: dupin fanzui anjian sixing shiyong wenti)' (11 January 2016) <http://www.360doc.com/content/16/0111/12/15644092_527076156.shtml> accessed 24 February 2019.

73 Shanon Tiezzi, 'China's Growing Drug Problem' *The Diplomat* (28 March 2015) <https://thediplomat.com/2015/05/chinas-growing-drug-problem/> accessed 2 February 2019.

74 Xiong (n 30) 226–230; Moulin Xiong, Siyu Liu, and Bin Liang, 'Criminal Defense and Judicial Sentencing in China's Death Penalty Cases' (2018) 24 Psychology, Crime & Law 414, 420–421.

75 Siyu Liu, Moulin Xiong, and Bin Liang, 'The Death Penalty for Foreign Drug Offenders in China: Legal Protection and Equal Treatment' (2019) 25 European Journal on Criminal Policy and Research 427, 428; Qing Zonggen, 'An Analysis of the Causes of and Countermeasures for Foreign-related Drug Crimes (shewai dupin fanzui de yuanyin ji duice tanxi)' (2010) 6 Journal of Fujian Police College 52, 53.

76 David Eimer, 'Execution of Briton Akmal Shaikh: China Defiant in the Face of Criticism' *The Telegraph* (London, 29 December 2009) <www.telegraph.co.uk/news/worldnews/asia/china/6904175/Execution-of-Briton-Akmal-Shaikh-China-defiant-in-the-face-of-criticism.html> accessed 20 January 2018; Tonyo Cruz, 'Death

increasing prevalence of drug abuse in Chinese society arguably demonstrates the ineffectiveness of executions as a deterrent measure, the established philosophy of 'killing the chicken to scare the monkey' continues to be applied to drug crimes in much the same way as it is for murder and economic crimes.

Public rallies calling for the sentencing to death and execution of drug convicts have become an important denunciatory tool of mass education campaigns in recent decades. For example, on 16 December 2017, 12 people convicted of murder, robbery, and drug-related crimes were paraded at a 'sentencing rally' at a sports stadium in the city of Lufeng, Guangdong province. Immediately afterwards, ten of these criminals were publicly executed, seven of them having been charged with drug offences.[77] The reason for holding the rally was that Lufeng had become dubbed the 'city of ice' with a reputation for illegal drug production.[78] Lufeng's experience is just the tip of the iceberg in terms of recent drug executions in China.

Concluding Remarks

This chapter has briefly introduced the history of mercy law and practice in contemporary China, and has examined plausible reasons for the complete absence of executive clemency in PRC-era capital cases. The author finds that the values of legal tradition, equality, retributivism, and deterrence each serve to explain the dearth of capital clemency grants in recent decades. Fulfilling the legal potential of special amnesty in capital cases remains as elusive as ever.

Death penalty policy is a lens through which to observe the brutality of human beings; how the government treats criminals often reflects how offenders treat their victims.[79] Many states retain the legal power to kill offenders,

penalty in China: Last hours of Ramon, Sally and Elizabeth' *Asian Correspondent* (30 March 2011) <https://asiancorrespondent.com/2011/03/death-penalty-in-china-last-hours-of-ramon-sally-and-elizabeth/#tjbBRMGq3A9l0o6O.97> accessed 11 January 2018; Barbara Mae Dacanay, 'Philippine President Benigno Aquino writes to Chinese President Xi Jinping' (*Gulf News*, 27 June 2013) <https://gulfnews.com/news/asia/philippines/philippine-president-benigno-aquino-writes-to-chinese-president-xi-jinping-1.1202724> accessed 25 June 2018.

77 Beimeng Fu, '10 people Paraded, Sentenced to Death in China's "City of Ice"' *ABC News* (New York, 29 December 2017) <https://abcnews.go.com/International/10-people-paraded-sentenced-death-chinas-city-ice/story?id=51880568> accessed 2 March 2018; Yi Han, 'Sentencing Rally in Lufeng, Guangdong: 10 People Executed for Manufacturing and Trafficking Drugs (Guangdong Lufeng zhaokai xuanpan dahui 10 ren yin zhifandu bei zhixing sixing)' (*Guangcha*, 12 December 2017) <www.guancha.cn/society/2017_ 12_17_439474.shtml> accessed 2 March 2018.

78 Ibid.

79 Joanna M Shepherd, 'Deterrence versus Brutalization: Capital Punishment's Differing Impacts among States' (2015)104 Michigan Law Review 203, 206; John K Cochran and Mitchell B Chamlin, 'Deterrence and Brutalization: The Dual Effects of Executions' (2000) 4 Justice Quarterly 685, 688.

but inversely they also possess the power to spare their citizens' lives by exercising mercy.[80] I do not seek to defend the death penalty, nor am I truly abolitionist, but I believe that we ought to make legal provision to save the lives of criminals who are not among the most heinous. Given the large number of executions taking place in China each year, we should reconsider whether execution is appropriate and legitimate for each individual offender. If we cannot promise that the death penalty shall only be applied in the most exceptional cases, for the most serious crimes, and under the strictest limits,[81] then executive clemency ought to be granted as a final safeguard.

Although there are many factors which influence discretionary capital sentencing in China, such as victim–perpetrator reconciliation, victim compensation, confession, self-surrender, and so forth,[82] executive clemency is still an essential final safeguard to spare those undeserving of death. Pardons were granted to death row prisoners throughout most of Chinese history,[83] so contemporary China should be no exception. Although I remain optimistic that the SCNPC and the president will grant executive clemency for some death row prisoners in the near future, there is no way to know exactly when this policy change will occur. Looking back at the first special amnesty granted to war criminals in 1959, the prior instructions not to kill made by Chinese political leaders imply that, indirectly, executive clemency already existed as a means of mitigating punishment. If political mercy could be shown to war criminals then, it can be shown to murderers and drug traffickers now.

To create an opportunity for death row and other convicts to receive executive clemency in China, the first step required is to clarify the legal process of special amnesty from application right through to decision. To do so, the NPC should enact a separate mercy law, or at least add a special chapter to the existing Criminal Procedure Law to regulate the broad special amnesty power present within the 1982 Constitution.[84] China's laws will then not only meet the minimum international law standard by offering death row prisoners

80 See Pascoe and Novak, this volume, on the ubiquity of clemency powers worldwide, both in capital and non-capital cases.
81 Human Rights Committee, 'Draft General Comment on Article 6 of the International Covenant on Civil and Political Rights—Right to life' (*Office of the High Commissioner for Human Rights*) <www.ohchr.org/Documents/HRBodies/CCPR/GCArticle6/GCArticle6_EN.pdf> accessed 2 October 2018.
82 Xiong, Liu, and Liang (n 74) 425; Moulin Xiong and Michelle Miao, 'Miscarriages of Justice in Chinese Capital Cases' (2018) 41 Hastings International and Comparative Law Review 274, 282–289; Lu Hong, Bin Liang, and Siyu Liu, 'Serious Violent Offenses and Sentencing Decisions in China—Are There Any Gender Disparities?' (2013) 8 Asian Journal of Criminology, 159, 170; Michelle Miao, 'Defining Death-eligible Murder in China' (2019) 67(2) American Journal of Comparative Law 327.
83 Bakken (n 48) 37–46; McKnight (n 47) 112–113.
84 Liu (n 8) 161; Mei (n 26); Zhang (n 25).

the opportunity to apply for commutation or pardon,[85] but will also pave the way to save some offenders' lives. Having already signed the ICCPR, China should comply with its duty to domesticate international law standards regarding clemency rights for death row prisoners.[86] If individual applications for clemency are operationalised through legislation, the constitutional powers of the SCNPC and the president would surely be put to more frequent use.

Last, but most importantly, I warn of the urgent necessity of reviving executive clemency to avoid instances of wrongful execution. The cases of defendants such as Nie Shubing (聂树斌), Teng Xinshan (滕兴善), and Huge Jletu (呼格吉勒图) demonstrate the ongoing risk of wrongful execution in China.[87] These well-known tragedies represent only a handful of the total number of suspected wrongful executions; there have presumably been many more death sentences wrongfully carried out since 1949. In recent years, news of wrongful convictions, wrongful imprisonment and even wrongful executions in China has spread around the world, via news media and academic scholarship.[88] Moreover, examples of wrongful convictions in capital cases have emerged in numerous retentionist nations, but in only a few cases have such defendants ever been pardoned by a king, president, or governor.[89] In China, as with Jia Jinglong's case, Dong Wei's regrettable execution for murder demonstrates how the lack of an effective legal safeguard mechanism following SPC review has the potential to cost lives.[90] Thus, the difficulty of exonerating

85 ICCPR, art 6(4); UN Human Rights Committee, 'General Comment No. 36 (2018) on art 6 of the International Covenant on Civil and Political Rights, on the Right to Life' (2018) CCPR/C/GC/36, para 47; UN Safeguards guaranteeing protection of the rights of those facing the death penalty, approved by Economic and Social Council resolution 1984/50 of 25 May 1984, Safeguard 7. See also Sangiorgio, this volume.

86 Liu (n 8) 159; Mei (n 26). See also Novak and Pascoe, this volume.

87 Xiong and Miao (n 82) 276–328; Jiang Na, 'A Comparison of Wrongful Convictions in Death Penalty Cases Between China and the United States' (2013) 41 International Journal of Law, Crime and Justice 144, 147; Jiang Na, *Wrongful Convictions in China: Comparative and Empirical Perspectives* (Springer, 2016) 46–48, 260–261.

88 Ibid.

89 For instance, according to Death Penalty Information Center, only seven persons were pardoned for innocence in the United States out of 162 death row exonerations between 1976 and 19 April 2018 (Death Penalty Information Center, 'Description of Innocence Cases' (*Death Penalty Information Center*, 2019) <https://deathpenaltyinfo.org/innocence-list-those-freed-death-row> accessed 12 December 2019).

90 Dong Wei, then aged 27, was sentenced by the Yanan Intermediate Court to the death penalty with immediate execution for a murder committed on 2 May 2001. Although he was possibly innocent, Dong's case has so far not been widely regarded an instance of wrongful conviction. On 27 April 2002, Dong's defence lawyer Zhu Zhanping was suddenly informed that the Shanxi Higher People's Court had already upheld Dong's death sentence and that Dong would be executed on 29 April at 10:30 am. Zhu immediately took the case to the SPC to argue that Dong was acting in legitimate self-defence. Then, four minutes before Dong's scheduled execution, a judge of the SPC issued a suspension order by phone call to the local

the innocent through existing court procedures also justifies the activation of executive clemency in capital cases.

Irrespective of the stated justifications against extra-legal mercy such as legal tradition, equality, retributivism, and deterrence, China's lack of a functioning executive clemency procedure compromises a far more important cultural and political norm: the state's responsibility to protect and foster life. I am optimistic that the Chinese government will eventually ratify the ICCPR and fulfil the requirements of its Article 6(4), potentially through enacting an independent mercy law. At the very least, inserting a new section on executive clemency into the existing Criminal Law and Criminal Procedure Law will help China comply with Article 6(4)'s requirements. The long history of mercy in imperial China suggests that the PRC should practise executive clemency as the ancestors of the Chinese people once did. I hope that this practice will be realised within the next decade, as many Chinese scholars have urged.

judge supervising the execution. Nevertheless, following the SPC's reprieve, the Shanxi Higher People's Court issued a new verdict on 26 August 2002 which again upheld the death sentence. Dong was executed 5 September 2002. See Jiang Xue, '4 Minutes Before a Death Row Execution (Qiangxia liuren ganzai xingxing 4 fenzhong qian)' *Chinese Business View* (Xi'an, 12 July 2002); Xie Yongqiang, 'Shanxi Soldering Gun Case Made into a Movie (Shanxi qiangxia liuren an paicheng dianying)' *Chinese Business View* (Xi'an, 6 January 2015).

9 Emerging Trends and Best Practices in Comparative Clemency

Andrew Novak and Daniel Pascoe

> A pardon in our days is not a private act of grace from an individual happening to possess power. It is a part of the Constitutional scheme. When granted, it is the determination of the ultimate authority that the public welfare will be better served by inflicting less than what the judgment fixed.
>
> Oliver Wendell Holmes Jr, 1927[1]

As the preceding chapters have demonstrated, the traditional portrait of clemency is still very much alive: the typical structure continues to involve a head of state or head of government with virtually unlimited discretion to reduce, cancel, or substitute punishment with few, if any, checks from the other branches of government. This structure has proven durable across jurisdictions and over time, reinforced by customary international law and human rights treaties that preserve access to the clemency power but add minimal safeguards. Many former colonies, for instance, retain a similar clemency structure to that under the colonial period. The image of a benevolent executive bestowing mercy on a penitent subject is still the predominant paradigm in both the common and civil law worlds. Even countries that operate under Islamic Law, such as Libya, Sudan, Saudi Arabia, or the Maldives, have recast traditional Islamic principles such as *diya* ('blood money' compensation) and *afw* (victim's pardon) within the global clemency model.[2] From a comparative constitutional perspective, clemency provisions are widely replicated across borders due to inertia, colonial links, or a lack of imaginative drafting. The retention of death penalty provi-

1 *Biddle v Perovich* 274 US 480, 486.

2 Mary C Duncan, 'Playing by Their Rules: The Death Penalty and Foreigners in Saudi Arabia' (1998) 27 Georgia International and Comparative Law Journal 231; Mutaz M Qafisheh, 'Restorative Justice in Islamic Penal Law: A Contribution to the Global System' (2012) 7 International Journal of Criminal Justice Sciences 487–507, 494–95, 503; Daniel Pascoe and Michelle Miao, 'Victim–Perpetrator Reconciliation Agreements in Murder Cases: What Can Muslim-Majority Jurisdictions and the PRC Learn from Each Other?' (2017) 66(4) ICLQ 963, 978.

sions in the constitutions of countries that have abolished the death penalty is a clear example of this path dependence.[3] Indeed, as we observed in chapter 1, the most popular words used to describe clemency in national constitutions have remained unchanged since the 1970s.[4]

Nonetheless, our study of clemency law and practice around the world shows that some innovation and development is occurring, cross-fertilised by other comparative law and international law trends. One notable change in the last 50 years is a trend toward conceiving of the right to seek clemency in human rights terms, as reflected by clemency's presence in international human rights treaties like the International Covenant on Civil and Political Rights ('ICCPR') and the American Convention on Human Rights ('ACHR'). Viewing clemency as an extension of the right to a fair trial has contributed to changes in clemency practice over this period, as have concerns about arbitrary misuse and discriminatory decision-making.

As the contributions to this volume show, currents in comparative criminal justice and comparative constitutional law have also affected the clemency power. Clemency has been influenced by the restorative justice movement by, for instance, involving victims in the deliberation process. The 'justice cascade', that is, the global legal trend toward holding human rights abusers accountable for their crimes, is reflected in limitations on the power to grant amnesties for international crimes such as war crime and genocide.[5] DNA evidence and the Innocence Revolution have also altered clemency's purpose and procedure, as claims of actual innocence are perceived to have a special priority.[6] Finally, the global trend toward the professionalisation and judicial review of clemency decisions reflects the rise of the administrative state across the Western world over the twentieth century in which decision-making is increasingly guided and less subject to individual discretion.[7] During the remainder of this chapter we summarise the most important recent trends in clemency laws and practice, postulate on the future of clemency, and conclude by offering several best practice recommendations to take the clemency agenda forward.

3 Examples include the Constitution of Malta 1964, s 93(2); Constitution of Cyprus 1960, art 53(4); Constitution of Solomon Islands 1978, s 45(7), and Constitution of Fiji 2013, art 119(4)(c). See also Appendix.

4 See Pascoe and Novak, this volume.

5 Kathryn Sikkink, *The Justice Cascade: How Human Rights Prosecutions Are Changing World Politics* (WW Norton 2011).

6 Keith A Findley, 'Innocence Found: The New Revolution in American Criminal Justice' in Sarah L Cooper (ed), *Controversies in Innocence Cases in America* (Ashgate 2014) 3–4.

7 Rachel E Barkow, 'The Ascent of the Administrative State and the Demise of Mercy' (2008) 121 Harvard Law Review 1332.

Death Penalty Clemency and Customary International Law

The right to seek clemency in death penalty cases is an emerging norm of international human rights law, and potentially even represents a 'norm cascade', defined as a widespread norm that has hit a tipping point so as to become self-evident.[8] As Sangiorgio explains in Chapter 2, the right to seek clemency in death penalty cases is protected by international legal instruments such as the ICCPR and the ACHR, and is reinforced by increasingly stronger UN resolutions, decisions of the International Court of Justice and other tribunals, and the UN Human Rights Committee's guidance.[9] The statutes of several international courts also contain early release mechanisms that are reminiscent of clemency,[10] whereas the Universal Periodic Review mechanism at the UN Human Rights Council has provided an opportunity to scrutinise clemency practice in an open forum.[11] Of course, international law's disapproval of the death penalty has worked to clemency's benefit, as emphasis on the right to seek clemency has the consequence of increasing the costs and reducing the application of capital punishment.

As Sangiorgio describes, the first mention in international law of a right to seek clemency in capital cases arose in the *travaux préparatoires* of the ICCPR. In the 1990s, UN experts began to elaborate on this right, adding that applicants for clemency must have adequate time to pursue the right and that they could not be executed while a petition was pending. Jurisprudence from the Judicial Committee of the Privy Council and the Inter-American Human Rights System during the early 2000s called on clemency mechanisms to be 'effective', thereby providing a basis to review these mechanisms in subsequent challenges.[12] Since 2016, the biennial UN General Assembly death penalty moratorium resolutions have also embraced clemency as a tool to end the death penalty. In 2016 and again in 2018, the UN General Assembly called on states to ensure that their death penalty clemency procedures were fair and transparent.[13] However, clemency transparency remains an elusive goal. While

8 Martha Finnemore and Kathryn Sikkink, 'International Norm Dynamics and Political Change' (1998) 52(4) International Organization 887, 895.

9 See Sangiorgio, this volume.

10 Statute of the International Criminal Tribunal for the Former Yugoslavia (1993) 32 International Legal Materials 1159, art 28; Statute of the International Criminal Tribunal for Rwanda (1994) UN Doc. S/RES/995, art 27; Statute of the Special Tribunal for Lebanon (2006) UN Doc. S/RES/1757, art 30; Statute of the Special Court for Sierra Leone (2000) UN Doc. S/RES/1315, art 23.

11 Edward McMahon and Marta Ascherio, 'A Step Ahead in Promoting Human Rights: The Universal Periodic Review of the UN Human Rights Council' (2012) 18 Global Governance 231, 236, 242, 243.

12 *Edwards v Bahamas*, Inter-Am. Comm'n HR, Case Nos. 12/067, 12/068, 12/086, Report No. 48/01 (4 April 2001), 166–170; *McKenzie v Jamaica*, Inter-Am Comm'n HR, Case 12/023, Report No. 41/00 (13 April 2000), 228; *Lewis v Attorney General of Jamaica* [2000] UKPC 35, para 47.

13 UN General Assembly Resolution 71/187, adopted 19 December 2016; UN General Assembly Resolution 73/175, adopted 17 December 2018.

state practice has gradually shifted to accommodate more robust procedure and even some judicial oversight, few governments have gone so far as to reveal clemency statistics, reasons, or criteria.

Although we identify a 'right to seek' death penalty clemency as an emerging norm, we stop short of asserting that such a right has already attained customary international law status.[14] This is so for two reasons. The first is that customary international law depends on state practice in order to be binding on non-parties or objectors.[15] As the death penalty is increasingly restricted to the most hardcore group of retentionist jurisdictions, which are those least likely to have compliant clemency processes, state practice in favour of such a norm may deteriorate further. Second, while most states have positive obligations under international human rights law treaties such as the ICCPR, we have precious little evidence that non-ratifying parties and other states without an active 'right to seek' clemency consciously consider themselves as 'persistent objectors' to an otherwise-binding capital clemency norm.[16] At best, the 'right to seek' clemency is founded on positive obligations in international treaties and a broad array of international soft law documents that are as aspirational as they are objective descriptions of state practice. The Inter-American Court of Human Rights stated in *Fermin Ramirez v Guatemala* (2005) that the 'right to grace forms part of the international corpus juris', but in that case the Court was considering Guatemala's positive obligations under the ACHR when it abolished its clemency process.[17] It is not clear that the Court was making a statement about customary international law itself.

For foreign nationals on death row, the jurisprudence is somewhat stronger. The International Court of Justice implicitly endorsed robust capital clemency processes in *Avena and Other Mexican Nationals (Mexico v United States of*

14 The closest that clemency may have come to forming part of a customary international law right is in relation to the legal availability of a post-judicial mercy power per-se. In 2018, 94 of 96 death penalty retentionist nations retained a conventional, legislative or constitutional power for the executive to dispense post-judicial leniency (clemency *or* amnesty) for at least some capital offences, as opposed to a 'right to seek' pardon or commutation on the part of the prisoner. Yet even here, there are exceptions such as the constitutions of Iraq and Niger, which both prohibit clemency for certain capital offences (Constitution of Niger 2010, art 72; Constitution of Iraq 2005, art 73(A)), and the nations that have most strictly incorporated Islamic Law into their positive criminal laws, according to which no state-based pardon of a *qisas* or *hudud* crime is permitted (Pascoe and Miao (n 2) 977).

15 Niels Petersen, 'Customary Law Without Custom? Rules, Principles, and the Role of State Practice in International Norm Creation' (2008) 23 American University International Law Review 275. See also the Statute of the International Court of Justice 1945, art 38(1)(b), defining as a relevant source of law 'international custom, as evidence of a general practice accepted as law'.

16 See generally James A Green, *The Persistent Objector Rule in Customary International Law* (OUP 2016).

17 *Fermin Ramirez v Guatemala* (Inter-American Court of Human Rights, 20 June 2005), para 109.

America) when it found that Texas's clemency process did not provide sufficient assurances that consular rights would be respected under the Vienna Convention on Consular Relations.[18] If the right to seek clemency in capital cases is to harden into a rule of customary international law, perhaps this is most likely to occur with the treatment of foreign nationals on death row owing to the protection of consular rights in international treaties and state practice. The Vienna Convention on Consular Relations is widely considered to have codified customary international law on consular notification rights.[19]

International and supranational courts are nonetheless expanding the scope of the treaty-based right to apply for clemency in a death penalty case. The right is becoming broader, as a right to seek clemency increasingly extends to more than just death penalty cases, notwithstanding the unique urgency of capital cases. The decisions of the European Court of Human Rights holding that individuals serving life sentences without the possibility of parole or remission have the right to a mechanism for reviewing their sentence must be seen in this context. According to the European Court of Human Rights, clemency could provide a 'meaningful prospect of release' for life-term prisoners if the clemency process was clear and known to the applicant, among other criteria.[20] In some jurisdictions, the rights of non-capital clemency applicants have been protected under the right to a fair trial, the right to human dignity, the right to be free from cruel and degrading treatment, or other human rights. Jurisdictions such as South Africa and the Solomon Islands have extended due process rights inherent in the right to seek clemency to prisoners serving life sentences.[21] In this way, the right to seek clemency attaching to non-capital defendants, most notably those serving life sentences or mandatory sentences, is becoming increasingly robust in state practice and in international legal guidance. Due process protections relating to clemency applications will still have life left after the global abolition of the death penalty

18 *Avena and Other Mexican Nationals (Mexico v United States of America)* [2004] ICJ Reports 64.

19 Antônio Augusto Cançado Trindade, 'The Humanization of Consular Law: The Impact of Advisory Opinion No. 16 (1999) of the Inter-American Court of Human Rights on International Case-law and Practice' (2007) 6(1) Chinese Journal of International Law 1, 1, 3; Cara S O'Driscoll, 'The Execution of Foreign Nationals in Arizona: Violations of the Vienna Convention on Consular Relations' (2000) 32 Arizona State Law Journal 323, 328.

20 *Kafkaris v Cyprus*, App. No. 21906/04 (ECHR 12 February 2008); *Iorgov v Bulgaria*, App. No. 36295/02 (ECHR 2 September 2010).

21 The High Court of the Solomon Islands ruled that a prisoner serving a life sentence has a genuine expectation that the Committee on the Prerogative of Mercy would consider his petition. The Court therefore ruled that it could require the Committee to be appointed. See *Maniau v Governor General* [2004] SBHC 118 (6 October 2004). The South African Constitutional Court similarly ruled that clemency applicants had a right to have their petitions considered and decided upon 'rationally, in good faith, in accordance with the principle of legality, diligently and without delay'. See *Minister of Justice v Chonco* (2010) 1 SACR 325 (CC), 30. This case also involved a life sentence.

is complete. Indeed, in time, prisoners charged with all but the most minor offences may also enjoy a domestic or international law right to seek commutation or pardon.

The right to seek clemency in death penalty cases is also deepening. No longer does the right to 'seek' clemency under the ICCPR or its equivalent provisions in regional instruments mean simply the right to passively be considered for clemency or even just the right to apply. Under the Roman law principle *ubi jus ibi remedium* (no rights without remedies), the existence of a legal right requires a remedy for violations, and courts therefore have broad authority to fashion remedies.[22] Article 6(4) of the ICCPR now protects a more robust right beyond simply applying for capital clemency, extending to a right to have one's petition considered in good faith in which the possibility of clemency has not been foreclosed. Purported blanket denials of clemency, such as the President of Indonesia's 2014 vow not to grant clemency in any drug trafficking cases, or the Indian Home Minister's 2013 refusal to recommend clemency in any rape cases where death results would contravene this requirement.[23] To live up to its potential as a procedural safeguard, the 'right to seek' clemency must, at a minimum, include the right to be genuinely considered, the right to notification of the final outcome, the right to make representations to the decision-maker, the right not to be executed while a petition is pending, and perhaps even the right to legal representation throughout the process.

The UN Human Rights Committee's General Comment Number 36, on Article 6: Right to Life, passed in October 2018, reflects these aspirations. According to the General Comment, executions may not be carried out until a final clemency decision has been 'meaningfully considered and conclusively decided upon'. The General Comment requires that clemency procedures be specified by law and should not allow victims a preponderant role in determining whether clemency should be granted, as with *diya* and *afw* in Islamic Law.[24] The clemency procedure must offer several fundamental guarantees,

22 José Manuel and Cortés Martín, 'Ubi Ius, Ibi Remedium? Locus Standi of Private Applicants Under Article 230(4) EC at a European Constitutional Crossroads' (2004) 11 Maastricht Journal of European and International Law 233.

23 Roger Hood and Carolyn Hoyle, *The Death Penalty: A Worldwide Perspective* (5th edn, OUP 2015) 313. Hood and Hoyle describe the blanket denial of clemency by the former president of the Gambia, 'effectively nullifying the defendants' right under international law to seek clemency'. For Indonesia, see 'Bali Nine: Indonesian President Rules out Clemency for Inmates on Death Row' *The Guardian* (10 December 2014) <https://www.theguardian.com/world/2014/dec/10/bali-nine-indonesian-president-rules-out-clemency> accessed 17 December 2019 and Bradley Holland, 'Clemency and Constitutional Duties in Indonesia: A Promise Made Is a Promise Kept?' (2018) 19(1) Australian Journal of Asian Law 1. For India, see Dhananjay Mahapatra, 'Has Mercy Power Been Used Rationally?' *The Times of India* (21 January 2013) <https://timesofindia.indiatimes.com/india/Has-mercy-power-been-used-rationally/articleshow/18109489.cms> accessed 17 December 2019.

24 Sayed Sikandar Shah Haneef, *Homicide in Islam: Legal Structure and the Evidence Requirements* (AS Noordeen, 2000), 121–129. See also note 2 and associated text.

including certainty about the process and the criteria to be applied; a right to make representations to the clemency authority; a right to be notified of when the decision will be made, and a right to know the final outcome.[25] We caution that the General Comment is not itself a reflection of state practice; it is simultaneously both objective and aspirational. Its primary purpose is to interpret the rights set out in the ICCPR,[26] which by the end of 2018 had nonetheless been ratified by more than 80 per cent of death penalty retentionist states.[27] Sun observes that scholars have accorded the UN Human Rights Committee's General Comments varying degrees of authoritativeness, ranging from the status of advisory opinions to unsystematic statements without firm foundation.[28] Nonetheless, we observe that a substantial number of jurisdictions have over the last 30 years created more robust and more accountable clemency mechanisms. Although the General Comment's prescriptions do not represent a 'consensus' of state practice, they nonetheless accord with a slowly emerging norm favouring a more expansive interpretation of the right to seek clemency in death penalty cases.

Clemency and Professionalisation

Over the past 40 years, the clemency decision-making process has become more sophisticated and professionalised. We observe this trend with two related developments: first, the ever more elaborate constitutionalisation of clemency procedure in certain nations; and second, the involvement of a greater array and proportion of non-political secondary actors in the clemency decision-making process. Several of the book's chapters provide examples to this effect.

First, we have observed nations with novel constitutional arrangements for clemency designed to further particular purposes. These are states that, for one reason or another, have escaped the 'inertial' model of constitutional clemency drafting first described in Chapter 1. Although this group may be presently limited in size, we expect more states to join in the future. In chapter 4, Smailagić describes how the 1994 Constitution of the Federation of Bosnia and Herzegovina required the executive president to consult with the two vice-presidents representing the entity's other ethnic and religious communities

25 UN Human Rights Committee, 'General Comment No. 36 (2018) on art 6 of the International Covenant on Civil and Political Rights, on the Right to Life' (2018) CCPR/C/GC/36, para 47.

26 Helen Keller and Leena Grover, 'General Comments of the Human Rights Committee and Their Legitimacy' in Helen Keller and Geir Ulfstein (eds), *UN Human Rights Treaty Bodies: Law and Legitimacy* (CUP 2012).

27 See Pascoe and Novak, this volume. Furthermore, of the list of retentionist states in 2018, China, Comoros, Cuba and Saint Lucia had signed the Covenant but had not yet ratified it.

28 Shiyan Sun, 'The Understanding and Interpretation of the ICCPR in the Context of China's Possible Ratification' (2007) 6(1) Chinese Journal of International Law 17, 25.

before exercising clemency. This provision was removed after a 20-year transitional period following civil war in the former Yugoslavia.[29] Smailagić also notes the equally unusual case of Kosovo, whereby implementing legislation places qualitative limits on the frequency of pardons (not intended as a 'routine remedy', but as a 'seldom-used tool') and on the reasons that they are granted ('to reward extraordinary displays of character and conduct or to address serious humanitarian concerns').[30] Among national constitutions, only Turkey's 1982 Constitution similarly purports to restrict the *reasons* for which clemency can be granted, as opposed to restrictions on clemency for certain crimes, punishments or individuals.[31]

As for other idiosyncratic forms of regulation, in chapter 7 on India, Batra describes the unusual relationship between the Minister of Home Affairs and the President of India in the clemency process. Owing to a 1979 constitutional amendment, the president may reject the recommendation of the Minister a single time, but the second recommendation subsequently becomes binding. This structure produces the anomalous result that, if the president prefers not to authorise any executions, clemency petitions may remain pending indefinitely until courts commute the sentence on account of delay, increasing rather than reducing arbitrariness in the clemency process.[32] As Batra has written elsewhere, recent Indian presidents 'inherited' pending clemency petitions from their predecessors, as they were unable to reject the advice from the Minister of Home Affairs but were unwilling to sign off on the executions. President APJ Abdul Kalam (2002–2007) inherited eight petitions from his predecessor, KR Narayanan (1997–2002). On leaving office Kalam in turn passed on 23 pending clemency petitions to his successor Pratibha Patil (2007–2012). President Patil left 16 pending clemency petitions for her successor, Pranab Mukherjee (2012–2017).[33] Recent presidents' evident dissatisfaction with the constitutional clemency process in India (and, in particular, with the quality of the recommendations from the Ministry of Home Affairs) is a significant obstacle to a rational clemency process.

The increasing constitutionalisation of clemency that we see in the Caribbean is a by-product of the persistent constitutional challenges against the

29 See Smailagić, this volume.
30 Ibid.
31 Constitution of Turkey 1982, art 104 (chronic illness, disability or old age only); Appendix. See further Pascoe and Novak, this volume.
32 See Batra, this volume.
33 Bikram Batra, '"Court" of Last Resort: A Study of Constitutional Clemency for Capital Crimes in India' (2009) Centre for the Study of Law and Governance, Jawaharlal Nehru University, New Delhi Working Paper CSLG/WP/11 <https://www.jnu.ac.in/sites/default/files/u63/11-Court%20%28Bikram%29.pdf> accessed 24 February 2019; V Venkatesan, 'Keeping the Nation in the Dark' *The Hindu* (22 November 2012) <https://www.thehindu.com/opinion/lead/keeping-the-nation-in-the-dark/article4120378.ece> accessed 17 December 2019.

death penalty in Caribbean courts and at the Judicial Committee of the Privy Council in London.[34] Most obviously, in 1989, a constitutional amendment in Belize created one of the most elaborate constitutional clemency provisions in the world, accounting for the membership of the nation's mercy advisory committee, the conditions under which it must work, and the clemency application procedure.[35] In 2009, the Cayman Islands passed a new constitution creating an Advisory Committee on the Prerogative of Mercy; the prior constitution authorised an executive acting alone. The Cayman Islands provision sets out the Committee's membership, procedure, and conditions of appointment.[36] In 2019, Barbados amended its constitution to abolish the mandatory death penalty in order to comply with a previous decision of the Caribbean Court of Justice. The amendment substantially altered Section 78 on the prerogative of mercy, providing for the right to make written representations to the clemency authority, including through a representative. The new provision even grants the right to make oral submissions at a hearing.[37] Trinidad and Tobago similarly considered an elaborate clemency provision in 2011, which would have created a right to make written representations to the clemency authority.[38] As Bulkan relays in chapter 6, the Commonwealth Caribbean provides the most telling example of deepening regulation prompted by judicial and administrative oversight of the clemency process, a trend which we explore in further detail below.

The second major trend related to clemency's professionalisation is that secondary decision-makers, where they exist, are now increasingly non-partisan from a political standpoint, at least on paper. We first noted this trend in chapter 1. In Chapter 5, Cooper and Burrows describe familiar examples from individual US states, whereas in Chapter 3, Arias and Kouroutakis point to Brazil's 1988 constitutional provision allowing for optional advice by government departments, as well as Greek and Argentinian constitutional clauses mandating clemency advice from majority judicial bodies. In chapter 6, Bulkan lists numerous contemporary examples of unelected mercy committees from the Commonwealth Caribbean, including Guyana (with specific term limits for counsellors), St Kitts and Nevis, where the committee on the prerogative of mercy was recently reconstituted to consider prison overcrowding as a ground

34 For an overview, see Quincy Whitaker, 'Challenging the Death Penalty in the Caribbean: Litigation at the Privy Council' in Jon Yorke (ed), *Against the Death Penalty: International Initiatives and Implications* (Ashgate 2008) 101–124.

35 Constitution of Belize 1981, s 54.

36 Constitution of Cayman Islands 2009, s 40. Compare Cayman Islands Constitution Order in Council 1959, s 60 (authorising the governor to act alone in issuing pardons).

37 Constitution (Amendment) Act 2019 (Barbados), s 4, amending the Constitution of Barbados 1966, s 78.

38 Constitution (Amendment) (Capital Offences) Bill 2011 (Trinidad and Tobago), s 6M(5).

for seeking clemency, and Belize, whose detailed constitutional provisions are mentioned above.[39]

Although, as Bulkan explains in his chapter, the Commonwealth Caribbean has long had involvement of majority unelected advisory committees or other secondary actors in the clemency process, we also observe an acceleration of this trend outside the common law world. Our own analysis reveals the ever more popular involvement of judges in the advisory clemency process, particularly in civil law jurisdictions. Twelve countries espousing civil law or Islamic Law systems, mostly in Africa, have relatively new constitutions that require input from a judicial actor, typically either a supreme court or judicial governance body.[40] By comparison, only four nations from Sebba's sample of 100 jurisdictions possessed a similar system in the mid-1970s.[41]

The trend toward including non-political secondary actors in the constitutional clemency process is therefore one that transcends the common law world and is a striking point of convergence between common law and civil law systems. In the future, we may even see unelected mercy committees established in European civil law nations, within a region where clemency decision-making is still dominated by political actors, either as the head of state or as secondary parties.[42] A clemency board or advisory committee, as we describe below, can have multiple benefits for the political leaders who seek out and rely on its advice.

Clemency and Judicial or Administrative Review

A notable change in the clemency landscape since the early 1980s has been the opening of constitutional clemency deliberations to judicial review. In his chapter on the Commonwealth Caribbean, Bulkan traces the constitutional evolution of the traditional rule in the common law world that saw clemency as mercy beyond or outside legal rights, and therefore not subject to judicial review. Beginning in 1984 when the House of Lords began to subject royal prerogative powers to judicial scrutiny, clemency (in the guise of the royal prerogative of mercy) has similarly opened to judicial review.[43] In the

39 See Bulkan, this volume; 'St. Kitts and Nevis to Address Overcrowding at Prison' *Nation News* (Barbados, 2 January 2017); note 35 and associated text.

40 See Appendix: Algeria, Benin, Burkina Faso, Democratic Republic of Congo, Finland, Guinea, Iran, Rwanda, Somalia, Suriname, Togo, Paraguay.

41 Leslie Sebba, 'The Pardoning Power: A World Survey' (1977) 68 Journal of Criminal Law and Criminology 83, 115.

42 Arias and Kouroutakis, this volume; note 40 and associated text; Appendix. At the time of writing, Greece was the only European civil law nation with a specially designated clemency advisory committee, in this case consisting in its majority of judges (Constitution of Greece 1975, art 47(1)).

43 *Council of Civil Service Unions (CCSU) v Minister for Civil Service* [1983] UKHL 6 (opening prerogative powers to judicial review); *R v Secretary of State for the Home Department Ex p Bentley* [1994] QB 349 (applying *CCSU* to royal pardon decisions).

Caribbean, this occurred through a decision of the Judicial Committee of the Privy Council in the year 2000, *Lewis v Attorney General of Jamaica*, which followed a trend that developed in British courts and later in other common law jurisdictions, in finding that courts could review whether the executive followed proper mercy procedures, considered clemency petitions in good faith, and otherwise did not act rashly or arbitrarily.[44] An executive's final decision, however, is not subject to judicial review in the common law world. As Bulkan explains, the Privy Council's decision in *Lewis* was foreshadowed by a trend in Caribbean courts toward recasting the pardon power not as a prerogative of the sovereign but as a constitutionally defined power. In the years before *Lewis*, courts in the Caribbean had already begun to reject the conception that clemency does not implicate legal rights since it is an entirely discretionary power.[45]

The trend outlined in chapter 6 is not limited to the Commonwealth Caribbean. It is replicated across the English-speaking world. The Constitutional Court of South Africa ruled that the presidential pardon power in that jurisdiction 'entails a corresponding right to have a pardon application considered and decided upon rationally, in good faith, in accordance with the principle of legality, diligently and without delay'.[46] Another well-known example is the Supreme Court of India, as Batra explains in chapter 7. India went through a process of opening mercy to judicial review under its own constitution, separately from the countries that operate under the common law prerogative power. In *Kehar Singh v Union of India*, the Supreme Court of India recognised that it had the power to scrutinise grants of clemency in limited instances, including procedural impropriety, though it could not consider the substantive merits of the final decision,[47] as with the position in the Caribbean. As Batra explains, the Supreme Court refused to lay down guidelines or criteria framing the executive's decision-making on clemency petitions. However, both the courts and several presidents of India have been sceptical of the internal policy guidance of the Ministry of Home Affairs, which makes recommendations for clemency. In chapter 7, Batra describes how the Supreme Court of India is gradually developing standards for clemency, though these efforts are not entirely consistent.[48]

Some countries have resisted the trend to open clemency to judicial review. In Singapore, the Court of Appeal has recognised the theoretical right of judicial review, but did not establish a process by which a clemency petitioner could discover how the Cabinet and president came to a decision.[49] Indonesia

44 *Lewis v Attorney General of Jamaica* [2000] UKPC 35, para 50.
45 See Bulkan, this volume.
46 *Minister of Justice v Chonco* (2010) 1 SACR 325 (CC).
47 *Kehar Singh v Union of India*, AIR 1989 SC 653.
48 See Batra, this volume.
49 *Yong Vui Kong v Attorney General* [2011] SGCA 9.

(a civil law jurisdiction) and Malaysia (a common law jurisdiction) have also resisted judicial challenges to clemency decision-making.[50] Outside of the Southeast Asian context, Arias and Kouroutakis notice substantial variation among the civil law countries of Europe and Latin America as to judicial input in the clemency process. They note that in Argentina, judicial actors provide input in the clemency process before the decision is made. By contrast, in Brazil the judicial actor is more prominent after the decision and can review presidential pardons for propriety. They point to the Lithuanian constitution as one that specifically forbids judicial review, one of the reasons why the European Court of Human Rights found Lithuania's life without parole statute did not provide a meaningful opportunity for release and therefore violated the European Convention on Human Rights.[51]

Some courts have found grants of clemency unconstitutional, most frequently because the conditions on a conditional pardon were unlawful. The High Court of Fiji reviewed a conditional pardon in which the condition imposed included a compulsory supervision order that did not comply with the laws on such orders. The Court instead granted the pardon without the condition attached.[52] The Supreme Court of Palau has invalidated presidential pardons where the president did not follow the constitutional and legislative procedure of transmitting the petitions to the Minister of Justice, Attorney-General, Parole Board, and top law enforcement officer for their prior recommendations.[53] In chapter 6, Bulkan points to an even more consequential act of judicial review, whereby the Guyana Court of Appeal vacated a denial of clemency because of a conflict of interest in which the Attorney General and chair of the Advisory Council on the Prerogative of Mercy previously served as the petitioner's defence counsel.[54] It is on such conflict of interest grounds that clemency grants or refusals may be the most vulnerable to constitutional challenge. In the United States, the US Court of Appeal for the Eighth Circuit stayed a pending execution on account that the prosecutor threatened to dismiss an employee if that employee provided information to the state parole board and to the governor in support of clemency.[55] These decisions would have been inconceivable under the 'old' conception of clemency as an unreviewable sovereign prerogative even 40 years ago.

Coterminous with judicial review, clemency has also opened to administrative review in some common law jurisdictions, including under freedom of information laws. In the United States, the US Court of Appeals for the

50 For Malaysia, see *Juraimi bin Husin v Lembaga Pengampuanan Negeri Pahang* [2001] 3 Malaya LJ 458 (HC). For Indonesia, see Decision 92/PLW/2012/PTUN-JKT, 27 September 2012 (Central Jakarta Administrative Court) and Holland (n 23) 6.

51 See Arias and Kouroutakis, this volume.

52 *Commissioner of Prisons v Raikali* [1998] 44 FLR 205.

53 *Llecholch v Republic*, Civ App No 14–003 (24 July 2014) (Palau SC).

54 *Yasseen and Thomas v Attorney General* (1996) 62 WIR 98 (Guyana CA).

55 *Young v Hayes*, 218 F.3d 850 (8th Cir. 2000).

District of Columbia Circuit applied the Freedom of Information Act 1966 ('FOIA') to the deliberations of the Office of the US Pardon Attorney in the Department of Justice. In this case, *Judicial Watch, Inc. v US Department of Justice*, the DC Circuit ruled that a public interest watchdog could request documents related to President Clinton's pardon deliberations. The Department of Justice had argued that the presidential communications privilege would shield pardon deliberations from FOIA disclosure.[56] Similarly, in 2010, the High Court of Australia reversed the Supreme Court of Victoria's finding that Victoria's Freedom of Information Act 1982 required disclosure of clemency deliberations, as this was within the 'public interest'.[57] In the Australian litigation, the High Court ruled that legal professional privilege did not apply to clemency documents, as it was outweighed by the interests of public confidence and transparency.[58] These administrative law decisions have the same kind of impact as the due process cases cited above: they have eroded the traditional conception of clemency as an unreviewable prerogative.

We note that several newer constitutions contain transparency requirements in their clemency provisions, though most stop short of requiring an executive to provide reasons for a grant or denial. Some more recent constitutions contain provisions designed to permit public scrutiny of the clemency process, including by prohibiting secret pardons. Zimbabwe's 2013 constitution requires publication of grants of clemency in the official gazette, a provision that did not exist in the previous constitution.[59] Under Tuvalu's 1986 constitution, the prime minister is required to provide a statement to parliament after every grant of clemency, including providing the reasons for it.[60] Belize's constitution (as amended in 1989) requires the president to submit an annual report to the prime minister and the national assembly detailing all the grants of clemency in the previous year.[61] Most US states require the governor or clemency board to report clemency actions to the state legislature.[62] Yet this trend appears limited, for now, to common law jurisdictions. We still await the first civil law jurisdiction to provide for a transparency requirement within its constitutional clemency procedures. However, the robust history of constitutional 'borrowing', even between countries espousing differing legal systems, suggests that this is an entirely plausible future development.[63]

56 *Judicial Watch, Inc. v US Department of Justice*, 365 F.3d 1108 (DC Cir. 2004).
57 *Osland v Secretary to the Department of Justice* [2010] HCA 24.
58 Ibid., reversing *Secretary to the Department of Justice v Osland (No. 2)* [2009] VSCA 69.
59 Constitution of Zimbabwe 2013, s 112(3).
60 Constitution of Tuvalu 1986, s 80(2).
61 Constitution of Belize 1981, s 54(19).
62 Andrew Novak, *Comparative Executive Clemency: The Constitutional Pardon Power and the Prerogative of Mercy in Global Perspective* (Routledge 2015) 160–161.
63 Sujit Choudhry, 'Migration as a New Metaphor in Comparative Constitutional Law' in Sujit Choudhry (ed), *The Migration of Constitutional Ideas* (CUP 2006) 28–29.

While transparency requirements are undoubtedly helpful, they do not prevent all abuse. As Cooper and Burrows demonstrate in chapter 5, judicial review may not be a robust safeguard against all clemency impropriety. Because executives often keep poor records and do not elaborately state their reasoning, even a successful judicial review may not be particularly enlightening. In the United Kingdom, the Ministry of Justice was not even required to keep records of pardon deliberations until 2013.[64] Kobil has raised the possibility that too much transparency might discourage clemency, as it would expose decision-making to political fallout and thereby encourage risk-averse behaviour. He nonetheless agrees that some public oversight of the clemency process could improve confidence in the quality of clemency decisions.[65] We believe that this nascent constitutional trend toward making clemency more judicially accountable has antiseptic benefits, especially in closed or partially closed legal systems, not to mention that it benefits researchers like ourselves. But we also acknowledge that transparency contains a moral hazard that could reduce clemency's frequency.

Clemency and the Justice Cascade

Chapter 4, on clemency and amnesty in the former Yugoslavia, points to an additional trend in comparative constitutional law over the past 30 years or so: the trend toward holding human rights abusers accountable for mass atrocities such as war crimes or crimes against humanity. Smailagić calls this the 'international legal dimension' of clemency.[66] Sikkink has termed the overarching movement against impunity the 'justice cascade', defined as the 'dramatic new trend in world politics toward holding individual state officials, including heads of state, criminally accountable for human rights violations'.[67] Perhaps the most remarkable aspect of the justice cascade is the trend toward using foreign or international legal processes, as opposed to purely domestic processes, to hold human rights abusers accountable.[68] This norm derives from the adoption of international legal instruments, the emerging practice of international courts, and the pronouncements of UN and regional human rights organs.

The justice cascade has also influenced comparative law and practice as it relates to clemency and amnesty. Even in the United States, scholars have

64 See Cooper and Burrows, this volume.

65 Daniel T Kobil, 'Should Clemency Decisions Be Subject to a Reasons Requirement?' (2001) 13 Federal Sentencing Reporter 151, 151–52.

66 See Smailagić, this volume.

67 Kathryn Sikkink, *The Justice Cascade: How Human Rights Prosecutions are Changing World Politics* (WW Norton 2011) 5.

68 Ellen Lutz and Kathryn Sikkink, 'The Justice Cascade: The Evolution and Impact of Foreign Human Rights Trials in Latin America' (2001) 2 Chicago Journal of International Law 1.

suggested that the president cannot pardon international crimes.[69] Article II, Section 2 of the US Constitution states that the president can only pardon 'offenses against the United States', and not against state governments, foreign sovereigns, or international law.[70] Because all countries have an obligation to prosecute or extradite persons who have committed international crimes (and perhaps to allow reparations to the victims),[71] allowing pardons for such crimes would appear to contradict this policy, in spirit at least.

Looking at the constitutions of the former Yugoslav republics, in chapter 4 Smailagić explains how each nation has wrestled with the question of amnesty, though they have since moved in different directions. North Macedonia's amnesty law applies to all cases referred by the International Criminal Tribunal for the Former Yugoslavia, preventing the prosecution of human rights abusers. By contrast, the European Court of Human Rights has allowed prosecutions to proceed in Croatia, notwithstanding an amnesty law. Such mixed signals reflect a broader ambivalence about amnesty laws. Many jurisdictions have adopted amnesty laws in recent years, notwithstanding a growing global scepticism toward amnesty for human rights abuses.[72] The trend is also evident with individual clemency mechanisms. Smailagić notes that Bosnia and Herzegovina, Kosovo, and Slovenia have each passed legislation limiting use of the clemency power for atrocity crimes. In Bosnia and Herzegovina, legislation prohibits clemency for genocide, crimes against humanity, and war crimes. Kosovo's legislation uses the broader term 'international crimes', while Slovenia's limitation is narrower, excluding only persons sentenced by the International Criminal Court. Bosnia and Herzegovina has proposed legislation to partially remove this exception, allowing clemency for human rights abuses once an offender has served two-thirds of his or her sentence, a proposal that generated opposition from international justice and human rights advocates.[73]

Latin American constitutions were perhaps the most profoundly influenced by transnational democratic principles, including the justice cascade. During the 1990s, constitutional changes in the Southern Cone of South America and elsewhere established more inclusive selection processes for executives and legislatures, broader protection of socioeconomic rights, and more specific

69 Jordan J Paust, 'Contragate and the Invalidity of Pardons for Violations of International Law' (1987) 10 Houston Journal of International Law 51, 52–53.

70 Constitution of the United States 1787, art II, sec 2.

71 M Cherif Bassiouni and Edward M Wise, *Aut Dedere Aut Judicare: The Duty to Extradite or Prosecute in International Law* (Martinus Nijhoff Publishers 1995). Bassiouni and Wise determine, based on international conventions and state practice, that the duty to extradite or prosecute international criminal conduct has become part of customary international law.

72 Mark Freeman, *Necessary Evils: Amnesties and the Search for Justice* (CUP 2009) 4; Louise Mallinder, 'Amnesties' Challenge to the Global Accountability Norm? Interpreting Regional and International Trends in Amnesty Enactment' in Francesca Lessa and Leigh A Payne (eds), *Amnesty in the Age of Human Rights Accountability: Comparative and International Perspectives* (CUP 2012) 69–96.

73 See Smailagić, this volume.

rights provisions to prevent future atrocities.[74] Prohibitions on clemency for human rights abusers fit firmly within this trend. Chapter 3 demonstrates how presidential pardons for human rights abusers can remain controversial for years afterwards. Writing on the Argentinian context, Arias and Kouroutakis describe how presidential pardons by President Carlos Menem in 1989 and 1990 generated significant outrage and were ultimately reversed by one of Menem's successors. The beneficiaries of the pardons included about 1,200 people involved in the previous military dictatorship (1976–1983) and in leftist guerrilla movements during the 1970s.[75] Argentina's constitution does not limit clemency or amnesty for international crimes, though it does do so for some political offences.[76]

Five constitutions worldwide explicitly prohibit clemency or pardons for international crimes such as genocide, war crimes, and crimes against humanity: those of Ethiopia (1994), The Federation of Bosnia and Herzegovina (1994), Venezuela (1999), Iraq (2005), and Niger (2010), all of which were drafted after the end of the Cold War. Furthermore, Ecuador's 2008 Constitution prohibits 'amnesty' and 'pardon' for 'crimes perpetrated against public administration or for genocide, torture, forced disappearance of persons, kidnapping, or homicide on political or moral grounds', though this provision refers exclusively to political leniency granted by the legislature.[77] Ecuador's constitution does not preclude pardons or commutations of sentence for these crimes by the country's president.[78] Ethiopia's constitutional provision is similar, precluding 'amnesty or pardon of the legislature or any other state organ' for crimes against humanity as defined in international law, 'such as genocide, summary executions, forcible disappearance or torture'. However, where the death penalty is at stake, the Ethiopian head of state may commute a death sentence to life imprisonment, in accordance with the requirements of the ICCPR.[79] In a June 1993 letter to a UN official, the Meles Zenawi government rejected the possibility of an amnesty for human rights abuses by the Marxist Derg regime (1974–1987), believing that such a refusal was grounded in the fight against impunity. The transitional government noted that it was 'aware of its obligations concerning the duty to prosecute systematic violations of human rights and the grave breaches of humanitarian law.'[80]

74 Mila Versteeg and Emily Zackin, 'Constitutions Unentrenched: Toward an Alternative Theory of Constitutional Design' (2016) 110 American Political Science Review 657, 669–71.
75 See Arias and Kouroutakis, this volume.
76 Constitution of Argentina 1853, s 99(5).
77 Constitution of Ecuador 2008, art 120(13).
78 Ibid., art 147(18).
79 Constitution of Ethiopia 1994, art 28(1), 28(2), 71(7).
80 Kjetil Tronvoll, Charles Schaefer, and Girmachew Alemu Aneme, 'The "Red Terror" Trials: The Context of Transitional Justice in Ethiopia' in Kjetil Tronvoll, Charles Schaefer and Girmachew Alemu Aneme (eds), *The Ethiopian Red Terror Trials* (James Currey 2009) 7–8.

Iraq's constitution is stricter than Ethiopia's because it does not on its face allow commutation of death sentences for terrorism, genocide, or other international crimes. The Iraqi constitution allows the president to issue a special pardon on the recommendation of the prime minister, except for torts or convictions for 'committing international crimes, terrorism, or financial and administrative corruption'.[81] Deeks and Burton note that the drafters employed a framework in which the prime minister was the 'direct executive authority responsible for the general policy of the state', whereas the president possessed largely ceremonial powers.[82] Even though the president cannot pardon international crimes or terrorism, both of which are death penalty-eligible offences,[83] the Iraqi constitution may permit the president to refuse to ratify death sentences. During the constitution drafting process, the president's role in ratifying treaties was reduced to a pro forma signature—in other words, the president cannot refuse to sign—but the same is not true of the clemency power. Notably, the president's power to 'ratify death sentences' in article 73(A) does not state that death sentences may be carried out without the president's consent; therefore, presumptively, the president *can* decline to ratify a death sentence for international crimes in his own discretion.[84] Nevertheless, whether this provision ensures compliance with Article 6(4) of the ICCPR remains debatable at best. A prisoner convicted of terrorism or international crimes plays no active role in the decision whether or not to ratify, and nor is the death sentence permanently commuted to a lesser punishment by executive action.

A similar situation applies in Niger, with the president prohibited from awarding clemency for 'imprescriptible crimes' within the 2010 Constitution, which extends the prohibition to executive leniency to genocide, crimes against humanity and war crimes.[85] Each remain capital offences in Niger.[86] Although the country has not performed an execution since 1976, the inapplicability of clemency for all capital crimes brings Niger in breach of its international treaty obligations under the ICCPR's Article 6(4). However, unlike in Iraq, there is

81 Constitution of Iraq 2005, art 73(A).

82 Ashley S Deeks and Matthew D Burton, 'Iraq's Constitution: A Drafting History' (2007) 40 Cornell International Law Journal 1, 38.

83 See Cornell Center on the Death Penalty Worldwide, 'Death Penalty Database: Iraq' (*Death Penalty Worldwide*, 11 December 2019) <http://www.deathpenaltyworldwide.org/country-search-post.cfm?country=Iraq> accessed 17 December 2019.

84 Ibid.

85 Constitution of Niger 2010, art 72. Imprescriptible crimes refer to crimes not time-barred for prosecution (Luigi Corrias, 'Law, Time and Inhumanity: Reflections on the Imprescriptible' in Luigi Corrias and Lyana Francot (eds), *Temporal Boundaries of Law and Politics: Time out of Joint* (Routledge 2018) 53–70). See also Constitution of Bolivia 2009, art 111–112.

86 Cornell Center on the Death Penalty Worldwide, 'Death Penalty Database: Niger' (*Death Penalty Worldwide*, 11 December 2019) <http://www.deathpenaltyworldwide.org/country-search-post.cfm?country=Niger> accessed 17 December 2019.

no additional safeguard for the ratification of death sentences by the president.[87]

Venezuela's constitutional limitation applies to both legislative amnesty and executive clemency. Article 29 of the Constitution of Venezuela 1999 states that the government is 'obliged to investigate and legally punish offenses against human rights committed by its authorities'. Serious violations of human rights and war crimes are not subject to statutes of limitation and are 'excluded from any benefit that might render the offenders immune from punishment, including pardons and amnesty'.[88] Venezuela had previously passed two amnesty laws for political crimes, but these laws specifically excluded crimes against humanity, war crimes, and serious violations of human rights.[89] In 2011, the Venezuelan government reported to the United Nations Human Rights Council that it had an 'an obligation to punish crimes against humanity and war crimes, which are not time-barred and cannot be subject to pardon or amnesty'.[90] Constitutional provisions such as the ones in Venezuela and in the former Yugoslavia may become more common as the emerging norm against amnesties and pardons for human rights violators takes root.[91]

Clemency and the Innocence Revolution

As Cooper has written, executive clemency has enjoyed a revival of sorts since the Innocence Revolution of the 1980s, which revealed the systematic problem of wrongful convictions.[92] In many legal systems, the advent of new forensic technologies like DNA evidence and challenges to the reliability of old investigative methods have conflicted with traditional rules governing finality of court decisions.[93] Even authoritarian China has confronted the troubling

87 Ibid.

88 Constitution of Venezuela 1999, art 29.

89 General Amnesty Law 2000 (Venezuela) and Special Amnesty Law 2007 (Venezuela) (both amnesties included the proviso that 'those persons having committed crimes against humanity, serious violations of human rights and war crimes shall not benefit from the present law').

90 International Committee of the Red Cross, 'Venezuela: Practice Relating to Rule 159, Amnesty' (*Customary International Humanitarian Law Database*) <https://ihl-databases.icrc.org/customary-ihl/eng/docs/v2_cou_ve_rule159> accessed 17 December 2019.

91 It is debatable whether blanket amnesties are now generally unlawful under international law for the perpetrators of war crimes, crimes against humanity, and genocide. However, individual grants of executive clemency do not appear to be legally proscribed at the present time. See generally Josepha Close, *Amnesty, Serious Crimes and International Law* (Routledge 2019).

92 Sarah L Cooper, 'The State Clemency Power and Innocence Claims: The Influence of Finality and Its Implications for Innocents' (2015) 7 Charlotte Law Review 51, 53, 93–95.

93 Keith A Findley, 'Innocence Found: The New Revolution in American Criminal Justice' in Sarah L Cooper (ed), *Controversies in Innocence Cases in America* (Ashgate 2014) 3–5.

reality that not only might innocent people be on death row, but, as Xiong explains in Chapter 8, innocent people have likely been executed.[94] Yet, even though innocence remains a powerful reason for granting clemency, and in some jurisdictions the only way to avoid the full weight of a criminal punishment, it is an imperfect solution. Cooper notes that the clemency process was 'not built to shoulder a corrective function'.[95] Clemency does not necessarily remove the stigma of conviction, and applicants for clemency—even innocent ones—face formidable legal and procedural barriers to seeking release through pardon. Furthermore, pardons are frequently granted directly by, or on the advice of, an elected actor who may not be impartial, given political considerations. Pardons are ad hoc and reactive rather than systematic and consistent, making for a less than ideal solution in innocence cases.[96]

In the common law world, the principle of finality ordinarily attaches to criminal convictions, except in the most extraordinary circumstances.[97] In chapter 5, Cooper and Burrows argue that clemency practice and reform in the United States and England and Wales have been profoundly affected by the Innocence Revolution. The authors recount the 1998 US Supreme Court decision in *Ohio Adult Parole Authority v Woodard*, in which the Court found that only the most minimal due process protections attach to state clemency proceedings, even though clemency is the traditional 'fail-safe' for the criminal justice process.[98] Similarly, England and Wales employ a high threshold for clemency, requiring an applicant to be 'morally and technically innocent'.[99] Despite the high burden facing an innocent clemency applicant, pardons based on innocence have nonetheless occurred in many English-speaking jurisdictions,[100] including in various states of the US, where constitutional reforms have accorded special recognition to pardons for innocence.[101] Innocence cases have even led to posthumous pardons for the wrongfully executed. For example, in 1979, Massachusetts Governor Michael Dukakis pardoned Nicola Sacco and Bartolomeo Vanzetti, two anarchist immigrants wrongly executed in

94 See Xiong, this volume.

95 Cooper, 'The State Clemency Power and Innocence Claims' (n 92) 94.

96 David Hamer, 'Wrongful Convictions, Appeals, and the Finality Principle: The Need for a Criminal Cases Review Commission' (2014) 37(1) UNSW Law Journal 270, 287.

97 Brandon L Garrett, 'Towards an International Right to Claim Innocence' (2017) 105 California Law Review 1173, 1181.

98 118 S.Ct. 1244 (1998).

99 *Regina v Secretary of State for the Home Department, ex parte Bentley* [1993] 4 All 442.

100 Garrett (n 97) 1181–1208.

101 Sarah L Cooper and Daniel Gough, 'The Controversy of Clemency and Innocence in America' (2014) 51 California Western Law Review 55, 93: Georgia and Alabama exempt claims of actual innocence from waiting periods; North Carolina and Texas have created 'pardons of innocence' to remove the stigma of conviction; and the governor of Tennessee is empowered to grant an 'exoneration' in cases of actual innocence.

1922. In the United Kingdom, the Queen has granted posthumous pardons for Timothy Evans and Derek Bentley, executed in 1950 and 1953, respectively. In 2008 the Governor of Victoria, Australia, pardoned Colin Campbell Ross, wrongfully executed in 1922 for the sensational 'gun alley murder'.[102]

Cooper and Burrows describe an emerging innocence trend in England and Wales. Since it began its work in 1997, the Criminal Cases Review Commission has been able to review the safety of a conviction outside the ordinary pardon process. The Commission can refer a case to the Court of Appeal for a possible new trial or to the Justice Secretary for a pardon. Nonetheless, as noted above, the threshold for a pardon referral is high: according to the High Court of England and Wales in *R v Secretary of State for the Home Department Ex p Bentley*, an applicant must be both morally *and* technically innocent of the crime.[103] This has created an obstacle for reviewing old convictions, particularly where an offender was guilty of a crime that has since been abolished. In the United Kingdom, this problem has arisen in the context of anti-sodomy convictions, battered spouse murders, and the so-called 'shot at dawn' soldiers. The legal requirement that pardons be granted for 'moral and technical innocence' was an obstacle to the pardons for Alan Turing and thousands of other gay men convicted under now-repealed sodomy laws. Cooper and Burrows describe the parliamentary debate about whether to apply the standards of the time or current moral standards. Parliament made it very clear that the Turing pardons were exceptional.[104] Similarly, convictions of battered spouses who killed and of soldiers with 'shellshock' (post-traumatic stress disorder) who were executed for cowardice or desertion occurred at a time when medical knowledge was not yet advanced.[105] In considering pardon, it is debatable whether such persons should be held to the standards of the time or more modern standards.

Wrongful convictions still occur in the civil law world, but the pardon framework is different because a wrongfully convicted person does not face the same obstacles to reopen a case before the judiciary.[106] In inquisitorial systems,

102 Novak, *Comparative Executive Clemency* (n 62) 95–97.

103 *R v Secretary of State for the Home Department Ex p Bentley* [1993] 4 All 442.

104 Cooper and Burrows (this volume); Paolo Caroli, 'The Thin Line Between Transitional Justice and Memory Activism: The Case of the German and British "Pardons" for Convicted Homosexuals' (2018) 12 International Journal of Transitional Justice 499.

105 Simon Wessely, 'The Life and Death of Henry Farr' (2006) 99 Journal of the Royal Society of Medicine 440, 442–443; David Sharp, 'Shocked, Shot, and Pardoned' (2006) 368 Lancet 975, 975–976; Lizzie Seal, *Capital Punishment in Twentieth Century Britain: Audience, Justice, Memory* (Routledge 2014) 23, 159 (on Ruth Ellis, executed in 1955 for killing her batterer).

106 Garrett (n 97) 1196; Kent Roach, 'Wrongful Convictions: Adversarial and Inquisitorial Themes' (2010) 35 North Carolina Journal of International Law and Commercial Regulation 387, 435 (noting that many European continental systems 'allow generous fact-based appeals or retrials', whereas common law countries typically limit appeals to mistakes of law).

truth is privileged over procedural justice. In Finland, for instance, the president may only grant a pardon if the conviction was justified, and as such a pardon does not erase the stigma of conviction. In innocence cases, the proper remedy is to return to court and seek a rescindment of the conviction, which erases the conviction entirely.[107] The modern Finnish judicial procedure code generously allows revision of a sentence in the event of misconduct by the prosecutor or other officials, falsification of evidence, misinterpretation of law, discovery of new evidence in a case, or a change in law such that the previous conviction would not have been passed.[108] However, an open process comes with a cost, especially where compensation for wrongful convictions is on the line: Finland has seen wrongful imprisonment claims quadruple in the last decade.[109] Nonetheless, a legal and constitutional framework that broadly allows wrongfully convicted persons to reopen their cases with new evidence or in light of misconduct absolves much of the need for innocence-based clemency. Elsewhere, we have recently argued that the availability of an unlimited number of retrials for convicted prisoners has depressed individual clemency rates in both Taiwan and Japan.[110] Moreover, in civil law Indonesia, presidential clemency is explicitly denoted as a form of legal forgiveness, following a prisoner's guilt. The Supreme Court's case re-opening procedure (*peninjauan kembali*) is to be employed for claims of factual innocence.[111] The same trends may apply to other civil law jurisdictions.

Innocence-based clemency is a paradox. As we have observed, the traditional clemency process is an imperfect tool for clemency cases, given that it may be procedurally complex to apply for and the result is ultimately in the discretion of the political executive. Yet it remains a crucial remedy in jurisdictions that provide little recourse for wrongfully convicted persons. At the very minimum, a sensible policy move would exempt innocence-based applicants for clemency from barriers such as waiting periods, fees, notification requirements, and other onerous procedural hurdles.[112] Moreover, any innocence-based pardon should fully remove the stigma of a criminal conviction, including as a 'prior conviction' in the sentencing of any future criminal offence.

107 CH Rolph, *The Queen's Pardon* (Cassell 1978) 71–72.

108 Code of Judicial Procedure 2015 (Finland), ch 31, s 7, 8, 8a.

109 'Wrongful Imprisonment Claims in Finland Quadruple in 10 Years' (*YLE*, 7 May 2018) <https://yle.fi/uutiset/osasto/news/wrongful_imprisonment_claims_in_finland_quadruple_in_10_years/10194181> accessed 17 December 2019.

110 Daniel Pascoe and Andrew Novak, 'Deadly Justice Without Mercy in East Asia?' (2020) (forthcoming).

111 Daniel Pascoe, 'Legal Dilemmas in Releasing Indonesia's Political Prisoners' (2017) 3 Indonesia Law Review 313, 325–326.

112 See Cooper and Gough (n 101) 93.

Best Practices and Recommendations

Finally, we turn to a series of global best practices for clemency arising from the studies forming part of this volume. One benefit of the comparative method is that it exposes policy-makers to a variety of experiments, options, and case studies.[113] Comparative studies of clemency reveal novel legal mechanisms designed to benefit applicants, increase fairness and improve public legitimacy. Although not all policy transplants will work equally as well in the 'host' society as in the society of 'origin',[114] the future drafters of national constitutions and legislation would benefit greatly from a considered analysis of comparative clemency. Given access to a range of constitutional and legislative tools and the results of natural experiments regarding clemency,[115] there is no need to repeat the mistakes of previous regimes by inertially retaining an unrestricted and unaccountable executive clemency power.

Our first and most important recommendation is that all jurisdictions that retain the death penalty should provide a mechanism by which condemned prisoners may seek commutation or pardon. In chapter 8, Xiong notes that although China's National People's Congress has passed several 'special amnesties' since 1949, never has a clemency applicant been able to initiate the process. China is therefore not compliant with Article 6(4) of the ICCPR, which requires that death penalty jurisdictions provide a 'right to seek' clemency. Xiong makes the case for an active and bilateral clemency mechanism to prevent the worst inconsistencies of the criminal justice system. He indicates that China's cultural acceptance of retributivism and the government's policy of deterrence have been obstacles to creating a true clemency process, especially given the fear that the rich or the well-connected would disproportionately benefit from clemency—hardly an unfounded concern, as the country's repeated 'cash for clemency' controversies indicate.[116] Nonetheless,

113 Peter De Cruz, *Comparative Law in a Changing World* (3rd edn, Routledge 2008) 20–21.

114 Günter Frankenberg, 'Constitutional Transfer: The IKEA Theory Revisited' (2010) 8 International Journal of Constitutional Law 563, 572, 579 (noting that constitutions are drafted by elites and transnational legal experts and are not necessarily constructed by the societies that they represent). Frankenberg describes how constitutional experts and legal consultants have developed a kind of global template for constitution-drafting, discarding or ignoring particular or non-transferable constitutional devices.

115 Beyond the suggestions made in this section, comparative constitutional law reveals a number of policy options that constitutional drafters might consider, for example: a prohibition on transitional or 'lame duck' pardons (Constitution of Rwanda 2003, art 104; Constitution of Kenya 2010, art 134), requirements for victim involvement (Constitution of Kenya 2010, art 133(2)–(4); Constitution of Fiji 2013, s 119(4)(c)), an oral hearing for clemency applicants (Barbados; see note 37 and associated text), or a prohibition on self-pardons (Constitution of Malaysia 1957, art 42(12)).

116 See David T Johnson and Franklin E Zimring, *The Next Frontier: National Development, Political Change and the Death Penalty in Asia* (OUP 2009) 277;

given China's recent pattern of wrongful convictions and even several known wrongful executions, a petition-based clemency process would provide a welcome safety valve for inevitable errors at the judicial level. In China itself, relatively minor legislative changes would be required to realise a 'right to seek' special amnesty in death penalty cases. More broadly, several national constitutions, such as those of Armenia and Barbados (in all cases), Zambia and Zimbabwe (in death penalty cases) provide a model to follow, whereby prisoners are specifically granted a constitutional right to seek clemency from the head of state.[117]

Second, we suggest that clemency applicants, whether in death penalty cases or not, should enjoy a right to legal representation in making a clemency petition, including the provision of legal aid for indigent defendants. If clemency is to be seen, among its other functions, as a retributive tool to individualise sentences and prevent underserved punishment,[118] a truly fair trial requires the right to counsel to be extended to this post-appellate stage of proceedings. Several constitutions of common law nations already authorise legal counsel in the clemency process, although they do not mention legal aid. For example, the aforementioned right to request pardon or commutation found within the Zambian constitution may be exercised either directly by the prisoner or through a representative.[119] There is no systemic reason why civil law legal systems could not make the same allowances.

Moreover, in case the right to be legally represented is breached at any stage of the proceedings, including during clemency itself, lack of adequate legal defence should be a justified basis for receiving clemency. In chapter 7, Batra offers notable praise for the Indian Ministry of Home Affairs for including lack of legal defence as one of the justified grounds within the Ministry's clemency guidelines, a factor that had not previously received enough weight in Indian clemency decision-making.[120] If an inadequate legal defence can reduce punishment or abrogate guilt at the judicial phase of case processing, a retributive model of clemency demands the same result at the post-appellate stage, albeit to be exercised by a political actor.[121]

Sue Trevaskes, 'Lenient Sentencing and the "Cash for Clemency" Debate' (2015) 73 The China Journal 38. In this context, 'clemency' refers to more lenient sentencing by judges, rather than executive clemency.

117 Constitution of Armenia 1995, art 70; Constitution of Zambia 1991, art 97(2); Constitution of Zimbabwe 2013, s 48(2)(e); Constitution of Barbados 1966, s 78 (5).

118 See Kathleen Dean Moore, *Pardons: Justice, Mercy and the Public Interest* (OUP 1989) 188–192; Elizabeth Rapaport, 'Retribution and Redemption in the Operation of Executive Clemency' (1999) 74(4) Chicago-Kent Law Review 1501, 1516–1519; Xiong, this volume; Cooper and Burrows, this volume.

119 Constitution of Zambia 1991, art 97(2). See also Constitution of Barbados 1966, s 78(5).

120 See Batra, this volume.

121 We also believe that delay in hiring a lawyer or in having one appointed should not count against the clemency applicant during the executive's assessment, especially

Third, academic research indicates that the involvement of an advisory committee helps to improve clemency decision-making by the political executive, even where that committee's recommendation is non-binding.[122] Although this research is primarily drawn from the United States, we believe that clemency committees serve three very important benefits, irrespective of where they are used, which helps explain why committees have been such durable features in postcolonial constitutions around the world. The first benefit is that a committee structure is more economically efficient as a division of labour. It conserves the time of senior political officials and delegates their discretion to criminal justice experts.[123] The second benefit is that it removes one of the major obstacles to clemency by potentially shielding an executive from the risk of political fallout from individual decision-making.[124] The third, and related, benefit is that a committee structure has the potential to improve public trust in the clemency process, by signalling that the decision to award or reject clemency has been reached for criminological or utilitarian reasons, rather than for politically self-interested ones.

Nonetheless, while committee consideration of clemency petitions may well improve outcomes, committee involvement poses one significant drawback that we would be remiss not to mention: in death penalty cases it may allow an executive to avoid personal responsibility for carrying out an execution by hiding behind or deferring to the committee's decision.[125] Silverman argues that dilution of responsibility by involving more actors in the process 'could tend to reduce the chances for the condemned to have an opportunity to have his clemency appeal receive meaningful consideration', but proceeds to explain that this concern could be mitigated by limiting the size of the board,

where clemency petitions are subject to time limits. In Botswana, the High Court rejected a 'death row syndrome' challenge on the basis of delay, believing that a nine-month delay in the case was the fault of the death row inmate. The claimant had alleged that a portion of the delay was spent finding an attorney to make a clemency application. Since the claimant was indigent, a *pro deo* counsel had to be appointed for him. The claimant was eventually executed. See Kealeboga N Bojosi, 'The Death Row Phenomenon Comes to Botswana: *Lehlohonolo Bernard Kobedi v The State*' (2005) 38 Comparative and International Law Journal of Southern Africa 304, 309–310.

122 Margaret Colgate Love, 'Reinvigorating the Federal Pardon Process: What the President Can Learn from the States' (2012) 9 University of St. Thomas Law Journal 730, 744–47; Andrew Novak, 'Transparency and Comparative Executive Clemency: Global Lessons for Pardon Reform in the United States' (2016) 49 University of Michigan Journal of Law Reform 817, 851.

123 See, e.g. BC Naudé, 'The Pardoning Power as a Duty of Justice' (2002) 15 South African Journal of Criminal Justice 159, 171.

124 Rachel E Barkow, 'The Politics of Forgiveness: Reconceptualizing Clemency' (2009) 21 Federal Sentencing Reporter 153, 154.

125 Adam M Gershowitz, 'The Diffusion of Responsibility in Capital Clemency' (2001) 17 Journal of Law and Politics 669, 673: 'Social science and historical evidence demonstrate that when responsibility is diffused, actors will engage in behavior that they might otherwise believe to be immoral or unacceptable'.

broadening the grounds on which clemency can be granted, providing counsel to the condemned, and creating a board that is not overly aligned with prosecutors.[126] Adding 'process' has an additional benefit besides improving decision-making: it can 'ensure that the ***appearance*** of justice is satisfied', as well as the substance.[127]

The structure of the committee and the conditions of office will affect its overall effectiveness. For example, a committee that is overly aligned with law enforcement or prosecutorial interests may produce punitive results.[128] Committees that include public officials such as government legal advisers or the executive him or herself may not enjoy the full set of conceptual benefits we outlined above. Committees that have poor procedures can also hardly be said to improve executive decision-making. The procedure of the Texas Board of Pardons and Paroles is an example of a poorly functioning committee: no records are kept, no reasons are provided, and no public proceedings or even in-person meetings are held. Unsurprisingly, in Texas, death row clemency is vanishingly rare, and clemency in non-capital cases remains unusual.[129] Furthermore, the benefits of a committee structure may be limited where the committee is not sufficiently independent of legislative control, including over its budget; where it meets irregularly or only at the executive's initiative; or where it is wholly appointed by a single person without input from others.

From the jurisdictions considered in depth in this volume, the Commonwealth Caribbean jurisdictions are the ones that best attempt to provide a transferable clemency committee model that respects the rights of the clemency applicant, involve criminal justice expertise in the decision-making process (for instance, by requiring involvement by the minister responsible for justice or corrections), and provides adequate political accountability for bad decisions. In chapter 6, Bulkan identified a number of procedural irregularities with these committees, but judicial review provides some oversight to prevent the worst abuses.[130] At a minimum, the constitutionalisation of clemency

126 Stephen E Silverman, 'There is Nothing Certain Like Death in Texas: State Executive Clemency Boards Turn a Deaf Ear to Death Row Inmates' Last Appeals' (1995) 37 Arizona Law Review 375, 397.

127 Beau Breslin and John JP Howley, 'Defending the Politics of Clemency' (2002) 81 Oregon Law Review 231, 245 n 49, emphasis added.

128 Barkow (n 124) 155–156: clemency boards should mimic the most successful state sentencing commissions, which are careful to mix law enforcement interests with those of defence lawyers and former offenders so that each side can learn from the other and increase the likelihood that sound conclusions will be reached and be less subject to political attack later.

129 Allen L Williamson, 'Clemency in Texas: A Question of Mercy?' (1999) 6 Texas Wesleyan Law Review 131, 147–48; The Texas Board of Pardons and Paroles, 'Annual Statistical Report: FY 2018' (*Texas Department of Criminal Justice*, 2018) 23–24 <https://www.tdcj.texas.gov/bpp/publications/FY%202018%20AnnualStatistical%20Report.pdf> accessed 17 December 2019.

130 See Bulkan, this volume.

procedure is a positive trend insofar as it protects the rights of the applicant and allows some remedy non-compliant decision-making.

Our fourth and final recommendation is that all jurisdictions should make the numbers of executive clemency grants and denials public, if only in the aggregate. Good reasons may exist to keep the substance of a discretionary decision-making process secret (such as privacy concerns and political fall-out),[131] but we believe the public has a right to know how frequently these decisions are made. Such a policy would benefit clemency-seekers and their counsel, who could discern the relative prospects for success and may then produce a better application. We also believe that transparency would improve public confidence in the clemency process. In liberal democracies, the public can be rightly sceptical of clemency as it involves a departure from the law for unstated reasons that cannot be known in advance. Yet, the empirical and legal analyses in this volume have shown that clemency still serves valuable purposes in the modern day and age. At a minimum, releasing statistics on grants and denials of clemency would show that the pardon power is 'an integral, rationally defensible part of our system of justice, as opposed to a gift that is arbitrarily bestowed by presidents [or other heads of state]'.[132]

Based on the trends we have outlined in this chapter, clemency will likely exist for the foreseeable future across a range of different societies. Clemency has evolved before, and will do so again, all the while remaining ever-present within the world's constitutional laws. With its potential to permanently mitigate or abrogate judicial punishment at the stroke of a pen, within individual cases or across collective groups, clemency decision-making deserves the same academic and media scrutiny that other actors in the criminal justice system have long received. Our hope is that the research contained in this volume renews and expands the debate over the place of executive clemency within global criminal justice futures.

131 See note 65 and associated text.
132 Ibid.

Appendix

Country	*Legal Source*	*Primary Clemency Decision Maker*	*Compulsory Recommendation / Countersigning Body*	*Other Advisory Bodies*	*Special Categories or Provisions*	*Type of Clemency Mentioned*	*Death Penalty Provisions and Relevant Status (December 2018)*
Afghanistan	Constitution 2004, art 64 (18)	President				pardon, reduction	
Albania	Constitution 1998, art 92 (b) (revised 2016)	President				pardon	
Algeria	Constitution 1989, art 91 (7) (reinstated 1996, revised 2016)	President		High Council of the Judiciary (prior consultative opinion) (art 175)		pardon, reduction, commutation	
Andorra	Constitution 1993, art 46 (1)(a)	Coprinces				prerogative of grace	
Angola	Constitution 2010, art 119(o)	President				pardon, commutation	

(*Continued*)

Antigua and Barbuda	Constitution 1981, s 84	Governor-General	A Minister designated by him, acting in accordance with the advice of the Prime Minister	Advisory Committee on Prerogative of Mercy (non-binding opinion to the Minister, s 85–86)		pardon (free or conditional), remittance, substitution, respite	Retentionist. Where an offender has been sentenced to death, the Minister shall cause a written report of the case from the trial judge, together with other information, to be taken into consideration at a meeting of the Advisory Committee (s 86(1))
Argentina	Constitution 1853, art 99 (5) (reinstated 1983, revised 1994)	President		The Appropriate Court	Authors of acts of force against the institutional order and democratic system are excluded from the benefits of pardon and commutation (art 36). May grant pardons except in cases of impeachment by the House of Deputies	pardons, commutations	
Armenia	Constitution 1995, art 135 (revised 2015)	President			Convict has the right to request pardon (art 70)	pardon	

Australia	*Royal Prerogative of Mercy (clemency not included in Constitution 1901, revised 1977)*	*Governor-General*		*Attorney-General*		*full pardon, conditional pardon, commutation, order of inquiry*
Austria*	Constitution 1920, art 65 (2)(c) (reinstated 1945, revised 2013)	Federal President	Compulsory recommendation: Federal Government or the Federal Minister authorised by it (art 67(1)) Counter-signature: Federal Chancellor or the competent Federal Minister (art 67(2))		Only exercisable in cases with no remaining right of appeal	pardon, mitigation, commutation, annulment, remission
Azerbaijan	Constitution 1995, art 109(22) (revised 2016)	President				mercy

(*Continued*)

Bahamas	Constitution 1973, art 90	Governor-General	A Minister designated by the Governor-General, acting in accordance with the advice of the Prime Minister	The Minister may consult with the Advisory Committee on the Prerogative of Mercy before tendering any advice to the Governor-General (art 92(2)) but is not obliged to act on the Committee's views (92 (3))		pardon (free or conditional), respite, substitution, remittance	Retentionist. Where an offender has been sentenced to death, the Minister shall cause a written report of the case from the trial Justice of the Supreme Court, together with such other information, to be taken into consideration at a meeting of the Advisory Committee (art 92(1))
Bahrain	Constitution 2002, art 41 (revised 2017)	King				abatement, commutation	
Bangladesh	Constitution 1972, art 49 (reinstated 1986, revised 2018)	President	Prime Minister (art 48 (3)) (President acts in accordance with the advice of)			pardons, reprieves, respites, remittances, suspensions, commutations	

Barbados*	Constitution 1966, s 78 (revised 2007)	Governor-General	Privy Council		Right to submit written representations directly or through a legal representative. Governor-General may direct that there shall be time-limits within which persons may appeal to, or consult, any person outside Barbados regarding pardon. Where a time limit has expired, the Governor-General and Privy Council may exercise their functions, notwithstanding that such an appeal or consultation has not been concluded	pardon (free or conditional), respite, substitution, remittance	Retentionist. Where any person has been sentenced to death, the Governor-General shall cause a written report of the case together with other information to be forwarded to the Privy Council.The power to require such information shall be exercised by him on the recommendation of the Privy Council or, in any case of urgency, in his discretion
Belarus	Constitution 1994, art 84 (19) (revised 2004)	President				pardon	

(Continued)

Belgium	Constitution 1831, art 110 (revised 2014)	King	Countersignature of a Minister (art 106)		Can grant pardons to Ministers but only upon request of the House of Representatives (art 103). Cannot grant pardons to Ministers convicted by the Supreme Court, except upon request of the House of Representatives (art 111). Cannot pardon members of a Community or Regional Government convicted by the Appeal Court except upon request by the Community or Regional Parliament concerned (art 125)	remittances, reductions	
Belize	Constitution 1981, s 52, 54 (revised 2011)	Governor-General	Belize Advisory Council		Requires a report to the Prime Minister each year detailing the activities of the Advisory Council	pardon (free or conditional), respite, substitution, remittance	Retentionist. Where any person has been sentenced to death, the Attorney-General shall cause a written report of the case from the trial judge together with other information to be taken into consideration at a meeting of the Belize Advisory Council, so that the Council may advise the Governor-General whether to exercise any of his powers (s 53))

Benin	Constitution 1990, art 60	President		Superior Council of the Magistrature, reasoned opinion to the President (art 130)		pardon
Bhutan	Constitution 2008, art 2(16)	Druk Gyalpo (King)		Lhengye Zhungtshog (Council of Ministers) (art 20 (3)). Prime Minister (art 20(4))		amnesty, pardon, reduction
Bolivia	Constitution 2009, art 172(14)	President	Pluri-National Legislative Assembly			amnesty, pardon
Bosnia and Herzegovina (Federation of)	Constitution 1994, part 4B, art 7(a) (viii) (revised 2008)	President			Cannot grant pardons or reprieves for war crimes, crimes against humanity and genocide	reprieves, pardon

(*Continued*)

Botswana	Constitution 1966, s 53 (revised 2016)	President	Advisory Committee on the Prerogative of Mercy (President may consult with the Committee in non-death penalty cases) (s 54, 55(2))		pardon (free or conditional), respite, substitution, remittance	Retentionist. Where any person has been sentenced to death, the President shall cause a written report together with other information to be considered at a meeting of the Advisory Committee on the Prerogative of Mercy. After obtaining the advice of the Committee he or she shall decide whether to exercise his or her powers (s 55(1))
Brazil	Constitution 1988, art 84(12) (revised 2017)	President	The 'agencies instituted by law' if necessary		pardons, sentence reductions	
Brunei	Constitution 1959, art 9 (revised 2006)	Sultan	Pardons Board (not currently in operation). Privy Council (Brunei Darussalam (Suspension) Order 2006 (S 15/06))		pardon (free or conditional), respite, substitution, remittance, discharge	

Bulgaria	Constitution 1991, art 98 (11) (revised 2015)	President	Countersignature of the Prime Minister or the Minister concerned (art 102 (2))			pardon
Burkina Faso*	Constitution 1991, art 54 (revised 2012)	President		Superior Council of the Magistrature (art 133) (opinion)		pardon
Burundi	Constitution 2018, art 114	President				pardon
Cabo Verde	Constitution 1980, art 135(1)(n) (revised 2010)	President		Government (consultation)		pardon, commutation
Cambodia	Constitution 1993, art 27 (revised 2008)	King	Proposed by the Council of Ministers (art 28)			pardons, amnesties

(*Continued*)

Cameroon	Constitution 1972, art 8 (7) (revised 2008)	President		Higher Judicial Council (consultation)		clemency	
Canada	*Royal Prerogative of Mercy. Governed by Criminal Code 1985, s 748 (uncodified Constitution)*	*Governor-General, Governor in Council*		*Cabinet, Parole Board*		*free pardons, conditional pardons, respites, remission*	
Central African Republic	Constitution 2016, art 33	President				pardon	
Chad*	Constitution 1996, art 89, 91 (revised 2015)	President				pardon	
Chile*	Constitution 1980, art 32 (14) (revised 2015)	President			Not applicable in the absence of a final judgment. Officials impeached by the Chamber of Deputies and condemned by the Senate may be pardoned by the Congress only. Terrorism excepted from clemency, except for commutations from death to life (art 9)	pardon, commutation	Abolitionist for ordinary crimes only. Individual pardon will not proceed concerning terrorism, except to commute the death penalty to life imprisonment (art 9)

China, People's Republic of	Constitution 1982, art 67 (18), 80 (revised 2018)	President (art 80) (issues)	Standing Committee of the National People's Congress (art 67 (18)) (decides)			special amnesty
China, Republic of (Taiwan)	Constitution 1947, art 40 (revised 2005)	President			Legislature (decides, amnesty only) (art 63)	pardon, amnesty, remissions, restitution of civil rights
Colombia*	Constitution 1991, art 201(2) (revised 2016)	Government (President; Cabinet; Directors of Administrative Departments, art 115)			May only be granted for political crimes. Must inform Congress about grants. In no case may these exonerations affect responsibility vis-à-vis private individuals	pardon
Comoros*	Constitution 2001, art 12 (revised 2009)	President				pardon

(*Continued*)

Congo, Democratic Republic of	Constitution 2005, art 87 (revised 2011)	President		Superior Council of the Magistrature (provides opinions only) (art 152)	pardon, remittance, commutation, reduction
Congo, Republic of	Constitution 2015, art 92	President			pardon
Costa Rica	Constitution 1949, art 147 (revised 2015)	Council of Government (President and Ministers)			pardon
Cote d'Ivoire	Constitution 2016, art 66	President			pardon
Croatia	Constitution 1991, art 98 (revised 2013)	President		Advisory Bodies appointed by the President / Office of the President of the Republic (art 106)	pardon
Cuba	Constitution 1976, art 90 (ll), 93(j) (revised 2002)	President	Council of State		pardon

Cyprus	Constitution 1960, art 47–49, 53 (revised 2016)	President and/or Vice President	Attorney-General and Deputy Attorney-General (in cases not involving a death sentence) (President/ Vice President must follow, but only on unanimous recommendation (art 53(4))				prerogative of mercy, remission, suspension, commutation of sentences	Abolitionist for all crimes. The President or the Vice-President of the Republic shall have the right to exercise the prerogative of mercy with regard to persons belonging to their respective community who are condemned to death (art 53 (1)). Where the person injured and the offender are members of different communities, such prerogative of mercy shall be exercised by agreement between the President and the Vice-President of the Republic; in the event of disagreement between the two the vote for clemency shall prevail (art 53(2)). In such cases, the death sentence shall be commuted to life imprisonment (art 53(3))

(Continued)

Czech Republic	Constitution 1993, art 62 (g), 63(1) (k) (revised 2013)	President			Countersignature of Prime Minister or a member of the Government designated by him required (art 63(3)) (for amnesties only)	pardon, commutation, expungement, amnesties	
Denmark	Constitution 1953, s 24	King			Ministers can only be granted a pardon for sentences passed by the High Court of the Realm if there is the consent of the Folketing (Parliament)	prerogative of mercy, amnesty, pardons	
Djibouti	Constitution 1992, art 32 (revised 2010)	President				pardon	
Dominica	Constitution 1978, s 73 (revised 2014)	President	Minister designated by the President, acting in turn in accordance with the advice of the Prime Minister	Advisory Committee on Prerogative of Mercy (s 74–75) (advises Minister)		pardon (free or conditional), respite, substitution, remittance	Retentionist. Where any person has been sentenced to death, the Minister shall cause a written report together with other information to be taken into consideration at a meeting of the Advisory Committee. After obtaining the advice of the Committee, the Minister shall decide in his own deliberate judgment whether to advise the President to exercise his powers (s 75(1))

Dominican Republic	Constitution 2015, art 128(1)(j)	President			Pardons can only be granted on the 27th of February, 16th of August, and 23d of December of each year. Pardons to be granted in accordance with 'international conventions'	pardon	
Ecuador	Constitution 2008, art 147(18) (revised 2018)	President				pardon, reductions, commutations	
Egypt	Constitution 2014, art 155	President		Cabinet (consultation)		pardon, mitigation	
~~El Salvador~~							Abolitionist for ordinary crimes only (note: ICCPR state party)
Equatorial Guinea	Constitution 1991, art 41 (l) (revised 2012)	President				pardon	
Eritrea	Constitution 1997, art 42 (12)	President			A declaration of a state of emergency or any measures undertaken or laws enacted pursuant to such a declaration cannot grant pardon or amnesty to a person who, acting under the authority of the state, has committed illegal acts (art 27(5)(b))	reprieve, pardon, amnesty	

(*Continued*)

Estonia	Constitution 1992, art 78 (19) (revised 2015)	President			Granted only at a convict's request	clemency, release, commutation	
Ethiopia	Constitution 1994, art 71 (7)	President			Crimes against humanity, defined by international agreements ratified by Ethiopia, may not be subject to amnesty or pardon. Examples are 'genocide, summary executions, forcible disappearances or torture' (art 28(1))	pardon, commutation	Retentionist. In the case of persons convicted of crimes against humanity and sentenced with the death penalty, the Head of State may commute the punishment to life imprisonment (art 28(2))
Fiji	Constitution 2013, s 119	President	Mercy Commission	Mercy Commission may consider the views of the victims of the offence; Mercy Commission must consider report from trial judge or the Chief Justice	Requires a petition by the offender. Mercy Commission to report regularly to Parliament on its 'functions and responsibilities'	pardon (free or conditional), postponement, remittance	

Finland	Constitution 2000, s 105 (revised 2018)	President		Supreme Court (compulsory statement)		pardon (full or partial)
France	Constitution 1958, art 17 (revised 2008)	President	Countersigned by Prime Minister, and, where required, by the Ministers concerned (art 19)			individual pardon
Gabon*	Constitution 1991, art 23 (revised 2011)	President				pardon
Gambia	Constitution 1996, s 82 (revised 2018)	President		Committee (compulsory consultation)		pardon (free or conditional), respite, substitution, remittance
Georgia	Constitution 1995, art 52 (1)(f) (revised 2018)	President				pardon

(*Continued*)

Germany	Basic Law 1949, art 60 (2) (revised 2017)	Federal President. May delegate this power to other authorities	Countersignature of Federal Chancellor or competent Federal Minister (art 58)			pardon	
Ghana	Constitution 1992, art 72 (1)(a) (revised 1996)	President		Council of State (compulsory consultation)		pardon (free or conditional), respite, substitution, remittance	Abolitionist in practice. Where a person is sentenced to death for an offence, a written report, together with other information shall be submitted to the President (art 72(2))
Greece	Constitution 1975, art 47 (revised 2008)	President		Minister for Justice and a Council, composed in its majority of judges (compulsory recommendation and consultation, respectively)	The President shall have the right to grant pardon to a Minister convicted as provided in art 86 (crimes committed during discharge of duties), only with the consent of Parliament	pardon, commutation, reduction, revocation	

Grenada	Constitution 1973, s 72 (1) (reinstated 1991, revised 1992)	Governor-General	Minister designated by the Governor-General, acting in accordance with the advice of the Prime Minister	Advisory Committee on the Prerogative of Mercy (advises Minister) (s 73)		pardon (free or conditional), respite, substitution, remittance	Abolitionist in practice. Where any person has been sentenced to death (otherwise than by a court-martial), the Minister shall cause a written report of the case from the trial judge together with other information to be taken into consideration at a meeting of the Advisory Committee on the Prerogative of Mercy. After obtaining the advice of the Committee he shall decide in his own deliberate judgment whether to advise the Governor-General to exercise any of his pardon powers (s 74))
~~Guatemala~~							Abolitionist for ordinary crimes only (note: ICCPR state party)
Guinea	Constitution 2010, art 49	President		Superior Council of the Magistrature (provides opinion) (art 111))		pardon	

(*Continued*)

Guinea-Bissau	Constitution 1984, art 68 (t) (revised 1996)	President			pardons, commutations	
Guyana	Constitution 1980, art 121, 188–190 (revised 2016)	President	Minister designated by the President (compulsory consultation). A second Minister specially designated in relation to persons convicted by courts-martial (compulsory consultation). First Minister may consult the Advisory Council on the Prerogative of Mercy in non-death penalty cases		pardon (free or conditional), respite, substitution, remittance	Retentionist. Where a person has been sentenced to death, the Minister designated by the President shall cause a written report of the case from the trial judge, together with other information to be taken into consideration at a meeting of the Advisory Council on the Prerogative of Mercy. After obtaining the advice of the Council, the Minister shall express his own deliberate opinion to the President as to whether he should exercise any of his powers
Haiti	Constitution 1987, art 146 (revised 2012)	President		Except for sentences handed down by the High Court of Justice (i.e. impeachment, art 186). May only be granted in res judicata cases	commutation	

Holy See (Vatican City State)	Fundamental Law of Vatican City State 2000, art 19	Supreme Pontiff			amnesties, indults, remissions, favours	
Honduras	Constitution 1982, art 245(24) (revised 2013)	President			pardons, commutations	
Hungary	Constitution 2011, 9(4)(g) (revised 2018)	President	Countersigned by a Member of the Government (art 9(5)). Except upon legislation to that effect			individual pardon
Iceland	Constitution 1944, art 29 (revised 2013)	President	Ministers (art 13, 16, 19)	The President may not absolve a Minister from prosecution or from a punishment imposed by the Court of Impeachment, unless approved by Althingi (Parliament)	pardon, amnesty	

(*Continued*)

India	Constitution 1950, art 72 (1), 161 (revised 2018)	President (Union cases); The Governor of a State (state cases); Officer of the Armed Forces of the Union (Court Martial)	Advice to President from the Council of Ministers (art 74). President must follow this advice. However, President may ask the Council of Ministers to reconsider their advice			pardons, reprieves, respites, remissions, suspensions, commutations	Retentionist. The President shall have the power to grant pardons, reprieves, respites or remissions of punishment in all cases where the sentence is a sentence of death. State Governors retain the power to suspend, remit or commute a sentence of death (art 72(1)(c), 72(3))
Indonesia	Constitution 1945, art 14 (reinstated 1959, revised 2002)	President		Supreme Court (clemency); Parliament (amnesty). Compulsory opinion in both cases		clemency, restoration of rights, amnesty, dropping of charges	
Iran	Constitution 1979 art 110(11), 155 (revised 1989)	Leader or Leadership Council. The Leader may delegate part of his duties and powers to another person		Head of the Judiciary Power (only on the recommendation of)	Within the framework of Islamic criteria (i.e. no clemency for *qisas* or some *hudud* crimes)	pardon, reduction	

Iraq	Constitution 2005, art 73 (A)	President		Prime Minister	Cannot issue pardon for anything concerning a private claim (i.e. *qisas* crimes) and for those who have been convicted of committing international crimes, terrorism, and financial and administrative corruption	special pardon
Ireland	Constitution 1937, art 13 (6) (revised 2018)	President	Only on the advice of the Government (art 13(9))			pardons, commutations, remittances
Israel	*Basic Law: The President of the State 1964, s 11(b) (uncodified constitution)*	*President*	*Countersignature of the Prime Minister or of such other Minister as the Government may decide (art 12)*			*pardons, lightening of penalties*
Italy	Constitution 1947, art 87 (revised 2012)	President	Countersignature of proposing Minister (s 89)			pardons, commutations

(*Continued*)

Jamaica	Constitution 1962, s 90, 91 (revised 2015)	Governor-General	Privy Council		pardon (free or conditional), respite, substitution, remittance	Retentionist. Where any person has been sentenced to death, the Governor-General shall cause a written report of the case and a notice to be delivered to the person sentenced so that the Privy Council may make a recommendation to the Governor-General (s 91)
Japan	Constitution 1946 art 7, 73	Emperor	Cabinet (decides)		general amnesty, special amnesty, commutations, reprieves, restoration of rights	
Jordan	Constitution 1952, art 38 (revised 2016)	King	Countersignature of Prime Minister and the Minister or Ministers concerned (art 40)		special pardon, remittances	Retentionist. No death sentence shall be executed except after ratification by the King, and every such sentence shall be placed before him by the Council of Ministers accompanied by its opinion thereon (art 39)

Kazakhstan	Constitution 1995, s 44 (15) (revised 2017)	President				pardon
Kenya	Constitution 2010, art 133	President		Advisory Committee. The Advisory Committee may take into account the views of the victims of the offence in respect of which it is considering making recommendations to the President	Prisoner must petition	mercy, pardon (free or conditional), postponement, substitution, remittance
Kiribati	Constitution 1979, s 50 (revised 2013)	Beretitenti (President)		Cabinet		pardon (free or conditional), respite, substitution, remittance
Korea, Democratic People's Republic of	Constitution 1972, art 103 (revised 2016)	Chairman of the State Affairs Commission				special pardons
Korea, Republic of	Constitution 1948, art 79 (revised 1987)	President	National Assembly (general amnesty) (art 79(2))	State Council (amnesty, commutation, restoration of rights) (art 89 (9))		amnesty, commutation, restoration of rights, general amnesty
Kosovo	Constitution 2008, art 84 (29) (revised 2016)	President				individual pardons

(*Continued*)

Kuwait	Constitution 1962, art 75 (reinstated 1992)	Amir			pardon, attenuate punishment
Kyrgyzstan	Constitution 2010, art 64 (10)(4) (revised 2016)	President			pardon
Laos*	Constitution 1991, art 67 (11) (revised 2003)	President			amnesty
Latvia	Constitution 1922, art 45 (reinstated 1991, revised 2016)	President	Countersignature by the Prime Minister or by the appropriate Minister (art 53)		clemency
Lebanon	Constitution 1926, art 53 (9) (revised 2004)	President	Countersignature by the Head of Government and the Minister or Ministers concerned (art 54)		special pardon
Lesotho	Constitution 1993, s 101 (revised 2018)	King	Pardons Committee on the Prerogative of Mercy (art s)		pardon (free or conditional), respite, substitution, remittance
Liberia	Constitution 1986, art 59	President		Except impeachment	remittances, reprieves, pardons, restoration of civil rights
*Libya**	*Penal Code 1954, art 124–125 (not present in Constitution 2011, revised 2012)*	*President*			*special pardon*

Liechtenstein	Constitution 1921, art 12 (revised 2011)	Prince Regnant			Compulsory recommendation required from Parliament (if remission or mitigation granted in favour of a member of the Government sentenced on account of his official acts)	remittances, mitigations, commutations, quashing convictions
Lithuania	Constitution 1992, art 84(23) (revised 2006)	President				pardons
Luxembourg	Constitution 1868, art 38, 83 (revised 2017)	Grand Duke	Countersignature of a member of the Government (art 45)		Does not apply to members of the Government. The Grand Duke may only pardon a condemned member of the Government at the request of the Chamber (legislature) (art 83)	remittances, reduction of penalties
Macedonia, North	Constitution 1991, art 84 (revised 2011)	President				pardons
Madagascar	Constitution 2010, art 58	President				pardons

(*Continued*)

Malawi	Constitution 1994, s 89(2) (revised 2017)	President		Advisory Committee on the Granting of Pardon (consultation)	Judgments in cases of impeachment of the President or Vice-President shall not be liable to pardon by the President	pardons, stays of execution, reduce sentences, remittances
Malaysia	Constitution 1957, art 38(2)(e), 42 (revised 2007)	Yang di-Pertuan Agong (King, court martials and federal cases); Yang di-Pertua Negeri (State Governor, state cases); Ruler of a State (state cases)		Pardons Boards (State and Federal). Pardons Boards must consider optional written advice by Attorney General	Self-pardons or pardons in favour of immediate family members by Yang di-Pertua Negeri to be exercised instead by the Yang di-Pertuan Agong; self-pardons or pardons in favour of consort by Yang di-Pertuan Agong or State Rulers to be exercised instead by the Conference of Rulers	pardons, reprieves, respites
Maldives*	Constitution 2008, art 115(s)	President			Only exercisable in cases with no remaining right of appeal	pardons, reductions of sentences

Mali	Constitution 1992, art 45	President			pardon	
Malta	Constitution 1964, art 93 (revised 2016)	President	Cabinet or a Minister acting under the general authority of the Cabinet (art 85(1))		pardon (free or conditional), respite, substitution, remittance	Abolitionist for all crimes. Where any person has been sentenced to death, the President shall cause a written report of the case from the trial judge, or, in the case of a court-martial the person presiding, and other information to be sent to the Minister responsible for justice. The Minister shall send the written report and information to the Cabinet, and the Cabinet shall advise the President whether he should grant the offender a pardon or respite
Marshall Islands	Constitution 1979, art 5, s 1(3)(f) (revised 1995)	Cabinet			pardons, reprieves	
Mauritania	Constitution 1991, art 37 (revised 2017)	President			pardon, reduce, replace	

(*Continued*)

Mauritius	Constitution 1968, s 75 (revised 2016)	President	Commission on the Prerogative of Mercy (President acts in accordance with advice of). However, President may order Commission on the Prerogative of Mercy to reconsider its advice			pardon (free or conditional), respite, substitution, remittance	Abolitionist for all crimes. Where any person has been sentenced to death (otherwise than by a court martial) for an offence, a report on the case by the judge (or a report on the case by the Chief Justice), together with other information shall be taken into consideration at a meeting of the Commission which shall then advice the President whether or not to exercise his powers
Mexico*	Constitution 1917, art 89 (14) (revised 2015)	President			Pardon may not be granted to an accused public servant, provided that the crime was perpetrated during his term (art 111)	pardon	

Micronesia	Constitution 1979, art 10 s(2)(c) (revised 1990)	President (federal cases); Chief Executive of a state (state cases)			pardons, reprieves
Moldova	Constitution 1994, art 88 (e) (revised 2016)	President			individual pardon
Monaco	Constitution 1962, art 15 (revised 2002)	Prince		Crown Council (must be consulted)	pardon, amnesty
Mongolia	Constitution 1992, art 33 (1)(8) (revised 2001)	President			pardon
Montenegro	Constitution 2007, art 95 (9) (revised 2013)	President			amnesty
Morocco	Constitution 2011, art 58	King	Counter-signature of the Head of Government (art 42)		pardon

(*Continued*)

Mozambique	Constitution 2004, art 158(k) (revised 2018)	Head of State				pardons, commutations
Myanmar	Constitution 2008, s 204 (revised 2015)	President			National Defence and Security Council (advises, amnesty only)	pardon, amnesty
Namibia	Constitution 1990, art 32 (3)(d) (revised 2014)	President				pardons, reprieves (both unconditionally or subject to conditions)
Nauru	Constitution 1968, art 80 (revised 2015)	President				pardons (free or conditional), respites, substitutions, remittances
Nepal	Constitution 2015, art 276 (revised 2016)	President	Mandatory consent and recommendation of Council of Ministers, through the Prime Minister (art 66(2))			pardons, suspensions, commutations, remittances
Netherlands	Constitution 1815, art 122 (revised 2008)	King	One or more Ministers or State Secretaries (art 47)	Court designated by Act of Parliament		pardons

New Zealand	*Letters Patent Constituting the Office of the Governor-General of New Zealand 1983, s 11 (uncodified constitution)*	*Governor-General*		*Minister of Justice*		*pardons (free or conditional), respites, remittances*	
~~Nicaragua~~							
Niger	Constitution 2010, art 72 (revised 2017)	President			Cannot be granted in cases of imprescriptible crimes	pardon	
Nigeria	Constitution 1999, s 175, 212 (revised 2011)	President (Federal cases); Governor (State cases)		Council of State (Federal cases), Advisory Council (State cases) (consultation)		pardons (free or conditional), respites, substitutions, remittances	
Norway	Constitution 1814, art 20 (revised 2018)	King		Council of State	The criminal shall have the choice of accepting the King's pardon or submitting to the penalty imposed. Ban on clemency for impeachment	pardons	Abolitionist for all crimes. In proceedings which the Storting (legislature) causes to be brought before the Court of Impeachment, no pardon other than deliverance from the death penalty may be granted, unless the Storting consents

(*Continued*)

Oman	Constitution 1996, art 42 (revised 2011)	Sultan				pardons, commutations
Pakistan	Constitution 1973, art 45 (reinstated 2002, revised 2018)	President	President shall act on and in accordance with the advice of the Cabinet or the Prime Minister. However, President may ask the Cabinet or Prime Minister to reconsider their advice (art 48(1))			pardons, reprieves, respites, remittances, suspensions, commutations
Palau	Constitution 1981, art 8, s 7(5) (revised 1992)	President			Power does not extend to impeachment	pardons, commutations, reprieves, suspension, remittance
Palestine	Basic Law 2003, art 42 (revised 2005)	President of the National Authority				special pardon, commutation
Panama	Constitution 1972, art 184(12) (revised 2004)	President			Pardons for political offences only, reduction of penalties and grants of conditional freedom for common crimes only	pardons, reduce penalties, grant conditional freedom

Papua New Guinea	Constitution 1975, s 151–152 (revised 2016)	Head of State (Governor-General, via s 82 (2))	National Executive Council (Governor-General acts with and in accordance with the advice of)	Advisory Committee on the Power of Mercy (National Executive Council shall consider the report of)	(2) Free or conditional pardon may be granted to an accomplice who gives evidence that leads to the conviction of a principal offender (3) Except in a case referred to in subsection (2) or as otherwise permitted by or under an Act of the Parliament, the exercise of the power shall not be held out, offered or promised in advance of conviction (s 151)	pardons (free or conditional), remissions, respite, less severe form of punishment, remittances
Paraguay	Constitution 1992, art 238 (10) (revised 2011)	President		Supreme Court of Justice (compulsory report)		pardons, commutations
Peru*	Constitution 1993, art 118 (21) (revised 2009)	President			Executive clemency may be granted only in cases where the stage of criminal proceedings has exceeded double the term plus extension	pardons, commutations, executive clemency

(*Continued*)

Philippines	Constitution 1987, art 7, s 19	President			Only applies to convictions after final judgement. Power does not extend to cases of impeachment. Must have a favourable recommendation of the Commission on Elections (art 9, s 5), only for 'violation of election laws, rules, and regulations'. Congress advises President on amnesty only	pardons, commutations, reprieves, remittances, amnesty
Poland	Constitution 1997, art 139 (revised 2009)	President		Presidential Chancellory (art 143)	Power does not extend to individuals convicted by the Tribunal of State (i.e. for impeachment)	pardon
Portugal	Constitution 1976, art 134 (f) (revised 2005)	President	Government (compulsory consultation, and countersignature) (art 140(1))			pardons, commutations
Qatar	Constitution 2003, art 67(6)	Prince				pardon, commutation
Romania	Constitution 1991, art 94(d) (revised 2003)	President	Prime Minister (art 100(2))			individual pardons
Russia	Constitution 1993, art 89(c) (revised 2014)	President				pardons

Rwanda	Constitution 2003, art 109 (revised 2015)	President		Supreme Court (consultation)	The incumbent President cannot, during a transitional period, grant mercy to persons definitively sentenced by Courts of law (art 104)	prerogative of mercy	
Saint Kitts and Nevis	Constitution 1983, s 66	Governor-General	Minister designated by the Governor-General, acting in accordance with the advice of the Prime Minister	Committee on the Prerogative of Mercy (advises Minister, s 67)		pardons (free or conditional), respites, substitutions, remittances	Retentionist. Where any person has been sentenced to death (otherwise than by a court-martial), the Minister shall cause a written report together with other information to be taken into consideration at a meeting of the Advisory Committee of the Prerogative of Mercy. After obtaining the advice of the Committee, he shall decide in his own deliberate judgment whether to advise the Governor-General to exercise any of his powers (s 68(1))

(*Continued*)

Saint Lucia	Constitution 1978, s 74	Governor-General	Committee on the Prerogative of Mercy			pardons (free or conditional), respites, substitutions, remittances	Retentionist. Where any person has been sentenced to death (otherwise than by a court-martial), the Minister shall cause a written report of the case from the trial judge, together with other information, to be taken into consideration at a meeting of the Committee on the Prerogative of Mercy, so that the Committee may advise the Governor-General whether to exercise any of his or her powers (s 76))
Saint Vincent and the Grenadines	Constitution 1979, s 65	Governor-General	Minister designated by the Governor-General, acting in accordance with the advice of the Prime Minister	Advisory Committee on the Prerogative of Mercy (advises Minister, s 67)		pardons (free or conditional), respites, substitutions, remittances	Retentionist. Where any person has been sentenced to death (otherwise than by a court-martial), the Minister shall cause a written report together with other information to be taken into consideration at a meeting of the Advisory Committee of the Prerogative of Mercy. After obtaining the advice of the Committee he shall decide in his own deliberate judgment whether to advise the Governor-General to exercise any of his powers (s 67(1))
Samoa	Constitution 1960, art 110 (revised 2017)	Head of State		Minister designated by the Prime Minister (consultation)		pardons, reprieves, respites, remittances, suspensions, commuta-	

~~San Marino~~							
Sao Tomé and Principe	Constitution 1975, art 80(f) (revised 2003)	President		Government (consultation)		pardons, commutations	
Saudi Arabia	*Sharia Law; Law on Criminal Procedure 2001, art 1, 22–23 (clemency not included in Basic Law 1992)*	*King*			*Tazir, some Hudud crimes only. No clemency for Qisas crimes*	*pardon*	*Retentionist. No execution may be carried out withough the King's approval (art 220 (a))*
Senegal	Constitution 2001, art 47 (revised 2016)	President				pardon	
Serbia	Constitution 2006, art 112 (7), 145	President				amnesty	
Seychelles	Constitution 1993, art 60 (revised 2017)	President		Advisory Committee on the Power of Pardon (compulsory advice, art 60–61)		pardons (free or conditional), respites, substitutions, remittances	
Sierra Leone	Constitution 1991, s 63 (reinstated 1996, revised 2013)	President	Committee appointed by the Cabinet (President acts in accordance with the advice of)			pardons (free or conditional), respites, substitutions, remittances	Abolitionist in practice. Where any person has been sentenced to death, the Committee shall cause a written report of the case together with other information, to be submitted to it as soon as possible

(*Continued*)

Singapore	Constitution 1965, art 22P (revised 2016)	President		Cabinet	President may grant a pardon to any accomplice in any offence who gives information which leads to the conviction of the principal offender	pardons (free or conditional), reprieves, respites, remittances	Retentionist. Where any offender has been condemned to death, the President shall cause the reports to be forwarded to the Attorney-General with instructions that, after the Attorney-General has given his opinion thereon, the reports shall be sent, together with the Attorney-General's opinion, to the Cabinet so that the Cabinet may advise the President on the exercise of the power
Slovakia	Constitution 1992, art 102, 121 (revised 2017)	President; Government	Countersignature by the Prime Minister of the Slovak Republic or a Minister authorised by him (art 102(2))		The Government (Prime Minister, Deputy Prime Ministers and Ministers) shall have the power to award amnesty for misdemeanors (only) (art 109(1), 121)	amnesty, pardon, lowers punishments, nullification, individual clemency	

Slovenia	Constitution 1991, art 107 (revised 2016)	President					clemency	
Solomon Islands	Constitution 1978, s 45 (revised 2018)	Governor-General	Committee on the Prerogative of Mercy (President acts in accordance with the advice of)				pardons (free or conditional), respites, substitutions, remittances	Abolitionist for all crimes. Whenever any person has been sentenced to death, a report on the case by the judge together with other information shall be taken into consideration at a meeting of the Committee, which shall then advise the Governor-General whether or not to exercise his powers
Somalia*	Constitution 2012, art 90(p)	President		Judicial Service Commission (on the recommendation of)			pardons, commutations	

(*Continued*)

South Africa	Constitution 1996, s 84(2)(j) (revised 2012)	President		Executive Deputy Presidents (must consult before pardoning or reprieving) (Schedule 6 Annexure B added to s 84)		pardons, reprieves, remittances	
South Sudan*	Constitution 2011, art 101(h) (revised 2013)	President				pardons, remittances	Retentionist. President confirm s death sentences
Spain	Constitution 1978, s 62(i) (revised 2011)	King	Counter-signature of President of the Government (Prime Minister) and, when appropriate, competent Ministers (art 56, 64)		If the President (Prime Minister) and other members of the Government shall be held criminally liable for treason or any offence against the security of the State committed in the discharge of office, the Royal prerogative of pardon shall not apply (art 102). No power for the King to authorise general pardon (art 62(i))	clemency	

Sri Lanka	Constitution 1978, art 34 (revised 2015)	President		(2) The President may in the case of any person who is or has become subject to any disqualification specified in paragraph (d), (e), (f), (g) or (h) of, art 89 (disqualification as an elector) or sub-paragraph (g) of Paragraph (1) of, art 91 (disqualification as a member of parliament) – (a) grant a pardon (free or conditional); or (b) reduce the period of such disqualification (3) The President may grant a pardon to any accomplice in such offence who shall give such information as shall lead to the conviction of the principal offender	pardons (free or conditional), respites, substitutions, remittances	Abolitionist in practice. Where any offender shall have been condemned to suffer death, the President shall cause a report to be made to him by the Judge and shall forward such report to the Attorney-General with instructions that after the Attorney-General has advised thereon, the report shall be sent together with the Attorney-General's advice to the Minister in charge of the subject of Justice, who shall forward the report with his recommendation to the President
Sudan*	Constitution 2005, art 58(1)(i)	President			pardons, lift convictions, remittances	Retentionist. President confirm s death sentences
Suriname	Constitution 1987, art 109 (revised 1992)	President	Sentencing Judge (opinion)		pardons	

(*Continued*)

Swaziland	Constitution 2005, s 64(4)(d), 78	King	Committee on the Prerogative of Mercy (for death and life sentences); Cabinet or a Minister acting under the authority of the Cabinet (for other sentences)		reprieves, commutations, pardon, pardon (free or conditional), respite, substitution, remittance	Abolitionist in practice. In cases of death sentence or life imprisonment, the King may grant pardon (free or conditional); respite (indefinite or for a specified period); substitution; or a remittance. In the exercise of these powers, the King shall act on the advice of a Committee on the Prerogative of Mercy. Whenever any person has been sentenced to death by any court other than a court-martial, the Chairman of the Committee on the Prerogative of Mercy shall cause a report on the case by the judge together with other information to be taken into consideration at the meeting of the Committee so that the Committee may advise the King whether or not to exercise these powers
Sweden	Constitution 1974, ch 12, art 9 (revised 2015)	Government (Prime Minister and other Ministers, ch 6, art 1)			remit, reduce	

~~Switzer-land*~~									
Syria	Constitution 2012, art 108	President					special amnesty, reinstatement		
Tajikistan*	Constitution 1994, art 69 (revised 2003)	President					pardons		
Tanzania	Constitution 1977, art 45(1) (revised 2005)	President					pardons (free or conditional), respites, substitutions, remittances		
Thailand	Constitution 2017, s 179	King					pardons		
Timor Leste	Constitution 2002, art 85(i)	President		Government (Prime Minister, Ministers, Secretaries of State, art 104(1)) (consultation)			pardons, commutations		

(*Continued*)

Togo	Constitution 1992, art 73 (revised 2007)	President	Superior Council of the Magistrature (opinion)		pardons	
Tonga	Constitution 1875, s 37 (revised 2013)	King	Privy Council	Cannot pardon cases of impeachment	pardons	
Trinidad and Tobago	Constitution 1976, s 87 (revised 2007)	President	Minister designated by the President, acting in accordance with the advice of the Prime Minister; Advisory Committee on the Power of Pardon (opinion not binding on Minister, s 89)	The power of the President may be exercised either before or after the person is charged with any offence and before he is convicted thereof	pardons (free or conditional), respites, substitutions, remittances	Retentionist. Where an offender has been sentenced to death, the Minister shall cause a written report of the case from the trial judge, together with other information to be taken into consideration at a meeting of the Advisory Committee on the Power of Pardon (s 89)

Tunisia	Constitution 2014, art 77	President				special pardons
Turkey	Constitution 1982, art 104 (revised 2017)	President			Commutation or revocation by President on the grounds of chronic illness, disability, or old age only	commutation, revocation
Turkmenistan	Constitution 2008, art 71(18) (revised 2016)	President				pardons, amnesty
Tuvalu	Constitution 1986, s 80 (revised 2010)	Head of State (Governor-General, s 51(2))	Cabinet (acts in accordance with advice)		The Prime Minister shall present to Parliament –(a) if the power is exercised during a meeting of Parliament – during that meeting; or(b) if the power is exercised at any other time – during the next meeting of Parliament,a statement giving details of the exercise of the power and of the reasons for it. The Head of State may relieve a person from any disability imposed by this Constitution or by or under an Act of Parliament because of a conviction under, or a contravention of, or a failure to comply with, a law of a country other than Tuvalu (i.e. extra-territorial relief)	pardon (free or subject to lawful conditions), relieve a person from any disability, grant delays for the enforcement of penalties, substitutions, remittances

(*Continued*)

Uganda	Constitution 1995, art 121 (revised 2017)	President		Advisory Committee on the Prerogative of Mercy		pardons (free or conditional), respites, substitutions, remittances	Retentionist. Where a person is sentenced to death for an offence, a written report of the case from the judge together with other information shall be submitted to the Advisory Committee on the Prerogative of Mercy
Ukraine	Constitution 1996, art 106(27) (revised 2016)	President				pardons	
United Arab Emirates	Constitution 1971, art 54(10), 107 (revised 2009)	President		Federal Minister of Justice, with the approval a Committee formed and chaired by the Federal Minister of Justice		pardons, commutations, substitution	Retentionist. A final death penalty delivered by a Federal Judicial Authority is executed only after the President of the UAE approves the sentence. The President of the UAE may substitute a lesser sentence for the death penalty (art 108)

United Kingdom	*Royal Prerogative of Mercy (uncodified constitution)*	*Queen*	*Justice Secretary*		*pardons (free or conditional), respites, substitutions, remittances*
United States of America	Constitution 1789, art 2, s 2 (revised 1992)	President		Not applicable in cases of impeachment	pardons, reprieves
~~Uruguay~~					
Uzbekistan	Constitution 1992, art 93(23) (revised 2017)	President			pardons
Vanuatu	Constitution 1980, art 38 (revised 2013)	President	Committee provided by Parliament		pardons, commutations, reductions

(Continued)

Venezuela	Constitution 1999, art 236(19) (revised 2009)	President		The State is obliged to investigate and legally punish offences against human rights committed by its authorities. These offences are excluded from any benefit that might render the offenders immune from punishment, including pardons and amnesty (art 29)	pardons	
Vietnam	Constitution 1992, art 88(3) (revised 2013)	President		National Assembly (advises, amnesty only)	pardons, amnesties	
Yemen	*Republican Decree 12/1994 Concerning Crimes and Penalties (clemency not included in Constitution 1991, revised 2015)*	*President*			*pardon*	*Retentionist. A death sentence shall not be executed unless endorsed by the President of the Republic (Constitution of Yemen 1991, art 123)*

Zambia	Constitution 1991, art 96–97 (revised 2016)	President		Advisory Committee on the Prerogative of Mercy		pardons (conditional or unconditional), substitutions, remittances, commutation	Abolitionist in practice. A person who is sentenced to death may request the President, either directly or through a representative, for a pardon or commutation of the sentence
Zimbabwe	Constitution 2013, s 112 (revised 2017)	President		Cabinet (consultation)	(2) Where a person who is resident in Zimbabwe has been convicted in another country of an offence against a law in force in that country, the President may declare that the conviction is not to be regarded as a conviction for the purposes of this Constitution or any other law in force in Zimbabwe (i.e. exta-territorial declaration). (3) The grant of a pardon or respite from execution of sentence or the substitution or suspension of a sentence must be published in the Gazette	pardons (unconditional or conditional), respites (unconditional or conditional), substitutions (unconditional or conditional), suspension (unconditional or conditional), declaration	Retentionist. Offender has a 'right to seek' pardon or commutation in death penalty cases (s 48(2)(e))

Note Italic text (e.g. ***Yemen***) = States with no codified constitution, or where the clemency power is found outside the codified constitution
Asterisk (e.g. **Tajikistan***) = States whose constitutions have been further amended up to 31 December 2018, the amendments for which are not reflected in the table
Strikethrough (e.g. **~~Guatemala~~**) = States with a legislative amnesty power but no executive clemency power within the constitution
Except where more recent versions were available, the editors consulted the English-language version of each constitution at ConstituteProject <https:\\www.constituteproject.org\search?lang=en>
The editors noted the death penalty status of each relevant state from Amnesty International, 'Death Sentences and Executions 2018' (*Amnesty International*, 2019) <https:\\www.amnesty.org\en\documents\act50\9870\2019\en\>

Index

For Product Safety Concerns and Information please contact our EU representative GPSR@taylorandfrancis.com
Taylor & Francis Verlag GmbH, Kaufingerstraße 24, 80331 München, Germany

www.ingramcontent.com/pod-product-compliance
Ingram Content Group UK Ltd.
Pitfield, Milton Keynes, MK11 3LW, UK
UKHW022205190926
475702UK00003B/208
* 9 7 8 0 3 6 7 2 4 3 5 7 9 *